THE
INDIAN
VEGETARIAN

THE INDIAN VEGETARIAN

NEELAM BATRA

WITH SHELLY ROTHSCHILD-SHERWIN

MACMILLAN PUBLISHING COMPANY   *New York*

MAXWELL MACMILLAN CANADA   *Toronto*

MAXWELL MACMILLAN INTERNATIONAL
New York   Oxford   Singapore   Sydney

MACMILLAN
A Simon & Schuster Macmillan Company
1633 Broadway
New York, NY 10019-6785

Library of Congress Cataloging-in-Publication Data
Batra, Neelam.
    The Indian vegetarian/Neelam Batra with Shelly Rothschild-Sherwin.
      p.   cm.
    Includes index.
    ISBN 0-02-862285-5
    1. Vegetarian cookery. 2. Cookery, India. I. Rothschild-Sherwin, Shelly. II. Title.
TX837.B339   1994
6415′636 — dc20   93-41193   CIP

Macmillan Publishing books may be purchased for business or sales promotional use.
For information please write:
Special Markets Department, Macmillan Publishing USA,
1633 Broadway, New York, NY 10019.

MACMILLAN is a registered trademark of Macmillan, Inc.

10 9 8 7 6 5 4 3 2 1

Printed in the United States of America

To my parents for giving me the gift of life.
To my husband for teaching me the meaning of life.
To my daughters for giving my life a new meaning.

CONTENTS

Acknowledgments

Little did I dream that standing by my mother's side and watching as she prepared our food would one day lead me to author a book on Indian cooking. I am truly blessed that my avocation is also my profession and it is entirely the support and encouragement of my family and friends that changed me from an amateur cook to a professional teacher.

It was a huge step to take from behind the stove to the front of a class but the journey has been a rewarding one. I share my recipes, my culture, and ultimately myself with an ever expanding circle of old friends and new.

My husband knew that I would write a cookbook ten years before I actually did and so dear Pradeep, here is the product of your prophecy. To my daughters Sumita and Supriya, who are becoming wonderful cooks in their own rights, eighteen years of thank yous for your love and smiles, and unflagging confidence in me.

The next circle of family to whom I truly owe my gratitude are my parents Prakash and Rani Bhatla, my mother-in-law Prakash Batra, my brother and sister-in-law Rakesh and Renu Bhatla, my sisters-in-law Veena, Asha, and Amita and my brothers-in-law Sushil Dua and Raj Puri, who in their own individual ways encouraged and supported my efforts. Our bond is so strong that there are no adequate words.

What would I have done without my cousins and extended family who did everything from typing to tasting, shared their knowledge and recipes and all unselfishly helped me wherever and with whatever I asked. My heartfelt thanks to Poonam and Billoo Bhatla, Mini and Rajan Aneja, Sunita and Romesh Chopra, Upma and Vikram Budhraja, Kiran and Ashok Malik, Uma and Arun Ahuja, Reita and Virender Bhalla, Anita and Sunil Vora, Poonam and Lalit Pant, Neelam and Raghu Rai, Bharti and Ashwani Dhalwala, Madhu and Harish Seth, Anju and Ashok Khanna, Peggy and Lalit Monga, Peggy and Jim Eickman.

Many thanks to my husband's cousin Sanjokta Budhraja whose encyclopedic knowledge answered every inquiry any time of the day or night. Special thanks to Bonnie Atlas who spent endless hours typing and testing my recipes.

During my years of teaching I met other renowned cooks and authors who offered me their advice and support. Thank you Linda Burum, Faye Levy, and Carolyn Thacker.

All those people I have already mentioned ultimately led me to those who are responsible for turning Pradeep's vision and my dreams into this hardbound reality. Thanks from my heart to Rachel Dourec the owner of Montana Mercantile—a cooking school in Santa Monica, who initiated the process by introducing me to Maureen Lasher, my agent. To Maureen and Eric Lasher for working so diligently on my behalf. To Pam Hoenig my editor at Macmillan, for devoting her time, expertise and knowledge during the writing of this book and with whom I had a most pleasant working relationship.

Now for the proverbial last but not least thank you to Shelly Rothschild-Sherwin for slipping into my mind and turning my innermost thoughts and memories into just the right words. What I can create with food, she does with language.

"Hardic Shukriya, Meherbani aur Dhanyavad" (Thank you from my heart).

INTRODUCTION

INDIAN FLAVORS FOR THE
AMERICAN KITCHEN

India. The very name conjures up exotic and mysterious visions in the American mind, and eating Indian food, consequently, seems adventurous and exciting. But growing up in India, what would seem exotic to Americans was perfectly normal and commonplace to me. Living in an ancient Eastern country, we derived our pleasures in much the same way as our ancestors did. Entertainment occurred every time the doorbell rang and a new guest arrived. Family, friends, neighbors, children—there never seemed to be a time when someone was not dropping by for some food for the soul as well as the body. Magically timed with the arrival of the guests came the appearance of plates offering savory treats and pitchers of liquid refreshment to help while away the hot humid hours. And the air was always laden with aromas promising new delicacies that had not yet made their way to the table. Much of our social life revolved around the home and hearth, where repaying a guest for enriching our existence came in the form of generous hospitality. Preparing food to honor those in our home took on an almost spiritual quality and was never regarded as burdensome.

Today, as I prepare my native recipes in my own kitchen, the smell of spices drying in the sun, dry-roasting over a flame, or being ground in a mortar and pestle still arouses pleasant memories of my mother's kitchen. Those aromas, which clung to my clothing and permeated the homes and streets, intoxicated my senses.

My memories of growing up in India are swirls of vivid colors. Outside of my house, the street was constantly filled, from dawn to dusk, with street vendors pushing carts of ripe, vibrant fruits and vegetables. Young and old carried huge trays on their heads and portable stands that they used to set down their wares. Each vendor sang the praises of his goods as he made the rounds on his established route. You could choose from fresh fruits and vegetables or prepared and "ready to eat" healthy and nutritious snacks. For a few pennies (*paise*) you could have a fresh mung bean salad mixed with sweet, vine-ripened, chopped tomatoes, slivers of flavor-packed baby red onion, and cilantro, or slices of fresh, seasonal fruits topped with delicate spices, herbs, and fresh lime juice. You could also buy freshly boiled or barbecued corn served with a spicy tamarind sauce or tender ginger-flavored garbanzo beans garnished with a tangy mint chutney and served with crispy fried bread. These street vendors cum chefs became famous for their specialties. They lived within the district they sold to, so when I desired a particular kind of food, I knew who to look for. It was like growing up in the largest extended family possible.

Under colorful awnings, sidewalk shops had tables piled high with inviting fruits, vegetables, herbs, and spices. It seemed that the lush countryside was delivered to our doorstep. In America a carnival or a street fair is the only event that produces the same type of visual explosion of colors and fills the air with all kinds of aromas.

I realize now how insular my "world" was. When I was growing up, people did not travel to the extent they do now. Few outside influences found their way into Indian culture. Upon my arrival in America, culture shock was immediately apparent in the Western style of making appointments for social visits and the seeming reluctance to "just drop by" unexpectedly. This more formal arrangement crept into my cooking habits; I was suddenly freed from the kitchen and started to follow the American custom of fixing just three meals a day. But as my circle of Indian friends grew, the more familiar patterns of food preparation reemerged. I felt the urge to relight the fires of creativity and use the opportunity to take advantage of the seemingly limitless variety of foodstuffs available in America.

Not all of my first experiments were without flaws, but my confidence never flagged because of a lesson I learned from my mother when I was ten or eleven years old. I had been asked to attend to the basic onion paste (*masala*) cooking on the stove. With deliberate delay, I made my way to the kitchen, picked up a spatula, and started to stir, when, to my horror, I noticed that it looked dark brown on the underside and almost white on top. I started to scream and told my mother that the *masala* was burnt and it was all her fault for not realizing the intensity of the heat. In my innocence, I was actually happy to see this happen; maybe next time my mother wouldn't send me back to the kitchen and I would be free to read the book I was so engrossed in!

Of course, that did not happen. My mother pointed out to me that there was nothing unusual in what had happened. She just removed the saucepan from the heat, stirred the contents, added a sprinkle of water, and put the pan back on the heat. (Nonstick pans were unheard of in those days.) She told me to watch the *masala* more carefully this time and keep stirring until it was a rich brown color. What else could I do except stand there and fix what was not my mistake? How was I to know that my mother had taught me a lesson that would last me a lifetime? Today, I can proudly say that my mother gave me a gift that has guided me in my cooking experiments and given me a confidence that I eagerly want to share with everyone.

It was this incident and many similar ones that taught me that feelings of despair or guilt have no place in the kitchen. If something goes wrong, fix it, and if you don't like it—change it. Cooking is not always doing the right thing, but is being able to create a new masterpiece when something goes wrong. It truly is an evolutionary process.

The exposure to all that is available to me here in the United States has led me to adapt my native savory recipes to a heart-healthy, earth-friendly, modern, easy, and fun method of cooking. By sharing some of my life and by giving you some of my favorite recipes, I hope to introduce you to this delightful world of Indian flavors.

Today, living in California, I find myself influenced by what I see around me. As a cook, my memories inspire me to try many new combinations of the green vegetables and fruits that one takes for granted here. I religiously make it a point to go to the farmers market in Santa Monica that is held every Wednesday. This market day reminds me of India. Farmers from central California load their flatbed trucks with produce that has been picked from the fields just before departure. The colors and earthy smells of vegetables and fruits lying in profusion on the tables, the warmth of the sun eliciting each food's perfume, surround me and stimulate all my senses simultaneously. Almost like a child in an old-fashioned candy store, overwhelmed by the choices, I walk from stall to stall, buying, sampling, touching, mentally cooking hundreds of dishes. Yellow peppers the color of pure butter, red peppers that are dazzling in their intensity, and the infinite shades of green vegetables make a lush vernal background. This is my paradise.

At home as I unload the produce and lay it out to be washed and stored, I start to mentally group and divide the quantities of each vegetable needed for all those different dishes I had envisioned. Before I can stop myself, I have already cooked a meal and laid it on the table. This time the table looks entirely different from last week, though it seems to me that I've essentially bought the same things as I did last week. Well, maybe not exactly.

An excursion through Indian cuisine requires traveling no farther than your local supermarket and, perhaps, one adventurous journey to an Indian market or placing an order by mail (see page 377 for a list of mail-order sources). The preparation necessary to understand and begin the immersion process of learning about Indian cuisine requires no sophisticated cooking methods. It is almost like taking an ordinary, storebought bouquet of flowers and rearranging them yourself to produce an entirely new creation. I hope to dispel any trepidation the cook may have about working with Indian cuisine by pointing out that most of the foods used are already staples in the American diet, and the procedures are as basic as chopping, boiling, frying, and grilling. When the lack of knowledge of some of the spices is replaced with a comfortable familiarity, the challenge will come from using these recipes and changing them to create your own personally arranged "bouquet" of meals.

The nature of American cuisine today has evolved from the meat and potatoes menu of the 1950s to the incorporation of many international dishes. There is no hesitaion about preparing pasta dishes or stir-fry meals. These dishes have become so familiar that the labels of "Italian" or "Chinese" have ceased to be affixed, and that is exactly what I hope will happen to many of the Indian dishes that you will learn to prepare. I would like nothing better than for them to become mainstreamed into American cooking. Their nutritional benefits are self-evident and after all, "variety is the spice of life."

My humble request to all of you living in America is this: In experimenting with my recipes, think of cooking as an adventure and not a chore. Look forward to wonderful results and the pleasure of sharing them with those you care about. Whether you use my recipes only on special occasions or, hopefully, on a more regular basis, I hope you will enjoy the process of acquiring new skills, be successful at duplicating these recipes, and at the same time create recipes anew.

ABOUT THIS BOOK

This Indian cookbook departs from the more traditionally oriented ones in that it takes the best of both American and Indian cultures and blends them to create a flavorful marriage between the abundance of the New World with the treasures of the Old. Some traditional Indian recipes are presented here exactly as they are prepared in India, but there are many dishes that have taken their inspiration from other cuisines and have been transformed anew with an Indian Influence.

Authentic Indian cuisine has no equivalent of green salads or salad dressings. Neither does it make provision for separate sauces or gravies. Keeping American food habits in mind, I have included both of these as separate chapters along with easy recipes for breads and sandwiches, homemade cheese and yogurt, and quick and simple Indian desserts that will appeal to American taste buds.

With the exception of two or three, none of the entrées are spicy hot; however, they can be made more robust simply by breaking the peppers in the dish. Whole green or red peppers have been added to impart special flavor accents. They can easily be removed from the dish before it is served or allowed to remain in the dish to be enjoyed only by the daring. (Remember to warn your guests about them.)

A large number of the recipes can be served with everyday American meals. You do not have to make a complete Indian menu to enjoy them. In fact, my American students and friends often serve Indian chutneys as dips with their appetizers, or as a relish on their sandwiches. They prepare a curry or a vegetable dish to serve with their everyday bread rolls, whole-wheat tortillas, pita bread, or rice. Most of the dishes can mingle easily with all types of cooked pasta or even with something as simple as instant rice.

Running an "American" kitchen for my American children has profoundly affected my approach to cooking. I do things in a manner that would have seemed foreign to my grandmother. I am constantly developing shortcuts to reduce my time in the kitchen. I find that one long session of advance preparation of ginger, onion, tomatoes, etc., pays off a thousandfold when all I have to do is reach into my freezer and grab as much of these prepared ingredients as needed.

I have given freezing instructions in individual recipes, but here is a list of some of the more commonly used ingredients that I prepare to make everyday life in the kitchen much easier:

TOMATOES: Puree fresh tomatoes in a food processor and transfer them to a heavy saucepan. Place the saucepan over high heat and cook, stirring, until most of the liquid dries up. Cool to room temperature and freeze in ice cube trays. When frozen, transfer to freezer bags and freeze up to 3 to 4 months. Frozen tomatoes can be used in their frozen state or thawed.

GINGER: Peel fresh ginger and cut it into ½-inch pieces, crosswise. With the motor of the food processor running, drop the pieces through the feed tube and process until minced finely. Spread the minced ginger on a salad plate in a thin layer and place in the freezer. When frozen, break the thin layer of ginger into smaller pieces with your fingers and freeze in freezer bags. (Don't let the frozen ginger thaw.) This allows you to remove any amount of ginger you need. Stays fresh for 3 to 4 months. Frozen ginger does not need any thawing; it can go straight into a dish.

GARLIC: Peel your garlic cloves ahead of time and refrigerate; they will keep for 15 to 20 days. Peeled garlic is much easier to use. I do not care for frozen garlic.

ONION: Dice or thinly slice onions and freeze in freezer bags. Before using, place in a nonstick skillet and cook, stirring every once in a while, over medium-low heat until all the water evaporates and the onion starts to brown. Then add the oil called for in the recipe and continue cooking. Be aware that chopped onion spreads a strong odor in the refrigerator, even after triple bagging, so it is a good idea to freeze chopped onion initially in an outside freezer if you have one. Once it is frozen, the chopped onion becomes odorless. It stays fresh for 3 to 4 months.

LEMON OR LIME JUICE: Juice your lemons, then measure the juice by the tablespoon and freeze in ice cube trays. You will have premeasured lemon juice all the time. (This juice makes wonderful fresh lemonade.)

BELL PEPPERS: Seed and finely dice bell peppers of various colors and freeze them in individual bags. Remove by the handful and use in all types of dishes from casseroles and pasta to stir-fries and as instant garnishes.

CILANTRO: Wash and dry the cilantro with kitchen towels until most of the water is wiped off. Then air-dry for 1 to 2 hours, until almost dry. Finely chop the leaves and the soft stems and store in the refrigerator. If your cilantro has been dried well, it should stay fresh for 4 to 5 days. The harder stems can be pureed and used in soups and curries.

MENU PLANNING

Perhaps the thought of preparing an entire Indian meal is a little daunting. Which entrées go with which vegetables? Which menus are lighter and which more substantial? There is a logic to combining dishes. The guidelines I use balance the palate so that the diner is not assaulted by a barrage of exotic flavors colliding with each other. No one dish should entirely dominate; rather, each dish should complement the others. Since there is no separation of courses, the dinner is more of a smorgasbord, which dictates the necessity that some of the dishes function as palate cleansers, such as yogurt.

A very important factor in choosing the recipes for a dinner is the inclusion of dishes with colorful vegetables. Nothing stimulates the appetite better than vibrant colors.

A family dinner in India consists of one "wet" dish (meaning one with a gravy), one "dry" dish (without a gravy), a yogurt, and rice or bread. Chutneys are welcome but not mandatory. A typical menu for entertaining, on the other hand, has appetizers (served with drinks), one or two "wet" main dishes and one or two "dry" side dishes. The most common accompaniments are yogurt raita, rice, and/or bread. Other standard dishes are chopped salads and an array of chutneys and pickles. The number of dishes might seem daunting at first, but many of them can be prepared well in advance, reheated, and served. The condiments need no further attention other than a quick garnish.

Let's try to put together a simple dinner menu for eight people. Suppose we decide to prepare baby potatoes in a curry sauce—a "wet" dish as our main entrée; we immediately visualize its yellow-brown-caramel color. To add protein to this carbohydrate, we should choose a "dry" vibrantly colored bean, lentil, or paneer cheese accompaniment. For a vegetable, any green, yellow, or red will not only round out the nutritional requirements but simultaneously spark the visual appeal. To any menu the presence of yogurt, rice, or bread is almost an unwritten law. You do not of course have to serve all of the above-mentioned simultaneously, but the absence of all of them will certainly diminish the authencity of a traditional Indian meal. The convenience of commercially available yogurt and Indian breads adds to the ease of their inclusion. Appetizers, chutneys, and desserts are optional.

The recipes with yields of eight servings will serve at least twelve or more when you prepare elaborate menus that contain many dishes. With the abundance of dishes offered, it follows logically that the individual portion of each one will be small.

To create an Indian ambiance, use paisley prints on napkins and tablecloths, and play a tape of Ravi Shankar sitar music or Bismillah Khan shehnai music (Indian bagpipes).

SAMPLE MENUS

A FESTIVE HOLIDAY

Appetizers and chutneys
Vegetable Turnovers
Cauliflower and Green Bean Fritters or Mixed Vegetable Fritters
Hot and Sour Chili Pepper Chutney
Green Mint Chutney

Main dishes
Black Urad Beans in Fragrant Butter Sauce
Paneer Cheese in Fresh Tomato Sauce

Side dishes
Barbecued Eggplant with Onion and Tomatoes
Cauliflower, Potatoes, and Red Bell Pepper
Baby Zucchini with Spices
Yogurt with Spinach, Scallions, and Roasted Coriander
Classic Indian Confetti Salad

Breads and Rice
Plain Paranthas or Naan and/or
Spinach and Sweet Pepper Rice or Three Mushroom Rice

Dessert
New Delhi Rice Pudding or Carrot Halvah
Vanilla and Mango Ice Cream

AN ELABORATE PARTY

Appetizers and Chutneys
Potato and Tapioca Fingers
Mint and Tomato Chutney or Yogurt Mint Chutney

Main dishes
Curried Baby Potatoes
Fresh Spinach with Paneer Cheese

Side dishes
Cut Okra with Sautéed Baby Pear Tomatoes
Green and Yellow Beans with Red Bell Peppers
Cucumber, Tomato, and Scallion Yogurt

Breads and Rice
Spiced or Herbed Paranthas
Rice with Fresh Fenugreek Leaves or Rice with Peas and Tomatoes

Dessert
An assortment of burfees or kulfi

A SIMPLE LUNCH
Flour Chips with Yogurt and Tamarind Chutney
Garbanzo Beans with Roasted Pomegranate Seeds
Paneer Cheese with Tomatoes and Onion
Naan, Kulcha, or Bhatura
Ground Rice Custard

A MODEST BRUNCH
Yogurt Cooler or Mango Lassi
Diced Potatoes in Gravy
Crispy Fried Bread with Carom Seeds
Semolina Halvah or Dried Vermicelli with Almonds and Pistachios

A HUMBLE BREAKFAST
Hot Tea with Cardamom
Stuffed Potato or Cauliflower Paranthas
Scallion and Mint Raita with Roasted Peppercorn
Slices of fresh melon or mango

Garnishes on Indian food are as important as flowers on the table. If you can visualize works of Indian art, you remember the attention that is paid to detail and intricate patterns. Garnishing food is another expression of the Indian appreciation of color and beauty, applied to the art of food preparation. It is an easy habit to form and might even carry over into other areas of your cooking. The Indian use of garnishes to enhance foods visually does not have to be any more complicated or time-consuming than the addition of vegetables, herbs, and nuts. The contrast of colors and textures truly does have a stimulating effect on one's appetite. The following is a list of my favorite fast and easy garnishes:

- Sautéed cherry tomatoes
- Seeded and finely diced red, green, and yellow bell peppers
- Grated cauliflower heads for a "white on green" effect
- Grated broccoli heads for a "green on white or red" effect
- Shredded paneer or ricotta cheese
- Finely diced red Swiss chard stems, especially when added to cooked white rice
- Finely sliced scallion whites or greens
- Finely chopped cilantro (fresh coriander)
- Sprigs of fresh parsley, cilantro, or mint
- Lemon or lime slices or twists
- Paprika and ground roasted cumin (see pages 9 and 16) on yogurt dishes
- Garam masala (see page 23)
- Crispy fried onion slices
- Crispy fried julienned fresh ginger (see page 11)
- Crispy fried grated potato
- Fried raisins, cashews, and/or almonds
- Ground or slivered and toasted (see page 76) nuts, especially on desserts
- Edible silver leaves (*chandi ke verk*): Authentic silver leaves, made from pure silver, are thinner than the finest quality tissue paper. They are extremely fragile and should be handled very carefully. Silver leaves are made by sandwiching paper thin sheets of silver between 5- to 6-inch sheets of ordinary paper and pressing (or pounding) on them until they become almost totally weightless (they disintegrate if you blow on them). The pressing causes the silver to actually cling to one side of the paper.

  To use them as a garnish, pick up one sheet of paper with the clinging silver leaf and place it, silver side down, on the dessert or dish to be garnished. Press lightly on the paper, then lift up the paper, leaving the silver adhering to the dish.

  Silver leaves are available in the Indian markets and in some upscale American markets.

CRISPY FRIED FRESH GINGER

BHUNA HUA ADRAK

Crispy fried ginger can be added as a garnish to almost any dish. It can be crumbled (like bacon) and then added to soups and salads, sandwiches, and casseroles or eaten on the side to perk up the flavor of even the blandest of foods.

Choose only plump and healthy looking fresh ginger with thin, shiny, buff-colored skin. Avoid pieces that show any type of decay. Peel and cut into 1- to 1 ½-inch sections. Then cut each section into thin, long julienne-style pieces in the food processor or by hand.

Heat ½ to 1 cup *desi ghee* (see page 30) or peanut oil in a medium-size saucepan and fry the ginger over high heat for 1 to 2 minutes, then over medium heat, stirring as necessary, until it turns crispy and brown, 4 to 6 minutes. Drain on paper towels and store in a small container in the refrigerator. It stays fresh for 3 to 4 months.

The catch in this recipe is to have enough ghee (or oil) so that the ginger can move easily as it fries. The ghee in which the ginger is fried becomes extremely fragrant and can be added as a flavor enhancer to ordinary steamed vegetables and sauces.

Serve rolled in fresh chapatis (see page 320) that are first basted with the ghee in which the ginger is cooked and then top with salt and pepper to taste.

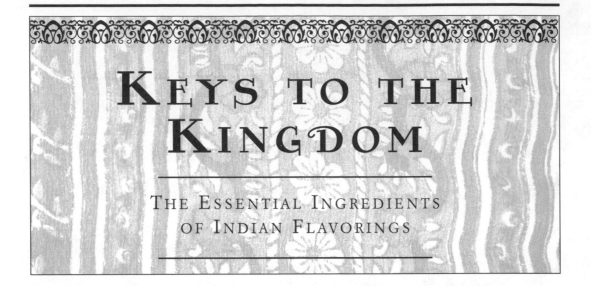

KEYS TO THE KINGDOM

THE ESSENTIAL INGREDIENTS OF INDIAN FLAVORINGS

HERBS, SPICES, AND SEEDS

The one factor that distinguishes one country's cuisine from another's is its use of herbs and spices. Indian cuisine is universally known for its distinctive flavorings. It was the quest to obtain India's prized spices that led to the discovery of the New World. And now, here I am introducing you, in America, to the secrets of my country's native treasures.

I am grouping all the herbs, spices, and seeds together in this chapter for the simple reason that some of them come from the same plant. For example, the coriander plant produces two vastly different seasonings: a spice (coriander seed) and an herb (cilantro, also called fresh coriander). Also, most of the herbs, spices, and seeds are used in combination with a common ultimate purpose in mind—to season foods.

I will discuss the spices and their preparation individually to familiarize you with their culinary uses and nutritional benefits, in addition to long-held Indian beliefs about their medicinal effects.

Spice preparation, which sometimes involves dry-roasting (also known as pan-roasting), is an age-old cooking process in India. Dry-roasting not only enhances the flavor of the spices but actually gives them a brand-new texture and identity. Spices such as coriander, cumin, fennel, sesame, pomegranate, mustard seeds, and also black peppercorns are often pan- or dry-roasted before they are added to various dishes. Whole or ground spices can be dry-roasted, though there will be subtle flavor differences.

To dry-roast whole spices, place them individually in a heavy skillet and roast, stirring constantly, over moderately high heat until they turn a few shades darker and become highly fragrant, 30 seconds to 2 minutes (depending on the quantity). Remove from the heat and use them whole or grind them coarsely or finely in a coffee or spice grinder, using a mortar and pestle, or with the back of a spoon. This dry-roasting technique is commonly used when toasted nuts and seeds are called for.

To dry-roast ground spices, place them individually or in combination in a heavy nonstick skillet and roast, stirring constantly, over moderately high heat until they start to brown, 30 seconds to 1 ½ minutes (depending on the quantity). Then reduce the heat to low and continue to roast, stirring constantly, until they are medium to dark brown, 1 minute. Remove from the heat, transfer to another container, and set aside to cool. Remember, spices will turn a few shades darker as they cool.

Dry-roasted spices can be used immediately or stored in an airtight bottle for 8 to 10 days. They are best when used fresh.

Spice preparation also involves creating several combination blends to elicit unique flavors. Following the individual spice descriptions are the spice combinations that are used routinely in all Indian households and in my recipes.

ASAFETIDA (*HING*). This pungent, almost unpleasant-smelling spice is a resinous gum that is available in its lumpy and ground forms. Use in very small portions and sauté in oil before adding the other ingredients. It imparts a pleasant garlic-onion flavor to dishes and has numerous beneficial properties, the most important one being an aid to digestion and relieving flatulence. This spice is available only in Indian markets.

BASIL (*TULSI*). This highly aromatic herb belonging to the mint family is popular mainly for its leaves, which impart a fragrant and rich flavor to dishes. The Indian variety of basil has small egg-shaped leaves and is called holy basil. Any type of basil can be used in its place. Basil is excellent for digestion, insect bites, and respiratory ailments.

BAY LEAVES (*TEJ PATTA*). There are two types of bay leaves, the bay laurel and the Indian bay cassia. These oval leaves with pointy tips are found generally in their whole dried form. They are at their fragrant best when fresh (don't pass them by if you ever find them) and should be used as soon as possible after they have been dried. The Indian bay leaves are sweeter and milder than the bay laurel, which is the one most commonly available in America, but both can be used interchangeably. Bay leaves are prized as digestive and appetite stimulants.

BLACK PEPPERCORNS (*KALI MIRCH*). This is one of the oldest known spices. Black peppercorns are the dried berries of the pepper plant. These berries are initially green. The green berries are picked and dried in the sun. As they dry, they shrivel up and turn almost black. White peppercorns are made by soaking the black ones in water, removing the black skin, and then redrying them.

Black peppercorns are peppery hot (though their heat does not linger for too long) and very flavorful. Besides using them as a savory seasoning, the Indians use black peppercorns to flavor certain desserts and drinks. They are invaluable for the digestion and are a common home remedy to soothe sore throats (when mixed with honey) and clear the sinuses.

BLACK SALT (KALA NAMAK). This lumpy rock salt is pinkish gray in color, but is popularly called black salt. When ground into a powder, it has an unpleasant odor, but imparts a pleasant fragrance to the dishes it is added to. It is commonly associated with savory appetizers, chutneys, and drinks and is considered to aid the digestion. It definitely cannot be replaced by common table salt. It is available only in Indian markets.

CARDAMOM PODS (ILLAICHI). Regarded as the world's third most valuable spice, next to saffron and vanilla, the oval cardamom pods have a sharp initial bite that soon mellows into a delicate and refreshing fragrance.

There are two types of cardamom pods available in India, the small green and the larger black ones. The first, called *choti* or *hari illaichi* (small or green cardamom), is green in color and about ⅓ to ½ inch in size. It contains eighteen to twenty sticky, black, slightly sweet, yet strong and highly aromatic seeds that have a hint of eucalyptus. This variety is sometimes bleached and puffed and sold in American supermarkets. (This process, in my opinion, is totally unnecessary, as it destroys the inherent aroma and flavor of the pods and makes them rather bland.) The green cardamom pods are available as whole pods, as seeds only, or ground into a powder. They are used as a flavoring in almost all spheres of Indian cooking, from main dishes to desserts and drinks. They are excellent breath fresheners that aid digestion as well. Indians chew them as Westerners chew gum.

The second variety, called *bari* or *kali illaichi* (big or black cardamom), is dark brown to black in color and about ¾ inch in size. Available mostly as whole pods, this variety has a nuttier flavor and, in most instances, can be used interchangeably with the green pods to flavor various spice blends, curries, and desserts. It is phenomenal when used in combination with cinnamon to season basmati rice preparations. As a home medicine it helps flatulence and is often boiled in water with fennel and carom seeds to make a mild tonic water (see page 34) that helps relieve colic problems in infants.

Black cardamom pods are available only in Indian markets, though the greens ones are found in most American supermarkets as well. (They are cheaper in the Indian markets.)

CAROM SEEDS (AJWAIN). Sometimes called lovage, omum, or bishop's weed in Indian books, these tiny purple-brown seeds look like celery seeds but have a pungent and hot bite. When crushed, they release a strong and highly aromatic, thymelike fragrance, which mellows down and permeates dishes as they cook. Invaluable for its flavor and medicinal properties, these seeds are irreplaceable in the Indian spice closet. They are used whole, crushed, or ground in pickles, appetizers, and breads. Carom seeds are an important part of various savory spice blends like chaat masala (see page 26).

These seeds are often chewed raw to relieve flatulence and stomachaches. They are combined with fennel seeds and black cardamom pods to make tonic water for infants (see page 34). Carom seeds are available only in Indian markets.

CINNAMON (DALCHINI). Cinnamon is the dried inner bark derived from two different trees of the laurel family. Both varieties resemble each other in look and flavor and are often used interchangeably. The true cinnamon has tightly rolled "quills" or tubular sticks, with a delicate, sweet aroma. False cinnamon (sometimes called cassia or the Indian variety) has thicker, more loosely rolled, almost flat quills and is stronger in flavor than the true variety. (The Indian variety of bay leaves come from this tree.)

Cinnamon is available in 3- to 4-inch sticks, small broken pieces, and ground, and can be used in any form to suit individual recipes. In Indian cuisine it is often used in combination with black cardamom pods to flavor curries, rice pullaos, and spice blends like garam masala (see page 23). It is not popular as a dessert spice, as it is in the West. The Indian people prefer to use green cardamom pods, saffron, or rose water in desserts.

CLOVES (LAUNG). These nail-shaped, dried, unopened flower buds are dark red-brown in color. They have a sharp, pungent, almost bitter bite, and a warm and familiar aroma. Available in their whole or ground form, they are widely used in the preparation of vegetables and basmati rice pullaos. They are an essential ingredient in certain spice blends. Whole cloves and clove oil are helpful home remedies for tooth and gum problems.

CORIANDER AND CILANTRO (SUKHA AUR HARA DHANIA). The dried seeds of the dainty coriander plant are known as coriander seeds or *sukha dhania*, and the greens are called fresh coriander, cilantro, Chinese parsley, or *hara dhania*.

Sukha dhania (coriander seeds) are small, ribbed, and spherical. Two varieties of coriander seeds are available in America, the pale green-buff Indian variety that has a sweet and citruslike aroma (especially when ground to a powder), and the brown Moroccan variety, which is not quite as flavorful. Coriander seeds can be purchased whole and ground. Since the packaged ground coriander seeds lose their aroma very quickly, I prefer to buy only the whole seeds of the Indian variety and grind them myself. (You can grind a pound at one time and store it in airtight containers in the refrigerator.) The Indian variety is found only in Indian markets. Coriander seeds add a wonderful flavor to cooked dishes.

Hara dhania (cilantro) is one of the most flavorful herbs in the world. Its popularity has increased in the past decade as more and more people have discovered the unique impact it has on food. Fresh coriander leaves look like a thinner version of the flat Italian parsley, only it is much more aromatic. The leaves and soft stems should be used, as the stems are also loaded with flavor. (Try biting on one and see for yourself.)

Cilantro is available in most supermarkets in California. It is also available in Indian, Mexican, Oriental, Middle Eastern, and gourmet markets. To store, trim and wash the cilantro, spin in a salad spinner then air-dry it until most of the moisture has been removed. Transfer to plastic bags and store in the refrigerator for 6 to 8 days. (Drying is crucial, as moisture encourages spoilage.) Moisture-free leaves can be chopped and stored in the refrigerator for 4 to 5 days.

Unlike other herbs such as mint, basil, and fenugreek, cilantro does not dry well. Dried cilantro leaves lose most of their flavor and therefore are an unacceptable substitute. It does not freeze well either

CUMIN (JEERA). Cumin seeds are actually the dried fruit of the cumin plant. There are two types of cumin seeds, the familiar brown seeds called *safaid jeera* (white cumin) and the more exotic variety known as *kala* or *shah jeera* (black or royal cumin).

Safaid jeera has strongly flavored, ¼-inch, oval brown seeds that look like those of caraway and fennel. They are widely available as whole or ground seeds in most American supermarkets. (Unless otherwise specified, this is the variety that has been used in most of the recipes.) Cumin seeds play a very important part in Indian cuisine and are used in numerous preparations, from spice blends to main dishes (though definitely not in desserts). Dry-roasted, they impart an irreplaceable flavor to yogurt raitas and savory appetizers and chutneys.

Kala jeera is a rare variety that grows in the Vale of Kashmir. It has thinner, darker seeds that resemble those of caraway but have a delicate, sweet aroma. These expensive and uncommon seeds add an exotic touch to basmati rice pullaos. They are available only in Indian markets and are generally used whole.

Cumin seeds are considered effective in treating digestive disorders, morning sickness, insomnia, and flatulence.

CURRY LEAVES (MEETHI NEEM OR KARI PATTA). The small oval leaves of the curry plant impart an aromatic currylike flavor to dishes. They are available fresh or dried at Indian markets only. The fresh ones are preferred over the dried as drying causes a considerable loss of flavor. (These leaves are hard to find, so simply omit them from the recipe if there is a problem getting them.) Curry leaves are a mild laxative and also effective in treating morning sickness, diarrhea, and dysentery.

FENNEL (SAUNF). These plump, oval, pale yellowish green seeds bear a resemblance to cumin seeds and taste like anise and licorice. They are available only as whole seeds at most American and ethnic markets. Fennel seeds are renowned for their medicinal properties and are often eaten raw or dry-roasted (see page 13) to aid digestion and freshen the breath after meals. As a cooking spice they are popularly added (whole or ground) to various meat and vegetable dishes, cooked chutneys, and special spice blends. They are also used as a pickling spice in combination with nigella, cardamom, and fenugreek seeds.

FENUGREEK SEEDS AND GREENS (DANA AUR PATTA METHI). Fenugreek is also called Greek hay and belongs to the legume family. The dried seeds of the fenugreek plant are called *dana methi* or *methere* and the greens *patta*. The fresh greens are treated as a vegetable (like spinach) or are dried and used as a spice. The dried fenugreek greens are called *sukhi* or *kasoori methi*.

Dana methi, the yellowish brown seeds, are about the size of mung beans and have a powerful currylike aroma. They are bitter raw but when cooked right are wonderful flavor enhancers. Fenugreek seeds are available whole, crushed, or ground, and are used in combination with other spices to make a variety of cooked chutneys, pickles, meats, vegetables, and spice blends.

Sukhi methi, the dried leaves, are ground to a powder and then generally used as a seasoning in small amounts to add a fragrant allure to various meats, vegetables, rice pullaos, and spice blends. However, in the absence of fresh fenugreek greens, the Indian people (who love the familiar slightly bitter taste of *methi*) use them instead of fresh greens to make special dishes with them.

All types of fenugreek (seed, dried leaves, and fresh greens) are available in Indian and Middle Eastern markets. Lately, I have been very successful in finding fresh fenugreek leaves in my local farmers' market, and at certain greengrocers also. The dried fenugreek leaves generally contain little dry stems that should be removed. (You can dry your own fenugreek by washing it and airing it in the shade until it becomes dry and crumbly, 3 to 4 days. Then grind and store in airtight containers in the refrigerator for up to 2 years. You could also try growing your own by sprinkling some fenugreek seeds in your backyard or in pots and covering them with soil. With normal watering, these seeds will sprout and turn into lovely plants.)

Fenugreek seeds are beneficial in the treatment of indigestion, flatulence, diabetes, respiratory infections, and skin irritations, and purify the blood.

GARLIC (*LASUN*). Belonging to the onion family, garlic really needs no introduction. Besides imparting a tremendous flavor boost to dishes, it is one of the best herbs for the entire body, including the heart and lungs.

Indian cooking uses only fresh garlic. Water-packed minced garlic may be substituted, but the dried varieties are not recommended.

GINGER, DRIED AND FRESH (*ADRAK, SUKHA AUR TAZA*). Ginger is the buff-colored, knotty rhizome of a tropical plant. The dried variety, called *sonth*, is available as small pieces or in its powdered form. It is dried by setting pieces of fresh ginger in the sun until they are brittle, then grinding them to a fine powder. Ground ginger has a spicy and sweet citruslike aroma and a hot bite. It is a crucial spice in savory blends like mint and chaat masala (see pages 28 and 26), and is added to cooked chutneys, vegetables, and meats.

When buying fresh ginger, look for large, plump rhizomes with shiny skin. (The skin is always peeled before cooking.) Fresh ginger stays fresh in the refrigerator for 2 to 3 weeks. To freeze, peel the ginger and cut it into ½-inch slices, crosswise. Then mince them in a food processor fitted with the metal S-blade (with the motor running, drop the pieces through the feed tube). Spread the minced ginger in a thin layer on a platter that will fit into your freezer. Place it there until frozen, 1 to 2 hours. Remove from the freezer, break the frozen ginger into smaller pieces, and store in plastic zipper bags in the freezer for 3 to

4 months. To use, simply remove from the freezer and add to the dish. There is no need to thaw it.

Ginger is one of the most beneficial of the herbs. In India it is often referred to as *maha aushadhi*—the great medicine—and provides the best home remedy for indigestion, nausea, motion sickness, fever, muscle aches and pains, and respiratory disorders. Both fresh and dried ground ginger are available in most American and ethnic supermarkets.

MANGO POWDER (*AMCHUR*). Like dried ginger, this spice is available as small buff-colored dried pieces or ground into a powder. Ripe mangoes flood the Indian markets in the hot summer months. This is the time they are preserved in most ingenious ways so they can be enjoyed in their different forms for the rest of the year. The excessively sour raw mangoes are cut into small pieces, dried in the scorching summer sun, and then ground into a fine powder that is used as a souring agent instead of lime or lemon juice in cooked dishes, especially those without gravy. It is also used in the preparation of various drinks, chutneys, spice blends, and salads. Mango powder is available only in Indian markets.

MINT, FRESH AND DRIED (*PUDINA, TAZA AUR SUKHA*). The highly aromatic, dark green, oval mint leaves play a crucial part in Indian cuisine. Fresh mint leaves are available year round in most American supermarkets and greengrocers. These are used extensively to make chutneys, yogurt raitas, and sauces. As a flavoring herb, mint is added to curries, rice pullaos, salads, and salad dressings.

Sukha pudina, dried and ground mint leaves, are made simply by drying fresh ones. This can be done in the sun or shade. (I prefer to air-dry my own leaves in the shade so they retain their deep green color.) Once they are dry, grind them in a coffee or spice grinder and store in an airtight bottle for 2 to 3 months at room temperature and for over a year in the refrigerator. Alternatively, purchase dried mint leaves in any American supermarket.

Mint is a valuable herb that helps digestion and stomachaches. It is also a natural antiseptic that keeps the mouth fresh and the taste buds healthy.

MIXED MELON SEEDS (*CHAR MAGAZ*). *Char* means four and *magaz* brain, and this name is given to a special mixture of shelled seeds from four melon varieties: cantaloupe (*kharbuza*), cucumber (*kheera*), white pumpkin (*kaddu*), and watermelon (*tarbooz*). Along with almonds, this mixture is held in high esteem as a provider of good nourishment to the brain. It is popularly added to various drinks and desserts and occasionally to cooked foods. It is available in Indian markets.

Shelling the tiny melon seeds is very time-consuming and labor intensive, so it is best to purchase this mixture or substitute sunflower, pumpkin, and other similar seeds that are more readily available in American markets. Always store the seeds in the refrigerator, as their high oil content causes them to turn rancid very fast.

MUSTARD (*RAI*). There are three types of mustard seeds, black, brown and white, or yellow. Indian cuisine uses the brown variety which is mistakenly referred to as "black" because of their dark color. (I also refer to them in the same manner in my recipes, because that is the way they are sold at the Indian markets.) They can replaced with the black or yellow ones quite successfully.

These tiny round seeds are dark brown to black on the outside and yellow inside. They have a sharp, pungent flavor which mellows after they are fried in hot oil or dry-roasted (see page 13). They impart a mild, tangy flavor and tremendous visual appeal to numerous chutneys, rice, vegetable, and lentil dishes. Indian cuisine uses both the whole and ground forms.

The greens of the mustard plant called *sarsoon ka saag* (mustard greens) are available in most American supermarkets and are eaten as a delicious main dish.

NIGELLA *(KALONJI)*. These charcoal black, triangular seeds bear an uncanny resemblance to onion seeds, and are often mistakenly referred to as such. Nigella seeds have a mild, oreganolike flavor that becomes positively fragrant when they are added to baked flat breads. (I often add a teaspoon to the breads that I make in my commercial bread maker.) They are also used as a pickling and chutney spice, along with fennel, cardamom pods, and fenugreek seeds. They are available in Indian markets and often contain impurities that have to be removed.

NUTMEG *(JAIPHUL)*. Nutmeg is the sun-dried kernel of the seed contained inside the apricotlike fruit of the nutmeg tree. (The lacy covering that surrounds this seed is dried and sold as mace.)

This medium brown, 1-inch-long, oval kernel has a rich, warm fragrance and a sweet antiseptic flavor. Although it is used extensively in different cuisines of the world, Indians use it sparingly, adding it only to rich and creamy dishes. More popularly it is added to various spice blends.

It is available in most American supermarkets, as whole and ground nutmeg. I prefer to buy it whole and grind it fresh before every use, as it loses its fragrance rapidly.

PAPRIKA *(RANG VALI MIRCH)*. Paprika is the ground powder of dried mild to sweet red peppers. *Rang* means color and *mirch* pepper. Paprika is called *rang wali mirch* because it lends color to cooked dishes without making them spicy hot. Since most Indian paprika comes mainly from the Vale of Kashmir, it is also called *Kashmiri degi mirch*.

Valued for the aesthetic beauty and brilliant color it adds to the recipes, paprika has an enviable spot in the spice closet. The sweet Hungarian paprika available in American supermarkets is very similar to Indian paprika and can be used in its place.

PEPPERS, FRESH GREEN AND DRIED RED *(MIRCHI, TAZI HARI AUR SUKHI LAL)*. Used fresh and dried, these members of the genus *Capsicum* provide spicy hot flavor to foods. All types of hot green peppers can be used interchangeably in my recipes (even when I specify serrano or jalapeño peppers). As a general rule I do not like to seed my green peppers because the seeds provide a welcome hot bite to the dish. If you want to make your dishes milder, add the peppers whole with their skins punctured (this lets the steam escape and prevents the peppers from bursting and causing injury to the eyes), and remove them from the dish before serving, or leave them in for those who may want to try them. (Don't forget to post a warning.) Use caution when working with all type of peppers and wear gloves, especially when chopping them.

Dried red peppers impart a different flavor to foods and are used in numerous savory dishes. Leave them in or remove them before serving a dish. Dried red peppers are also available in their ground form and are called cayenne pepper or ground red pepper. Under whichever name you purchase them, they can be used interchangeably.

All peppers are rich in vitamin C and are very effective in clearing the sinuses.

POMEGRANATE SEEDS, DRIED (ANARDANA). These are the sun-dried seeds of sour pomegranates. The flesh around the seeds dries and forms a brown-black sticky coating on the seed. These seeds have a predominantly sour taste, yet there is a latent sweetness in them. They are available in their whole or ground form in Indian and Middle Eastern markets and are used in various breads, chutneys, and bean dishes. When they are ground and dry-roasted (see page 13), they impart a rich brown color and a welcome tanginess to various sauces.

POPPYSEEDS (KHUS KHUS). There are two types of poppyseeds, the familiar blue-gray variety and the lesser known white ones. Indian cuisine uses only the white variety (the blue-gray ones can be used in their place, but the color of the dish will be very different).

These minute kidney-shaped seeds have a hint of almond and are often ground with almonds, cashews, and other nuts to flavor and thicken numerous sauces and drinks.

White poppyseeds are available only in Indian markets. If you buy them in large quantities, store them in the refrigerator, like nuts, because they can turn rancid in 3 to 4 months.

ROSE ESSENCE AND WATER (RUH GULAB AUR GULAB JAL). Both are made from the petals of highly fragrant deep pink roses (called *succha* or "pure" *gulab*) that are specially cultivated for this purpose. The concentrated rose essence is available in small bottles and is used as a flavoring in numerous drinks, desserts, rice pullaos, and nonvegetarian curries. Just a few drops are adequate as a flavor enhancement. Rose water, on the other hand, is a much more diluted version of the essence, and is available in large bottles. The rose essence and water are both available in Indian and Middle Eastern markets.

SAFFRON (KESAR). Saffron, the dried, threadlike stigmas of the saffron crocus, is the most expensive spice in the world. These hand-picked deep red stigmas have a distinctly rich and enticing aroma and impart a lovely yellow color to various white sauces, rice pullaos, and desserts. Saffron also adds an excellent flavor to vegetables and meats.

Saffron is available in its thread and ground forms in Indian, Mexican, Middle Eastern, and some American markets. I prefer to buy and use only the saffron threads. To use, soak them in some milk for 15 to 30 minutes to release the flavor and color, then add to the dish. Some people pan-roast (see page 13) the threads lightly before soaking them.

SESAME SEEDS (TIL). These small oval flat seeds ranging in color from white to brown-black are quite tasteless in their raw state, but after pan-toasting they offer a wonderful nutty flavor to foods. These high-protein seeds are considered to have a warming effect on the body and are often found as a coating on special winter desserts and candies.

Sesame seeds are available in Indian and Oriental markets and also in American supermarkets.

TAMARIND (IMLI). Tamarind is the predominantly sour and slightly sweet pulp obtained from the bean-shaped pods of the tamarind tree. Enclosed in the brittle light brown shell is the reddish to dark brown tamarind pulp and the seeds. Extracting the usable pulp from the whole pods, though very simple, involves a few time-consuming steps (remove the shell, soak in water until it becomes soft, mash with your fingers, then pass through a strainer). It is much simpler to purchase packaged seedless pulp, thickened tamarind paste, or tamarind powder. (Of late I have been using tamarind powder in all my recipes with positive results.) All these forms of tamarind are available in Indian markets and some are also found in Oriental, Mexican, and some American markets.

Tamarind has a cooling effect on the body and is also a mild laxative.

TURMERIC (HALDI). Belonging to the ginger family, turmeric is the rhizome of the tropical turmeric plant. This rhizome is shaped like fresh ginger with short "fingers," but has bright orange flesh. This rhizome is boiled, skinned, and then dried before it is ground into the familiar orange-yellow powder. Turmeric imparts a characteristic yellow color and an aromatic flavor to curries and other dishes ranging from vegetables and paneer cheese to beans and lentils.

Turmeric is a natural antiseptic, an anti-inflammatory, and a blood purifier. It helps relieve aches and pains in the body and soothes a sore throat. This spice is highly regarded as a home remedy for various other problems also.

It is available as dried pieces only in Indian markets and in its ground form in most American markets also.

CONVENIENT SPICE BLENDS
CURRY POWDER

KARI KA MASALA

Curry in Indian terminology means a sauce or a gravy and curry powder is a blend of spices that are popularly used in the preparation of authentic curries. The term *curry* does not automatically refer to dishes that are enriched with curry powder. Only a dish that has some type of a sauce, be it thick or thin, qualifies to be labeled as a curry. This is how we differentiate between "wet" and "dry" dishes.

I would also like to mention that in the old days no such blend was available, and though today it is marketed in the larger Indian cities, it is not utilized in traditional home cooking. The Indian people prefer the freedom and creativity of adding assorted spices to different dishes to capture a variety of flavors that would otherwise be impossible. India's vast rural population has probably never even heard of this blend.

This combination was put together by the British people, who wanted to re-create flavorful Indian curries with a minimum of effort. The main disadvantage in using prepackaged curry powder is that all the dishes come out looking and tasting the same. There is no variety to the meal and the authenticity of home cooking is sacrificed.

I think this blend is excellent if you limit it to the use of certain curries for example, Classic Curry Sauce (see page 123) or Garbanzo Beans with a Curry Sauce (page 271), but if you try to add it to all the preparations, then it loses its alluring attraction. It is full of flavor but is not spicy hot. If you wish to make it hot, add some cayenne or any other hot chili pepper.

Commercially packaged curry powder is generally not acceptable, unless you happen to find one that you like. Homemade curry powder, on the other hand, is a blessing in the kitchen, but please be selective about its use. I often add it to other non-Indian foods to perk up their flavor. (Hamburgers, chicken salad, and guacamole top my list.)

½ cup coriander seeds
¼ cup cumin seeds
2 tablespoons fenugreek seeds (see page 16)
1 tablespoon black peppercorns
1 tablespoon fennel seeds
1 tablespoon black mustard seeds
1 tablespoon white poppyseeds
15 to 20 green cardamom pods
Seeds from 7 to 10 black cardamom pods
2 tablespoons turmeric
1 tablespoon ground ginger
2 teaspoons ground nutmeg

Combine the coriander, cumin, fenugreek, peppercorns, fennel, black mustard, poppyseeds, and cardamom pods and seeds in a small bowl, then transfer them to a coffee or spice grinder and grind them into a fine powder (you may have to do this in three or four batches). Mix in the turmeric, ginger, and nutmeg.

Store in an airtight container in a cool, dark place. This masala stays fresh for 6 to 8 months in the refrigerator. Keep some in the kitchen and refrigerate the rest.

MAKES ABOUT 1 CUP

Garam Masala

Garam masala is to Indian cuisine what salt and pepper are to American cooking. It is so basic an ingredient that its absence would be immediately noticed. Although the garam masala combination of spices can vary from region to region and even from family to family, it is a staple found in every single Indian kitchen.

Garam means "hot" in the Hindi language. This particular mixture is a blend of four different spices that produce internal heat in the body. It is also spicy hot because of the black pepper. Even though garam masala mixtures are available commercially, most of them contain other spices to increase their volume, so I strongly suggest that you make your own, unless you happen to find one that you especially like.

25 black cardamom pods (or more if they are very small)
3 tablespoons ground cloves
2 tablespoons ground cinnamon
2 tablespoons ground black pepper

Grind the cardamom pods with their skin in a spice or coffee grinder until powdered. Pass through a sieve and discard the husk. Place, along with the cinnamon, cloves, and black pepper, in a small nonstick skillet and roast over medium heat until heated through, 30 to 40 seconds. Shake the skillet to stir the spices. Cool completely and store in an airtight container in a cool, dark place or in the refrigerator for 6 to 8 months. (Keep some on hand in the kitchen and refrigerate the rest.)

Garam masala is generally added as a garnish on cooked dishes, just prior to serving, to enhance their flavor. If you desire to make a dish very fragrant and spicy, use the garam masala during cooking also.

Makes ⅔ cup

Korma Masala

The term *korma* refers to a special cooking technique that involves simmering meats, paneer cheese, or vegetables in a fragrant yogurt and nut sauce. Korma masala is a blend of nuts and spices that are essential to obtain the distinct flavor that is associated with authentic *korma* curries.

This blend is especially flavorful when used in combination with sautéed onion and yogurt or cream. Though it is used mainly as a seasoning blend to make Yogurt Sauce with Caramelized Onion (see page 132), it can unhesitatingly be used to flavor any chicken, seafood, paneer cheese, or vegetable preparation. Try it as a fragrant thickening agent in other sauces, or add it to soups to perk up the flavors.

Simmer 1 to 2 teaspoons of korma masala with 1 cup milk to make a nutritious cool weather drink. (The black pepper and ginger will add a certain amount of heat.)

20 green cardamom pods
Seeds of 5 black cardamom pods
2 tablespoons raw pistachios (35 to 40)
2 tablespoons raw almonds (20 to 25)
2 tablespoons pine nuts
2 tablespoons cashew pieces
2 tablespoons white poppyseeds
2 tablespoons ground ginger
1 tablespoon ground cinnamon
1 teaspoon ground cloves
2 teaspoons ground black pepper, or to taste

Place the cardamom pods and seeds in a coffee grinder and grind until powdered. (If it doesn't grind properly, add some pistachios or almonds and grind once again. This will increase the volume and facilitate the grinding.) Remove to a bowl.

Grind the nuts and poppyseeds together in two or three batches until powdered. Remove to the bowl with the cardamom. Mix in the ginger, cinnamon, cloves, and black pepper.

Store in an airtight container in the refrigerator. Stays fresh for up to 2 months.

MAKES ABOUT 1 ¼ CUPS

TANDOORI MASALA

Tandoori masala is a specific blend of spices used in the preparation of foods that are cooked in the *tandoor*, a cylindrical clay oven that uses live coals and cooks the food at a very high temperature. The closest American substitute is a covered barbecue.

The distinct character and flavor of tandoori meats, vegetables, and breads cannot truly be equaled. Most of the meats and vegetables are marinated in a combination of garlic, ginger, yogurt, and tandoori masala. This process tenderizes and flavors them before they are quickly cooked in the high heat of the tandoor.

This masala consists of spices that combine superbly to give tandoori foods their characteristic intriguing flavor. Red food coloring is traditionally added for visual impact, and in my opinion is totally unnecessary. For that reason, I have not included it in my recipe. Paprika does a better job of appealing to the senses, besides imparting flavor.

If you want a spicy "hot" tandoori masala, be sure to include the cayenne pepper. Prepackaged tandoori masala contains too much color and in my opinion is not very desirable.

2 tablespoons coriander seeds
2 tablespoons cumin seeds
2 tablespoons fenugreek seeds (see page 16)
1 tablespoon black peppercorns
1 tablespoon cloves
Seeds of 8 black cardamom pods
¼ cup paprika
1 tablespoon ground dried fenugreek leaves (see page 17)
1 tablespoon ground cinnamon
2 teaspoons ground ginger
1 teaspoon ground cayenne pepper, or to taste (optional)

Place the coriander, cumin, fenugreek seeds, peppercorns, cloves, and cardamom seeds in a medium-size heavy nonstick skillet and roast on moderately high heat until heated through, about 1 minute. Remove from heat, let the spices cool for a few minutes, and then grind them in a spice or coffee grinder until reduced to a fine powder. Transfer to a bowl and mix in the remaining ingredients.

Cool and store in an airtight container in a cool, dark place. This blend stays fresh for 6 to 8 months in the refrigerator.

To use it as a marinade, add it to sizzling hot oil and then mix in some yogurt (and/or sour cream, lemon juice, orange juice, vinegar, pureed tomatoes, etc.) and some salt. Add it to fresh homemade cheese, boiled potatoes, steamed baby cauliflower, and other vegetables, or lamb, chicken, and seafood. The marinated foods can then be barbecued, grilled in the oven, or pan-fried with or without the marinade. Tandoori masala can also be used to make special curries with a tandoori flavor.

MAKES ABOUT ½ CUP

CHANNA MASALA

Channa is the Indian name for garbanzo beans, and channa masala is a blend of selected spices that enhances the flavor of the prepared garbanzo bean dishes. The unique rich brown color and complex flavor of this masala can be obtained only by dry-roasting the spices. The process causes them to release their essential oils which in turn imparts an intense flavor and visual appeal to the cooked beans.

This unusual blend has absolutely no substitute and though it is authentically used with garbanzo beans, it can also be used to create significant variations of authentic curry sauces.

Prepackaged channa masala, available at Indian markets, is quite acceptable, but remember, it is very hot and must be used with caution.

3 tablespoons ground dried pomegranate seeds (see page 20)
3 tablespoons ground cumin
2 tablespoons ground coriander
1 tablespoon ground fenugreek seeds (see page 16)
1 tablespoon ground ginger
1 tablespoon mango powder (see page 18)
1 tablespoon tamarind powder (see page 21)
1 tablespoon black salt (see page 14)
2 teaspoons asafetida (see page 13)
2 teaspoons freshly ground black peppercorns
2 teaspoons ground carom seeds (see page 14)
1 teaspoon ground cayenne pepper (optional)
½ teaspoon ground cinnamon
½ teaspoon ground cloves

Place all the spices in a medium-size, heavy nonstick skillet and roast, stirring constantly, over high heat for about 1 minute and then over medium until brown and fragrant, about 3 to 4 minutes. Remove the skillet from the heat. (Remember, the spices will turn a shade darker as they cool.) Transfer to a bowl and set aside.

Cool completely and store in an airtight container in a cool, dark place. Channa masala stays fresh for 6 to 8 months, if stored in the refrigerator. (Keep some on hand in the kitchen and refrigerate the rest.)

MAKES ABOUT 1 CUP

CHAAT MASALA

The word *chaat* has a very broad meaning, but it is primarily used to classify foods that have a complex sweet, salty, tart, and spicy flavor. *Chaat* is a category of Indian food that takes some explaining. A synonym of *chaat* might be "mélange." For example, if you were to take an American dinner of home-fried potatoes, bite-size chunks of meat, and peas and carrots, toss them together and then top them with a special chutney or sauce and spices, it would be a *chaat*. Or a fruit salad likewise tossed and topped with appropriate chutneys and spices, this too would be considered a *chaat*. A whole array of salads and appetizers fall in the *chaat* category, for example, Indian-Style Fruit Salad (see page 110) or Flour Chips with Yogurt and Tamarind Chutney (page 71). All these dishes use chaat masala in combination with lemon juice and tamarind or mango chutney to create sumptuous, finger-licking preparations that can be enjoyed any time of the day. In India these "combo" dishes are typical street food and are eaten with the fingers.

Use this blend with fresh lime or lemon juice on freshly cut vegetables and fruits. Sprinkle on any yogurt raita or on vegetable fritters. Chaat masala is also delicious on barbecued corn, sweet potatoes, and yams.

Commercially packaged chaat masala sold at Indian supermarkets is quite acceptable.

2 teaspoons carom seeds (see page 14)
3 tablespoons cumin seeds
¼ cup mango powder (see page 18)
3 tablespoons tamarind powder (see page 21)
2 talespoons black salt (see page 14)
1 tablespoon ground ginger
1 teaspoon ground nutmeg
1 teaspoon ground black pepper
1 teaspoon salt, or to taste
1 teaspoon ground cayenne pepper, or to taste (optional)

Place the carom seeds in a small, heavy nonstick skillet and roast over moderately high heat until they start popping, about 2 minutes. Transfer to a bowl and set aside.

Place the cumin seeds in the same skillet and roast over moderately high heat until it is fragrant and turns a few shade darker, 2 to 3 minutes. Transfer to the bowl with the carom seeds. Cool for a few minutes and grind in a coffee or spice grinder and transfer back to the bowl.

Mix in the remaining ingredients.

Return the mixture to the skillet and roast for 1 to 2 minutes to blend the flavors. Cool and store in an airtight container in a cool, dark place. Chaat masala stays fresh for 6 to 8 months in the refrigerator.

MAKES ABOUT 1 CUP

MINT MASALA

PUDINA MASALA

This mint-flavored spice mixture is a refreshing seasoning when added to sautéed or steamed vegetables. Sprinkle it on different curries for a unique touch, add it to yogurt raitas or to lemonade or orange juice for a refreshing yet zesty flavor. Use as a flavor enhancer when you desire a minty lemon twist on barbecued meats, vegetables, and corn. This masala can also be used on baked or deep-fried finger foods.

    3 tablespoons mango powder (see page 18)
    2 tablespoons ground dried mint leaves
    1 tablespoon tamarind powder (see page 21)
    1 tablespoon black salt (see page 14)
    2 teaspoons ground ginger
    ½ teaspoon carom seeds (see page 14)

In a small bowl, mix together all the ingredients. Store in an airtight container in a cool and dark place. This mixture stays fresh for 6 to 8 months in the refrigerator.

MAKES ABOUT ½ CUP

SAMBAR MASALA

Sambar masala is a unique spice blend that is used in the preparation of South Indian-Style Lentil Soup vibrantly flavored with fresh tamarind and lemon juice (see page 264). It is also used in Coconut Chutney (see page 90) and in certain other lentil and vegetable dishes.

Generally, this blend is made very hot to suit the taste of the people in southern India, but you can make yours as hot or as mild as you desire. To make it milder, reduce or eliminate the cayenne pepper.

    ½ cup coriander seeds
    3 tablespoons cumin seeds
    2 tablespoons fenugreek seeds (see page 16)
    1 tablespoon dried yellow urad beans (see page 254)
    1 tablespoon dried split yellow chick-peas (see page 255)
    1 tablespoon black peppercorns

½ cup crushed dried curry leaves (see page 16)
2 teaspoons ground asafetida (see page 13)
1 teaspoon ground cayenne pepper, or to taste (optional)

Place the coriander, cumin, fenugreek, urad beans, chick-peas, peppercorns, curry leaves, and asafetida in a medium-size, heavy nonstick skillet and roast the spices over moderately high heat until they turn lightly golden, about 3 to 5 minutes. Remove the skillet from the heat and cool for 3 to 4 minutes. Place the roasted spices in a spice or coffee grinder and process them into a fine powder. Mix in the cayenne pepper.

Cool completely and store in an airtight container in a cool, dark place. This masala stays fresh for 6 to 8 months in the refrigerator.

MAKES ABOUT 1 CUP

DESSERT MASALA

MITHAI KA MASALA

Pistachios, almonds, cashew nuts, walnuts, raisins, melon seeds, black and green cardamom pods, rose water, and saffron all are used to flavor Indian desserts. They can be used together, in various combinations, or individually.

Try this cardamom-flavored nut mixture over your rice, bread, or tapioca pudding, or add it to cakes as a layer in the center or a sprinkling on top. The pale green color supplied by the pistachios makes this a very attractive garnish over casseroles and rice dishes.

¾ cup raw pistachios
½ cup raw almonds
¼ cup cashew pieces
25 to 30 green cardamom pods
Seeds from 1 black cardamom pod

Grind all the ingredients together in a spice grinder in one or two batches. Store in an airtight bottle in the refrigerator. This mixture stays fresh in the refrigerator for 2 to 3 months.

MAKES ABOUT 1 ½ CUPS

Tea Masala

An occasional touch of herbs and spices brewed with tea leaves adds more than just flavor. The natural oils contained in various seeds, leaves, and barks impart a myriad of beneficial effects also.

This is a multipurpose mixture which combines an array of spices to provide a perfect ending to an Indian meal.

This blend can also be used with vegetables, curries, and rice dishes.

1 black cardamom pod
Seeds from 25 green cardamom pods
4 cloves
½ teaspoon fennel seeds
¼ teaspoon black peppercorns
¼ teaspoon carom seeds (see page 14)
1 teaspoon ground ginger
1 teaspoon ground cinnamon

Grind the cardamom pod and seeds, cloves, fennel seeds, peppercorns, and carom seeds in a spice grinder until fine, then add the ginger and cinnamon. Grind once more to mix the spices. Remove to a small bottle and store in a cool and dark place. This blend stays fresh for about 6 months.

Use ¼ to ½ teaspoon per cup of water. Follow the instructions on page 33 to make Indian-style masala tea.

MAKES ABOUT 3 TABLESPOONS

Clarified Butter

DESI GHEE

This recipe is included in this chapter because it is so basic and essential to Indian cooking. Even though oil is used in most recipes, if you want an authentic taste, this is what you should use.

A lovely aroma fills the air as the butter gradually melts and transforms into a super-fragrant *ghee* that can be used as a cooking medium or a flavor enhancer.

Desi ghee is authentically made by churning clotted or heavy cream into fluffy whipped butter and then simmering it over low heat until all the milk solids separate from the fat and settle to the bottom of the pan. Once this happens, the clarified fat is passed through a strainer. This clarified butterfat is called *desi, usli,* or *khara ghee.*

The shelf life of butter is vastly increased after it is clarified. It is the milk solids in the butter that turn rancid and spoil it, and once these solids are removed from the butter, it stays fresh for a long time (4 to 6 months) at room temperature. Its shelf life in cool weather is even longer.

To make clarified butter, place 1 pound of unsalted butter in a heavy medium-size saucepan and simmer, stirring occasionally, over medium-low heat until the milk solids turn golden and settle to the bottom of the pan, 15 to 20 minutes. (At first the butter will start to foam, but this will eventually subside.) Once this happens, pass everything through a sieve and save the clarified butter in a clean jar. The milk solids that remain in the sieve should not be discarded. They combine superbly with whole-wheat flour to make one of the most delicious parantha breads (see page 325).

VARIATIONS: To make flavored clarified butter, add any of the following flavorings to the pan as you start melting the butter.

- ½ cup minced fresh mint leaves
- ½ cup minced fresh basil leaves (or lemon or purple basil)
- 2 tablespoons peeled and minced fresh ginger
- 1 tablespoon coarsely chopped garlic
- 3 to 4 bay leaves (preferably fresh)
- 1 to 2 teaspoons cumin seeds
- 1 teaspoon carom seeds (see page 14)

Season this flavored *ghee* with some fresh lemon juice, salt, and pepper and use it as a dipping sauce with cooked lobster or shrimp, as a final glaze on barbecued meats, poultry, or seafood, or serve it with freshly baked breads.

THE THIRST QUENCHERS— SPICED BEVERAGES

The adventurous nature of the Indian cook prompts frequent and imaginative uses of all kinds of spices extending into the preparation of even ordinary beverages. (You'd never recognize Coca-Cola after we've finished with it!) Adding slices of lemon or lime to cold water is considered quite chic in trendy restaurants in this country, while in India we have always stirred in all sorts of herbs and spices to continually surprise, quench, and refresh our thirsty palates. Our creativity is not limited to common hot or cold drinks. The diversity of the ingredients is indeed ingenious yet logical when you consider the tropical climate of the Indian peninsula.

Some additions are made just for fun, while others have medicinal purposes. It is quite common to cure a stomachache by adding lemon juice, salt, and spices to bottled Coke. I've included a centuries-old recipe for infant tonic water that generations have used successfully to treat colic.

You may not live in a tropical climate, but do try some of these exotic-sounding beverages at your next barbecue or winter gathering. You may never go back to plain soda, coffee, or tea again.

SPICED TEA

Each family has its own collection of spicy and beneficial tea recipes.

This recipe is the most common version served in Indian restaurants. The spices in this tea are an aid to the digestion process and therefore provide a perfect ending to any meal.

2 ½ cups water
1 teaspoon tea masala (see page 30)
1 ½ to 2 teaspoons loose tea leaves
¼ cup (or more) low-fat or regular milk
Brown or white sugar to taste

Place the water and tea masala in a stainless steel saucepan or kettle that can be washed, and bring to a boil over high heat. Reduce the heat to medium-low, cover the pan, and simmer for 5 minutes. Add the tea leaves (the amount depending upon the variety of the tea and the strength required). Continue to boil for about 1 minute, then add the milk. Boil once more, strain, and pour into individual cups or a large kettle or flask. Serve with sugar on the side.

Alternatively, brew the tea without any spices. Add about ⅓ teaspoon of the spice mixture to each cup and then pour in the brewed tea.

MAKES 3 CUPS

VARIATIONS: To warm you on a cold day, make your tea with black cardamom pods, cinnamon, and cloves. (These spices are also a crucial part of garam masala—see page 23—as they are believed to produce internal heat in the body.)

For a sore throat, boil the water with black peppercorns, a piece of fresh ginger, a few lemon slices, and then sweeten it with honey. (This tea has a peppery hot touch.)

To soothe indigestion and stomachache, boil the tea water with carom seeds (see page 14), fennel seeds, and black cardamom pods.

To make a pure and simple fragrant tea, add ⅛ teaspoon coarsely crushed green cardamom seeds to each cup and then top with the brewed tea. Cardamom is probably the most popular and quick addition to ordinary tea.

Hot Milk with Almonds and White Poppyseeds

BADAAM AUR KHUS KHUS KA GARAM DOODH

This deliciously flavored hot milk drink is also a home remedy for allergies and insomnia.

The ground mixture stays fresh in the refrigerator for 1 to 2 months. Use 2 to 3 table-spoons per 8-ounce serving.

¼ cup blanched almonds
4 ½ teaspoons white poppyseeds
Seeds from 7 to 10 green cardamom pods
⅛ teaspoon black peppercorns, or to taste (optional)
Sugar to taste (optional)
2 to 3 cups nonfat, low-fat, or regular milk

Place the almonds, poppyseeds, cardamom seeds and peppercorns in a coffee or spice grinder and grind until reduced to a fine powder.

In a medium-size heavy nonstick saucepan (not Teflon coated), combine the milk with the ground mixture and bring to a boil, stirring, over high heat. Reduce the heat to medium and simmer, stirring, for 2 to 3 minutes. Serve hot with a spoon in each cup, as part of the mixture settles to the bottom.

This can also be done in a microwave oven. Combine everything and place in an open microwave-safe bowl and boil on high power 3 ½ to 4 minutes per cup of milk.

MAKES 2 TO 3 SERVINGS

Infant Tonic Water

SAUNF ILLAICHI KA PANI

This excellent recipe from my mother-in-law is a natural remedy for infants who suffer from colic. My own daughters were relieved from hours and hours of pain and I honestly feel an obligation to pass this recipe on to you. My students have been very thankful for it.

Adults can also benefit from it. Increase the quantity, add some teabags (or loose tea leaves), and this drink instantly turns into a spicy tea.

⅔ cup water
1 teaspoon fennel seeds
1 black cardamom pod, crushed
⅛ teaspoon carom seeds (see page 14)
¼ teaspoon brown or white sugar

Combine everything except the sugar in a small saucepan and bring to a boil over high heat. Reduce the heat to low, cover the pan, and simmer until the water is reduced by half, 8 to 10 minutes.

Stir in the sugar and set aside to cool. Pass through a very fine sieve or a piece of muslin. Discard the whole spices.

Give 2 to 3 teaspoons only when colic strikes. Discard after 24 hours or add to soups and sauces for additional flavor.

MAKES ABOUT ⅓ CUP

FRESH LEMONADE

SHAKANJVI

Imagine yourself in a faraway land, sitting in the shade of a mango tree, eating exotic dishes, and sipping on a tall glass of intriguingly spiced lemonade made with the juice of freshly squeezed lemons. India!

¾ cup sugar
3 cups water
½ cup or more fresh lemon juice (from 2 to 3 lemons)
1 or 2 teaspoons mint masala (see page 28)
Several thin slices lemon
Several fresh mint leaves, bruised

Dissolve the sugar in the water, then add the lemon juice. Refrigerate until needed. Stir in the mint masala and serve over crushed ice or ice cubes and thin slices of lemon and mint leaves.

MAKES 4 TO 6 SERVINGS

VARIATION: Make limeade instead.

Sparkling Limeade

SODÉ VALI SHAKANJVI

In the scorching summer heat, cool yourself with sparkling *shakanjvi*, a drink that is popularly served at the more expensive Indian restaurants in India. Pakoras, samosas, and puff pastry appetizers are perfect accompaniments.

¾ cup sugar
1 ½ cups water
½ cup or more fresh lime juice (from 4 to 5 large limes)
2 cups club soda
Lime twists for garnish
Chaat masala (see page 26) or black salt (page 14) for additional flavor

Dissolve the sugar in the water, then add the lime juice. Refrigerate until needed.

Prior to serving, add crushed ice or ice cubes to four to six individual glasses and divide the limeade among them. Top with soda, garnish with lime twists, and serve. Serve chaat masala or black salt on the side. A pinch of these spices adds an unexpected pizzazz.

MAKES 4 TO 6 SERVINGS

Carbonated Guava Soda

SODÉ VALA AMROOD KA RASSA

Indian guavas are very different from the small green pineapple guavas available in this country. Ranging anywhere from 1 ½- to 3-inch rounds with a smooth yellow skin and white or reddish pink flesh embedded with innumerable tiny edible seeds, Indian guavas are similar to Mexican guavas.

As a fruit for eating, choose the slightly firm and fragrant ones. (I love them when they are very firm and slightly underripe.) The softer and riper ones are excellent for jams, jellies, sauces, and drinks.

5 very ripe 2-inch guavas, coarsely chopped
2 tablespoons fresh lemon juice
¼ cup sugar, or to taste

1 teaspoon freshly ground black pepper
1 teaspoon salt, or to taste
1 teaspoon chaat or mint masala (see page 26 or 28) or ½ teaspoon black salt
   (page 14)
Chilled club soda or water

Process the guavas in a food processor or blender until smooth, then pass through a sieve and discard all the seeds. Add the lemon juice, sugar, pepper, salt, and chaat masala. Refrigerate until needed. This puree can be refrigerated for 1 to 2 days or frozen for 2 to 3 months.

Divide the puree among six to eight glasses, add the soda, adjust the seasonings, and serve.

MAKES 6 TO 8 SERVINGS

VARIATION: This drink can be made with kiwis, mangoes, strawberries, peaches, nectarines, and fresh or canned lychees also. A few fresh mint leaves make a lovely addition.

COLD COFFEE FLOAT

THANDI KAFFEE

This is a coffee float with one difference: the coffee is made entirely with milk, no water. Like Sparkling Limeade (see page 36), this drink is a special treat to be enjoyed at outdoor cafés, as tea reigns supreme at home. At these trendy eateries this beverage is often accompanied by an assortment of Indian appetizers such as pakoras and kebabs with spicy mint chutney.

   ¾ cup nonfat or low-fat milk
   1 teaspoon sugar, or to taste
   ½ teaspoon instant coffee
   2 scoops coffee or vanilla ice cream

Place the milk, sugar, coffee, and 1 scoop of the ice cream in a blender and process for a few seconds, until foamy. Place the second scoop of ice cream in the serving glass and pour the blended coffee over it. Serve with a straw and a tall spoon.

MAKES 1 SERVING

YOGURT COOLER

MEETHI LASSI

This yogurt drink has its origin in ancient times. It is served mainly in the summer months with plain or stuffed paranthas at breakfast or as an all-day reliable thirst quencher.

This is the most basic home recipe. To this *lassi* you can also add a few drops of rose water or mint leaves. It can be made as thick or thin as you prefer.

2 cups nonfat plain yogurt
2 to 3 cups water
½ cup sugar

In a blender, process together the yogurt, water, and sugar. Serve.

MAKES 6 SERVINGS

VARIATION: To make **Mango Lassi**, blend the pulp of one or two large ripe mangoes or 1 cup canned mango pulp with the above ingredients.

Lassi that is served with meals is generally thinner and made without any sugar and contains a touch of salt, pepper, and ground roasted cumin (see page 16).

BAKED MANGO DRINK

PANNA

This savory drink with complex flavors is made with baked unripe green mangoes. More authentically, the mangoes should be baked by burying them in the dying coals of the *angithi* (a coal-burning stove), but an oven works fine. Choose the hardest raw mangoes you can find.

2 large green unripe mangoes, washed and dried
2 tablespoons finely chopped fresh mint leaves
¼ cup sugar
1 tablespoon chaat masala (see page 26)
½ tablespoon ground roasted cumin (see page 16)
1 teaspoon salt, or to taste

½ teaspoon black salt (see page 14)
4 cups water
Freshly ground black pepper to taste for garnish
Fresh mint leaves for garnish

Place the mangoes on a baking sheet and bake in a preheated 350° F oven until tender, 50 to 60 minutes. Cool, peel the skin, and separate the pulp from the seeds. (This is quite messy.) Mash the pulp and set aside. (If the pulp seems too fibrous, pass it through a sieve.)

Combine the mashed pulp with the mint leaves, sugar, chaat masala, cumin, salt, and black salt. Refrigerate until needed (up to 5 days). Mix in the water and serve over crushed ice or ice cubes. Garnish each serving with a touch of freshly ground pepper and mint leaves.

MAKES 6 TO 8 SERVINGS

SAVORY TAMARIND AND MINT COOLER

JAL JEERA

This is predominantly a summer drink. Flavored with roasted cumin seeds and black salt, this tangy cooler can be made as peppery as you like. The Indians like it very hot. The sweat induced by the peppers has a pleasant cooling effect on the body.
For each 8 ounce serving:

1 cup water
1 tablespoon tamarind powder (see page 21)
1 tablespoon fresh lime juice
1 teaspoon minced fresh mint leaves
½ teaspoon ground roasted cumin (see page 16)
¼ teaspoon black salt (see page 14)
⅛ teaspoon ground cayenne pepper, or to taste (optional)

Combine the ingredients and serve chilled or over ice cubes.

CARDAMOM-FLAVORED CHILLED MILK WITH ALMONDS AND MELON SEEDS

SARDAI OR THANDAI

This nutritious drink is fun to make for your immediate family and classy enough to be served at large gatherings. In India, people do not generally serve beer, wine, or liquor at weddings or religious ceremonies and often rely on this old-fashioned drink as an celebratory beverage. Sometimes they add saffron and rose water.

The ground mixture can be stored in the refrigerator for 1 to 2 months. Packaged mixed melon seeds (see page 18) are available in the Indian markets.

½ cup blanched almonds
½ cup mixed melon seeds or mixed pumpkin and sunflower seeds
2 tablespoons shelled pistachios
½ teaspoon black peppercorns
Seeds from 20 to 25 green cardamom pods
2 cups low-fat milk
1 cup water
¼ cup sugar, or to taste

Place the almonds, melon seeds, pistachios, peppercorns, and cardamom seeds in a spice or coffee grinder in one or two batches and grind until reduced to a fine powder. Set aside.

Combine the milk and water and stir in the sugar. Then mix in the ground nut mixture. Chill for at least 2 to 3 hours. Serve over crushed ice.

MAKES 4 TO 6 SERVINGS

Savory Appetizers and Snacks

India seems ageless to me, as seamless in the passing of time as the eternally smooth, flowing Ganges. Life in an Indian household is in a constant state of intermingling people, whether friends, family, business associates socializing, or tradesmen making their rounds. This continued daily ebb and flow of people contributes to the ease of hospitality and confident casualness associated with Indian hostesses. Rather than focusing on the few times a year when formal invitations are sent out and setting an artificial time frame for "entertaining" (which is a more Western approach), Indian families do not let the clock dictate the hours in which they receive people. Consequently, the style of providing food matches the manner of visitation. Small and varied dishes which are quick to prepare allow the hostess to spend more time with the guests and less in the kitchen.

The method of fast food preparation most frequently employed in Indian households is frying, primarily because of the short amount of time between preparation and consumption. The other reason is the historical lack of access to an oven in most Indian households. Even today electricity and gas are still not commodities taken for granted in India.

So when I devote a major part of this chapter to fried food, I want to reassure my readers that I am not rejecting my dedication to sound nutritional and healthy guidelines. The oil I use and recommend is peanut oil, which is monounsaturated and cholesterol free. Careful attention is paid to oil temperature and draining afterward to ensure that the most minute amount of oil is actually absorbed by the cooked food. Deep-frying foods correctly adds no more fat to the food than steaming or boiling and then adding margarine or a dressing. To the point that your conscience and diet allow you, please enjoy!

ABOUT PAKORA FRITTERS

Pakoras are the ultimate finger food. These deep-fried fritters are made with an eggless garbanzo bean (chick-pea) flour batter. (This flour is readily available in Indian and Middle Eastern markets and in some health food stores.) India grows two varieties of garbanzo beans, the commonly available white beans and the unfamiliar black ones (see page 275). This flour is customarily made with the black garbanzo bean variety, though sometimes regular white garbanzo beans are also used.

Pakoras are the Indian cousins of the Japanese tempuras and though both are batter fried, the end results are very different. Made with an infinite array of meats, paneer cheese, vegetables and greens, pakoras are almost a specialty cuisine in themselves. They are healthy, wholesome, and deeply satisfying, and can be served as upscale sophisticated finger foods on fancy platters with elaborate garnishes or as ordinary everyday snacks rolled in a chapati (see page 320) or sandwiched between two pieces of bread. They are generally served with an assortment of dips and chutneys, the most popular being the mint- and cilantro-based ones.

Authentic Punjabi-style pakoras are fried in mustard oil, although peanut and vegetable oils are also quite popular. Mustard oil has a high smoking point and it does not burn easily, so it is a favored choice as a deep-frying medium. Also, mustard grows almost wild in Punjab and its pungent oil (which adds a rustic aroma to foods) is highly regarded by the Punjabi population.

A vast variety of pakoras are prepared all over India, from private homes to the roadside stalls, to even the more classy restaurants. This is one snack that I was "officially" permitted to eat outside of my home, perhaps because the pakoras are generally refried before they are served and are therefore considered hygienic. In fact, these "outside" pakoras were routinely served by my Aunt Swarna, especially when she relaxed in the evening (after feeding a constant flow of relatives three to four times a week). I still remember licking my fingers after stuffing myself with cauliflower, potato, and hot chili pepper pakoras. My cousins and I loved them with *basi roti* (leftover chapatis, see page 320) and tomato ketchup (which we called sauce). The grownups, however, enjoyed them with authentic chutneys. My aunt had standing requests from us to always make extra chapatis in the afternoon, so we could enjoy some with pakoras at teatime.

The popularity of pakoras has prompted the creation of an infinite number of unusual recipes, with each region adding its own special touches. To bring this unpretentious addictive snack food to your home, I am giving you some simple recipes that can be prepared in about the time it takes to cut the vegetables and make the batter. The batter ingredients are quickly mixed manually in a work bowl (there is no need for a blender or a food processor), and the actual frying takes no more than a few minutes per batch. I have mentioned double frying for certain vegetable pakoras. This is not absolutely necessary, especially if the pakoras are going to be consumed right away. This procedure is a blessing when you make pakoras in large quantities or ahead of time.

A word about vegetable types and sizes: The firmer vegetables like cauliflower and potatoes take a longer time to soften, as do vegetables cut in large pieces. The softer ones like eggplant and zucchini become limp very fast and are a little difficult to handle (especially if they are cut in large round slices). This is when a slightly heavy coating of batter is helpful. Mushrooms and tomatoes are very delicious, but they contain too much water and sometimes tend to splatter, so take care when cooking with them. All types of cooking greens, the commonly available spinach and mustard as well as the more exotic, like colocassia (*arbi patta*), turnip, beet and white daikon greens, green and red Swiss chard, and kale, are wonderful when dipped into batter and fried or when chopped into the batter and then transformed into pakoras.

The spices mentioned in the following recipes should act just as a guideline. You can alter the spice combinations to suit your taste. Sometimes, especially if the pieces are large, I season my cut vegetables with salt and spices prior to dipping them in the batter.

I like my pakoras to be crispy and lightly battered. This allows the flavor of the vegetables to shine through and not be overpowered. A thicker coating of batter tends to become "doughy" and masks the true taste of these delicate fritters.

Before serving pakoras, I always sprinkle them with chaat masala (see page 26). This extra step adds a terrific last touch to the already flavorful pakoras, like a squeeze of fresh lime on barbecued chicken.

Always serve pakoras on large attractive platters with julienned carrots, daikon radishes, turnips, colorful bell peppers, or finely shredded colorful lettuce, purple cabbage, radicchio, or flowering white or purple kale as natural garnishes. (Make sure there is no moisture on the vegetables or leaves, because this could make the pakoras soggy.)

With this introduction, I leave you free to roam in the wonderful world of pakora cuisine.

CAULIFLOWER FRITTERS

GOBI KE PAKORÉ

Made with florets of sparkling white cauliflower, dipped in a light cumin- and coriander-flavored garbanzo bean flour batter, these crispy pakoras are an instant success wherever they are served.

This batter is also wonderful with thinly sliced potatoes and sweet potatoes, broccoli and broccoflower florets, whole or halved mushrooms, and eggplant, zucchini fingers, and even jalapeño peppers (if you are adventurous).

1 cup garbanzo bean flour (see page 254)
1 tablespoon ground coriander
2 teaspoons ground cumin
½ teaspoon garam masala (see page 23)
½ teaspoon crushed carom seeds (see page 14)
½ teaspoon paprika
⅛ teaspoon baking soda
1 teaspoon salt, or to taste
3 tablespoons finely chopped cilantro (fresh coriander)
¾ to 1 cup water
2 to 3 cups peanut oil for deep-frying
1 large cauliflower, cut into 55 to 60 florets
Sprigs cilantro or parsley for garnish
1 teaspoon chaat masala (see page 26) for garnish

Sift the flour in a medium-size bowl and mix in the coriander, cumin, garam masala, carom seeds, paprika, baking soda, and salt. Then add the cilantro and enough water to make a medium thick batter.

Heat the oil in a wok or a skillet to 350° to 375° F. (Drop ⅛ teaspoon batter into the hot oil, and if it bubbles and rises to the top immediately, then the oil is ready to be used.) Dip each cauliflower floret into the batter, shake off the excess by slapping it lightly against the bowl, and put it into the hot oil carefully to avoid splattering. Add as many as the wok can hold at one time without crowding. Fry until all the pakoras are light brown and partially cooked, 2 to 3 minutes. Remove to a cookie sheet lined with paper towels to drain.

Refry the pakoras in hot oil until crisp and golden or place the cookie sheet (with the paper towels removed) in a preheated 400° F oven for 8 to 10 minutes (or broil 6 inches from the source of heat for 3 to 4 minutes), turning them once or twice until they are crispy.

Remove to paper towels to drain. Arrange on a platter, garnish with cilantro, sprinkle the chaat masala on top, and serve.

Pakoras can be lightly fried, cooled completely, and refrigerated for 4 to 5 days. Bring to room temperature and refry or place on a cookie sheet and bake or broil as per the instructions above.

MAKES 55 TO 60 PAKORAS

GREEN BEAN FRITTERS

HARI PHALLI KE PAKORÉ

Even though the batter used in this recipe is almost the same as the one for Cauliflower Fritters, this dish is different. No Indian household or restaurant ever uses green beans to make pakoras, and I think this is rather unfortunate. In my opinion green beans are one of the finest and easiest vegetables to use for this purpose.

Choose 5- to 6-inch-long straight beans (avoid the curved ones) of the "stringless" variety or purchase any other young and tender bean and remove the strings before you start. I often use the young, round green and yellow "strike" beans that flood my farmers' market in the summer months. When made into fritters, these delicate beans magically transform into spectacular, crispy, moist "sticks," alive with flavor from the spices in the light batter. They disappear very fast, so make at least 6 to 8 per person.

Try this recipe with asparagus also.

1 cup garbanzo bean flour (see page 254)
1 tablespoon ground coriander
1 teaspoon ground cumin
1 teaspoon dried fenugreek leaves (see page 17)
½ teaspoon crushed carom seeds (see page 14)
½ teaspoon paprika
⅛ teaspoon baking soda
1 teaspoon salt, or to taste
1 tablespoon peeled and finely minced or ground fresh ginger
¾ to 1 cup water
2 to 3 cups peanut oil for deep frying
50 to 60 green and yellow stringless beans, trimmed
Sprigs cilantro (fresh coriander) or parsley for garnish
1 teaspoon chaat masala (see page 26) for garnish

Sift the garbanzo bean flour in a medium-size bowl and mix in the coriander, cumin, fenugreek leaves, carom seeds, paprika, baking soda, and salt. Then add the ginger and water and make a medium-thick batter.

Heat the oil in a wok or skillet over high heat until it reaches 350° to 375° F. (Drop ⅛ teaspoon batter into the hot oil, and if it bubbles and rises to the top, then the oil is ready to be used.) Dip each bean into the batter, shake off the excess batter by slapping it lightly against the side of the bowl, and put it into the hot oil carefully to avoid splattering. Add as many as the wok can hold at one time. Fry until they are partially cooked, 1 to 2 minutes.

Remove to a cookie sheet lined with paper towels. Finish frying all the beans and set aside. (This can be done up to 5 days ahead of time.)

When ready to serve, bring the beans to room temperature, heat the oil again, and refry the beans until they become lightly brown and crisp, 2 to 3 minutes. Drain on paper towels and arrange on a platter. Garnish with cilantro, sprinkle with the chaat masala, and serve with any green or yogurt-based chutney.

MAKES 50 TO 60 PAKORAS

SPINACH FRITTERS

PALAK KE PAKORÉ

Picture this: tender leaves of baby spinach, dipped into a spicy garbanzo bean flour batter, and then deep-fried individually until each transforms into a crunchy, dark green and golden piece of art that crackles and explodes with flavor at every bite.

Working with spinach is a little bit more labor-intensive and time-consuming, but the results are spectacular. Try to choose same size leaves if possible. This recipe is good with sorrel and amaranth leaves also.

    1 cup garbanzo bean flour (see page 254)
    1 teaspoon crushed carom seeds (see page 14)
    1 teaspoon peeled and minced fresh ginger
    1 teaspoon ground coriander
    1 teaspoon ground cumin
    ⅛ teaspoon baking soda
    1 teaspoon salt, or to taste
    About ½ cup water
    70 to 80 leaves baby spinach, with 1 ½-inch stems attached, well washed
    2 to 3 cups peanut oil for deep-frying
    1 teaspoon chaat masala (see page 26) for garnish

Sift the flour in a medium to large bowl and mix in the carom seeds, ginger, coriander, cumin, baking soda, and salt. Then add enough water to make a medium thick batter. Add the spinach leaves and mix gently (preferably with your fingers) to coat each leaf lightly with the batter. (If the batter is not thick enough or becomes too thin from the water sticking to the leaves, add some more garbanzo bean flour.)

Heat the oil in a wok or skillet over high heat until it reaches 350° to 375° F. (Drop a small leaf into the hot oil and if it sizzles and rises to the top immediately, the oil is ready to be used.) Shake off excess batter by slapping the leaf against the side of the bowl and put each batter-coated leaf into the hot oil carefully to avoid spattering and fry until it becomes crispy and golden, 1 to 2 minutes. (Add as many as the wok will hold at one time without crowding.) Remove to a cookie sheet lined with paper towels and drain for a few seconds. Transfer to a platter, sprinkle the chaat masala on top, and serve as appetizers with Yogurt Mint Chutney (see page 88).

Spinach pakoras can be made up to 2 to 3 hours in advance. Leave them on a cookie sheet lined with paper towels, at room temperature. (Do not cover them, or they will become soggy.) About ½ hour before serving, place in a 150° F oven. Transfer to a platter, garnish with the chaat masala, and serve.

MAKES 70 TO 80 PAKORAS

VARIATION: Remove the tough stems from the spinach (or any other greens), chop them coarsely, and add to the batter with all the spices. Heat the oil and drop the spinach batter in (in 2 or 3 batches) with your fingers or a serving spoon. They will fry in loose clusters. When they become crisp, remove them to a platter lined with paper towels. Separate the leaves with your fingers or leave them together. Sprinkle chaat masala on top and serve.

MIXED VEGETABLE FRITTERS

SABZ PAKORÉ

These crispy, light, intricately flavored vegetable fritters are a great way to start an evening of adventurous eating. Served with any of the enticing mint or cilantro chutneys (see pages 85 to 89) and a glass of Indian beer, they excite the palate and hint at the other great foods that have yet to appear.

Almost all types of vegetables work well in this recipe. (This is a delicious way of using leftover bits of fresh vegetables.)

1 cup grated zucchini
1 cup grated cauliflower
1 cup grated carrot
1 cup peeled and grated potatoes
1 cup finely shredded cabbage
1 cup finely chopped onion
2 or 3 serrano peppers, finely chopped (optional)
½ cup firmly packed finely chopped cilantro (fresh coriander), soft stems included
2 tablespoons peeled and minced fresh ginger
2 cups garbanzo bean flour (see page 254)
2 tablespoons ground coriander
2 teaspoons ground cumin
1 tablespoon dried fenugreek leaves (see page 17)
1 teaspoon crushed carom seeds (see page 14)
1 ½ teaspoons salt, or to taste
¼ teaspoon baking soda
2 to 3 cups peanut oil for deep-frying
1 teaspoon chaat masala (see page 26) for garnish
Few sprigs fresh parsley or cilantro for garnish

Combine the zucchini, cauliflower, carrot, potatoes, cabbage, onion, peppers, cilantro, and ginger in a medium-size bowl. Sift in the flour, then add the coriander, cumin, fenugreek, carom seeds, salt, and baking soda. (If the mixture is too soft, add a little extra garbanzo bean flour.) Make forty to forty-five 1 ½-inch round balls and set aside.

Heat the oil in a wok or a skillet to 350° to 375° F. (Drop a piece of the mixture into the hot oil, and if it bubbles and rises to the top immediately, then the oil is ready to be used.) Deep-fry the pakoras (in three to four batches), turning occasionally, until golden, about 3 to 4 minutes. Drain on paper towels and set aside. When the pakoras are slightly cool, press them lightly between the palms of your hands into small discs with ragged edges. Refry them in hot oil until crisp, 2 to 3 minutes. Drain on paper towels again. Transfer to a platter, garnish with the chaat masala and parsley sprigs, and serve with Green Mint (see page 85) or any yogurt-based chutney.

These pakoras can be made (up to the "disc" stage), cooled completely, and frozen. Thaw and refry before serving. They can also be placed on a cookie sheet in a single layer and then baked at 400 F for 8 to 10 minutes or broiled 6 inches from the source of heat for 5 to 6 minutes until crispy. Turn them over once or twice.

MAKES 40 TO 45 PAKORAS

PANEER CHEESE FRITTERS

PANEER KE PAKORÉ

This culinary triumph is nothing fancy or intimidating, just modest and simply delicious. When made well, these pakoras melt in the mouth, leaving behind a feeling of pure satisfaction.

Served with Sparkling Limeade (see page 36) or a glass of Cold Coffee Float (page 37), they remind me of my childhood, when I used to feast on this combination at least once a week.

Process some potatoes or cauliflower with the paneer cheese to increase the number and get a different flavor.

2 to 5 serrano peppers, stemmed (optional)
¼ cup loosely packed fresh mint leaves
1 recipe Basic Paneer Cheese (see page 230)
1 teaspoon salt
½ teaspoon freshly ground black pepper
1 cup garbanzo bean flour (see page 254)
1 teaspoon dried fenugreek leaves (see page 17)
1 teaspoon ground cumin
⅛ teaspoon baking soda
1 tablespoon finely chopped fresh mint leaves
¾ to 1 cup water
2 to 3 cups peanut oil for deep-frying
1 teaspoon chaat masala (see page 26) for garnish

With the food processor fitted with the metal S-blade and the motor running, process the serrano peppers and mint leaves until minced. Then add the paneer cheese, ½ teaspoon of the salt, and the pepper and process until the mixture starts to gather into a ball. Remove to a bowl and shape into 30 to 35 finger-shaped rolls. Set aside.

Sift the flour in a medium-size bowl and mix in the fenugreek leaves, cumin, baking soda, and remaining salt. Then add the chopped mint and enough water to make a medium thick batter.

Heat the oil in a wok or a skillet to 350° to 375° F. (Drop ⅛ teaspoon batter into the hot oil, and if it bubbles and rises to the top immediately, then the oil is ready to be used.) Dip each paneer cheese finger into the batter, shake off the excess batter by slapping it lightly against the work bowl, and put it in the hot oil carefully to avoid splattering. Add as many as the wok can hold at one time without crowding. Fry until all the pakoras are medium brown and crisp, 3 to 4 minutes. Remove to a cookie sheet lined with paper towels to drain.

Arrange on a platter with a bowl of Yogurt Mint Chutney (see page 88) in the center, garnish with chaat masala, and serve any time of the day.

Paneer pakoras should not be reheated or fried a second time. They are at their tastiest when served straight from the wok.

MAKES 30 TO 35 PANEER CHEESE PAKORAS

VARIATION: Cut the paneer cheese into any size squares or rectangles, season with salt and pepper, and then dip into the batter and fry. These pakoras are not as soft as the ones in the above recipe, but they are wonderful in their own right. (This is the most popular way of making paneer cheese pakoras.)

You can also make sliced onion fritters (*pyaz ke pakoré*) using thin slices of red, white, or brown onions, separated into rings if you like, dipped into the same batter.

GARBANZO BEAN FLOUR DUMPLINGS FOR KADHI

KADHI KE PAKORÉ

Made specially to add to yogurt sauce (see page 132), these pakoras contain more garbanzo bean flour than any of the other pakoras to prevent them from completely disintegrating after they are added to the sauce. As a result they are slightly more dense.

These pakoras can be served as appetizers with any mint or cilantro chutney, or added to pita pockets to make falafels.

1 ⅔ cups garbanzo bean flour (see page 254)
1 large potato, peeled and very finely diced
1 small onion, finely chopped
2 tablespoons peeled and minced fresh ginger (or less)
¼ cup loosely packed finely chopped cilantro (fresh coriander), soft stems included
1 to 3 serrano peppers, finely chopped (optional)
1 tablespoon ground coriander
1 teaspoon ground cumin
1 ½ teaspoons salt, or to taste
1 teaspoon dried fenugreek leaves (see page 17)
½ teaspoon crushed carom seeds (see page 14)

¼ teaspoon baking soda
About ¾ cup water
3 to 4 cups peanut oil for deep-frying

Sift the flour into a bowl and mix in the potato, onion, ginger, cilantro, peppers, coriander, cumin, salt, fenugreek, carom seeds, and baking soda. Add enough water to make a medium thick batter. (If the mixture is too soft, add a little extra garbanzo bean flour.)

Heat the oil in a wok or a skillet to 350° to 375° F. (Drop a piece of the mixture into the hot oil, and if it bubbles and rises to the top immediately, then the oil is ready to be used.) Gently drop 1-inch balls of batter into the hot oil with your fingers or with the help of a spoon. Deep-fry all the pakoras in three or four batches, turning occasionally, until medium brown, about 3 to 4 minutes. Drain on paper towels and set aside.

Add them to yogurt sauce, or serve them as appetizers. These pakoras can be made and refrigerated for 4 to 5 days or frozen for 2 to 3 months. To serve as appetizers, thaw and refry, bake at 400° F for 8 to 10 minutes, or broil 6 inches from the source of heat for 3 to 4 minutes, turning two or three times.

MAKES 40 TO 45 PAKORAS

VARIATION: Add 1 to 2 cups finely chopped well-washed spinach (with any tough stems removed) or any other green to the batter, adjust the seasonings, and proceed with the recipe.

BREAD AND
MINT CHUTNEY FRITTERS

DOUBLE ROTI AUR PUDINA CHUTNEY KE PAKORÉ

These flavorful and spicy pakoras are a savory, eggless, and vegetarian version of French toast. They are perfect for brunch or a light summer lunch (and picnics too), hot or at room temperature. Serve them with slices of fresh melon or peaches, and a glass of Mango Lassi (see page 38) or a banana milkshake to soothe the burning sensation from the mint chutney.

½ cup or more Green Mint Chutney (see page 85)
12 thin slices white or whole-wheat bread
1 large extra-firm tomato, very thinly sliced
¼ cup loosely packed finely chopped cilantro (fresh coriander), soft stems included
½ cup or more grated mild cheddar cheese
1 cup peanut oil for deep-frying
1 recipe batter for Spinach Pakoras (see page 46)
Chaat masala (see page 26) for garnish

Spread the mint chutney generously on six slices of the bread. Place the tomato slices on top of the chutney. Sprinke the cilantro and cheese over the tomatoes, and cover with the remaining slices of bread. Then cut each one diagonally into two triangles.

Heat the oil in a skillet (not a wok) to 325° to 350° F. (Drop a piece of bread into the hot oil, and if it bubbles and rises to the top immediately, then the oil is ready to be used.) Carefully coat each triangle with the batter (don't allow the tomatoes to slip out), then add them to the hot oil (in two or three batches). Deep-fry all the pakoras, turning occasionally, until medium brown, about 3 to 4 minutes. Drain on paper towels, cut into smaller triangles, garnish with the chaat masala, and serve fresh.

MAKES 24 TO 36 PAKORAS

BASIC SAMOSA PASTRY RECIPE

SAMOSA BANAO

An original from India, these savory triangular pastries packed with irresistible flavor are impossible to pass by. The pastry crust is traditionally made with a slightly leavened flour, shortening, and water dough. (Health-conscious people sometimes use part whole-wheat flour.) A fairly large range of fillings is used, the most popular being potatoes and peas. (Others include lentils, paneer cheese, minced lamb or chicken.) These fillings can be made mild or spicy as desired.

These already appetizing little packets are further enhanced when served with one or more of the piquant chutneys. Spicy Garbanzo Bean Chutney (see page 93) and Yogurt Mint Chutney (page 88) are my favorites.

In America, samosas are popularly served as appetizers before meals, whereas in India they are an anytime snack and are extensively served as part of afternoon or evening teas, especially at the arrival of unexpected company.

TO MAKE THE DOUGH
3 cups self-rising flour
¼ cup vegetable oil
1 teaspoon crushed carom seeds (see page 14)
¾ to 1 cup water

TO FOLD THE SAMOSAS
1 cup all-purpose flour
½ cup water
1 recipe filling of your choice

TO FRY THE SAMOSAS
2 to 3 cups peanut oil for deep-frying

To make the dough, place the flour, oil, and carom seeds in a food processor fitted with the metal S-blade and process to mix. With the motor running, pour the water in a slow stream and process until it gathers into a ball. Remove the dough from the food processor, cover, and set aside for 1 to 4 hours.

To make this dough by hand, place the flour and carom seeds in a bowl and add the oil slowly, mixing with your fingers, until all of it is incorporated in the flour. Then add half the water and keep mixing and rubbing with your fingers, adding more as needed, until it gathers together. Dip one hand in water and knead the dough with the back of your fin-

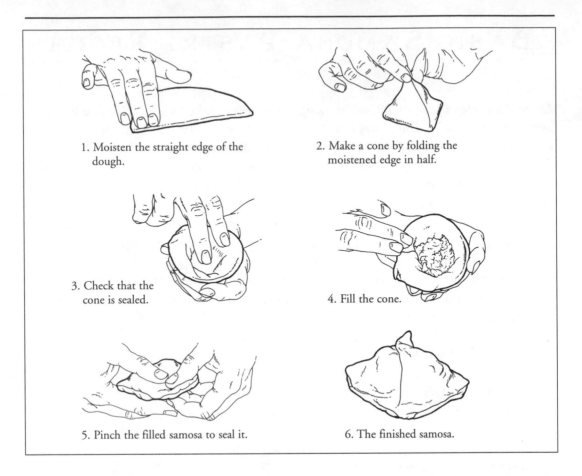

1. Moisten the straight edge of the dough.

2. Make a cone by folding the moistened edge in half.

3. Check that the cone is sealed.

4. Fill the cone.

5. Pinch the filled samosa to seal it.

6. The finished samosa.

gers, kneading and gathering it into a ball three or four times until it becomes smooth. Cover and set aside for 1 to 4 hours.

To fold the samosas, place the flour and water in two separate small bowls. With oil on your fingers, divide the dough into twenty-five 1 ½-inch round balls. Working with each ball separately, flatten with your fingertips and coat with flour. Roll into a 6- to 7-inch circle. Cut the circle in half. Moisten the straight edges with water.

Pick up each half one at a time and make a cone, as demonstrated in the illustration. The moistened edge helps seal the cone.

Fill each cone with 1 tablespoon or more of the filling and seal the opening with water. Set aside until ready to fry. Repeat with all the other balls.

Heat the oil in a wok or skillet until it reaches 350° to 375° F. (Drop a piece of the dough into the hot oil and if it bubbles and rises to the top immediately, then the oil is hot enough to be used.) Fry the samosas, as many as the wok can hold at one time without crowding, turning them a few times, until they become crispy and golden on all sides, 4 to 5 minutes. (If the samosas brown too fast, they will not cook well from the inside.) Remove to paper towels to drain the excess oil. Transfer to a platter and serve.

Samosas can be lightly fried and stored for 5 to 6 days in the refrigerator. They can also be frozen for 2 to 3 months. Bring to room temperature first and fry again until crisp and golden, or finish by baking in a preheated 400° F oven for 8 to 10 minutes, turning them once or twice. Drain on paper towels and serve.

MAKES 50 SAMOSAS

SPLIT CHICK-PEA STUFFING FOR SAMOSAS

SAMOSÉ VALI CHANNA DAL

Channa dal is made from split black garbanzo beans from which the skin has been removed. These deep yellow beans look a lot like yellow split peas, but they taste different. Yellow split peas are a good substitute.

This stuffing is superb in paranthas (see page 322) and pooris (see page 340) and in eggplant, zucchini, tomatoes, and colorful bell peppers.

3 cups dried split yellow chick-peas (see page 255), picked over and washed
5 cups water
1 teaspoon salt, or to taste
1 tablespoon peanut oil
2 teaspoons cumin seeds
1 teaspoon ground asafetida (see page 13)
1 ½ tablespoons tamarind powder (see page 21)
1 tablespoon ground coriander
1 cup firmly packed finely chopped cilantro (fresh coriander), soft stems included
1 cup finely chopped onion
2 to 5 serrano peppers, finely chopped (optional)

Place the chickpeas, water, and salt in a pressure cooker. Secure the lid and cook on high heat for 3 to 4 minutes after the pressure regulator starts rocking. Turn off the heat and let the pressure drop by itself, 15 to 20 minutes. Open the lid and set aside. The beans should be dry and firm, yet soft. (To make them without a pressure cooker, place in a large saucepan with 1 cup additional water, cover, and cook, initially on high heat for 5 to 7 minutes, then over low, until the beans are done, 45 to 60 minutes.)

Heat the oil in a heavy, medium-size pan over moderately high heat and cook the cumin seeds, stirring, until they sizzle, about 10 seconds. Stir in the asafetida, then add the tamarind powder and coriander. Mix in the cooked chick-peas and cook, stirring as necessary, over high heat until all the water from the beans evaporates and they become absolutely dry, 3 to 5 minutes.

Add the cilantro, onion, and peppers and set aside to cool. Use as a stuffing for samosas.

MAKES ENOUGH FILLING FOR 50 SAMOSAS

POTATO AND PEA STUFFING FOR SAMOSAS

SAMOSÉ VALÉ ALU MATTAR

Remember your willpower! Don't fill up on these, and allow yourself the luxury of sampling the rest of the meal.

This filling makes a charming side dish also, and can be used as a filling for a puff pastry turnovers or to make stuffed tomatoes and bell peppers.

    3 tablespoons peanut oil
    1 teaspoon cumin seeds
    2 tablespoons ground coriander
    1 teaspoon ground cumin
    1 teaspoon mango powder (see page 18)
    ½ teaspoon paprika
    1 cup firmly packed finely chopped cilantro (fresh coriander), soft stems included
    3 to 4 serrano peppers, finely chopped (optional)
    4 large potatoes, boiled until tender, peeled, and finely diced
    1 ½ cups frozen peas, thawed
    1 teaspoon salt, or to taste
    ½ teaspoon garam masala (see page 23)

Heat the oil in a medium-size nonstick skillet over moderately high heat and cook the cumin seeds, stirring until they sizzle, 10 seconds. Stir in the coriander, ground cumin, mango powder, and paprika, then add the cilantro and peppers. Add the potatoes, peas, salt, and garam masala, reduce the heat to medium-low, and cook, stirring occasionally, until the potatoes are lightly golden, 20 to 25 minutes.

Remove from the heat and set aside. Let them cool completely and use as a filling for samosas.

MAKES ENOUGH FILLING FOR 50 SAMOSAS

VEGETABLE TURNOVERS WITH CURRY POWDER

SABZI VALÉ ANGREZI SAMOSÉ

It was the British who introduced the Indians to the popular Western-style turnovers, which they made with a variety of fillings, not sweet, but savory and curry-flavored. "Mutton" (goat), chicken, and vegetables perked up with Indian spices were stuffed into puff pastry triangles or rounds to make these charming turnovers, which are called *patties* in India.

When I was a child, no one thought turnovers could be made at home. A special trip had to be made to special British-style bakeries to purchase these exotic items. It's a different story today, particularly in America, where the availability of prerolled puff pastry sheets facilitates the preparation of all types of turnovers.

Make twice the recipe at one time. These curry-flavored appetizers freeze very well (for 3 to 4 months) and can go straight from the freezer to a preheated oven.

2 tablespoons vegetable oil
½ cup finely chopped onion
1 tablespoon peeled and finely chopped fresh ginger
3 tablespoons all-purpose flour
1 ½ cups finely chopped mushrooms
½ cup grated carrots
1 to 2 serrano peppers, finely chopped (optional)
¼ cup fresh lemon juice
2 teaspoons curry powder (see page 21)
½ teaspoon salt, or to taste
Freshly ground black pepper to taste
One 20-ounce package frozen puff pastry sheets, thawed for 20 minutes
1 large egg white, beaten with 1 tablespoon water

Heat the oil in a medium-size nonstick saucepan over high heat and cook the onion and ginger, stirring, until the onion becomes transparent, 2 to 3 minutes. Add the flour and continue to cook, stirring, until everything turns golden, 3 to 4 minutes. Then add the mushrooms, carrots, peppers, lemon juice, curry powder, salt, and pepper. Reduce the heat to medium and cook, stirring occasionally, until all the liquid from the mushrooms evaporates and the carrots are soft, 3 to 4 minutes. Remove from the heat and let the filling cool before using it.

Divide the filling into two equal parts. Cut each puff pastry sheet into nine squares. Roll out each square and make it slightly larger. Baste the edges with water, place 1 tablespoon filling in each and fold it into a triangle. Seal the edges by pressing with a fork. Brush the top of each turnover with the beaten egg white and then poke a few holes so the steam can escape.

Preheat the oven to 375° F. Place the turnovers on an ungreased cookie sheet and bake until puffed and golden, about 30 minutes.

Serve hot or cold with Hot and Sour Chili Pepper Chutney (see page 91).

MAKES 18 TURNOVERS

VARIATIONS: Try different vegetables as fillings. Asparagus and scallion, cauliflower and potatoes, peas and chopped spinach are some wonderful combinations. Cooked chicken or fish is also delicious.

PUFF PASTRY STUFFED WITH FRESH MOREL MUSHROOMS

GUCCHIYAN KI TUKRI

Morels, known as *gucchiyan*, are native to Kashmir, which lies along the northern border of India. They are harvested during the summer monsoon months, then dried and distributed to the rest of India. Being one of the rarest and most expensive mushroom varieties found in India, these dark brown, cone-shaped mushrooms with an uneven ridgelike surface are reserved primarily for festive occasions, like marriage banquets and special religious ceremonies. They are especially favored when only vegetarian food is the order of the day.

In America, fresh morels are available from March to May. My own exposure to this gastronomic delight was limited to the dried variety until one day I saw fresh morels at my farmers' market. Now I look forward to the spring months when I can experience their delicate flavor. During the rest of the year, the dried ones impart a rich and smoky flavor in my kitchen experiments.

Fresh and dried morels are available in specialty stores, though of late I have been spotting them in the gourmet food sections of some supermarkets also. To reconstitute dried morels, wash them in a thin stream of water, then scrub lightly with a brush to remove all the grit. Rinse once more, then soak them in warm water for 20 to 30 minutes. Dry and use as required. The soaking liquid should be passed through a coffee filter or a sieve lined with a paper towel to remove all the grit. This liquid can be used in curries, soups, or as stock for rice.

3 tablespoons vegetable oil
1 ½ cups finely chopped onion
½ cup finely chopped fresh green garlic (see page 17) or 1 teaspoon minced garlic
1 to 4 serrano peppers, finely chopped (optional)
4 ½ teaspoons ground coriander
1 ½ cups peeled and grated russet potatoes
¾ teaspoon salt, or to taste
½ teaspoon freshly ground black pepper, or to taste
½ cup firmly packed finely chopped cilantro (fresh coriander), soft stems included
1 cup or more sliced morel mushrooms (fresh or reconstituted dried)
One 20-ounce package frozen puff pastry sheets, thawed
1 large egg white
1 tablespoon water

Heat the oil in a large nonstick skillet over moderately high heat and cook the onion, garlic, and peppers, stirring, until the onion turns medium brown, 5 to 7 minutes. Stir in the coriander, then add the grated potatoes, salt, pepper, and cilantro. Reduce the heat to medium-low, cover the pan, and cook until slightly crusty on the bottom, 5 to 7 minutes. Stir the potatoes gently, top with the sliced morels, cover the pan, and continue to cook 3 to 4 minutes longer.

Remove from the heat and set aside to cool.

Roll the thawed puff pastry sheets to make them slightly larger. Place one sheet on a cookie tray and moisten the edges with a pastry brush or your fingers. Spread the cooked potato-and-mushroom mixture evenly over it and then top with the other puff pastry sheet. Press lightly to seal the edges, then use a fork to make tine marks all around the puff pastry.

Combine the egg white with the water and brush it on top of the puff pastry. Poke plenty of holes in the top sheet. Bake in a preheated 375° F oven until it turns a rich golden color, about 30 minutes.

Remove from the oven and let it rest for 5 to 7 minutes. Then cut into desired-size pieces. These appetizers are delicious as is or served with Hot and Sour Chili Pepper Chutney (see page 91) or any other chutney. They can be served hot or at room temperature.

Cut into larger pieces, they can be the main meal themselves. Serve with Tossed Green Salad with Basil Paneer Cheese, Version 4 (see page 232) and a glass of peach-flavored ice tea.

MAKES FIFTY 1 ½-INCH PIECES

YOGURT CHEESE CUTLETS

DAHI KI TIKKI

Though the taste and flavor may seem familiar, these appetizers will keep your guests guessing. Made with tangy yogurt cheese and roasted garbanzo bean flour, these delicious cutlets can either be deep- or pan-fried. They are extraordinary with any mint or cilantro chutney. Stuff them with dry cooked beans or lentils (see pages 253 and 254), mixed vegetables, or toasted and coarsely chopped nuts and shape them into 4-inch rounds, and you have a nutritious lunchtime treat that is ideal with a cup of soup and salad.

2 cups nonfat plain yogurt
⅓ cup garbanzo bean flour (see page 254), plus 2 to 3 tablespoons for dusting
1 teaspoon ground coriander
½ teaspoon ground cumin
½ teaspoon ground ginger
½ teaspoon salt, or to taste
½ teaspoon freshly ground black pepper, or to taste
2 to 3 tablespoons peanut oil
1 teaspoon chaat masala (see page 250) for garnish

Drain and press the yogurt according to the instructions on page 146. Place in a medium-size bowl.

Sift the flour and place in a small nonstick skillet. Roast, stirring, over moderately high heat for 2 to 3 minutes, then reduce the heat to medium-low and continue to roast until it turns golden and fragrant, 2 to 4 minutes. Transfer to the bowl with the yogurt cheese. Add the spices, salt, and pepper and mix everything with a spoon or your fingers until it becomes like a soft dough. (This can also be done in a food processor.)

With lightly greased hands, divide the dough into 20 to 24 uneven balls and shape them into flat discs. Coat with flour and set aside.

Heat the oil in a large nonstick skillet over moderately high heat. Place all the cutlets in it in a single layer and fry, turning once, until golden on both sides. Transfer to a platter, garnish with the chaat masala, and serve.

Tikkis can be made 4 to 5 days in advance. Cool completely and store in the refrigerator. Reheat in a skillet with additional oil over medium heat. They can be reheated in a preheated 400° F oven for about 10 minutes. Do not freeze or reheat in a microwave oven.

MAKES 20 TO 24 TIKKIS

POTATO CUTLETS

ALU KI TIKKI

*Tikki*s are made with spicy mashed potatoes shaped into round cutlets and skillet-fried until a thick crust develops on both sides. Professional cooks in India fry these on a huge 3-foot concave griddle called a *tava* (see pages 317 and 320). Initially they are placed in the center, where the heat is high, and as they cook they are gradually moved toward the peripheries, which are less hot. Here the *tikki*s lie, sometimes for 1 to 2 hours, cooking slowly until they become crusty and deep brown.

Served open-faced or sandwiched between two pieces of bread, topped with plain whipped yogurt, Dried Mango and Fruit Chutney (see page 101), and a sprinkling of chaat or mint masala (see page 26 or 28), this appetizer snack is indeed something to rave about.

3 to 4 large russet potatoes, boiled until tender, peeled, and mashed (about 1 ½ pounds)

2 slices white bread, soaked in water until softened, then squeezed until dry and crumbled

1 ½ tablespoons ground coriander

1 teaspoon ground cumin

1 teaspoon ground ginger

½ teaspoon garam masala (see page 23)

1 teaspoon salt, or to taste

½ cup peanut or vegetable oil (or less)

Combine the mashed potatoes with the bread in a food processor or by hand, then mix in the spices and salt.

With lightly greased hands, shape the mashed potatoes into sixteen 3-inch discs. Roll each disc on a cutting board (like a wheel) to make the edges even. (Each *tikki* should be about ¾ inch thick.)

Heat 3 tablespoons of the oil in a large, heavy nonstick skillet over high heat. Place eight tikkis in the skillet (without overcrowding) and, after 1 minute, reduce the heat to medium. Cook undisturbed until the bottom becomes golden and the *tikki* does not stick to the pan, 6 to 8 minutes.

Carefully turn each *tikki* over with a spatula. Add 1 to 2 tablespoons more oil to the pan and increase the heat to high for about a minute. Then reduce the heat to medium and cook the second side undisturbed for 6 to 8 minutes.

Let the tikkis remain over low heat until they develop a rich brown color and a thick crispy crust. Turn as necessary. Repeat the process with the remaining *tikki*s.

*Tikki*s can be made 4 to 5 days in advance. Cool completely and store in the refrigerator. Reheat in a skillet with additional oil if needed over medium heat. They can be reheated in a preheated 400° F oven for about 10 minutes. Do not freeze or reheat in a microwave oven.

MAKES 16 TIKKIS

POTATO AND TAPIOCA FINGERS

ALU AUR SABUDANA KE TUKRE

This 40-year-old recipe is straight from my mother's kitchen. The starch from the cooked tapioca adds an unexpected lightness to these finger-shaped mashed potato cutlets, and the ground tapioca coating (as suggested by my friend Bharti.) forms a crunchy crust that gives an impression of freshly fallen snowflakes.

These fingers are irresistible with a glass of chilled Indian beer or a cup of Indian Spiced Tea (see page 33).

3 tablespoons tapioca
½ cup boiling water
1 tablespoon peeled and minced fresh ginger
4 to 5 scallion whites, minced
3 tablespoons finely chopped cilantro (fresh coriander)
1 tablespoon ground coriander
1 teaspoon ground cumin
½ teaspoon garam masala (see page 23)
3 large potatoes, boiled until tender, peeled, and mashed (1 ½ pounds)
2 to 3 cups peanut oil for deep-frying

Place 1 tablespoon of the tapioca in the boiling water and set aside to soak for 15 to 20 minutes. Then cook over medium heat until it becomes starchy and transparent, 4 to 5 minutes. Set aside to cool.

Coarsely grind the remaining 2 tablespoons of tapioca in a coffee or spice grinder. Transfer to a flat dish and set aside for coating the cutlets.

Add the ginger, scallions, cilantro, coriander, cumin, and garam masala to the mashed potatoes and mix. Then mix in the tapioca-water solution and shape the potatoes into thirty to thirty-five 2 ½- by ¾-inch fingers. (You may need to apply some oil to your hands when doing this.) Roll each cutlet in the ground tapioca, then between the palms of your hands. (This allows the tapioca to adhere nicely to the cutlets.) Set aside.

Heat the oil in a large wok or skillet over high heat until it reaches 350° to 375° F or until a small piece of potato thrown in the oil bubbles and rises to the top immediately. Add the potato fingers and fry until they become crisp and golden. (Somehow, after frying, these potatoes become very airy—kind of hollow—and light.)

Serve on a bed of shredded green and red cabbage. These appetizers can be made 2 to 3 days ahead of time and refrigerated. Bring to room temperature and refry. They can be frozen for 2 to 3 months. Thaw and refry or place on a cookie sheet and heat 6 inches from the broiler for 3 to 4 minutes on each side. Turn occasionally.

MAKES 30 TO 35 FINGERS

YELLOW URAD BEAN PATTIES

URAD DAL KE BADÉ (OR VADÉ)

Badé are protein-rich, crispy fried patties made with pureed lentils and/or beans. Over the centuries, creative Indian minds have figured out ingenious ways of flavoring and serving these patties. They can be served as appetizers with a chutney, as a side dish with whisked yogurt, or as an entrée when combined with Classic Curry Sauce (see page 123).

2 cups dried yellow urad beans (see page 254), picked over
About 4 ½ cups water
One 1 ½-inch piece fresh ginger, peeled
5 serrano peppers, stemmed (optional)
2 tablespoons dried fenugreek leaves (see page 17)
2 tablespoons ground coriander
1 tablespoon ground cumin
1 ½ teaspoons salt, or to taste
1 teaspoon coarsely ground black pepper
¾ teaspoon baking soda
3 large potatoes, boiled until tender, peeled, and grated
1 cup finely chopped onion
1 cup loosely packed finely chopped cilantro (fresh coriander), soft stems included
3 to 4 cups peanut oil for deep-frying
1 teaspoon chaat masala (see page 26) for garnish

Wash the urad beans in three to four changes of water, stirring lightly with your fingers until the water runs almost clear. Then soak them overnight in 4 cups of the water. Rinse the soaked beans, drain completely, and set aside.

In a food processor fitted with the metal S-blade and the motor running, mince the ginger and peppers by dropping them through the feed tube. Stop the motor, add the drained urad beans and about ½ cup water to the work bowl and process once again until the urad beans become smooth. Scrape the sides of the work bowl two or three times with a spatula. Stop the motor and add the fenugreek, coriander, cumin, salt, pepper, and baking soda and process to mix.

Transfer to a bowl, cover, and set it in a warm place for 6 to 8 hours or longer to ferment. (This fermented batter can be stored in the refrigerator for up to 3 days.) Stir occasionally.

Mix the potatoes, onion, and cilantro into the fermented batter. (The batter should be textured and thick, somewhere between a soft dough and a thick batter. You should actually be able to pick up this batter with your fingers and shape it into an irregularly shaped ball.)

Heat the oil in a large wok to 350° to 375° F, or until a pinch of batter dropped into the oil bubbles and rises to the top immediately. Gently drop 1-inch balls of batter into the hot oil with your fingers or with the help of a spoon. (Don't worry about the shape when you drop the batter to the oil.) Add as many as the wok will hold at one time without crowding. Fry the round balls partially, until they start to turn golden, then remove them to a paper towel–lined tray. Deep-fry all the *badé* in this manner, in three to four batches.

When the partially fried *badé* are cool enough to handle, press each one lightly between the palms of your hands to form thick 2-inch discs. Refry these discs in hot oil once again until crisp and brown and remove them to a tray lined with paper towels. If you wish to avoid the second frying, place the discs on a cookie sheet in a single layer and bake in a preheated 400° F oven, or broil 6 inches from the heat source, turning once or twice.

Transfer them to a platter, sprinkle chaat masala on top, and serve with Cilantro Coconut Chutney (see page 89) or Coconut Chutney (page 90).

Once the *badé* have been pressed into discs, they can be cooled completely and stored in the refrigerator for 5 to 6 days, or in the freezer for 2 to 3 months. Thaw and refry, or finish cooking them under the broiler.

MAKES 50 TO 55 *BADÉ*

BLACK GARBANZO BEAN PATTIES WITH SWISS CHARD

KALE CHANNE AUR SAAG KE BADÉ (OR VADÉ)

This recipe is a variation of the authentic Yellow Urad Bean Patties (see page 63). A little time-consuming in prep time but nevertheless very easy to follow, this recipe takes you a step further with your bean family repertoire.

Sandwich these patties between hamburger buns and smear with Zucchini Chutney (see page 94) or Cilantro Coconut Chutney (page 89) to create unparalleled vegetarian hamburgers.

1 cup dried black garbanzo beans (see page 275), picked over
About 2 ½ cups water
One 1-inch piece fresh ginger, peeled
5 serrano or jalapeño peppers, stemmed (optional)
7 to 10 red radishes, trimmed
1 cup firmly packed coarsely chopped Swiss chard or spinach, with any tough stems
    removed
1 cup firmly packed cilantro (fresh coriander), soft stems included
1 cup or more garbanzo bean flour (see page 254)
1 tablespoon dried fenugreek leaves (see page 17)
1 tablespoon ground coriander
2 teaspoons garam masala (see page 23)
2 teaspoons ground cumin
1 teaspoon coarsely ground black pepper, or to taste
1 teaspoon baking soda
1 ½ teaspoons salt, or to taste
2 to 3 cups peanut oil for deep-frying
1 teaspoon chaat masala (see page 26) for garnish

Wash the beans and soak them in 2 cups of the water for 24 hours or longer. Rinse, drain, and set aside.

In a food processor fitted with the metal S-blade and the motor running, puree the ginger, serrano peppers, and radishes. Add the Swiss chard and cilantro and process until smooth. (You will have to stop the motor and scrape the sides of the work bowl with a spatula.) Add the garbanzo beans and remaining ½ cup water and process once again, scraping the sides with a spatula, until smooth. Remove to a bowl and stir in the fenugreek, coriander, garam masala, cumin, black pepper, baking soda, and salt. Cover and keep in a warm, draft-free place for 8 to 10 hours or longer to ferment. Correct the consistency with additional garbanzo bean flour or water as required. (You should be able to pick the batter up with your fingers and shape it onto an irregularly shaped ball.)

Heat the oil in a large wok to 350° to 375° F or until a pinch of batter dropped into the oil bubbles and rises to the top immediately. Gently drop 1- to 1 ½-inch balls of batter into the hot oil with your fingers or with the help of a spoon. (Don't worry about the shape when you drop the batter into the oil.) Add as many as the wok will hold at one time without crowding. Fry the round balls partially, until they start to turn golden, and then remove them to a paper towel–lined tray. Deep-fry all the *badé* in this manner, in three or four batches.

When the partially fried *badé* are cool enough to handle, press each one lightly between the palms of your hands to form thick 2-inch discs. Refry these discs in hot oil until crisp and brown and remove them to a tray lined with paper towels. To avoid the second frying, place the discs on a cookie sheet in a single layer and broil, turning once or twice, 6 to 7 inches under the broiler, or bake them in a preheated 400° F oven.

Transfer them to a platter and sprinkle chaat masala on top.

Once the *badé* have been pressed into discs, they can be cooled completely and stored in the refrigerator for 5 to 6 days or in the freezer for 2 to 3 months. Thaw and refry, or finish cooking them under the broiler as instructed above.

MAKES 50 TO 55 *BADÉ*

YELLOW SPLIT PEA AND MUNG BEAN PUFFS WITH RAISINS

KISHMISH VALÉ PEELI MATTAR AUR MUNG DAL KE LADOO

Ladoo means round and plump. (Little babies are sometimes called *ladoo* with affection.) Falling somewhere between the *bade* (see page 63) and pakora (page 42) categories, these irregularly shaped puffs are made with split peas and yellow mung beans.

The procedure of this recipe may sound very similar to that of Yellow Urad Bean Patties (see page 63), but the finished product is very different. Each bean lends a unique texture, color, and flavor. When made into patties, these appetizers are crisp and almost crunchy, whereas as "puffs" they tend to be crisp on the outside and moist and spongy inside.

Serve with Cilantro Coconut Chutney (see page 89) or Coconut Chutney (page 90).

1 cup dried yellow split peas, picked over
1 cup dried yellow mung beans (see page 254), picked over
4 ⅔ to 4 ¾ cups water

2 cloves garlic, peeled

One 2-inch piece fresh ginger, peeled and cut into 3 or 4 pieces

5 jalapeño peppers, stemmed (optional)

2 tablespoons ground coriander

1 teaspoon ground cumin

1 ½ teaspoons salt, or to taste

¼ teaspoon baking soda

⅓ to ½ cup raisins

2 to 3 cups peanut oil for deep-frying

1 teaspoon chaat masala (see page 26) for garnish

Wash the peas and beans in three to four changes of water, stirring with your fingers until the water runs almost clear. Then soak them overnight in 4 cups of the water. Rinse, drain, and set aside.

In a food processor fitted with the metal S-blade and with the motor running, mince the garlic, ginger, and peppers by dropping them through the feed tube. Stop the motor, add the drained peas and beans and ⅔ cup of the water and process once again until they become smooth. Scrape the sides of the work bowl two or three times with a spatula. Stop the motor and add the coriander, cumin, salt, and baking soda and puree until smooth. Add more water if needed. (The batter should be textured and thick, somewhere between a soft dough and a thick batter. You should actually be able to pick up this batter with your fingers and shape it into an irregularly shaped ball.) As you shape the batter into 1-inch balls, place two raisins in the center of each one.

Heat the oil in a large wok to 350° to 375° F or until a pinch of batter dropped into the oil bubbles and rises to the top immediately. Gently drop the raisin-stuffed balls into the hot oil with your fingers or with the help of a spoon. (Don't worry about the shape when you drop them into the oil.) Add as many as the wok will hold at one time without crowding. Fry partially, until they start to turn golden, and then remove them to a tray. Deep-fry all the puffs in this manner in three to four batches.

Prior to serving, refry in hot oil until crisp and brown and remove them to a tray lined with paper towels. If you wish to avoid the second frying, place the puffs on a cookie sheet in a single layer and broil, turning once or twice, 6 inches under the broiler heat, or bake in a preheated 400° F oven.

Transfer them to a platter, sprinkle chaat masala on top, and serve. These puffs can be cooled completely and stored in the refrigerator for 5 to 6 days or in the freezer for 2 to 3 months. Thaw and refry, or finish cooking them under the broiler or in the oven as instructed above.

MAKES 55 TO 60 PUFFS

VARIATION: GREEN SPLIT PEA PUFFS *(sukhi mattar dal ke ladoo):* Use 2 cups dried yellow or green split peas instead of the combination of mung beans and split peas, increase the garlic to 4 cloves, reduce the ginger to a 1-inch piece, use 3 serrano peppers instead of 5 jalapeños, add a small onion cut into four to six wedges, add ½ teaspoon garam masala (see page 23), and reduce the amount of water added to the food processor to ½ cup. Omit the raisins. Proceed as for the original recipe, adding the onion along with the garlic, ginger, and pepper.

MUNG BEAN PUFFS FOR YOGURT

RAITE VALÉ MUNG DAL KE LADOO

Made with the easy to digest yellow mung beans and flavored just with fresh ginger and salt, these deep-fried puffs are round in shape, as the word *ladoo* suggests.

Besides being added to yogurt to make a raita (see page 147), these versatile puffs can be partnered with any fresh green or cooked chutney and served as appetizers. They are often added to the *Papri Chaat* platter (see page 71) or served with slices of marinated onion, grated daikon radish, and a tamarind chutney. My cousin Sunita Chopra often presents them in a curry sauce as a main dish.

    1 cup dried yellow mung beans (see page 254), picked over
    About 2 ½ cups water
    One 1-inch piece fresh ginger, peeled
    ½ teaspoon salt, or to taste
    ⅛ teaspoon baking soda
    2 to 3 cups peanut oil for deep-frying

Wash the beans in three to four changes of water, stirring with your fingers until the water runs almost clear. Then soak them overnight in 2 cups of the water. Rinse, drain, and set aside.

In a food processor fitted with the metal S-blade and the motor running, mince the ginger by dropping it through the feed tube. Stop the motor, add the drained beans and a little less than ½ cup of the water, and process once again until smooth. Scrape the sides of the work bowl down two or three times with a spatula. Stop the motor, add the salt and baking soda, and puree until smooth. (The batter should be textured and thick, somewhere between a soft dough and a thick batter. You should actually be able to pick up this batter with your fingers and shape it into an irregularly shaped ball.) Form the batter into 1-inch balls.

Heat the oil in a large wok to 350° to 375° F, until a pinch of batter dropped into the oil bubbles and rises to the top immediately. Gently drop the balls of batter into the hot oil with your fingers or with the help of a spoon. (Don't worry about the shape when you drop them into the oil.) Add as many as the wok will hold at one time without crowding. Fry, turning with a large slotted spoon, until they are crisp and deeply golden, 2 to 3 minutes. (A knife inserted in the middle should come out clean.) Remove them to a tray lined with paper towels. Deep-fry all the puffs in this manner, in three to four batches.

These puffs can be cooled completely and stored in the refrigerator for 5 to 6 days or in the freezer for 2 to 3 months. To use as appetizers, thaw and refry, or finish cooking them under the broiler or in the oven as instructed above, or thaw and use in other recipes.

Makes 25 to 30 puffs

Vegetarian Shammi Kebab Patties

SHAKAHARI SHAMMI KEBAB

"These are delicious. Which meat have you used with the garbanzo beans?" asked my husband, Pradeep, when I asked him to critique these vegetarian-style *shammi kebab* made with black garbanzo beans. I somehow knew that they would pass the "Pradeep" test.

It is very easy to pass these kebabs off as the authentic ones made with minced lamb or goat meat, because they look, taste, and smell like them. It's a shame when they get thrown in the trash by vegetarian friends (especially at large gatherings) who mistakenly think they are being served forbidden foods.

Make twice the recipe, serve some, and freeze the rest.

1 cup dried black garbanzo beans (see page 275), picked over
3 cups water
1 teaspoon garam masala (see page 23)
1 teaspoon salt, or to taste
2 large cloves garlic, peeled
One 1-inch piece fresh ginger, peeled
1 cup firmly packed cilantro (fresh coriander), soft stems included
¾ to 1 cup garbanzo bean flour (see page 254)
2 to 3 cups peanut oil for deep-frying

Wash the garbanzo beans and soak them in 2 cups of the water overnight or longer. Rinse, drain, and set aside. (Soaked garbanzo beans can be refrigerated for 4 to 5 days.)

Place the garbanzo beans and the remaining 1 cup water in a pressure cooker. Add the garam masala and salt, secure the lid of the pressure cooker, and boil for 4 minutes after the regulator starts rocking. Turn off the heat and let the pressure drop by itself, 10 to 15 minutes. Open the pressure cooker and check to see if the garbanzo beans are tender. If not, cook for another minute or two under pressure, with additional water if required. (The garbanzo beans should be soft with almost no water.) (To make them without a pressure cooker, place in a large saucepan with 1 cup additional water, cover, and cook, initially over high heat for about 10 minutes, then over low, until the beans are tender, 60 to 80 minutes.)

With the food processor fitted with the metal S-blade and the motor running, puree the garlic and ginger together. Stop the motor, add the cilantro, and process until smooth. Stop the motor and add the cooked garbanzo beans and liquid and process until smooth. (You will have to stop the motor and scrape the sides of the work bowl with a spatula.) Add ¾ cup of the flour and process (scraping the bowl) until everything starts to gather almost like soft dough. (Add more garbanzo bean flour if required.) Remove to another bowl and shape into ¼- by 2-inch flat discs. (You should be able to make 25 to 30 of them.)

Heat the oil in a wok or a skillet to 350° to 375° F. (Drop a piece of the mixture into the hot oil, and if it bubbles and rises to the top immediately, the oil is ready to be used.) Deep-fry all the kebabs (in three to four batches, being careful not to crowd the wok), turning occasionally, until golden, about 3 to 4 minutes. Drain on paper towels. Transfer to a platter and serve with Green Mint Chutney (see page 85) or Yogurt Mint Chutney (page 88).

The kebabs can be fried once, cooled completely, and refrigerated for 5 to 6 days or frozen for 2 to 3 months. To reheat, place on a cookie sheet in a single layer and broil 6 inches away from the source of heat until crisp, 3 to 4 minutes on each side (thaw the frozen kebabs before reheating them in the broiler), or in a preheated 400° F oven.

MAKES 25 TO 30 KEBABS

FLOUR CHIPS WITH YOGURT AND TAMARIND CHUTNEY

PAPRI CHAAT

Traditional to the state of Punjab, this ingenious specialty looks like a colorful piece of modern art, especially if served on a black or red platter. It is as easy to make and serve to one person as it is to assemble it for large gatherings. The tamarind chutney freezes very well (over 1 year), and the chips stay fresh for up to 3 to 4 weeks. The potatoes and garbanzo beans can be mashed up to 2 days in advance (or simply omitted). The final assembly takes only a few minutes. I often combine the spices together and store them separately to make it easy for myself.

The chips are also delicious with Avocado or Zucchini Chutney (see page 95 or 94).

1 package 8-inch thin flour tortillas (12 pieces), preferably vegetarian style
2 to 3 cups peanut oil for deep-frying
1 large potato, boiled until tender, peeled, and very coarsely mashed
1 cup canned garbanzo beans, drained, rinsed, and coarsely mashed
1 ½ to 2 cups nonfat plain yogurt, whisked until smooth
½ cup or more Tamarind and Ginger Chutney (see page 100)
1 teaspoon roasted ground cumin (see page 16)
½ teaspoon black salt (see page 14)
2 teaspoons chaat masala (see page 26)
Ground cayenne pepper, red pepper flakes, or chopped jalapeño peppers to taste
    (optional)
½ cup loosely packed finely chopped cilantro (fresh coriander) for garnish

Cut the flour tortillas into 1-inch pieces. Heat the oil in a large wok or skillet over high heat until it reaches 350° to 375° F, or until a small piece of a tortilla dropped into the oil immediately bubbles and rises to the top. Deep-fry the tortillas in three to four batches, turning them with a large slotted spoon, until they become golden, 2 to 3 minutes. Drain on paper towels, cool, and set aside. When completely cool, spread the chips on a serving platter. Add the mashed potatoes and garbanzo beans. Pour the yogurt evenly over the top and sides, making sure that most of the chips are covered. Drizzle the chutney all over the top of the yogurt. Sprinkle the spices and pepper on top, then garnish with the cilantro and serve immediately. The chips get soggy in about 10 to 15 minutes, but this platter should be finished within that amount of time.

MAKES 8 GENEROUS SERVINGS

CHERRY TOMATOES FILLED WITH YELLOW MUNG BEANS

MUNG DAL SE BHARÉ HUÉ CHOTÉ TAMATAR

Cherry tomatoes make perfect garnishes when added to salads and entrées, but to get maximum enjoyment both visually and taste-wise, cut, fill, and serve them as finger foods, on a bed of baby greens or parsley, or intersperse them with different baked or deep-fried appetizers.

I have seen tomatoes filled with numerous delicious fillings but have never come across one that used lentils or beans, so I developed this spicy, high-protein, and easy recipe.

3 tablespoons vegetable oil
1 cup finely chopped onion
1 tablespoon peeled and finely chopped fresh ginger
1 teaspoon cumin seeds
½ teaspoon turmeric
¾ teaspoon salt, or to taste
½ cup finely chopped cilantro (fresh coriander), soft stems included
¾ cup dried yellow mung beans (see page 254), picked over and washed
1 ½ cups water
½ teaspoon mango powder (see page 18)
½ teaspoon garam masala (see page 23)
2 to 4 jalapeño peppers, finely chopped (optional)
45 to 50 firm cherry tomatoes
3 cups baby greens or sprigs fresh parsley

Heat the oil in a medium-size saucepan over moderately high heat and cook the onion and ginger, stirring, until golden, 5 to 7 minutes. Add the cumin seeds, turmeric, and salt, then add the cilantro and stir until wilted. Add the mung beans and water and bring to a boil. Reduce the heat to low, cover the pan partially (to prevent the froth from spilling over), and cook the beans until all the water is absorbed and the beans are tender, 10 to 12 minutes. Stir occasionally. Then stir in the mango powder and garam masala and set aside. (Add some chopped jalapeño peppers if you wish to make the filling spicy hot.)

Spread the greens on a large platter. Cut a thin slice from the top of each cherry tomato and scoop out the pulp and seeds with a small spoon (a grapefruit spoon works well). Fill each tomato with the cooked beans and arrange on the platter and serve.

The platter can be assembled 8 to 10 hours in advance. Cover and refrigerate until needed. The mung beans can be prepared up to 3 days in advance.

MAKES 45 TO 50 STUFFED TOMATOES

Baked Potato Skins Stuffed with Ricotta Cheese

PANEER SE BHARÉ HUÉ ALU KE CHILKÉ

My original recipe was made with paneer cheese (see page 230), but I made the switch to ricotta when I found that it makes the whole recipe go much faster.

This stuffing can be made 4 to 5 days ahead of time and can be used to stuff vegetables like zucchini, tomatoes, and eggplant. Reheat in a microwave oven or over high heat before filling the potatoes.

12 medium-size russet potatoes (¼ pound each), baked at 350° F until tender
2 tablespoons plus 1 teaspoon vegetable oil
1 cup finely chopped onion
1 ½ cups finely chopped fresh tomatoes
1 ½ cups part-skim ricotta cheese
1 tablespoon ground coriander
1 teaspoon ground cumin
1 teaspoon garam masala (see page 23)
1 teaspoon salt, or to taste
½ cup firmly packed finely chopped cilantro (fresh coriander), soft stems included
3 to 5 serrano peppers, finely chopped (optional)
¼ cup grated mild cheddar cheese

Cut the baked potatoes in half lengthwise and scoop out the insides, leaving a ¼-inch boat. Using a pastry brush, lightly brush the potato skins on both sides with 1 teaspoon of the oil. Place on a cookie sheet and bake in a preheated 400° F oven until they become golden, 30 to 40 minutes, or deep-fry them. (Use the scooped-out potato in a different recipe.)

Meanwhile, prepare the cheese stuffing. Heat the remaining oil in a medium-size nonstick saucepan over moderately high heat and cook the onion, stirring, until it turns golden, 5 to 7 minutes. Add the tomatoes and cook, stirring occasionally, until all the liquid from the tomatoes evaporates, 5 to 7 minutes. Add the ricotta cheese and continue to cook, stirring occasionally, until all the liquid from the ricotta cheese evaporates, 5 to 7 minutes. Stir in the coriander, cumin, garam masala, and salt and cook for another 4 to 5 minutes. Mix in the cilantro and peppers and set aside off the heat.

Remove the potato skins from the oven and fill with the prepared ricotta cheese stuffing. Top with cheddar cheese and bake in a preheated 400° F oven until the cheddar cheese melts and becomes golden, 4 to 5 minutes. Serve with Yogurt Mint Chutney (see page 88) or just by themselves.

The potato skins can be assembled up to 3 days in advance and refrigerated. Final baking can be done just prior to serving. They can be frozen for 2 to 3 months. Thaw and finish baking.

MAKES 24 PIECES

VARIATION: My sister-in-law Veena Dua suggests stuffing potato skins with sautéed onion, grated bitter melon skin, and spices. The slightly bitter taste of bitter melon gives this appetizer a brand-new identity.

WALNUT AND CHEESE LOGS

AKHROAT AUR PANEER KE TUKRÉ

A new flavor for your cheese platter. In this recipe, walnut oil and balsamic vinegar–flavored paneer cheese is pureed with raisins and then shaped into small logs that are rolled in toasted ground walnuts.

Walnuts are considered the "hottest" (producing internal heat in the body) of all the nuts and are traditionally paired with raisins or raw sugar. (The general opinion is that this combination counters any reaction that the walnuts may have.) This common belief prompted me to add some raisins to the cheese before coating it with walnuts.

Serve with an array of crackers or use as a spread on toasted bread. Almonds and peanuts are wonderful in this recipe also.

½ cup coarsely chopped walnut pieces
1 recipe Flavored Paneer Cheese, Version 2 (see page 232)
½ cup coarsely chopped raisins
1 tablespoon fresh lemon juice
½ teaspoon salt
½ teaspoon freshly ground black pepper
2 to 4 tablespoons whey (left over from making the paneer) or milk

Toast the walnut pieces by placing them in a small nonstick skillet and toasting over moderately high heat until they turn golden and fragrant, 4 to 5 minutes. (Regulate the heat if it seems too high.) Cool for 5 to 7 minutes and process in a food processor fitted with a metal blade until finely ground. Transfer to a flat dish and set aside.

Place the paneer cheese, raisins, lemon juice, salt, and pepper in the same food processor and process until it gathers into a ball. You may need to add 2 to 4 tablespoons whey or yogurt if the mixture seems too dry. Remove to a bowl. Divide the mixture into three equal parts and shape each into a 4- by 1 ½-inch log. Roll these logs in the ground walnuts, making sure they are well coated. Then roll each log on another flat surface to make it smooth. As you roll, the logs will become slightly longer and thinner.

These logs stay fresh in the refrigerator for 4 to 5 days and can be frozen. Wrapped individually in colorful plastic sheets, they make great hostess gifts. You can make one large log, or numerous small balls in the same manner.

MAKES 3 LOGS

PANEER CHEESE LOGS WITH ROASTED PEPPERCORNS

KALI MIRCH VALA MULLAIYAM PANEER

These silky smooth paneer and cream cheese logs, perked up with lemon juice and roasted peppercorns, stimulate the taste buds and indulge your senses. My sister-in-law Amita Batra loves to serve them as a part of morning breakfast with wedges of crispy paranthas (see pages 329 and 332), slices of fresh mango, and hot cardamom-flavored tea.

Pressed Ricotta Paneer Cheese (see page 248) can replace the paneer cheese if desired.

½ recipe Basic Paneer Cheese (see page 230)
One 4-ounce package light cream cheese
1 tablespoon fresh lemon juice
1 teaspoon ground roasted peppercorns (see page 13)
½ teaspoon salt, or to taste
1 teaspoon coarsely ground roasted peppercorns (see page 13)

Place the paneer cheese in a food processor fitted with the metal S-blade and puree until it becomes very smooth. Add the cream cheese, lemon juice, ground peppercorns, and salt and process until smooth. Remove to a plate and refrigerate until very cold, 45 to 50 minutes. (Processed cheese is very sticky, so use a spatula to remove it from the work bowl.)

Divide the cheese into two parts and shape each one into a 4- by 1 ½-inch log. Roll each log in the coarsely ground peppercorns, making sure each is well coated with them. Serve with crackers or chopped vegetables. This cheese is sumptuous on freshly toasted bread or bagels.

To store, wrap each log in plastic wrap and refrigerate for 8 to 10 days. This cheese can also be frozen. Thaw in the refrigerator, or at room temperature.

MAKES 2 LOGS

SAVORY SNACK MIX

MILA-JULA NAMKEEN

Most Indian homes are well stocked with a variety of healthful dry snack mixtures. The spicy equivalent to the trail mixes available in America, they are made with pressed or puffed rice, crunchy garbanzo bean flour noodles, crispy lentils, garbanzo beans, seeds, and nuts, all mixed in novel combinations with aromatic herbs and spices. These mixtures can be served as a snack with a cup of tea or coffee, as an appetizer before dinner, or with a cold glass of beer or wine.

This version, though not exactly like those available in India, is still a wonderful snack to keep at home.

2 tablespoons peanut oil
3 tablespoons ground coriander
3 tablespoons chaat masala (see page 26)
2 teaspoons mango powder (see page 18)
½ to 1 teaspoon ground cayenne pepper (optional)
3 cups Rice Krispies cereal
2 cups cornflakes cereal
2 cups toasted (see note below) peanuts, with skins on
1 cup raw or toasted (see note below) sunflower seeds
2 cups canned shoestring potatoes

Heat the oil in a large wok over moderately high heat and add the ground coriander, chaat masala, mango powder, and cayenne pepper and stir for about 30 seconds.

Stir in the Rice Krispies, cornflakes, peanuts, sunflower seeds, and potatoes. Reduce the heat to low and cook, stirring occasionally, for 3 to 4 minutes, making sure that everything is well coated with the spices.

Remove the mixture from the heat and let it cool completely. Transfer it to an airtight container and store at room temperature. This mixture stays fresh for 1 ½ to 2 months.

MAKES ABOUT 10 CUPS

Note: To toast the peanuts and sunflower seeds, place them separately on a cookie sheet and bake them at 350° F until they are fragrant and lightly golden, 10 to 15 minutes. Stir two or three times.

Savory Mung Bean Snack

NAMKEEN MUNGI KI DAL

This simple preparation of lightly salted, crunchy yellow mung beans is as popular among the Indians as toasted seeds and nuts are among Americans.

Try it in place of bacon bits to add a delicate crunch to salads and cooked rice. It is very attractive as a garnish, especially on green, red, or white casseroles.

2 cups dried yellow mung beans (see page 254), picked over
Scant pinch of baking soda
4 cups hot water
3 to 4 cups peanut oil for deep-frying
½ teaspoon salt, or to taste

Wash the beans in three to four changes of water, stirring with your fingers, until the water runs almost clear. Stir in the baking soda and soak them overnight in the hot water.

Drain the beans well and spread them on a cookie sheet lined with several layers of paper towels until completely dry, 30 to 40 minutes. Stir a few times with your fingers to ensure proper drying. (This is essential, because water drops on the beans will cause the oil to splatter when they are fried.)

Heat the oil in a large wok over high heat to 375° to 400° F, or until a few beans dropped into the hot oil bubble and rise to the top immediately. Have ready another cookie sheet lined with paper towels. Put about one-third of the beans in a large, fine sieve and place the sieve (with the beans in it) in the hot oil. The oil will immediately start to foam, and some of the beans may escape into the oil. Fry the beans until the foaming subsides, about 1 minute, then transfer them to the cookie sheet. (Remove the beans in the oil with a spoon.) Repeat this process with the remaining beans.

When all the beans are fried, transfer them to a bowl and mix in the salt. Let everything cool to room temperature, then transfer to an airtight container. This snack should stay fresh for 2 to 3 months.

MAKES ABOUT 4 CUPS

VARIATION: Add 1 to 2 teaspoons of chaat masala (see page 26) or mint masala (page 28) instead of the salt.

CRUNCHY GARBANZO BEANS

CHANNA JOR GARAM

Crunchy, spicy, and fiery-flavored is how I remember these beans. The first bite gets you hooked, and even the intensity of the chili peppers cannot stop you from finishing your share. Sold in 8- to 10-inch conical paper cups, with an opening no larger than 1 ½ inches, these munchies were a must (like popcorn in movie theaters) each time we went for a stroll in the gardens outside the Rashtrapati Bhavan (Indian Presidential Quarters). By this time even the strongest of us had a raging fire inside our mouths, so we would continue our walk down to the majestic India Gate, a memorial constructed to commemorate the Indian soldiers who fought in World War I, and head straight to the ice-cream vendor to put out the flames.

I promise this recipe won't be as hot. To make it even milder, simply omit the cayenne pepper.

2 cups dried garbanzo beans, picked over
½ teaspoon baking soda
4 cups very hot water (not boiling)
2 teaspoons mango powder (see page 18)
1 teaspoon salt, or to taste
½ teaspoon black salt (see page 14)
½ teaspoon freshly ground black pepper, or to taste
½ teaspoon ground cayenne pepper, or to taste (optional)
¼ teaspoon citric acid (optional; found in the baking section of the supermarket)
3 to 4 cups peanut oil for deep-frying

Wash the beans in three to four changes of water, stirring with your fingers, until the water runs almost clear. Stir in the baking soda and soak them for 20 to 24 hours in the hot water.

Drain the beans well, then wipe them with kitchen towels until completely dry. Spread them on a cookie sheet lined with paper towels and further air-dry them for 7 to 10 minutes. (This is essential, because water drops on the beans will cause the oil to splatter when they are fried.)

While the beans are drying, mix all the spices and the citric acid together and place them in a medium-size bowl.

Heat the oil in a large wok over high heat to 350° to 375° F, or until a bean dropped into the hot oil bubbles and rises to the top immediately. Put the garbanzo beans in the hot oil. (The oil will immediately start to bubble vigorously, then slowly stop bubbling.) Fry the beans until they are lightly golden and crispy, 15 to 18 minutes. (Frying causes the water in the beans to evaporate, and makes them much lighter.) Remove them with a slotted spoon to a cookie sheet lined with paper towels. Drain for 2 to 3 minutes.

Transfer the beans to the bowl containing the spices. Mix with a large spoon, making sure that all the beans are well coated with the spices. Taste and adjust the seasonings while the beans are still hot.

Cool to room temperature, then transfer to an airtight container. These beans should stay fresh for 1 to 2 months.

MAKES ABOUT 4 CUPS

VARIATION: Add 1 to 1 ½ tablespoons chaat masala (see page 26) or mint masala (page 28) instead of mixing the beans with the spices.

SANDWICHES WITH AN INDIAN FLAVOR

HINDUSTAN KI DOUBLE ROTI

Though the whole world starts with the same basic flour and water, they end up with totally different breads. Breads as we know them in the Western world are very different from Indian ones. As a general rule, Indian breads are made with unleavened dough that is rolled into flat rounds and then cooked on a griddle.

Western-style bread loaves (introduced to India by the British) are made with dough that has risen to twice its volume, therefore they are referred to as "double roti" (bread). Today this bread has become a very important part of the Indian household, especially in the larger cities, and the Indians have developed countless recipes made with this invaluable staple.

White bread, cut into medium-thick slices, is by far the most popular bread in India, mainly because it provides a variation from the indigenous whole-wheat breads. It is topped with a variety of raw and cooked vegetables; tomatoes top the raw vegetable list, with cucumbers and an uncooked green mint or cilantro chutney a close second. All types of cooked "dry" vegetable dishes, especially Barbecued Eggplant with Onions and Tomatoes (see page 165) and Paneer Cheese with Tomatoes and Onion (page 239) are wonderful served on or with toasted breads or in combination with greens to make sandwiches.

Listed below are just a few ways this bread can be transformed into savory treats.

CRISPY TOMATO AND CHEESE TOAST SQUARES

TAMATAR AUR CHEESE KI DOUBLE ROTI

Oven grilled and crispy, these savory open-faced toasts can be served as an appetizer or a light lunch. Serve them with a glass of freshly squeezed orange or grapefruit juice perked up with some carbonated soda and a pinch of chaat or mint masala (see page 26 or 28). Seasonal fruits are a lovely accompaniment.

My family loves these sandwiches on sourdough bread, but rye, oatmeal, and whole-wheat are also excellent choices.

2 tablespoons (or less) unsalted butter, at room temperature
Eight 4-inch-square slices bread
2 cups ripe tomatoes, finely chopped
½ cup scallion whites, finely chopped
2 to 5 serrano peppers, finely chopped (optional)
Salt and freshly ground black pepper to taste
1 cup or more grated mild cheddar (or cheddarella) cheese
½ cup loosely packed finely chopped cilantro (fresh coriander) for garnish

Spread a light coating of butter on each piece of bread. Place the chopped tomatoes, scallion whites, and serrano peppers on top of each slice, then sprinkle with salt and pepper. Top with the grated cheese, place on an ungreased cookie sheet, and bake in a preheated 400° F oven until the bread is crisp and the cheese melts and gets dotted with golden spots, 10 to 12 minutes.

Remove from the oven, garnish with the chopped cilantro, cut into small squares or triangles (or leave them whole), and serve.

MAKES EIGHT 4-INCH SLICES OF BREAD

DAINTY CUCUMBER AND MINT CHUTNEY SANDWICHES

KHEERÉ AUR CHUTNI KE SANWICH

It is imperative to use extra-thin bread to make these attractive and extremely addictive sandwiches. These were occasional lunch box treats when we were growing up. They can be prepared about a day in advance, covered tightly with plastic wrap, and stored in the refrigerator. This makes them a perfect choice for large gatherings.

One 1-pound loaf extra-thin white or whole-wheat bread (24 slices)
⅔ cup Green Mint Chutney (see page 85)
½ cup (or less) unsalted butter, at room temperature
1 large English hothouse or 4 pickling cucumbers, peeled and thinly sliced
Finely shredded red cabbage or grated carrot for garnish
Delicate bean sprouts for garnish

Cut off the crust from all sides of the bread slices. Place the chutney in a fine sieve to remove most of the liquid, 1 to 2 minutes (do not let it drain completely dry, or it won't spread).

Spread a light coating of butter on each slice. Divide the loaf into two parts. Spread about 1 teaspoon chutney on half the slices, then place cucumber slices over the chutney, making sure that you reach all the corners. Top with the remaining bread slices.

Cut into triangles or rectangles and transfer to a platter. Do not pile one on top of another, but place them in an overlapping manner. Garnish with shredded cabbage and bean sprouts and serve.

MAKES ABOUT 24 SANDWICHES

VARIATION: Mash 1 hard-boiled (or ¾ boiled) egg and mix it in with the butter. Season the butter with 1 teaspoon dry mustard, salt, and pepper and use it in place of the mint chutney.

Add thin slices of Swiss cheese, tomatoes, colorful bell peppers, and delicate sprouts such as onion, alfalfa, clover, or radish.

GRILLED MUSHROOM AND CHEESE SANDWICHES

KHUMB AUR CHEESE KE SANWICH

This spread is excellent on English muffins, long French or sourdough loaves, and also on ordinary everyday bread slices. Serve Hot Pepper Chutney with Ginger and Lemon Juice (see page 92) on the side to add fire, along with a hot soup and a green salad with Lime and Peppercorn Dressing (page 118). Round off the meal with Layered Vanilla and Chocolate Fudge (see page 363).

¼ cup light mayonnaise
½ cup light sour cream
½ cup grated mild cheddar or Colby cheese
3 cups finely chopped mushrooms (about 8 ounces)
¼ cup finely chopped scallion greens
2 tablespoons finely chopped fresh basil or ½ teaspoon dried
½ teaspoon curry powder (see page 21)
½ teaspoon salt, or to taste
½ teaspoon freshly ground black pepper to taste
One 1-pound long French or sourdough loaf, cut into 16 diagonal slices
Shredded or whole leaves curly lettuce for garnish

Place the mayonnaise, sour cream, and cheese in a medium-size bowl. Stir in the mushrooms, scallion greens, basil, curry powder, salt, and pepper.

Divide the mixture and spread it evenly on each slice of bread. Then place on a cookie sheet and bake in a preheated 400° F oven until the bread becomes crisp, 10 to 12 minutes. Place under the broiler till the tops turn slightly golden, 2 to 3 minutes. Serve on a platter lined with lettuce leaves.

MAKES 16 SANDWICHES

TASTY TOAST WITH COOKED PANEER CHEESE

SANCHÉ VALÉ BUND SANWICH

Made in electric or manual grills, these sandwiches, served hot, are very popular with all Indians and are distinguished by their characteristic of completely enveloping or sealing in their contents.

Use any type of "dry" cooked vegetables as a stuffing. (I make them with fresh finely chopped tomatoes and grated mild cheddar cheese also.)

1 tablespoon safflower oil
½ cup finely chopped onion
½ teaspoon cumin seeds
1 teaspoon ground coriander
⅛ teaspoon turmeric
2 tablespoons nonfat plain yogurt, whisked lightly

1 cup crumbled Basic Paneer Cheese (see page 230) or Pressed Ricotta Paneer Cheese (page 248)
¼ cup loosely packed finely chopped cilantro (fresh coriander), soft stems included
1 tablespoon butter or more
Eight 4-inch-square slices bread

Heat the oil in a medium-size saucepan over moderately high heat and cook the onion, stirring, until golden. Stir in the cumin seeds, coriander, and turmeric. Add the yogurt and paneer cheese and cook, stirring, until all the liquid from the yogurt evaporates and the cheese becomes slightly golden, 4 to 5 minutes. Add the cilantro and remove from the heat.

Lightly butter the bread slices. Place 1 ½ to 2 tablespoons of the filling in the center of the unbuttered side of four of the slices. Cover with the remaining slices (keeping the buttered side outside). Place the sandwich in a sandwich grill and grill according to the manufacturer's instructions.

MAKES 4 SANDWICHES

VARIATIONS: Add diced cooked potatoes, diced summer squash, grilled and mashed or diced eggplant, chopped greens, etc., instead of the paneer cheese.

"SUBMARINE" SANDWICHES WITH VEGETABLE FRITTERS

SABZ PAKORÉ VALI LAMBI DOUBLE ROTI

12 to 15 Mixed Vegetable Pakoras, Vegetarian Shammi Kebab Patties, or *bade* (see page 47, 69, or 63)
½ cup or more Green Mint or Yogurt Mint Chutney (see page 85 or 88)
One 1-pound long French or any other soft loaf, cut in half lengthwise
Shredded bronze or red oakleaf lettuce to cover one side of the bread
2 medium-size red onions, thinly sliced
2 large firm tomatoes, thinly sliced
1 large yellow bell pepper, seeded and thinly sliced
½ cup or more grated mild cheddar cheese
1 cup clover, onion, or radish sprouts (or mixed)

Press the pakoras between the palms of your hands to flatten them into disks. Spread the chutney generously on the cut sides of both halves of the bread loaf. On the bottom half, spread the lettuce, onions, tomatoes, pepper, cheese, and sprouts (in that order). Top with the flattened pakoras. Cover with the top half of the loaf. Slice and serve with additional chutney.

MAKES 1 LARGE SANDWICH

Lost in the Chutney World

There are some Hindi words that don't translate well into English. Although *chutney* has become as familiar a term to American cooks as other foreign culinary terms such as *pesto* or *salsa*, to native Indians the word simply means an unrecognizable mush. Whether it is cooked or uncooked, its intended use in Indian cuisine is to bring a distinctive zest and diversion to the palate. It can be sweet or sour, spicy or soothing, but it is always a looked-for addition on an Indian table, used to personally customize a meal. That is one of the unique characteristics about Indian meals. With the table laden with so many different types of dishes and condiments, an individual can select and create a dish quite different from that of the person sitting right next to her or him.

A chutney can be used as a dipping sauce for appetizers, with main entrées, or even mixed with sweetened yogurt for dessert. My father's favorite ending to a meal is yogurt with mango chutney added to it. As with all my recipes, you can substitute your favorite fruit or vegetable for those listed and create your own new and exciting "mush."

You can freeze the processed chutney in ice cube trays, then place the cubes in plastic freezer bags and use when needed.

Green Mint Chutney

PUDINA CHUTNI

A traditional Indian chutney with extraordinary flavors, this basic chutney is the ultimate companion to all types of Indian appetizers. It can be served with meals as a condiment, added to plain yogurt to make a raita (see page 147), or to freshly steamed vegetables for additional flavor. It is excellent as a spread for sandwiches or as a "spice" when added to dishes while they are cooking. I often combine it with more lemon juice and use it as a quick marinade for fish or chicken.

It is so easy to make and also to freeze that you can have it on hand almost all the time. Frozen, this chutney retains its brilliant green color, whereas the refrigerated chutney starts to become pale as the days go by. This, however, does not affect the flavor.

3 to 5 serrano peppers, stemmed
6 scallions, cut into 3 to 4 pieces
1 small green bell pepper, seeded and cut into 4 to 5 pieces
1 cup firmly packed fresh mint leaves
2 cups firmly packed cilantro (fresh coriander), soft stems included
¼ cup fresh lime or lemon juice
1 teaspoon sugar
1 teaspoon salt, or to taste
½ teaspoon freshly ground black pepper
Cilantro or mint leaves for garnish

In a food processor fitted with the metal S-blade, process the serrano peppers, scallions, and bell pepper until smooth. Add the mint and cilantro. Start the machine and add the lime juice in a fine stream and blend until smooth. Then add the sugar, salt, and black pepper and process until well blended. (Stop the machine and scrape the sides of the work bowl a few times.)

Transfer to a bowl, garnish with cilantro, and serve. This chutney stays fresh in the refrigerator 10 to 15 days and in the freezer for up to 6 months.

MAKES ABOUT 2 ½ CUPS

GARLIC, GINGER, AND CILANTRO CHUTNEY

LASUN ADRAK AUR DHANIA KI CHUTNEY

Since garlic, ginger, and carom seeds are excellent digestive aids, this chutney should be paired with foods that are hard to digest, such as legumes, beans, and cruciferous vegetables (cauliflower, broccoli, and brussel sprouts).

1 tablespoon ground cumin
1 teaspoon freshly ground black pepper, or to taste
1 teaspoon carom seeds (see page 14)
One 1-inch piece fresh ginger, peeled
2 to 3 large cloves garlic, peeled
3 to 4 serrano peppers, stemmed (optional)
4 scallions, cut into 3 pieces each
1 small green bell pepper, seeded and cut into 4 to 5 pieces
3 cups firmly packed cilantro (fresh coriander), soft stems included
¼ cup fresh lime or lemon juice
1 ½ teaspoons salt, or to taste
1 teaspoon sugar

Place the cumin, black pepper, and carom seeds in a small nonstick skillet and roast, stirring gently, over moderately high heat until they turn dark brown, 1 to 2 minutes. Remove from the hot skillet and set aside.

In a food processor fitted with the metal S-blade, process the ginger, garlic, serrano peppers, scallions, and bell pepper until smooth. Add the cilantro. Start the machine and add the lime juice in a fine stream and blend until smooth. Add the salt, sugar, and the roasted spices and process until smooth. (Stop the machine and scrape the sides of the work bowl a few times.)

Transfer to a serving bowl and serve as a dip with appetizers or as a condiment with meals. This chutney stays fresh in the refrigerator 10 to 15 days. It also freezes well up to 6 months.

MAKES ABOUT 2 CUPS

MINT AND TOMATO CHUTNEY

PUDINA AUR TAMATAR KI CHUTNI

This Indian version of Mexican-style salsa has universal appeal. It can be served with traditional Indian meals or other cuisines of the world or as a dip with vegetables and chips. (Flour tortilla chips, as made for *Papri Chaat*—see page 71—are an excellent choice.) Add some garlic and this chutney instantly becomes a fragrant marinade for meats, poultry, and seafood.

One ½-inch piece fresh ginger, peeled
4 scallions, cut into 3 to 4 pieces
5 jalapeño peppers, stemmed (optional)
2 large ripe tomatoes, quartered (about 1 pound)
1 cup firmly packed fresh mint leaves
½ cup firmly packed cilantro (fresh coriander), soft stems included
3 tablespoons fresh lime or lemon juice
½ teaspoon garam masala (see page 23)
1 ½ teaspoons salt, or to taste
½ teaspoon freshly ground pepper, or to taste
Several fresh mint leaves for garnish

In a food processor fitted with the metal S-blade, process the ginger, scallions, jalapeños, and tomatoes until smooth. Add the mint and cilantro. Start the machine and add the lime juice in a fine stream and blend until the chutney is smooth. (Stop the machine and scrape the sides of the work bowl a few times with a spatula.) Add the garam masala, salt, and pepper and process once again.

Transfer to a bowl, garnish with mint leaves, and serve. This chutney stays fresh in the refrigerator for about 15 days and in the freezer for 6 months.

MAKES ABOUT 2 CUPS

YOGURT MINT CHUTNEY

DAHI PUDINA CHUTNI

This multipurpose, tangy, and refreshing yogurt chutney is a dish in itself. Present it as a condiment, side dish, a dip, or as a topping to liven up the flavor of cooked vegetables and rice. Served with baked or mashed potatoes, it raises their status to "gourmet food."

5 serrano peppers, stemmed (optional)
4 scallions, cut into 3 to 4 pieces each
1 cup firmly packed fresh mint leaves
1 cup firmly packed cilantro (fresh coriander), soft stems included
2 tablespoons fresh lemon or lime juice
1 cup nonfat plain yogurt, whisked until smooth
1 tablespoon ground roasted cumin (see page 16)
½ teaspoon freshly ground black pepper, or to taste

½ teaspoon black salt (see page 14; optional)
1 teaspoon salt, or to taste
Several fresh mint leaves for garnish

In a food processor fitted with the metal S-blade, process the serrano peppers and scallions until smooth. Add the mint and cilantro. Start the machine and add the lemon juice in a fine stream and blend until smooth. (Stop the machine and scrape the sides of the work bowl a few times with a spatula.)

Place the yogurt in a serving bowl, and mix in the processed chutney. Stir in the roasted cumin, pepper, black salt, and salt and refrigerate until needed. Garnish with mint leaves and serve.

This chutney stays fresh in the refrigerator for 6 to 8 days. It cannot be frozen because the yogurt becomes watery when thawed. The greens can be processed and frozen separately for about 6 months. Mix with the yogurt and spices when needed.

MAKES ABOUT 2 CUPS

CILANTRO COCONUT CHUTNEY

DHANIA AUR NARIYAL KI CHUTNI

When pureed in the food processor, fresh coconut does not become completely smooth, and manages to retain its delicate crunch, which in turn adds a new dimension to this everyday green chutney.

This chutney is unparalleled when served with all types of bean and lentil appetizers. It is also outstanding when enriched with toasted nuts and offered with barbecued meats and vegetables.

3 to 5 jalapeño peppers, stemmed (optional)
4 scallions, cut into 3 pieces each
½ cup shelled and peeled fresh coconut pieces
2 cups firmly packed cilantro (fresh coriander), soft stems included
¼ cup fresh lime or lemon juice
1 teaspoon sugar
1 teaspoon salt, or to taste
½ cup nonfat plain yogurt
Cilantro sprigs for garnish

In a food processor fitted with the metal S-blade, process the peppers, scallions, and coconut until smooth. Add the cilantro. Start the machine and add the lime juice in a fine stream and blend until smooth. (Stop the machine and scrape the sides of the work bowl a few times with a spatula.)

Add the sugar, salt, and yogurt and process once more until smooth. Transfer the chutney to a bowl, garnish with cilantro sprigs, and serve. This chutney stays fresh in the refrigerator for 8 to 10 days. It cannot be frozen because the yogurt becomes watery when thawed. It can, however, be frozen without the yogurt for about 6 months. Add the yogurt when you're ready to serve.

MAKES ABOUT 1 ½ CUPS

COCONUT CHUTNEY

NARIYAL KI CHUTNI

Using fresh coconut is essential in this traditional favorite. Preparing the coconut is quite a tedious process, but once it is done, this chutney is very easy to make and enjoy.

Like Cilantro Coconut Chutney (see page 89), this authentic chutney, originating from southern India, is superb with all types of bean and lentil appetizers. It is especially good when served with South Indian-Style Lentil Soup (see page 264) and Potatoes with Onion and Mustard Seeds (page 191).

    4 or 5 jalapeño peppers, stemmed (optional)
    1 fresh coconut, shelled, peeled, and coarsely chopped
    3 tablespoons fresh lime or lemon juice
    ½ cup firmly packed cilantro (fresh coriander), soft stems included
    3 tablespoons sambar masala (see page 28)
    1 teaspoon salt, or to taste
    1 cup nonfat plain yogurt
    1 tablespoon mustard or vegetable oil
    1 teaspoon black mustard seeds

In a food processor fitted with the metal S-blade, process the peppers, coconut, and lime juice until smooth. Add the cilantro, and process until smooth. (Stop the machine and scrape the sides of the work bowl a few times with a spatula.) Add the masala, salt, and yogurt and process once more until smooth.

Transfer the chutney to a serving bowl and set aside. Heat the oil in a small saucepan over high heat and fry the mustard seeds until they pop, 20 to 30 seconds. Pour them immediately over the chutney, stir gently to mix, and serve.

This chutney stays fresh in the refrigerator for 8 to 10 days, or in the freezer for about 6 months.

MAKES ABOUT 2 ½ CUPS

HOT AND SOUR CHILI PEPPER CHUTNEY

SIRKA MIRCH CHUTNI

Made simply by mixing sliced green chili peppers and spices in vinegar, this modest chutney adds a tangy flavor and hot bite to even the blandest of foods. Serve as a condiment with appetizers, barbecued foods, or with meals. This chutney is especially superb with all puff pastry treats. If you want it even hotter, add some of the super-hot orange habañero peppers.

Be careful when you slice the peppers; they leave a long-lasting effect on the fingers and can cause a burning sensation if you accidentally touch your mouth or eyes. Use gloves to protect your hands. The slicing can be done in a food processor if you like.

¼ cup finely sliced serrano or jalapeño peppers
1 tablespoon salt, or to taste
½ cup red wine or any flavored vinegar
1 teaspoon coarsely ground roasted peppercorns (see page 13)
1 teaspoon dried mint leaves (optional)

Place the peppers in a small glass bottle. Mix in the salt and set aside for 2 to 3 hours at room temperature.

Stir in the vinegar, peppercorns, and mint. Refrigerate at least 24 hours before using. This chutney stays fresh for over a year in the refrigerator. Use sparingly as needed. To get flavor without too much heat, season your food only with the pepper-flavored vinegar, avoiding the peppers.

MAKES ¾ CUP

Hot Pepper Chutney with Ginger and Lemon Juice

MIRCHI AUR ADRAK KI KHATTI CHUTNI

This brilliant red chutney is a head-clearing blend of serrano peppers, ground red chilies, fresh ginger, and spices. Even my most daring Indian friends eat this one with caution. I always keep a supply of this chutney in my refrigerator. Half a teaspoon is exceptional on pizza or pasta or with Mexican food. My friends Raghu and Neelam Rai love it on all types of salads, including fruit salads. They insist that this chutney livens up the flavors of the otherwise bland nonfat salad dressings.

Add some habañero peppers to make this chutney into dynamite. To make it really mild, combine jalapeño peppers with green or red bell peppers and then proceed with the recipe. (Always wear gloves when working with serrano peppers.)

4 ounces serrano peppers, stemmed
One 2-inch piece fresh ginger, peeled and cut into 3 to 4 pieces
1 ½ teaspoons salt, or to taste
1 tablespoon coarsely ground carom seeds (see page 14)
¼ cup ground cayenne pepper
1 tablespoon coarsely ground black pepper
½ cup or more fresh lemon juice

In a food processor fitted with the metal S-blade, process the peppers and ginger until smooth.

Add the salt, carom seeds, cayenne, black pepper, and lemon juice. Process once again to mix well. Refrigerate at least 24 hours before using. This chutney stays fresh for 6 to 8 months in the refrigerator. Do not freeze. Use sparingly as needed.

MAKES ABOUT 1 CUP

VARIATION: To give this chutney a new character, add ground dried mint, basil, dill, or any other herbs of your choice.

SPICY BEAN CHUTNEY

CHATPATI CHANNÉ KI CHUTNI

This high-protein cooked chutney is popularly served with samosas (see page 53) and pakoras (page 42), but it can just as easily be served as a main dish with *Ajwain Poori* (see page 340) if the amount of tamarind in it is reduced.

1 tablespoon mustard or peanut oil
1 teaspoon minced garlic
1 teaspoon peeled and minced fresh ginger
½ cup finely chopped onion
1 teaspoon ground cumin
⅛ teaspoon turmeric
One 15 ½-ounce can garbanzo beans, drained and rinsed
1 ½ cups water
¼ cup tamarind powder (see page 21)
2 tablespoons finely chopped cilantro (fresh coriander)

Heat the oil in a small nonstick wok or saucepan over moderately high heat, then stir-fry the garlic and ginger until golden, 1 to 2 minutes. Add the onion and cook, stirring as necessary, until it turns brown, 2 to 3 minutes. Stir in the cumin and turmeric, then add the garbanzo beans and water. Reduce the heat to medium-low, cover the pan, and cook until the beans become very soft, 10 to 15 minutes. (Crush some of the beans to thicken the chutney.) Add the tamarind powder and cook, stirring, for another 5 minutes. (Add 2 to 4 tablespoons boiled water if the chutney looks too thick; tap water encourages spoilage.)

Transfer to a serving bowl, garnish with the cilantro and offer as a condiment with deep-fried appetizers. This chutney stays fresh in the refrigerator for 5 to 6 days and can be frozen for up to 4 months.

MAKES 1 ½ CUPS

ZUCCHINI CHUTNEY

GHIA KI CHUTNI

This southern Indian–style chutney, often served by my friend Gayatri Sirohi, has a very refreshing flavor that marries well with grilled or pan-sautéed seafood, especially shrimp. As a dip it provides a tangy zip to freshly cut vegetables, and it can be used as a sandwich spread or be added to yogurt to make an unusual raita (see page 150).

1 tablespoon olive oil
2 large cloves garlic, coarsely chopped
½ cup finely chopped onion
1 teaspoon brown mustard seeds
½ heaped teaspoon asafetida (see page 13)
¾ cup diced zucchini or any other squash
2 to 4 serrano peppers, stemmed (optional)
½ cup firmly packed coarsely chopped cilantro (fresh coriander) leaves, soft stems
  included
¼ cup loosely packed coarsely chopped fresh mint leaves
1 tablespoon fresh lemon juice
3 tablespoons nonfat plain yogurt
½ teaspoon salt, or to taste
½ teaspoon freshly ground black pepper, or to taste
Cilantro or mint leaves for garnish

Heat the oil in a small saucepan over moderately high heat and cook the garlic and onion, stirring, until golden, 3 to 4 minutes. Add the mustard seeds and asafetida and cook, stirring, about 1 minute. Add the zucchini, peppers, cilantro, and mint and cook over medium heat until the zucchini becomes tender, 7 to 10 minutes. Remove from the heat and set aside to cool for 10 to 15 minutes.

Place in a blender or a food processor with the lemon juice, yogurt, salt, and pepper and blend until smooth. Remove to a serving bowl, garnish with cilantro, and serve.

This chutney stays fresh in the refrigerator for 5 to 6 days and can also be frozen for 2 to 3 months. Serve cold or at room temperature.

MAKES ABOUT 1 CUP

VARIATION: Add 1 tablespoon unsweetened dried coconut when you add the mustard seeds and asafetida.

Avocado Chutney

AVOCADO KI CHUTNI

This chutney is very similar to guacamole. Serve with paneer cheese with colorful peppers or add to pita pockets with Mixed Vegetable Fritters (see page 47) to make "falafels." This chutney is superb with deep-fried or baked appetizers and as a condiment with meals.

Adding yogurt to pureed avocadoes prevents them from discoloring.

3 scallions, cut into 3 to 4 pieces each, greens included
1 large clove garlic, peeled
One 1-inch piece fresh ginger, peeled
2 to 4 serrano peppers, stemmed (optional)
½ cup firmly packed cilantro (fresh coriander), soft stems included
½ cup firmly packed fresh mint leaves
2 tablespoons fresh lemon juice, or to taste
1 large avocado, peeled, stoned, and cut into 1-inch pieces
3 tablespoons nonfat plain yogurt, or to taste
1 teaspoon salt, or to taste
1 teaspoon ground roasted cumin (see page 16)
1 teaspoon curry powder (see page 21)
Cilantro or mint leaves for garnish

In a food processor fitted with the metal S-blade, process the scallions, garlic, and ginger. Add the remaining ingredients except the garnish and process until smooth. (Scrape the work bowl a few times with a spatula.) Adjust the seasonings, remove to a serving bowl, garnish with cilantro leaves, and serve. This chutney stays fine in the refrigerator for 2 to 3 days, though it is best when served within a few hours.

MAKES ABOUT 1 CUP

MANGO CHUTNEY

AAM KI CHUTNI

Translucent and shimmering pieces of raw green mangoes and a myriad of whole spices, glittering in perfectly caramelized sugar, make this chutney a piece of art. Once you taste this rare preparation, you will be hooked. This mango chutney is vastly different from anything you've ever tasted before.

Use as a condiment with meals or with toasted bread, in place of jam. My father often adds it to plain yogurt to make a quick dessert.

Choose mangoes that are hard as rocks so that they will retain their shape even after prolonged cooking and not turn into one big "mush." A vegetable peeler works well to remove the peel and the julienne disc of the food processor does a fine job of cutting the mangoes.

2 large green mangoes (over ¾ pound each)
1 teaspoon fenugreek seeds (see page 16)
1 teaspoon black peppercorns
20 cloves
One 3-inch stick cinnamon
5 black cardamom pods, pounded lightly to break the skin
½ teaspoon nigella seeds (see page 19)
1 ½ teaspoons salt, or to taste
2 cups sugar
6 tablespoons white vinegar

Peel the mangoes and cut them into 1 ½-inch julienne pieces. Discard the center seed. Place the mangoes in a large, heavy stainless steel (or other nonreactive) saucepan. Stir in the fenugreek seeds, peppercorns, cloves, cinnamon, cardamom pods, nigella seeds, salt, and sugar.

Bring to a boil over high heat, stirring, 4 to 5 minutes. Reduce the heat to medium-low, cover the pan, and simmer until slightly thickened, 15 to 20 minutes. Add the vinegar and continue to simmer until the syrup becomes thick and golden like honey, another 15 to 20 minutes. (Don't allow the chutney to become too thick, because it will thicken slightly as it cools.)

Let the chutney cool completely and then put it in sterile glass jars. Store in a cool place. Mango chutney does not need to be refrigerated, and it stays fresh for over 1 year. The color of the chutney deepens with the length of time, but that does not affect the taste. Always use a dry spoon when ladling it out, as added moisture will cause it to go bad.

MAKES ABOUT 2 ½ CUPS

VARIATION: Make the chutney with grated raw mangoes. This can be combined with nonfat plain yogurt to make a wonderful salad dressing or a sauce for grilled seafood, chicken, or vegetables.

PINEAPPLE CHUTNEY

ANNANAS KI CHUTNI

This chutney is very similar to the preceding Mango Chutney. I have included it because mangoes are a seasonal fruit and may not be easily available all over America.

Use as a condiment with meals, as a spread on toasted bread, or puree and combine with lemon juice to use as a marinade for chicken or fish.

    1 large pineapple (preferably unripe), peeled and cut into ½-inch dice (3 ½ to 4
        pounds)
    2 tablespoon peeled and minced fresh ginger
    1 teaspoon fenugreek seeds (see page 16)
    1 teaspoon black peppercorns
    1 teaspoon fennel seeds
    One 3-inch stick cinnamon
    4 bay leaves
    5 black cardamom pods, pounded lightly to break the skin
    1 teaspoon red pepper flakes (optional)
    2 cups sugar
    1 ½ teaspoons salt, or to taste
    2 tablespoons fresh lemon juice
    3 tablespoons white vinegar

Place all the ingredients except the vinegar in a large, heavy stainless steel (or other nonreactive) saucepan. Bring to a boil over high heat, stirring. Reduce the heat to medium-low, cover the pan, and simmer until slightly thickened, 15 to 20 minutes. Add the vinegar and continue to simmer, uncovered, until the syrup becomes thick and golden like honey, 15 to 20 minutes. (You may increase the heat to speed the cooking time.) Don't allow the chutney to become too thick, because it will thicken slightly as it cools.

Let the chutney cool completely, then put it in sterile jars. Pineapple chutney does not need to be refrigerated after it is made. It stays fresh for over 1 year. The color of this chutney deepens with the length of time, but that does not affect the taste. Always use a dry spoon when ladling it out, as added moisture will cause it to go bad.

MAKES ABOUT 4 CUPS

CRANBERRY CHUTNEY

The students in my class at Santa Monica College were really excited when they tasted my Indian-style cranberry chutney a few years ago. This intricately flavored sweet and tart chutney is just the thing to lend an unexpected dimension to your Thanksgiving feast.

Two 12-ounce packages fresh cranberries
4 cups sugar
3 cups water
10 black cardamom pods, pounded lightly to break the skin
One 3-inch stick cinnamon
1 tablespoon fennel seeds
½ teaspoon nigella seeds (see page 19)
1 teaspoon fenugreek seeds (see page 16)
1 tablespoon ground ginger
1 ½ teaspoons salt, or to taste
5 tablespoons white vinegar
1 tablespoon blanched almond slivers, toasted (see page 76), for garnish
1 tablespoon pine nuts, toasted (see page 76), for garnish

Place the fresh cranberries, sugar, water, cardamom pods, cinnamon, fennel, nigella, and fenugreek seeds, ginger, and salt in a large, heavy stainless steel (or other nonreactive) saucepan and bring to a boil over high heat. Reduce the heat to medium, cover partially (to prevent spilling), and cook, stirring occasionally, until it turns slightly thick, 5 to 7 minutes.

Uncover the pan, add the vinegar and continue to cook until the chutney is quite thick, 5 to 7 minutes. (Remember that the chutney will continue to thicken as it cools.)

Transfer to a bowl and set aside until cold. Garnish with the toasted nuts and serve. This chutney is great on hot toasted bread, in plain yogurt, or with any rice pullao. It can be stored in the refrigerator for over a year. Do not freeze.

MAKES ABOUT 6 CUPS

TOMATO AND RAISIN CHUTNEY

TAMATAR AUR KISHMISH KI CHUTNI

My mother-in-law showed me how to make this dazzling red chutney with firm, garden-fresh tomatoes. It stays fresh for a long time and is an outstanding way to use the summer bumper crop of tomatoes.

Serve as a condiment with meals, or mix with yogurt to make a delicious salad dressing or dip. It is also great on hot toast or as a sandwich spread.

    1 tablespoon vegetable oil
    1 teaspoon finely chopped garlic
    One 1-inch piece fresh ginger, peeled and cut into julienne strips
    5 jalapeño peppers, whole (skin punctured to prevent bursting) or finely chopped
    1 teaspoon fennel seeds
    ½ cup dark or golden raisins
    2 large fresh tomatoes (1 pound), finely chopped
    1 ½ cups sugar
    2 teaspoons salt, or to taste
    1 teaspoon paprika
    Ground cayenne pepper to taste (optional)
    5 tablespoons white vinegar

Heat the oil in a medium-size, heavy stainless steel (or other nonreactive) saucepan over high heat and cook the garlic, stirring, until golden, about 30 seconds. Add the ginger, jalapeños, fennel seeds, and raisins and stir until the raisins puff up, 1 to 2 minutes. Add the tomatoes, sugar, salt, paprika, and cayenne pepper and bring to a boil over high heat. Cover the pan, reduce the heat to medium-low, and simmer for 5 to 7 minutes.

Uncover the pan, stir in the vinegar, and let the chutney simmer, uncovered, until it becomes semi-thick, about 15 minutes. (It will continue to thicken as it cools.) Remove from the heat and let it cool completely. Pour into sterile jars and store in a cool, dry place. This chutney does not need to be refrigerated and will stay fresh for 6 to 8 months.

Use a dry spoon when ladling the chutney from the jar. Added moisture will cause it to spoil.

MAKES ABOUT 2 ¼ CUPS

Tamarind and Ginger Chutney

IMLI KI SONTH

This brown chutney with a smooth saucelike consistency has a pronounced spicy, sweet and sour flavor. To expedite the customary drawn out and messy process of soaking, seeding, and then mashing the tamarind pods, I am using dried tamarind powder in this recipe.

This chutney or its variation made with mango powder repeatedly shows up with savory Indian appetizers, *chaat* (see page 26), or salad preparations. It is a crucial part of *Papri Chaat* (see page 71) and is extraordinary with Garbanzo Bean Salad with Tamarind Chutney (page 107).

1 ½ cups tamarind powder (see page 21)
4 cups water
1 ½ cups firmly packed dark brown sugar
1 tablespoon peeled and finely minced fresh ginger
1 tablespoon ground ginger
1 tablespoon salt, or to taste
1 tablespoon black salt (see page 14)
2 tablespoons ground roasted cumin (see page 16)
2 tablespoons chaat masala (see page 26)

Break the lumps in the tamarind powder by passing through a sieve. Then mix the tamarind powder and water in a medium-size, heavy stainless steel (or other nonreactive) saucepan and bring to a boil over high heat, stirring for about 5 minutes. Add the sugar, fresh and ground ginger, salt, black salt, roasted cumin, and chaat masala. Reduce the heat to medium-low and simmer, uncovered, stirring occasionally, until it reaches a thick saucelike consistency, 10 to 12 minutes. Remove from the heat and let it cool completely. (The chutney will thicken as it cools.)

Transfer to three or four different containers. Refrigerate one and freeze the rest. This chutney stays fresh in the refrigerator for 3 to 4 months. Frozen chutney stays fresh for over a year.

If the chutney seems too thick, add some boiled water to it. Tap water encourages spoilage and should be used only if the chutney is to be consumed within 24 hours.

MAKES ABOUT 6 CUPS

VARIATION: MANGO POWDER AND GINGER CHUTNEY: Make this chutney in exactly the same way but replace the tamarind powder with mango powder (see page 18).

DRIED MANGO AND FRUIT CHUTNEY

AMCHUR AUR MEVON KI SONTH

Although similar in appearance and flavor to Tamarind and Ginger Chutney (preceding recipe), this chutney is sweeter and contains tiny pieces of dried fruits that give it a slightly chewy texture. Serve it as a dipping sauce with appetizers, or as a topping with any yogurt raita (see page 147), especially the ones containing fresh fruits, particularly banana.

1 cup mango powder (see page 18)
1 tablespoon peanut oil
1 cup finely diced mixed dried fruits (raisins, peaches, apricots, plums, figs, etc.)
3 cups water
1 tablespoon peeled and finely minced fresh ginger
2 teaspoons ground ginger
1 cup firmly packed dark brown sugar
2 tablespoons ground roasted cumin (see page 16)
2 tablespoons chaat masala (see page 26)
1 tablespoon black salt (see page 14)
2 teaspoons salt, or to taste

Sift the mango powder to remove lumps. Heat the oil in a medium-size, heavy stainless steel (or other nonreactive) saucepan over moderately high heat and cook the mixed dried fruits, stirring, until they turn slightly golden, 30 to 45 seconds. Add the sifted mango powder and water and stir to mix. Bring to a boil, stirring, over high heat, 3 to 4 minutes. Reduce the heat to medium-low, add the fresh and ground ginger and continue to cook, stirring until the chutney is slightly thick, 3 to 4 minutes.

Add the sugar, cumin, masala, black salt, and salt and bring to a rolling boil over high heat, stirring, for about 1 minute. Reduce the heat to medium-low and simmer, uncovered, stirring occasionally, until it reaches a thick, saucelike consistency, about 10 minutes.

Cool completely and put in two or three different containers. Keep one in the refrigerator and freeze the rest. It stays fresh in the refrigerator for 2 to 3 months and in the freezer for over a year.

If the chutney seems too thick, add some boiled water. Use of tap water encourages spoilage. However, tap water can be used if the chutney is to be consumed within 24 hours.

MAKES ABOUT 3 ½ CUPS

Sun-Cooked Lime Pickle

This pickle (or a variation of it) is found in almost all the Indian homes in India and abroad. It is used as a condiment with meals, or its juice is added to cooked dishes to enhance their flavor and digestive properties. Pregnant women often suck on little pieces of this pickle to get relief from morning sickness.

The two crucial things to remember are that there should be enough salt (which acts as a preservative) and enough juice to cover the ingredients by at least ½ inch. Also, make sure that everything is completely dry because water encourages spoilage.

Once the pickle is ready, it stays fresh almost indefinitely, 10 to 15 years. In fact, it gets even better as it ages. The lime pieces become soft, and the juice starts to turn into jelly and eventually into fine crystals. The color becomes dark brown and the flavor intense. At this point this pickle is almost like a home remedy for indigestion, stomach upsets, and nausea.

To settle an upset stomach, my mother always serves this pickle with Soft Rice with Lentils *(Khitchree)* (see page 309).

12 to 15 fresh limes (about 1 ½ pounds)
¾ cup salt
1 tablespoon crushed carom seeds (see page 14)
2 cups fresh lime juice (from 10 to 12 large limes)
Small piece muslin or 4 layers cheesecloth (enough to cover the mouth of the jar)

Wash and dry the limes completely. Cut each lime into eight pieces and then place in a glass jar. Add the salt and carom seeds, cover the jar and shake vigorously to stir. Remove the cover and stir in the lime juice. Then cover the jar with muslin (secure the muslin with a rubber band) and place in the sun.

This pickle should stay in the sun for at least 15 to 20 days. Bring it inside in the evening. Shake the contents of the jar once or twice every day. At the end of this period, the pieces should have softened, the juice thickened, and the pickle become ready to be eaten, but the real flavors develop after a month and they keep getting better.

MAKES 2 ½ TO 3 CUPS

VARIATION: Add whole or slit serrano peppers and julienne strips of fresh ginger. If you want a touch of sweetness, add ½ cup sugar.

PICKLED JULIENNED GINGER

GULABI ADRAK NIMBOO

Indians are very fond of fresh ginger. They eat it raw, in cooked dishes, pickled in vinegar or lemon juice, they dry it and eat it as a digestive stimulant, and they even add it to fruit juices and tea. In fact, my husband's friend Vinay Goel adds it to his omelettes. I have to admit they're wonderful.

The taste of this ginger pickle is very similar to the one that is served with Japanese sushi. It is popularly served as a condiment with Indian meals, though I often serve it with salads and sandwiches also. The lemon juice in this pickle can be used to make salad dressings, or it can be added to cooked dishes to perk up their flavors. Mince some ginger with the lemon juice in the food processor and add it to milk to make paneer cheese (see page 230).

1 cup peeled 1 ½-inch-long fresh ginger julienne strips (about ⅓ pound)
3 ½ teaspoons salt
1 teaspoon coarsely crushed carom seeds (see page 14)
1 ¼ cups fresh lemon juice

Place the ginger in a glass bottle and stir in the salt. Set aside for 2 to 4 hours. Then add the carom seeds and lemon juice. Let stand at room temperature for another 2 to 4 hours, until it turns pink.

Keep refrigerated. Serve sparingly as it has a spicy, hot bite. This pickle stays fresh in the refrigerator for 4 to 6 months.

MAKES 1 ½ CUPS

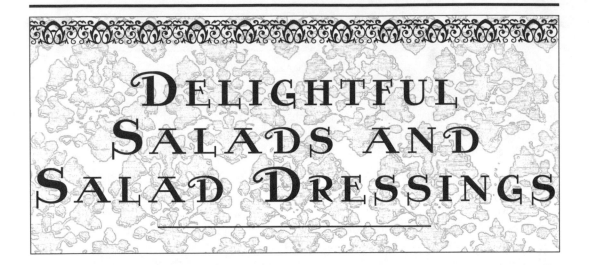

DELIGHTFUL SALADS AND SALAD DRESSINGS

Western "salad" has no true first cousin in the Indian cuisine. Our "salads" contain no lettuce because it is not freely availible in India. Our version is a combination of fresh vegetables chopped, diced, or sliced and then topped with salt, pepper, and lime juice. Another concept of what Westerners refer to as salad is Indian *chaat* preparations (see page 26). A cold *chaat* composed of beans, potatoes, or cracked wheat is akin to Western bean or potato salads or bulgur taboulehs.

This chapter then follows the Indian interpretation of salad, with just one or two recipes including salad greens. Even after living in America for over twenty years, I seem to confine my use of lettuce to garnishing my salads. I guess some habits die hard.

CRACKED WHEAT SALAD

DALIA KA SALAAD

This one-meal salad packed with wholesome and delectable ingredients is perfect to enjoy with your family or just by yourself.

My cousins Rajan and Mini habitually serve this salad, and often add frozen mixed vegetables instead of fresh and substitute the mint masala with commercial chaat masala (see page 26) to speed up the preparation.

3 tablespoons vegetable oil
4 bay leaves, broken

2 teaspoons cumin seeds

1 teaspoon fennel seeds

1 tablespoon ground coriander

1 ½ cups cracked wheat or bulgur

2 tablespoons blanched almond slivers

2 tablespoons shelled raw pistachios

½ cup raisins

4 cups fresh vegetables (diced green beans and carrots, broccoli and cauliflower florets, shelled peas, red and yellow bell pepper strips, etc.)

1 ½ teaspoons salt, or to taste

3 cups water

½ cup firmly packed finely chopped cilantro (fresh coriander), soft stems included

2 tablespoons mint masala (see page 28)

¼ cup fresh lemon juice, or to taste

2 cups shredded lettuce, any variety

2 small ripe tomatoes, cut into wedges for garnish

Heat the oil in a large saucepan over moderately high heat and cook the bay leaves, cumin and fennel seeds, and coriander, stirring, for 30 seconds. Add the cracked wheat, almond slivers, pistachios, and raisins and continue to cook, stirring, until the raisins puff up, 4 to 5 minutes. Add the vegetables and stir-fry for another 2 to 3 minutes. Stir in the salt and water, cover the pot, and cook over medium heat until all the water is absorbed and the vegetables are tender-crisp, 7 to 10 minutes. Stir occasionally.

Stir in the cilantro, mint masala, and lemon juice, and cook until all the lemon juice is absorbed, 1 minute.

Line a platter with the shredded lettuce and place the cooked salad on it. Garnish with tomato wedges and serve. This salad can be served hot, warm, or cold. It stays fresh in the refrigerator for 4 to 5 days.

MAKES 8 SERVINGS

SPROUTED MUNG BEAN SALAD

PHOOTI HUI MUNG DAL KA SALAAD

Whether you use beans you have sprouted yourself (see page 255) or those purchased at the market already sprouted, I advise cooking them a few minutes. Cooking makes them easier to digest and less gaseous.

This salad is great to take to potluck parties and picnics. It requires no last-minute attention and if you need to increase the quantity, simply add some shredded lettuce and adjust the seasoning.

2 tablespoons vegetable oil
4 serrano peppers, skin punctured to prevent them from bursting
1 teaspoon minced garlic
1 tablespoon peeled and minced fresh ginger
1 tablespoon ground coriander
1 teaspoon ground cumin
½ teaspoon turmeric
1 teaspoon salt, or to taste
2 tablespoons water
3 cups sprouted mung beans
1 cup seeded and finely diced red or yellow bell pepper
½ cup finely diced peeled and seeded cucumber
½ cup thinly sliced scallion whites
1 cup firmly packed finely chopped cilantro (fresh coriander), soft stems included
¼ cup Lime and Peppercorn Dressing (see page 118)
Cucumber slices for garnish
Red bell pepper rings for garnish

Heat the oil in a large nonstick skillet or wok over moderately high heat and cook, stirring, the serrano peppers until golden, 30 to 40 seconds. Stir in the garlic, ginger, coriander, cumin, turmeric, salt, and water, then add the sprouted beans. Cover and bring to a boil over high heat. Reduce the heat to medium and simmer until the beans are barely tender, 3 to 4 minutes. Stir occasionally. Add the bell pepper, cucumber, scallions, and cilantro, then gently mix in the dressing. Cover the pan and set aside until ready to serve.

Garnish with cucumber slices and pepper rings and serve hot or cold. This salad stays fresh in the refrigerator for 4 to 5 days.

MAKES 8 SERVINGS

VARIATION: To serve as a main dish, follow Kiran and Ashok Malik's recipe. Cook the beans with the garlic, ginger, turmeric, and salt until they become soft. Then heat the oil and stir-fry the remaining spices and stir them into the cooked *dal*. Top with cilantro and lemon juice and serve.

Garbanzo Bean Salad with Tamarind Chutney

IMLI VALÉ CHANNÉ KA SALAAD

An example of typical Indian street food, this finger-licking salad falls in the *chaat* (see page 26) category. Its wholesome and nutritious qualities, along with an unparalleled blending of spices, makes it so versatile that it can be served as a starter course, a side dish, or just as a snack all by itself.

This Indian-style bean salad can be made in large quantities very successfully and is an ideal food at summer picnics, potlucks, or winter lunches.

3 ½ tablespoons peanut oil
¼ cup ground coriander
½ cup loosely packed finely chopped cilantro (fresh coriander), soft stems included
2 large russet potatoes, boiled until tender, peeled, and cut into 1-inch pieces
Four 15 ½-ounce cans garbanzo beans, drained and rinsed
2 tablespoons fresh lemon juice
3 cups shredded green leaf lettuce (optional)
½ cup Tamarind and Ginger Chutney (see page 100)
One 1 ½- by 1-inch piece fresh ginger, peeled and cut into julienne strips
4 serrano peppers, minced, or cut into 4 long pieces each (optional)
2 teaspoons chaat masala (see page 26)
½ cup fresh pomegranate seeds for garnish (optional)

Heat 2 tablespoons of the oil in a large nonstick skillet over moderately high heat and cook 2 tablespoons of the coriander and the cilantro, stirring, for 30 seconds. Add the potatoes and cook, stirring occasionally, until they become slightly crusty, 4 to 5 minutes. Stir in the garbanzo beans, then add the remaining coriander and cook, stirring as necessary, until the beans are tender, 5 to 6 minutes. Add the lemon juice, cook for another minute, and remove from the heat. (This can be done up to 2 days ahead of time. Reheat and proceed with the recipe.)

Transfer to a serving platter lined with the shredded lettuce, drizzle and lightly mix in the chutney, and set aside.

Heat the remaining oil in a separate small saucepan over moderately high heat and fry the ginger, stirring, until golden brown and crisp, 3 to 4 minutes. Remove to paper towels to drain. Set aside. (This can be done up to 2 days ahead of time.)

Add the serrano peppers to the same oil and cook, stirring, for 1 minute. Stir in the chaat masala and immediately pour on top of the cooked garbanzo beans. Top with the fried ginger and fresh pomegranate seeds, and serve at room temperature or warm. (If the chaat masala sticks to the pan, remove it with a spatula, or with additional lemon juice.)

This salad stays fresh for 3 to 4 days in the refrigerator.

MAKES 8 SERVINGS

POTATO AND SWEET POTATO SALAD

ALU AUR SHAKARKANDI KI CHAAT

A delightful addition to your list of international potato salads. This savory salad is commonly sold by street hawkers in India. I always marveled at how easily and effortlessly these men would carry a huge basket, full of assorted prepared vegetables and an array of delicious chutneys and spice blends, on their heads, a lightweight stand in the crook of their arm, and walk around with a smile on their faces as they proudly sang the praises of the foods they were selling.

Boiled until tender, then peeled and diced, taro root and malanga root make a lovely addition to this salad.

3 large russet potatoes
1 medium-size sweet potato
1 medium-size yam
1 tablespoon peeled and minced fresh ginger
½ cup loosely packed chopped cilantro (fresh coriander), soft stems included
2 to 3 serrano peppers, finely chopped (optional)
2 tablespoons chaat masala (see page 26) or to taste
⅓ cup fresh lime or lemon juice
½ cup Tamarind and Ginger or Mango Chutney (see page 100 or 96; optional)

Place the potatoes, sweet potato, and yam in a large pot, cover with water and boil over high heat until tender, about 30 minutes. Drain, cool, peel, and cut into ¾-inch dice.

Transfer to a bowl and add the ginger, cilantro, and serrano peppers. Sprinkle the chaat masala on top, then stir in the lime juice. To make this salad even more exciting, stir in one of the chutneys.

Serve on a colorful platter as an appetizer salad, a snack, or as a part of a larger menu. This savory salad can be served at room temperature or cold from the refrigerator. It stays fresh for 4 to 5 days.

MAKES 8 SERVINGS

VARIATION: Cook the potatoes, sweet potato, and yam in a pressure cooker to speed the preparation. Pressure cook for 1 minute after the regulator starts rocking. Let the pressure drop by itself, 5 to 6 minutes. Remove the potatoes and yam, then proceed with the recipe.

CLASSIC INDIAN CONFETTI SALAD

CACHUMBER

A lot of finely diced vegetables, some crunchy, some soft, some spicy hot and some relatively bland, all very colorful and appealing, and brought alive with freshly squeezed lemon juice and dry-roasted cracked peppercorns, this salad is a perfect example of edible art.

I like to serve this salad in radicchio "cups" or in "bowls" made from the outer leaves of lettuce or cabbage.

8 cups finely diced vegetables (cucumbers, tomato, red radishes, daikon radishes, carrots, colorful bell peppers, jalapeño peppers, zucchini, scallions, etc.)
½ cup loosely packed chopped cilantro (fresh coriander), soft stems included
½ cup loosely packed chopped fresh mint leaves
3 tablespoons fresh lemon juice
1 tablespoon peeled and minced fresh ginger
2 teaspoons toasted (see page 76) sesame seeds
1 teaspoon coarsely ground roasted peppercorns (see page 13) or to taste
1 teaspoon salt, or to taste

Place the diced vegetables in a salad bowl and mix in the cilantro and mint.

Combine the lemon juice, ginger, sesame seeds, peppercorns, and salt and pour over the salad. Toss to mix evenly. Serve immediately.

To make in advance, cut the vegetables and store in the refrigerator. Combine the lemon juice with the spices and store in the refrigerator also. Toss and serve. (If the dressing is added ahead of time, the salad will become too watery.)

MAKES 8 SERVINGS

INDIAN-STYLE FRUIT SALAD

Some of my American friends find it rather strange when they see me add a touch of spice (sometimes even hot chili peppers) to freshly cut fruit, then toss it with fresh lime juice or a tamarind chutney. I am not alone in doing this; this common practice among most Indians helps satisfy the savory taste cravings that most of us develop at a very young age.

I serve this salad as a snack, or as a part of a light brunch, especially in the summer months, when there is an abundance of fruits and gorgeous berries in the market.

6 cups mixed ripe fruits, sliced or cut artistically into desired-size pieces (bananas, mangoes, guavas, peaches, apricots, kiwi, etc.)
1 cup seedless grapes (red, green, and black)
1 cup mixed fresh berries (raspberries, blueberries, etc.)
¼ cup fresh lime juice
1 ½ to 2 teaspoons chaat masala (see page 26)
Freshly ground black pepper to taste
Several sprigs fresh parsley or dill for garnish
2 tablespoons toasted (see page 76) sunflower seeds for garnish

Arrange all the fruits artistically on a platter. Top with the lime juice, chaat masala, and black pepper. Taste the seasonings and add more if desired. Garnish with the parsley and sunflower seeds and serve. This salad goes especially well with barbecued foods. It can be prepared 3 to 4 hours ahead of time and refrigerated.

MAKES 8 SERVINGS

VARIATION: For a different flavor, top with ½ cup Tamarind and Ginger Chutney (see page 100) instead of the lime juice.

PINK LENTIL SALAD WITH TOASTED SUNFLOWER SEEDS

MASOOR DAL KA SALAAD

This pastel-colored salad made with soaked and quickly cooked pink lentils and toasted sunflower seeds is enlivened with a zippy fresh lemon or lime juice dressing. This is a substantial, protein-rich salad.

There are two varieties of pink lentils available in most supermarkets, a larger kind and a smaller kind. Each of these is available in their whole and split form. In this recipe I have used the larger whole variety.

1 ½ cups dried whole pink lentils, picked over
2 cups warm water
½ teaspoon salt, or to taste
1 tablespoon safflower oil
1 teaspoon paprika
1 ½ cups toasted (see page 76) sunflower seeds
½ cup finely chopped scallion greens
3 cups mixed shredded lettuce and red cabbage
¼ cup Lime and Peppercorn Dressing (see page 118) or Lemon and Chaat Masala
    Dressing (page 119), or to taste

Wash the lentils and place them in a medium-size bowl with the water and salt. Heat the oil in a small saucepan over moderately high heat until very hot, 1 to 1 ½ minutes. Remove from the heat and add the paprika, shaking the pan to stir. Quickly transfer to the bowl with the lentils and stir. (Add some water to the saucepan to remove all the paprika.) Paprika burns easily, so work fast. Soak the lentils in the paprika water for 2 to 3 hours. Drain and set aside. (Use the paprika water for other purposes.)

Coat a heavy nonstick skillet with a thin film of oil or cooking spray and heat it over moderately high heat for 1 minute. Add the drained lentils in three to four batches and cook, stirring lightly with a spatula, until heated through, about 1 minute. (This is enough to get rid of their raw taste.) Make sure that the lentils remain whole and don't discolor. Stir in the sunflower seeds and the scallions and set aside to cool.

Line a platter with the shredded lettuce and cabbage and place the cooked lentils over it. Serve warm, at room temperature, or straight out of the refrigerator topped with the dressing of your choice.

This salad stays fresh in the refrigerator for 4 to 5 days.

MAKES 8 SERVINGS

PANEER CHEESE AND TOMATO SALAD

PANEER AUR TAMATAR KA SALAAD

Picnic or potluck, this salad brings color to all table settings. Serve this salad with a glass of Indian beer and any naan bread (see page 346).

As a variation, try using diced boiled potatoes, boneless chicken, or firm white fish instead of the cheese.

1 tablespoon vegetable oil
1 teaspoon Chinese sesame oil
¼ cup fresh lime or lemon juice
1 teaspoon minced garlic
1 tablespoon peeled and minced fresh ginger
1 teaspoon salt, or to taste
½ teaspoon freshly ground black pepper, or to taste
1 recipe Basic Paneer Cheese (see page 230), cut into ½-inch or larger pieces
1 cup peeled and diced pickling or Japanese cucumber
16 cherry tomatoes, each cut in half
12 medium-size mushrooms, quartered
1 cup finely chopped scallions
2 jalapeño peppers, finely chopped (optional)
1 ½ teaspoons chaat masala, or to taste (see page 26)
Red oak or bronze leaf lettuce to cover the platter
3 tablespoons chopped cilantro (fresh coriander) for garnish

Combine the oils, 2 tablespoons of the lime juice, the garlic, ginger, salt, and pepper and marinate the cheese in this mixture in the refrigerator for 1 to 2 hours or longer, up to 24 hours.

Place the paneer cheese with all the marinade in a large nonstick skillet and cook over high heat until it turns lightly golden and all the juices evaporate, 5 to 7 minutes. Stir in the cucumber, tomatoes, mushrooms, scallions, and jalapeños, cook, stirring, for 30 to 40 seconds, then remove from the heat. Top with the chaat masala and the remaining lime juice. Adjust the salt and pepper.

Transfer to a platter lined with lettuce leaves, garnish with the cilantro, and serve. This salad can be served warm or at room temperature.

If you make it ahead of time, do not sauté the vegetables, because they will release their juices and become soggy. Instead, add them raw and let them absorb the flavors of the chaat masala and lime juice.

MAKES 8 SERVINGS

TOSSED GREEN SALAD WITH BASIL PANEER CHEESE

HARÉ SALAAD MEIN TULSI KA PANEER

The newest convenience found at my local supermarket is an inviting array of individual or mixed baby greens. Try serving a colorful mixture of different greens, tossed with high-protein, flavor-laden pieces of homemade paneer cheese and a light dressing.

6 to 8 cups firmly packed mixed baby greens
1 cup quartered small mushrooms
1 cup mixed thin, 1-inch-long bell pepper strips
1 recipe Flavored Paneer Cheese, Version 4 (see page 232), cut into ½-inch cubes
¼ cup grated carrots
¼ cup toasted (see page 76) blanched almond slivers
2 teaspoons toasted (see page 76) sesame seeds
1 recipe Basil and Ginger Dressing (see page 120)
Freshly ground black pepper to taste

Wash and dry the greens in a salad spinner or on a kitchen towel, then tear the larger leaves into bite-size pieces. Place them in a salad bowl and add the mushrooms, bell peppers, paneer cheese, and carrots. Cover and refrigerate until needed. (This salad can be stored in plastic zipper bags in the refrigerator for 2 to 3 days.)

When ready to serve, sprinkle the almond slivers and sesame seeds over the salad, then drizzle half of the dressing over it. Toss to mix, top with black pepper, and serve with remaining dressing on the side.

MAKES 8 SERVINGS

VARIATION: Cut the paneer cheese into larger pieces and sauté them very lightly in 1 tablespoon extra virgin olive oil over medium heat, top with 1 tablespoon fresh lemon juice and black pepper, and offer as an appetizer on a bed of lettuce. You could also coat the cheese pieces with olive oil and grill them on a barbecue.

Fresh Spinach Salad with Cumin Yogurt Dressing

PALAK KA SALAAD

This salad was served by Sunil Vora at my husband's office Christmas party, along with baked whole salmon that had been marinated in Tandoori Masala (see page 24) and Barbecued Paneer Cheese and Vegetable Skewers (page 246). Garlic Naan (see page 347) is a perfect accompaniment with this meal.

½ cup shelled raw pistachios
1 cup nonfat plain yogurt, whisked until smooth
½ cup low-fat milk (1% or 2%)
2 tablespoons fresh lemon juice
1 tablespoon ground roasted cumin (see page 16)
1 teaspoon salt, or to taste
½ teaspoon freshly ground black pepper, or to taste
1 bunch fresh spinach, trimmed of tough stems, washed, and coarsely chopped
½ cup toasted (see page 76) blanched almond slivers
¼ teaspoon paprika for garnish

Place the pistachio nuts in a small saucepan with water to cover. Bring to a boil over high heat, then remove from the heat and let them soak for about 30 minutes. Drain and transfer to a kitchen towel and rub them gently to remove the skins. Set aside for garnish.

Combine the yogurt with the milk, lemon juice, cumin, salt, and pepper. Place the spinach in a salad bowl and drizzle half the dressing on top. Sprinkle with the pistachios and almonds. Garnish with the paprika and serve with the remaining dressing on the side.

MAKES 8 SERVINGS

Marinated Onion Salad

NIMBOO VALÉ PYAZ

This simple marination removes the bitter juices from the onion slices, making them delectable even to people who generally shy away from raw onions.

If you are able to locate small (1 ½-inch) onions, cut them into thin slices, then separate them into rings and proceed with the recipe. White pearl onions are marvelous. Indians generally eat this salad with their fingers.

2 to 4 small onions, cut in half lengthwise and thinly sliced
2 teaspoons salt, or to taste
1 teaspoon cumin seeds
½ teaspoon crushed carom seeds (see page 14)
½ teaspoon white peppercorns
3 tablespoons fresh lemon juice, or to taste
½ teaspoon finely minced jalapeño pepper (optional)
2 tablespoons minced scallion greens
Sliced firm red or yellow tomatoes or shredded red romaine or red oak leaf lettuce for garnish
½ teaspoon dried mint leaves for garnish

Place the onion slices in a medium-size bowl and mix in the salt with your fingers. Let the onions sweat for 30 minutes to 1 hour. Wash, drain, and dry them.

Place the cumin and carom seeds and peppercorns in a small nonstick skillet and roast over moderately high heat until the cumin turns dark brown and fragrant, 1 to 2 minutes. Remove from the skillet and let them cool for a few minutes. Then coarsely grind them in a mortar and pestle or with the back of a large spoon. Set aside.

Mix the onions with the lemon juice, jalapeño, scallion greens, and roasted spices. Refrigerate until ready to serve, up to 2 days.

Line a platter with tomato slices or shredded lettuce, top with the marinated onions, garnish with the dried mint, and serve.

(Any leftovers can be pureed in a food processor and used as a flavoring in other dishes.)

MAKES 8 SERVINGS

YOGURT SESAME DRESSING

DAHI AUR TIL KI DRESSING

This is a light and refreshing, low-calorie dressing, perfect for a hot summer day. Try making it with different types of nonfat fruit yogurts. (You will have to adjust the quantity of honey, because the fruit yogurts are sweeter.)

½ cup nonfat plain yogurt, whisked until smooth
3 tablespoons fresh lemon juice
1 tablespoon peeled and minced fresh ginger
1 tablespoon honey, or to taste
½ teaspoon Chinese sesame oil
1 tablespoon toasted (see page 76) sesame seeds
1 teaspoon salt, or to taste
Freshly ground black pepper to taste

Place the yogurt in a small bowl and add the remaining ingredients. Stir to mix, then refrigerate until needed.

This dressing stays fresh in the refrigerator for 8 to 10 days. Serve with any green or on any sprouted bean salad. This dressing can also be used as a delicate marinade for boneless chicken, fish, and vegetables.

MAKES ABOUT 1 CUP

YOGURT CILANTRO DRESSING

DAHI AUR DHANIA KI DRESSING

This dressing gives an unexpected and wonderful twist to even the most ordinary everyday salads. Serve it with any green or sprouted bean salad or try it as a dip with freshly cut vegetables.

1 large clove garlic, peeled
One 1-inch piece fresh ginger, peeled and sliced into 2 to 3 pieces
6 medium-size scallions, white and light green parts only
½ cup firmly packed cilantro (fresh coriander), soft stems included
2 tablespoons fresh orange juice
2 tablespoons fresh lemon juice
½ cup nonfat plain yogurt
1 tablespoon honey
1 tablespoon ground, lightly roasted coriander (see page 15)
1 teaspoon salt, or to taste
Freshly ground black pepper to taste

In a food processor fitted with the metal S-blade, process the garlic, ginger, and scallions until minced. Add the remaining ingredients and process until smooth. (Scrape down the sides of the work bowl with a spatula.)

This dressing stays fresh in the refrigerator for 5 to 6 days.

MAKES ABOUT 1 CUP

YOGURT CUCUMBER DRESSING WITH BLACK MUSTARD SEEDS

RYE VALI KHEERA AUR DAHI KI DRESSING

A revitalizing cool dressing, perfect for hot weather and a light summer salad. Add it liberally to a salad of baby greens or to slices of sweet vine-ripened orange and yellow tomatoes (if you can find them). This is also sensational as a dip with freshly cut vegetables, with deep-fried or baked appetizers, or served as a side dish with barbecued foods.

3 tablespoons blanched almond slivers
One 1-inch piece fresh ginger, peeled
1 to 2 serrano peppers, stemmed (optional)
2 scallions, cut into 3 pieces each
1 medium-size pickling cucumber, peeled
1 cup nonfat plain yogurt
½ cup low-fat milk (1% or 2%)
½ teaspoon salt, or to taste
Freshly ground black pepper to taste
1 tablespoon mustard or vegetable oil
1 teaspoon black mustard seeds

Soak the almond slivers in water to cover for 1 hour or longer. Drain and set aside.

In a food processor fitted with the metal S-blade, process the almonds, ginger, serrano peppers, scallions, and cucumber until smooth. Add the yogurt, milk, salt, and pepper and process to combine. (If you desire a thinner dressing, add more milk.) Remove to a bowl and set aside.

Heat the mustard oil in a small saucepan over moderately high heat. Add the mustard seeds, cover the pan, and cook until they splatter, about 30 to 45 seconds. (Shake the covered pan to ensure even cooking.) Immediately pour the contents over the dressing in the bowl and serve.

This dressing stays fresh for 6 to 7 days in the refrigerator.

MAKES ABOUT 1 ½ CUPS

YOGURT AND PINEAPPLE CHUTNEY DRESSING

DAHI AUR ANNANAS CHUTNI KI DRESSING

This creamy, sweet, and tangy blend with a gingery hot bite is irreplaceable when served on a mixed vegetable or potato salad. Try it as a final glaze on barbecued chicken or seafood or as a condiment with basmati rice.

Make it with different fruit chutneys for unusual flavors.

¼ cup Pineapple Chutney (see page 97)
½ cup nonfat plain yogurt, whisked until smooth
1 tablespoon fresh lemon juice
½ teaspoon salt, or to taste
½ teaspoon freshly ground black pepper, or to taste
Chopped cilantro (fresh coriander) or mint leaves for garnish

Process the chutney in a small food processor, blender, or a washable spice grinder until pureed.

Transfer the yogurt to a serving bowl. Add the lemon juice, salt, pepper, and processed chutney and stir to mix. Garnish with cilantro and serve. This dressing stays fresh in the refrigerator for 8 to 10 days.

MAKES ¾ CUP

LIME AND PEPPERCORN DRESSING

NIMBOO AUR KALI MIRCH KI DRESSING

To extract maximum flavor from spices, it is essential to expose them to some form of heat, either by pan-roasting without any oil or by frying them in a small amount of oil.

These methods produce distinctly different results. In this recipe the pan-roasted pepper-corns impart a smoky, aromatic flavor.

    3 scallions, cut into 3 to 4 pieces each
    1 small green bell pepper, seeded and cut into 3 to 4 pieces
    ½ cup loosely packed fresh mint leaves
    ½ cup fresh lime juice
    1 teaspoon ground roasted peppercorns (see page 13)
    1 teaspoon salt, or to taste
    1 to 2 teaspoons sugar (optional)

In a food processor fitted with the metal S-blade, process the scallions and bell pepper until minced. Add the mint, lime juice, peppercorns, and salt and process until smooth. Add the sugar if desired.

Refrigerate until needed. It stays fresh in the refrigerator for 10 to 15 days. Serve with any salad or with barbecued meats or vegetables. This dressing is great to use as a marinade, especially with lamb.

MAKES ¾ CUP

LEMON AND CHAAT MASALA DRESSING

NIMBOO AUR CHAAT MASALÉ KI DRESSING

The complex flavors of chaat masala give this dressing an exotic touch. This dressing is considered the simplest of the simple, because all Indian families have homemade or storebought chaat masala on hand to perk up their everyday foods.

Serve this very basic dressing as a topping for fruits and fruit salads, and individual or mixed vegetables like slices of cucumber, tomato, daikon and red radishes, onions and scallions, and colorful bell peppers.

    ¼ cup fresh lemon juice
    1 teaspoon minced lemon zest
    1 tablespoon firmly packed finely chopped cilantro (fresh coriander), soft stems
       included
    1 tablespoon chaat masala (see page 26)
    ½ teaspoon paprika

Combine all the ingredients and refrigerate until ready to use. This dressing stays fresh in the refrigerator for 4 to 5 days. Without the cilantro it stays fresh for another 8 to 10 days.

MAKES ABOUT ⅓ CUP

BASIL AND GINGER DRESSING

TULSI AUR ADRAK KI DRESSING

Tulsi, or holy basil, is popularly associated with religious ceremonies in India. Even though people often pluck off the leaves and eat them, or make occasional cups of remedial tea, it is not customarily used as a household seasoning in India. My exposure to this popular herb in America made me realize its tremendous flavor impact on foods, and today I try to incorporate it in my daily preparations.

This tangy blend of Italian and Indian seasonings is superb on tossed mixed green and tomato salads. It is also a wonderful marinade for vegetables and seafood.

½ cup Italian herb vinegar
1 tablespoon safflower or olive oil
1 teaspoon sugar
½ teaspoon ground ginger
½ teaspoon ground dried basil
¼ teaspoon crushed carom seeds (see page 14)
½ teaspoon salt, or to taste
Freshly ground black pepper to taste

Combine all the ingredients. Taste and correct the seasonings. Store in a airtight bottle in the refrigerator. This dressing stays fresh for 2 weeks or longer.

MAKES ⅔ CUP

Garlic and Red Pepper Dressing

LASUN AUR LAL SIMLA MIRCH KI DRESSING

I was introduced to this dressing (which was originally served to me as a chutney) by my cousins Upma and Uma. They serve it with a special Indian dish made with puffed rice, but in my opinion it is equally delicious as a salad dressing, especially when served over a tossed salad made with red romaine, curly leaf, arugula, and dandelion greens. Add crumbled paneer cheese, diced cooked potatoes or chicken, or toasted blanched almond slivers, pine nuts, or walnuts and you will have created a gourmet salad.

3 large cloves garlic, peeled
1 large red bell pepper, seeded and coarsely chopped (½ pound)
¼ cup firmly packed cilantro (fresh coriander), soft stems included
3 tablespoons fresh lemon juice
1 teaspoon chaat masala (see page 26)
½ teaspoon salt, or to taste
½ teaspoon freshly ground black pepper, or to taste

In a food processor fitted with the metal S-blade, process the garlic and bell pepper until smooth. Add the remaining ingredients and process until fairly smooth. (Stop the machine and scrape the sides of the work bowl a few times with a spatula.)

Transfer to a bowl and serve with the salad of your choice. This dressing stays fresh in the refrigerator for 5 to 6 days.

MAKES ABOUT 1 ½ CUPS

VARIATION: This dressing can be transformed into a delicate sauce in a matter of minutes. Heat 1 teaspoon safflower oil in a small nonstick skillet over moderately high heat and stir-fry ½ teaspoon black mustard seeds for 30 seconds. Immediately add the dressing and cook until it is reduced by half. Remove from the heat and stir in ½ cup non-fat plain yogurt that has been whisked until smooth. Taste and adjust the seasonings and serve with grilled chicken, seafood, or vegetables.

TOMATO AND VINEGAR DRESSING

TAMATAR AUR SIRKÉ KI DRESSING

The recipe for this simple blended tomato and vinegar dressing was given to me by Sunil Vora. He likes to marinate fresh mushrooms, diced cooked potatoes, or cauliflower florets in it before adding everything to a green salad.

 1 large ripe tomato
 1 large clove garlic, peeled
 1 tablespoon red wine or balsamic vinegar
 ½ teaspoon salt, or to taste
 ½ teaspoon freshly ground white pepper, or to taste

Blanch the tomato in boiling water to cover for 2 to 3 minutes. Remove, wash under cold water, then peel off the skin by pulling it with your fingers. Chop coarsely and place in a food processor fitted with the metal S-blade. Add the remaining ingredients and process until pureed. This dressing stays fresh for about 1 week in the refrigerator.

MAKES ⅔ CUP

 VARIATION: Blend 2 to 4 tablespoons ricotta cheese, cream cheese, or plain yogurt cheese with the tomato and serve it as a dipping sauce with freshly warmed rolls in place of garlic-flavored olive oil or herbed butter.

SAUCES FOR ALL OCCASIONS

There is nothing quite as satisfying as sopping up the last drops of a sauce or gravy. Indians especially enjoy this practice, using any remaining bread or rice as their sponge.

In America, sauces are generally served on the side, or drizzled lightly over cooked foods, but Indians almost never serve them as "stand alones." Most Indian sauces are made as a base in which vegetables, paneer cheese, beans, or various types of meats are cooked. Gentle simmering of various foods in the sauces enriches both the foods and the sauce. The sauce may be savory or sweet, mild or spicy hot, depending upon the components of the dish and the mood of the cook.

In this chapter, I use popular Indian sauce-making techniques to create sauces that are thick and creamy, thin and soupy. Most are made without any flour or cornstarch, yet they are full of character and unsurpassed flavor.

By grouping the sauces together in this chapter, my intention is to make them easily accessible in the hope that that they will become a part of your everyday cooking.

CLASSIC CURRY SAUCE

KARI, TARI AUR RASSA

More often than not, when Indian food is mentioned, most people picture a spicy-hot foreign dish with exotic flavors. In fact, however, *curry* is a blanket term in India that refers to all dishes that have a gravy, just as "pasta" refers to more dishes than just spaghetti. The word *curry* is probably a translation of the southern Indian word *kari*, which means gravy. This traditional sauce, thickened only with onion and tomato (with a little help from other herbs and spices), forms the basis of all Indian "curries."

An authentic curry involves three basic steps: The first is the grinding of the onion, ginger, and garlic to a smooth paste, called wet masala (see pages 6 and 21). This is authentically done in a stone mortar and pestle, though more affluent families use electric coffee grinders, blenders, and food processors. But even today an average household routinely grinds its onion masala in the more traditional manner.

In the second step this masala is cooked in oil over a medium to low flame until it turns a rich brown color and loses its raw taste. To this are added pureed or finely chopped tomatoes and/or yogurt and spices. The choice of oil depends entirely upon personal preference. Traditionally, all Indian cooking (with the exception of frying) was done in generous amounts of homemade clarified butter (see page 30), but today with more health awareness, people are moving toward using lesser quantities of the lighter poly- and monounsaturated oils.

The third step calls for the addition of a cooking liquid, which in most cases is water. Sometimes buttermilk or flavorful stock is added. Everything is then brought to a boil and then allowed to simmer until the desired consistency is obtained. I am partial to thick sauces because I feel their intense flavor and smooth texture marry very well with all types of breads. Thinner sauces, on the other hand, are a perfect partner to all kinds of rice dishes.

In India, generally a curry sauce like this one is never served by itself, on the side. A vegetable or meat is always cooked in it and that makes this sauce even more flavorful and alive. However, there are a few exceptions; for example, this sauce can be combined with halved hard-boiled eggs just before serving, to make an egg curry, or with deep-fried vegetable fritters to make a kofta curry.

In America, I feel it is quite important to plan meals so as to spend the minimum amount of time in the kitchen. This is where this versatile sauce steps in, as you can use it to make many different meals. For example, serve this sauce in a traditional manner with paneer cheese or koftas, cooked potatoes, sautéed mushrooms, or even cooked chicken or shrimp. Then you could use it to smother a steamed cauliflower or broccoflower, or add chopped steamed vegetables and greens (like spinach, chard, dandelions, etc.) to the sauce and serve it as an exotic soup. This sauce can also be used as a cooking medium for basmati rice dishes.

You do not have to use traditional spices; experiment with Italian, Asian, or any other kinds of herbs or spices to create your own trademark curries.

A nonstick pan works best for these sauces. If you don't have one, then use any other heavy pan. Avoid lightweight stainless steel pans as they do not conduct heat well and things tend to burn easily. Keep control of the heat and stir frequently, especially as the onion mixture starts browning. If it gets stuck to the bottom, then reduce the heat, sprinkle with 1 or 2 tablespoons water, and continue to cook. This mixture must actually turn medium to dark brown before the raw taste of the onion goes away and the curry develops its optimum flavor.

5 large cloves garlic, peeled
One 1-inch piece fresh ginger, peeled
1 large onion, cut into 8 wedges
1 large tomato, cut into 6 wedges
½ cup firmly packed cilantro (fresh coriander), soft stems included
3 tablespoons peanut oil
1 tablespoon ground coriander
2 teaspoons ground cumin
2 teaspoons dried fenugreek leaves (see page 17)
1 teaspoon paprika
½ teaspoon turmeric
1 ½ teaspoons salt, or to taste
½ cup nonfat plain yogurt, whisked until smooth
4 cups water
½ teaspoon garam masala (see page 23) for garnish
3 tablespoons chopped cilantro for garnish

In a food processor fitted with the metal S-blade, process the garlic, ginger, and onion together until smooth. Remove to a small bowl and set aside. (Do not clean the food processor.) Process the tomatoes and cilantro together until smooth and set aside.

Heat the oil in a medium-size nonstick saucepan over moderately high heat and cook the onion mixture, stirring, for 2 to 3 minutes. Reduce the heat to medium-low and continue to cook, stirring, until it turns medium to dark brown, 8 to 10 minutes. Add the tomato mixture, increase the heat to medium-high, and cook, stirring occasionally, until all the liquid evaporates, 8 to 10 minutes. Stir in the coriander, cumin, fenugreek, paprika, turmeric, and salt and cook, stirring, another 2 to 3 minutes. Add the yogurt a little at a time, stirring constantly to prevent it from curdling, until all of it is incorporated into the sauce.

Add the water, increase the heat to high, and bring to a rolling boil. Cover the pot and continue to boil for about 5 minutes, then reduce the heat to medium to low and cook until the sauce is reduced to about 3 ½ cups, 15 to 20 minutes.

Transfer to a serving bowl, garnish with the garam masala and cilantro, and serve. This will stay fresh in the refrigerator for about 5 days. It can be frozen for 2 to 3 months in an airtight container.

MAKES ABOUT 3 ½ CUPS

VARIATION: Substitute 2 to 3 tablespoons of homemade curry powder (see page 21) for the spices.

CURRY SAUCE WITH CARAMELIZED ONION SLICES

BHUNÉ HUÉ PYAZ VALI KARI

This is another authentic curry sauce, but the curry-making procedure here differs dramatically from the previous recipe. In this recipe, coarsely sliced onion, ginger, and garlic are first stir-fried in oil until they turn caramel colored, then ground to a paste (this was customarily done in a mortar and pestle) and added to the sauce toward the end, imparting a unique flavor. This can be used interchangeably with Classic Curry Sauce (see page 123). For a different flavor, try adding canned coconut milk instead of water.

1 teaspoon fenugreek seeds (see page 16)
1 tablespoon coriander seeds (see page 15)
1 teaspoon black cumin seeds (see page 16)
1 large tomato, coarsely chopped
¼ cup loosely packed fresh mint leaves
3 tablespoons peanut or safflower oil
1 large onion, cut in half lengthwise and sliced
3 large cloves garlic, peeled
One 1-inch piece fresh ginger, peeled and cut into 3 slices
¼ cup nonfat plain yogurt
½ teaspoon turmeric
1 teaspoon salt, or to taste
4 cups water
½ teaspoon garam masala (see page 23) for garnish

Place the fenugreek, coriander, and cumin seeds in a spice or coffee grinder and grind until reduced to a fine powder. Set aside. Puree the tomato and mint together in a food processor or blender and remove to a small bowl.

Heat the oil in a medium-size saucepan over moderately high heat and stir-fry the onion, garlic, and ginger until the onions are caramel colored, 8 to 10 minutes. Drain and transfer to the food processor. Add the yogurt and grind into a smooth puree. Remove to a bowl and set aside.

Add the tomato-and-mint puree to the pan the onions were cooked in and cook over moderately high heat, stirring, until all the liquid from the tomatoes evaporates, 5 to 7 minutes. Stir in the turmeric and salt, then add the onion paste. Cook, stirring, for 4 to 5 minutes, then add the water and bring to a boil over high heat. Reduce the heat to low, cover, and simmer until the sauce becomes thick and creamy, 20 to 25 minutes.

Garnish with the garam masala and serve.

MAKES ABOUT 3 CUPS

THE NO-ONION CURRY SAUCE

BINA PYAZ KI KARI

My friend Faye Levy, a renowned cookbook author, was amazed when I told her that traditional-style curries could be made without any onion. At her request, I am including this basic onionless sauce.

Curries made without onion contain extra tomatoes, yogurt, and spices. They are easier to make, less time-consuming, and can be made thick or thin, as desired. In fact, if made thin, this curry can make a lovely base for a vegetable soup. If you want it thicker, add ½ cup mashed potatoes.

2 tablespoons safflower oil
1 teaspoon cumin seeds
1 tablespoon ground coriander
1 teaspoon ground cumin
½ teaspoon paprika
¼ teaspoon turmeric
1 teaspoon salt, or to taste
1 cup canned crushed or pureed tomatoes
½ cup firmly packed finely chopped cilantro (fresh coriander), soft stems included
1 clove garlic, crushed or minced
One ½-inch piece fresh ginger, peeled and crushed or minced
¼ cup nonfat plain yogurt, whisked until smooth
3 cups water
1 teaspoon dried fenugreek leaves (see page 17)
½ teaspoon garam masala (see page 23)
Chopped cilantro for garnish

Heat the oil in a medium-size saucepan over moderately high heat and cook the cumin seeds, stirring, until they sizzle, 10 seconds. Stir in the coriander, ground cumin, paprika, turmeric, and salt, then add the tomatoes, cilantro, garlic, and ginger. Cook, stirring occasionally, until all the liquid from the tomatoes evaporates, 5 to 7 minutes.

Add the yogurt a little at a time to prevent it from curdling until all of it is incorporated into the sauce. Add the water, increase the heat to high, bring to a boil, and let boil for about 5 minutes. Cover the pot, reduce the heat to medium-low, and simmer for 15 to 20 minutes or longer. Add the fenugreek leaves and garam masala. (You can add more water if you wish a thinner sauce, or uncover and reduce further if you require a thicker sauce.)

Transfer to a bowl, garnish with chopped cilantro, and serve. This sauce stays fresh in the refrigerator for 5 to 6 days and can be frozen for 3 to 4 months.

MAKES ABOUT 2 CUPS

TOMATO CREAM SAUCE WITH CARDAMOM AND CLOVES

GAADHI MAKHANI KARI

Richer than rich and slightly sweet, this pale orange-red sauce made with vine-ripened tomatoes, fragrant cardamom and cloves, and heavy cream is absolutely divine. One of the most distinctive and versatile sauces of Indian cuisine, it is also the most exotic, making its appearance as part of more exclusive dinners at home or in restaurants.

My daughters, Sumita and Supriya, eat this sauce any time of the day. Their favorite way is to combine it with boneless pieces of chicken that have been cooked in the tandoor or barbecued. I love it with paneer cheese (see page 230), sautéed whole mushrooms, or smothered on steamed cauliflower and baked for about 30 minutes at 350° F. It is also superb over pan-fried fish, shrimp, and baby new potatoes that have been boiled until tender and peeled. All of these should be simmered in the sauce for 3 to 4 minutes prior to serving. Serve naan (see page 346) or paranthas (page 322) on the side. Cooked stuffed pasta simmered in this sauce is spectacular.

To make it heart healthy, use nonfat yogurt instead of the cream and substitute canola oil for the butter. (The taste will be different, but still extraordinary.)

4 large cloves garlic, peeled
One 1 ½-inch piece fresh ginger, peeled
6 to 8 serrano peppers, stemmed, or ½ mild Anaheim pepper, coarsely chopped
5 large tomatoes, coarsely chopped (2 ½ to 3 pounds)
15 green cardamom pods, pounded lightly to break the skin
20 cloves, pounded lightly
20 black peppercorns

One 1-inch stick cinnamon
1 tablespoon paprika
2 ½ cups water
1 teaspoon salt, or to taste
1 tablespoon dried fenugreek leaves (see page 17)
2 tablespoons butter
1 cup or less heavy cream
Chopped cilantro (fresh coriander) for garnish

In a food processor fitted with the metal S-blade, mince the garlic, ginger, and peppers together, then add the tomatoes and process until smooth. Transfer to a medium-size saucepan. Stir in the cardamom pods, cloves, peppercorns, cinnamon, paprika, and water, increase the heat to high, bring to a boil, and let boil uncovered until reduced to almost half, 20 to 25 minutes. Stir occasionally.

Pass through a food mill or sieve and discard the fiber. (Add an additional ½ cup water to extract the maximum pulp.) Return to the pan, add the salt and fenugreek, and boil for another 5 minutes over high heat. Add the butter and cream and simmer over low heat for 3 to 4 minutes. Garnish with cilantro.

This sauce stays fresh in the refrigerator for 4 to 5 days or in the freezer for 2 to 3 months. Reheat (with 2 to 3 tablespoons milk if needed) in a microwave oven or over medium heat.

MAKES ABOUT 4 CUPS

TOMATO CREAM SAUCE WITH CORIANDER

DHANIA VALI MAKHANI KARI

A scrumptious sauce made with clarified butter and garden ripe tomatoes. This sauce has universal appeal and makes a stunning presentation when served with contrasting white, yellow, and green vegetables (try baby yellow and green pattypan squash and zucchini, 3-inch cauliflower florets, and peas), paneer cheese (see page 230), chicken, or just by itself. (I love to scoop it up with bite-size pieces of naan, paranthas, or sourdough bread.)

This sauce also makes an inventive addition to pasta, meatloaf, and grilled seafood. Freeze it in ice cube trays or small soufflé cups and you have individual servings on hand all the time.

5 large tomatoes, coarsely chopped (2 ½ to 3 pounds)
5 serrano peppers, halved and seeded
2 teaspoons minced garlic
1 tablespoon peeled and minced fresh ginger
2 bay leaves, crushed
4 cups water
3 tablespoons melted clarified butter (see page 30) or vegetable oil
One 1-inch piece fresh ginger, peeled and cut into julienne strips
2 tablespoons ground coriander
1 teaspoon garam masala (see page 23), plus ½ teaspoon for garnish
½ teaspoon ground green cardamom seeds (see page 14)
2 teaspoons dried fenugreek leaves (see page 17)
2 teaspoons paprika
1 teaspoon salt, or to taste
½ cup heavy cream or milk

Place the tomatoes, peppers, garlic, ginger, bay leaves, and water in a large saucepan and bring to a boil over high heat. Reduce the heat to medium, cover the pan, and simmer until the tomatoes are completely mushy, 15 to 20 minutes. Pass through a food mill or puree in a blender or food processor (remove the bay leaves if using the blender or food processor), and return the smooth sauce to the saucepan.

Heat the butter in a small saucepan over moderately high heat and fry the ginger, stirring, until golden. Add the coriander, garam masala, cardamom, and fenugreek leaves. Turn off the heat, stir in the paprika, and quickly add to the smooth tomato sauce.

Stir in the salt and cream and simmer over low heat for 5 to 7 minutes. If the sauce seems too thick, add some milk or water to get the desired consistency. Serve as is on the side, or simmer for a few minutes with seafood, chicken, paneer cheese, or steamed vegetables before presenting it as a main dish.

This sauce stays fresh in the refrigerator for 4 to 5 days or in the freezer for 2 to 3 months. Reheat (with 2 to 3 tablespoons milk if required) in a microwave oven or over medium heat.

MAKES ABOUT 4 CUPS

Tomato Mustard Sauce

TAMATAR AUR RYE KI KARI

Mustard oil and black mustard seeds give this creamy sauce a distinct flavor and character that can lend a dramatic twist to grilled seafood and steamed or stir-fried tender-crisp vegetables. It is marvelous over cooked pasta and pan-sautéed cubes of paneer cheese (see page 230). Try making a grilled seafood pizza with this sauce and crumbled paneer cheese.

One 2-inch piece fresh ginger, peeled and cut into 3 or 4 pieces
5 or 6 scallions (white and light green parts only)
3 large tomatoes, cut into 8 wedges each
1 cup loosely packed cilantro (fresh coriander), soft stems included
2 tablespoons light sour cream or nonfat plain yogurt
1 tablespoon mustard oil
2 teaspoons black mustard seeds
½ teaspoon ground asafetida (see page 13)
½ teaspoon salt, or to taste
½ teaspoon freshly ground black pepper, or to taste
½ cup low-fat milk or light cream
½ teaspoon garam masala (see page 23) for garnish
1 tablespoon chopped cilantro for garnish

In a food processor fitted with the metal S-blade, process the ginger, scallions, and tomatoes until pureed. Add the cilantro and sour cream and process once again until smooth. Set aside.

Heat the oil in a medium-size saucepan over moderately high heat and fry the mustard seeds for 30 to 40 seconds. (Cover the pan immediately, as the seeds "pop" and fly out of the pan.) Stir in the asafetida and immediately add the tomato mixture and cook, stirring, until it comes to a boil. Reduce the heat to medium and continue to cook, stirring occasionally, until all the liquid from the tomatoes evaporates, 10 to 12 minutes. Season with salt and pepper and stir in the milk. Let simmer for 2 to 3 minutes over low heat.

Transfer to a serving bowl, garnish with the garam masala and cilantro, and serve hot. This sauce stays fresh in the refrigerator for 4 to 5 days or in the freezer for 2 to 3 months.

Makes about 1 ½ cups

SAUCES FOR ALL OCCASIONS   131

Yogurt Sauce with Caramelized Onion

KORMA KI KARI

This rich-tasting light brown sauce with a "cream added" look gets most of its color from the caramelized onion, its flavor from cardamom seeds, cinnamon, and cloves, and its texture from the nuts, which though ground to a powder still retain some of their granular structure.

All these features combine to create a fragrant and intriguing sauce. Serve with baked or mashed potatoes, sautéed mushrooms or paneer cheese pieces (see page 230), or with a rice pullao for a spectacular effect. As a fun experiment, try it over a pizza crust instead of tomato sauce (make sure it is thick) with some wild mushrooms, sliced red onion, and artichoke hearts.

1 ½ cups nonfat plain yogurt
1 ¼ cups water
2 tablespoons vegetable oil
1 ½ cups finely chopped onion
2 teaspoons minced garlic
½ cup korma masala (see page 23)
¼ teaspoon salt, or to taste
2 tablespoons chopped cilantro (fresh coriander) for garnish

Blend the yogurt and water in a blender until smooth. Set aside.

Heat the oil in a medium-size nonstick saucepan and cook the onion over high heat, stirring, for 4 to 5 minutes, then over medium heat until it turns dark brown and crisp, 18 to 20 minutes. Stir in the garlic and cook, stirring, for about 1 minute, then add the korma masala and salt and cook, stirring, for another minute. Increase the heat to high and add the blended yogurt a little at a time, stirring continuously, to prevent it from curdling. Bring to a rolling boil, then reduce the heat to medium-low, cover the pan, and simmer until thick and smooth, 15 to 20 minutes. Stir occasionally.

Transfer to a serving bowl, garnish with the cilantro, and serve. This sauce stays fresh in the refrigerator for 5 to 6 days or in the freezer for 2 to 3 months.

MAKES ABOUT 2 CUPS

INDIAN-STYLE BUTTERMILK SAUCE

LASSI VALI KARI

Thickened with vine-ripened tomatoes, garbanzo bean flour, and fragrant spices, this tangy buttermilk sauce is another versatile addition to your collection of international flavors.

This sauce can be served as a curry with any type of koftas (see index), or added to steamed vegetables or wilted greens. It is superb with baked potatoes, grilled chicken, or fish fillets.

2 large tomatoes, coarsely chopped
2 tablespoons peeled and coarsely chopped fresh ginger
2 large cloves garlic, peeled
4 bay leaves, crushed
1 cup nonfat plain yogurt
2 cups water
2 tablespoons garbanzo bean flour (see page 254)
2 tablespoons peanut oil
1 tablespoon ground coriander
1 teaspoon ground cumin
½ teaspoon paprika
½ teaspoon turmeric
1 teaspoon salt, or to taste

Place the tomatoes, ginger, garlic, and bay leaves in a medium-size saucepan, cover, bring to a boil over high heat, and let boil for about 5 minutes. Reduce the heat to medium-low and simmer for another 5 to 7 minutes. Remove from the heat, blend until smooth, then pass through a food mill or sieve. Discard the fiber and set the sauce aside.

Place the yogurt, water, and flour in a blender and process to make a smooth buttermilk. Set aside.

Heat the oil in a large nonstick saucepan over moderately high heat and stir in the coriander, cumin, paprika, turmeric, and salt, then add the tomato puree and cook over high heat for 2 to 3 minutes, then over medium heat, stirring occasionally, until most of the liquid from the tomatoes evaporates, 5 to 7 minutes.

Stir in the buttermilk mixture and boil over high heat for 3 to 4 minutes. Reduce the heat to medium and continue to cook until the sauce becomes thick and smooth, 12 to 15 minutes.

This sauce stays fresh in the refrigerator for 5 to 6 days. It does not freeze well.

MAKES ABOUT 4 CUPS

PUREED SPINACH SAUCE WITH GINGER AND GARLIC

PALAK KI KARI

Perfect with just about everything, this delicate sauce complements not only all types of Indian menus, but also works wonders on cooked pasta, vegetables, meats, and tofu.

½ pound fresh spinach, trimmed of tough stems and washed
1 small green bell pepper, seeded and cut into 5 to 6 pieces
¼ cup water
2 tablespoons mustard or peanut oil
1 tablespoon peeled and minced fresh ginger
1 teaspoon minced garlic
1 tablespoon ground coriander
1 teaspoon ground cumin
1 teaspoon dried fenugreek leaves (see page 17)
½ teaspoon salt, or to taste
Freshly ground black pepper to taste
1 tablespoon fresh lemon juice, or to taste
¼ cup nonfat plain yogurt, whisked until smooth
½ teaspoon garam masala (see page 23) for garnish
Tomato wedges for garnish

Place the spinach, bell pepper, and water in a medium-size saucepan and cook over medium heat, stirring, until the pepper becomes soft, about 5 minutes. Cool, then puree in a food processor or blender and set aside.

Heat the oil in another saucepan over moderately high heat and cook the ginger and garlic, stirring, until golden, about 1 minute. Stir in the coriander, cumin, fenugreek, salt, and pepper, then add the lemon juice. Mix in the pureed spinach and peppers and bring to a boil over high heat. Reduce the heat to medium-low, cover the pan, and simmer for 4 to 5 minutes to blend the flavors. Stir in the yogurt and remove from the flame. (If you prefer a thinner sauce, just add some water or stock.)

Transfer to a bowl, garnish with the garam masala and tomato wedges, and serve. This sauce stays fresh in the refrigerator for 5 to 6 days. It can also be frozen for 2 to 3 months.

MAKES ABOUT 2 CUPS

VARIATION: Make this sauce with 2 tablespoons curry powder (see page 21) and add some chopped serrano peppers, or make it with different greens, for example sorrel, Swiss chard, and chicory.

CREAMY SAFFRON SAUCE

KESARI KARI

Fragrant with saffron and green cardamom, this multi-purpose sauce is creamy without the addition of any cream. Serve with Nine Jewel Vegetables (see page 208) or lightly grilled vegetables. It is great over cooked pasta and broiled or sautéed shrimp.

½ teaspoon saffron threads
1 cup low-fat milk
2 tablespoons peanut oil
1 cup coarsely chopped onion
5 green cardamom pods, pounded lightly to break the skin
½ cup nonfat plain yogurt
4 ½ teaspoons cornstarch
¾ teaspoon salt, or to taste
Freshly ground black pepper for garnish

Stir the saffron into the milk and set aside.

Heat the oil in a small saucepan over high heat and cook the onion and cardamom pods, stirring, until the onion turns golden, 4 to 5 minutes. Transfer to a food processor fitted with the metal S-blade. Add the saffron milk, yogurt, and cornstarch and process until smooth.

Return to the pan, add the salt, and cook over moderately high heat, stirring constantly, until it becomes smooth, 4 to 5 minutes. Garnish with pepper and serve hot. This sauce stays fresh in the refrigerator for 5 to 6 days and in the freezer for 2 to 3 months.

MAKES ABOUT 2 CUPS

Mushroom Sauce

Try making this sauce with different varieties of mushrooms. To serve, place sautéed mushrooms on a bed of rice and spoon the sauce on top, drizzle over a platter of cooked ravioli or tortellini, present on the side with barbecued chicken or seafood, or dilute with milk or cream to make a soup.

2 tablespoons vegetable oil
2 teaspoons cumin seeds
½ cup chopped scallions (whites and light green parts only)
2 large cloves garlic, chopped
2 teaspoons white poppyseeds
6 large mushrooms, diced
½ cup regular or low-fat milk
1 cup water
1 tablespoon ground coriander
½ teaspoon garam masala (see page 23)
½ teaspoon paprika
½ teaspoon salt, or to taste
3 tablespoons nonfat plain yogurt, whisked until smooth
1 tablespoon fresh lemon juice

Heat 1 tablespoon of the oil in a small nonstick saucepan over moderately high heat and fry the cumin seeds until they sizzle, 10 seconds. Immediately add the scallions and cook, stirring, until they turn golden, 1 to 2 minutes. Add the garlic, poppyseeds, and mushrooms and cook, stirring as necessary, until all the water from the mushrooms evaporates and they turn golden, 5 to 7 minutes.

Transfer the mixture to a blender or food processor, add the milk, and process until smooth. Remove to a bowl and set aside. Add the water to the blender and blend for 15 seconds (to recover the leftover mushrooms pieces). Set aside.

Heat the remaining oil in the saucepan in which the mushrooms were cooked over moderately high heat and fry the ground coriander, garam masala, paprika, and salt for 30 seconds, stirring, then add the mushroom mixture. Cook, stirring, for about 10 minutes. Add the water from the blender and simmer until most of the water is evaporated, 5 to 7 minutes. Stir in the yogurt and lemon juice and heat through.

This sauce stays fresh in the refrigerator for 5 to 6 days and in the freezer for 2 to 3 months.

MAKES ABOUT 1 ½ CUPS

ALMOND AND POPPYSEED SAUCE

BADAAM AUR KHUS KHUS KI KARI

A little on the rich side, this textured brown sauce derives its heavenly flavor from soaked, blanched, and sautéed almonds, poppyseeds, and cinnamon. Serve with grilled or baked chicken breasts, sautéed mushrooms, or baked potatoes. Add some turkey drippings and create a scrumptious sauce for your next holiday dinner.

½ cup almonds
1 ½ cups water
¼ cup white poppyseeds
2 large cloves garlic, peeled
One 1-inch piece fresh ginger, peeled and cut into 3 slices
2 tablespoons vegetable oil
One 3-inch stick cinnamon
4 black cardamom pods, pounded lightly to break the skin
1 teaspoon salt, or to taste
½ teaspoon garam masala (see page 23)
2 ½ cups buttermilk

Soak the almonds in 1 cup of the water for at least 4 hours (preferably overnight). Drain, peel off the brown skin, and set aside. (This can be done up to 3 days in advance.)

Soak the poppyseeds in the remaining water for 1 hour or longer.

In a food processor fitted with the metal S-blade, process the almonds, poppyseeds and their soaking liquid, garlic, and ginger until smooth. (Stop the motor to scrape the sides two or three times.) Heat the oil in a small to medium-size nonstick saucepan over moderately high heat and stir-fry the cinnamon and cardamom pods for 30 to 40 seconds. Add the almond mixture, reduce the heat to medium-low, and cook, stirring as necessary, until the mixture turns golden to brown in color, 10 to 15 minutes. Add the salt and garam masala and stir for 2 to 3 minutes. Add the buttermilk and continue to cook, stirring occasionally, until all the buttermilk is absorbed and the sauce becomes thick, 20 to 25 minutes. To make it thinner, add some more buttermilk or water.

This sauce stays fresh in the refrigerator for 5 to 6 days and in the freezer for 2 to 3 months.

MAKES ABOUT 2 CUPS

RED BELL PEPPER SAUCE WITH GARAM MASALA

LAL SIMLA MIRCH KI KARI

Though this is not an authentic Indian sauce, it has all the right flavors that could classify it as one. This creamy, no-butter sauce derives its intriguing aroma and visual appeal from pureed red bell peppers and Indian spices and is remarkably rich in flavor but not in calories.

Serve over steamed or grilled baby yellow or green squash, zucchini, cauliflower, or broccoli. Put ¼ cup of it in the center of a dinner plate, top with a piece of pan-sautéed chicken breast or fish, a green or yellow vegetable of your choice, and a rice pullao.

To make a green or yellow sauce with similar flavors, substitute the red bell pepper with green or yellow ones.

2 large cloves garlic, peeled
One ½-inch piece fresh ginger, peeled
1 medium-size red bell pepper, seeded and coarsely chopped
¼ cup firmly packed cilantro (fresh coriander), soft stems included
3 tablespoons fresh lemon juice
½ teaspoon salt, or to taste
½ teaspoon freshly ground black pepper, or to taste
2 cups low-fat milk
½ cup ground blanched raw almonds or cashews
1 teaspoon garam masala (see page 23)

In a food processor fitted with the metal S-blade, process the garlic, ginger, and bell pepper until fairly smooth. Add the cilantro, lemon juice, salt, and pepper and process once again until fairly smooth. (Stop the machine and scrape the sides a few times with a spatula.) Transfer to a bowl and set aside.

Combine the milk and ground almonds in a medium-size saucepan and bring to a boil over high heat. Reduce the heat to medium-low and simmer for about 5 minutes. Stir in the pureed peppers and continue to simmer for 5 to 7 minutes. Stir in the garam masala and serve.

If you desire a thicker sauce, stir 1 tablespoon cornstarch into ¼ cup additional milk and add it to the sauce. Cook for 3 to 5 minutes longer and serve.

This sauce stays fresh in the refrigerator for 5 to 6 days and can be frozen for 2 to 3 months only if you have not added the cornstarch.

MAKES ABOUT 3 CUPS

PUMPKIN SAUCE

PETHÉ KI KARI

This mustard-colored sauce is great when presented with turkey during holiday celebrations. Try it in place of Classic Curry Sauce to add a different flavor to vegetable or paneer cheese koftas (see pages 227 and 243), or serve it over a vegetable pullao.

2 cups peeled and diced pumpkin (or any other yellow squash)
½ cup diced potato (with peel)
½ cup diced onion
3 penny-size slices peeled fresh ginger
2 serrano peppers, stemmed (optional)
2 cups water
1 teaspoon cumin seeds
½ teaspoon fenugreek seeds (see page 16)
1 tablespoon vegetable oil
1 cup finely diced fresh tomato
¼ cup nonfat plain yogurt, whisked until smooth
½ teaspoon salt, or to taste
½ teaspoon garam masala (see page 23) for garnish

Place the pumpkin, potato, onion, ginger, peppers, and water in a medium-size saucepan and cook over high heat for 3 to 4 minutes, then over medium until the pumpkin and potatoes are tender, 20 to 25 minutes. Transfer to a food processor and puree until smooth. Return to the pan.

Coarsely grind the cumin and fenugreek seeds in a spice or coffee grinder or mortar and pestle. Set aside.

Heat the oil in a small nonstick saucepan over moderately high heat and cook the ground seeds, stirring, until they sizzle, 30 seconds. Add the tomatoes and cook, stirring, until all the liquid evaporates, 4 to 5 minutes. Add the yogurt a little at a time to prevent it from curdling. Transfer to the pan with the pureed pumpkin, season with salt, and simmer for 4 to 5 minutes over medium heat. Add more water if you desire a thinner sauce.

Transfer to a bowl, garnish with the garam masala, and serve hot. This sauce stays fresh in the refrigerator for 5 to 6 days and in the freezer for 2 to 3 months.

MAKES ABOUT 3 ½ CUPS

Indian White Sauce with Roasted Peppercorns

SAFAID KARI

This mildly flavored white sauce is a perfect example of the British influence on Indian cuisine. My memory takes me back to my childhood, when one of my special rewards was a visit to our family's favorite restaurant that served boneless chicken (which was unheard of in those days) in a delicately flavored white cream sauce. There was always more sauce than chicken, and it was this sauce that tasted divine to my developing taste buds, especially when I scooped it up with pieces of hot naan (see page 346). Even today, when I visit India, I make at least one trip to this restaurant.

The superb taste of that velvety sauce stayed with me and after many unsuccessful attempts, I was able to re-create the familiar flavor in a way I think is even better than the original.

My friend Shelly Sherwin ate this sauce when I served it at a school luncheon and has become addicted to it. She served it at one of her traditional Jewish holiday dinners, and now her family also loves it. Shelly, this recipe is for you.

3 tablespoons corn oil
½ cup minced onion
2 teaspoons minced garlic
1 tablespoon peeled and minced fresh ginger
5 serrano peppers, stemmed and skin punctured to prevent them from bursting
¼ cup cornstarch
1 tablespoon ground coriander
1 teaspoon ground cumin

½ teaspoon ground nutmeg
½ teaspoon paprika
2 cups Cauliflower Broth (recipe follows) or chicken stock
½ cup low-fat milk
¼ cup heavy or whipping cream (optional)
1 teaspoon coarsely ground roasted white peppercorns (see page 13)

Heat the oil in a medium-size nonstick saucepan over moderately high heat and cook the onion, garlic, ginger, and peppers, stirring, until the onion is soft, 2 to 4 minutes. Stir in the cornstarch and continue to cook until it becomes golden and fragrant, 2 to 3 minutes. Add the coriander, cumin, nutmeg, and paprika, then the cauliflower broth and milk, stirring constantly to prevent it from lumping.

Reduce the heat to medium-low and cook the sauce another 15 to 20 minutes, then stir in the cream. Cook another 3 to 4 minutes. This sauce should be thick and smooth. (If the sauce is too thin, thicken with another spoonful of cornstarch dissolved in additional milk or broth.) Transfer to a bowl, garnish with the roasted white peppercorns, and serve with any type of steamed vegetable, sautéed mushrooms, pieces of paneer cheese, cooked boneless chicken, or seafood.

This sauce stays fresh in the refrigerator for 5 to 6 days or in the freezer for 2 to 3 months.

MAKES ABOUT 3 CUPS

FRESH MANGO AND GINGER SAUCE

PISA HUA AAM AUR ADRAK

A simple sauce made with a fascinating blend of ripe mangoes and fresh ginger. Serve with sautéed vegetables or barbecued meats. I also like it with pakoras (see page 42), Chinese egg rolls, and fried won tons.

Choose fragrant, ripe mangoes. A perfect mango has a shiny skin and feels like a ripe avocado. Avoid mangoes that are too hard (unless you want to save them for a few days) or those that have brown spots and feel too soft.

To remove the pulp from a fresh mango, peel off the skin with a knife and then with the same knife remove the pulp around the center seed, or cut thick slices and then scoop the pulp out of the skin as with avocados.

One 1-inch piece fresh ginger, peeled
1 cup fresh or canned mango pulp
2 tablespoons fresh lemon juice
½ teaspoon salt, or to taste
½ teaspoon freshly ground black pepper, or to taste
2 tablespoons minced cilantro (fresh coriander)

In a food processor fitted with the metal S-blade, process the ginger until smooth. Add the mango, lemon juice, salt, and pepper and process once again until smooth.

Remove to a serving bowl, stir in the cilantro, and serve. This sauce stays fresh in the refrigerator for 4 to 5 days or in the freezer for 2 to 3 months. Serve cold or at room temperature.

MAKES ABOUT 1 CUP

VARIATION: Substitute peeled fresh ripe peaches, nectarines, or apricots for the mangoes.

CASHEW, POPPYSEED, AND MANGO SAUCE

KAJU AUR KACHCHÉ AAM KI GAADHI KARI

This tangy summer sauce is so delicious it can be eaten by itself. Its irresistible flavor makes it an exciting condiment to be served with meals. It could also be a dip for vegetables, or a sauce over steamed or grilled foods. Try it as a final glaze on barbecued chicken and seafood.

¼ cup raw cashews
1 tablespoon white poppyseeds
One 1-inch piece fresh ginger, peeled
1 large moderately hard, unripe mango, peeled, seeded, and coarsely chopped
2 tablespoons safflower oil
½ teaspoon cumin seeds
1 tablespoon ground coriander
1 teaspoon ground cumin
½ cup firmly packed finely chopped cilantro (fresh coriander), soft stems included
1 teaspoon salt, or to taste
1 cup water
Freshly ground black pepper for garnish
Cilantro sprigs for garnish

Grind the cashews and poppyseeds together in a coffee or spice grinder until reduced to a fine powder. Set aside.

In a food processor fitted with the metal S-blade, process the ginger until minced. Add the mango and process until smooth. (Scrape the sides with a spatula a few times.)

Heat the oil in a medium-size saucepan over moderately high heat and cook the cumin seeds, stirring, until they sizzle, about 10 seconds. Quickly add the ground coriander, cumin, and ground cashews and poppyseeds. Reduce the heat to low and cook, stirring, until the spices become fragrant, 2 to 3 minutes. Add the pureed mangoes, cilantro, and salt and cook, stirring occasionally, for 5 to 7 minutes. Increase the heat to high, add the water, and boil for 2 to 3 minutes. Reduce the heat to low, cover the pan, and simmer for 5 to 7 minutes.

Transfer to a serving bowl, garnish with freshly ground black pepper and cilantro sprigs, and serve. This sauce stays fresh in the refrigerator for 4 to 5 days or in the freezer for 2 to 3 months. Serve hot or cold.

MAKES ABOUT 2 CUPS

INDIAN BARBECUE AND BASTING SAUCE

TANDOORI ZAYAKA

To perk up their flavors and add a delicate glaze, baste your barbecued meats and vegetables with this simple blend.

    1 tablespoon peanut oil or clarified butter (see page 30)
    2 teaspoons ground roasted cumin (see page 16)
    ½ teaspoon paprika
    3 tablespoons fresh lime juice, or to taste
    ½ teaspoon salt, or to taste

Heat the oil in a small saucepan over moderately high heat and fry the cumin for 15 seconds. Remove the pan from the heat and stir in the paprika, lime juice, and salt.

Use as a basting sauce during the last 5 to 7 minutes of barbecuing. This sauce stays fresh in the refrigerator for about 2 months.

MAKES ABOUT ¼ CUP

CAULIFLOWER BROTH

GOBI KA SHORWA

Almost like a soup, this fragrant broth is splendid as a base for delicate sauces, soups, or for cooking rice. Add some plain nonfat yogurt (or cream) and a sprinkle of freshly ground white peppercorns and you have a nutritious soup.

This same recipe works well with carrots, zucchini, broccoli, brussels sprouts, and various other vegetables.

1 small head cauliflower, cut into florets, soft stems included
5 cups water
4 large cloves garlic, coarsely chopped
One 1-inch piece fresh ginger, peeled and chopped
½ cup firmly packed cilantro (fresh coriander), soft stems included
4 bay leaves (preferably fresh)
1 tablespoon ground coriander
½ teaspoon garam masala (see page 23)
1 teaspoon salt, or to taste

Place all the ingredients in a large saucepan and boil for 5 minutes over high heat. Reduce the heat to medium-low and simmer until the cauliflower florets are very soft, 10 to 15 minutes. Remove from the heat and cool for 10 to 15 minutes. Discard the bay leaves, and blend everything else in a blender. Set aside.

MAKES ABOUT 3 ½ CUPS

THE SOOTHING YOGURT

Yogurt flows through the Indian digestive system as blood through our veins. It is like wine to the French and pasta to the Italians. From infancy to old age it is a constant in our diets, as necessary to us nutritionally as it is satisfying to our palates. In the heat of the day it refreshes our bodies, at the end of the meal it is a pleasant and soothing conclusion and it is the one food of which one can never grow tired. Yogurt is a serene, lifelong friend.

All the raita dishes in this chapter use commercial nonfat plain yogurt. If you use homemade yogurt, just remember that it is delicate and light and the resulting raita will be slightly different.

HOMEMADE YOGURT

DAHI

The art of making fresh, wholesome yogurt at home is simple enough for everyone to understand and follow. No fancy yogurt makers or special equipment are required. Any type of pot will suffice.

This basic recipe calls for cooling boiled milk, then adding a starter (yogurt with live culture). This "starter added milk" is covered loosely and placed in a warm spot for 3 ½ to 4 hours, after which time the yogurt should be ready. The longer it takes to set, the stronger the taste of the yogurt.

Yogurt forms a crucial part of all meals in northern India. With my present knowledge of nutrition, I realize how much insight there was in India about the value of a daily serving of this perfect food, even before most of the world became aware of its healthful benefits. My mother still makes yogurt twice a day, for lunch and dinner. She collects all the leftover yogurt in a separate bowl and saves it for making lassi, a yogurt drink (see page 38), or for cooking purposes, especially to make Punjabi Kadhi (page 222). In America, I must confess, I don't make fresh yogurt for every meal, but I do make it once in every two or three days.

The yogurt bacteria stay active for about 15 days in the refrigerator, so if you make a fresh batch every 10 to 15 days, you will always have fresh homemade yogurt in your refrigerator.

Most plain yogurts sold in the supermarket are sour and contain thickening additives like pectin, tapioca, or gelatin. These ingredients are probably essential to increase its shelf life, but they mask the true and subtle flavor of this naturally delicate dairy item.

Homemade yogurt, on the other hand, is made solely with milk and a starter, and the resulting yogurt is delicate, sweet, and smooth. Yogurt can be made with any type of milk, full fat, 2 percent, 1 percent, or nonfat or by combining any of these in varying proportions. For obvious health reasons, I use nonfat or 1 percent milk or combine these two varieties when I make my own yogurt. This yogurt sets beautifully, and tastes superb, but is not as thick as the yogurt made with full fat or cream added milk. (Even today there are numerous Indian families who use only full fat milk to make their yogurt, but I assure you that once you get used to making yogurt with nonfat or 1 percent milk, you will never eat anything else.)

A word of reassurance: Don't be disappointed if your first yogurt-making attempt is unsuccessful. It's probably not your fault at all. Maybe the starter you used was not active enough (even though the carton said it was). If that was the case, you will notice some lumps at the bottom of the yogurt bowl. Use these yogurt lumps to start a new batch, and this time it should work. Do not throw the bowl of milk away. Boil it with some lemon juice and make paneer cheese (see page 230) with it. (When you boil this milk with lemon juice, it will automatically curdle and turn into curds and whey. Strain the contents through a piece of fine muslin or cheesecloth and you will have made a delicate cheese.)

The only crucial step in yogurt making is the temperature of the milk. The milk has to reach the boiling point (see page 147 for tips on how not to burn your milk in the process) and then cool down to the required temperature. If it remains too hot, then the yogurt bacteria die, and if it is too cold, they multiply very slowly or not at all, depending on the temperature. If you follow my directions, your yogurt should set in 3 to 4 hours.

If you want to make yogurt overnight, add half the starter to milk that is between 105° and 110° F. This will slow down the multiplication of the yogurt bacteria and thus the formation of the actual yogurt.

Milk can also be boiled in a microwave oven by placing it uncovered in a large glass or Corning Ware bowl and boiling it on high power for 15 to 20 minutes. Nonfat milk especially benefits from this because it does not burn at all.

½ gallon milk (regular, 1% or 2%, or nonfat)
¼ cup nonfat plain yogurt, whisked until smooth

Place the milk in a medium-size saucepan and bring to a boil over high heat. Stir constant-ly, especially if you are using nonfat milk, to prevent it from burning.

Transfer the milk to a yogurt pot (preferably ceramic, though glass, Pyrex, stainless steel, and even plastic containers are acceptable) and let it cool until it registers 118° to 120° F on a meat thermometer. Stir in the yogurt. Place two square pot holders or a fold-ed kitchen towel on a shelf in a kitchen cabinet. Cover the pot with a loose fitting lid and place it on top of the pot holders. Cover completely with another large towel folded in half. (This insulates the yogurt pot and helps maintain the ideal temperature for the multi-plication of the yogurt bacteria.)

Let the milk rest undisturbed for about 3 ½ to 4 hours. Check to see if the yogurt is made. (Do not pick up the pot to do this—this can disturb the bacteria and their subse-quent multiplication, causing the yogurt not to set properly; just pick the lid up.) When set, the yogurt should look almost like flan or Jell-O, with a smooth surface. Some liquid (whey) may be visible on the sides and the top, but that is quite normal. If the yogurt seems soft or liquidy, leave it for another 30 minutes or longer. Refrigerate as soon as the yogurt is made and chill for at least 5 to 6 hours before using.

Another way to make the yogurt is to place the "starter added milk" overnight in an oven with a gas pilot or to leave the oven light on in an electric oven. (The heat from the pilot or the oven light helps maintain the ideal temperature.)

It is important to remember that the longer the yogurt is left to set, the more sour and pungent it gets. This yogurt stays nice and sweet for about 3 to 4 days, then starts getting a little sour, though it still remains good for 12 to 15 days.

Another important fact to remember is that you should not cover the yogurt pot with any clinging plastic wrap or an airtight plastic lid. Yogurt bacteria need to breathe in order to multiply.

Makes ½ gallon

Plain Raita

SAADA RAITA

Whisked until smooth and seasoned just with salt and pepper, this simple preparation is unparalleled when served with Stuffed Paranthas (see page 334) or a complete meal.

Blend it in a blender with crushed ice cubes and you create a savory slush. Blended with water it makes a lovely yogurt drink that cools the body and protects it from the scorching summer heat.

Whatever way you make it, it is delicious.

1 ½ cups nonfat plain yogurt, whisked until smooth
¼ teaspoon salt, or to taste
¼ teaspoon freshly ground black pepper, or to taste

Combine and refrigerate. You can add chopped cilantro (fresh coriander) or mint also.

MAKES 2 SERVINGS

SCALLION AND MINT RAITA WITH ROASTED PEPPERCORNS

HARÉ PYAZ AUR PUDINÉ KA RAITA

Yogurt has a great way of masking the real "raw" taste of the onion. Even though this recipe calls for scallions, you can use almost any type of onion. Finely diced tomatoes make a remarkable addition to this dish.

4 cups nonfat plain yogurt, whisked until smooth
1 cup minced scallions (white and green parts included)
½ cup finely chopped fresh mint leaves or 2 teaspoons dried
1 teaspoon crushed roasted peppercorns (see page 13), or to taste
½ teaspoon salt, or to taste
¼ cup toasted (see page 76) blanched almond slivers

Place the yogurt in a medium-size serving dish. Stir in the scallions, mint, peppercorns, and salt. Cover and refrigerate until needed. Garnish with the almond slivers and serve with any meal.

To make ahead of time, combine everything except the scallions and almond slivers. Add these just before serving or they will lose their crunch.

MAKES 8 SERVINGS

VARIATION: A bit of cayenne pepper can be added as an extra bonus.

CUCUMBER RAITA

Cool and soothing and almost effortless to prepare, this simple dish is indispensable to most Indian families.

Use the small pickling or seedless Japanese or English hothouse cucumbers. Do not squeeze out the juice after grating the cucumbers.

3 cups nonfat plain yogurt, whisked until smooth
2 cups peeled and grated cucumber
½ teaspoon salt, or to taste
½ teaspoon freshly ground black pepper, or to taste
½ teaspoon paprika for garnish
1 teaspoon ground roasted cumin (see page 16) for garnish
Cilantro or mint leaves for garnish

Place the yogurt in a serving bowl. Stir in the cucumber, salt, and pepper. Garnish with the paprika, cumin, and cilantro or mint leaves, and serve.

This raita can be prepared 5 to 6 hours in advance and refrigerated. Serve cold.

MAKES 8 SERVINGS

CUCUMBER, TOMATO, AND SCALLION YOGURT WITH MINT MASALA

KHEERÉ TAMATAR AUR HARÉ PYAZ KA RAITA

This dressed-up version of the simple cucumber raita is wonderful to serve on festive occasions or as a side dish with any meal. It's almost like a salad and can actually pass for one if you add an extra cup of salad vegetables and less yogurt.

Use the small pickling or the seedless Japanese or English cucumbers. If you are unable to find a seedless variety, remove the seeds from regular cucumbers before grating them. The tomatoes should be firm and vine ripened.

3 cups nonfat plain yogurt, whisked until smooth
1 ½ cups peeled and grated cucumber
1 cup finely chopped fresh tomatoes
½ cup finely chopped scallions (white and green parts included)
1 tablespoon peeled and minced fresh ginger
¼ cup minced fresh mint leaves
1 teaspoon finely chopped jalapeño peppers (optional)
1 to 2 teaspoons mint masala (see page 28) or 1 teaspoon ground roasted cumin
    (page 16)
½ teaspoon salt, or to taste
½ teaspoon paprika for garnish
A few fresh mint leaves for garnish

Place the yogurt in a medium-size serving bowl. Stir in the cucumber, tomatoes, scallions, ginger, mint leaves, and jalapeños, then the mint masala and salt. Garnish with the paprika and mint leaves and chill in the refrigerator for 3 to 4 hours or until ready to use.

MAKES 8 SERVINGS

CUCUMBER AND ZUCCHINI YOGURT WITH TOASTED SESAME SEEDS

TIL VALÉ KHEERÉ AUR ZUCCHINI KA RAITA

A refreshingly cool yogurt dish that soothes your burning palate and enables you to enjoy your favorite spicy hot foods. Serve this on the side especially if you feel like giving a calcium and vitamin boost to a meal.

3 cups nonfat plain yogurt, whisked until smooth
1 cup peeled and grated pickling cucumber (squeeze out any excess water)
1 cup grated zucchini
1 teaspoon peeled and minced fresh ginger
½ teaspoon minced garlic
1 teaspoon ground roasted cumin (see page 16)
½ teaspoon salt, or to taste
1 tablespoon toasted (see page 76) sesame seeds
½ teaspoon freshly ground black pepper for garnish

½ teaspoon paprika for garnish
Several cilantro (fresh coriander) leaves for garnish

Place the yogurt in a medium-size serving dish and stir in the cucumber, zucchini, ginger, and garlic, then the cumin, salt, and half of the sesame seeds.

Garnish with the remaining sesame seeds, the black pepper, paprika, and cilantro and refrigerate for up to 4 hours.

MAKES 8 SERVINGS

BARBECUED EGGPLANT IN YOGURT

BHUNÉ BAINGAN KA RAITA

The roasting of eggplants on live coals was almost a weekly occurrence at my mother's home in India. We were very fond of most of my mother's eggplant dishes, but I could not understand her love for adding roasted eggplant pulp to perfectly good yogurt. It was much later, after I got married and came to live in California, that I found myself automatically stealing some barbecued eggplant pulp from the Barbecued Eggplant with Onion and Tomatoes recipe to make this raita.

1 large eggplant (1 ¼ pounds or more)
3 cups nonfat plain yogurt, whisked until smooth
1 teaspoon minced garlic
3 tablespoons finely chopped cilantro (fresh coriander)
2 teaspoons ground roasted cumin (see page 16)
2 teaspoons toasted (see page 76) sesame seeds
1 teaspoon paprika
½ teaspoon ground cayenne pepper (optional)
½ teaspoon salt, or to taste
½ teaspoon freshly ground black pepper, or to taste
Several fresh mint and cilantro leaves for garnish

Barbecue and mash the eggplant according to the directions on page 165.

Place the yogurt in a serving bowl and mix in the mashed eggplant pulp. Then stir in the garlic, cilantro, cumin, sesame seeds, paprika, cayenne pepper, salt, and black pepper. Refrigerate until needed. Garnish with mint and cilantro leaves and serve as a side dish or dip.

This raita can be prepared up to 2 days in advance. Top with additional roasted cumin and paprika before serving.

MAKES 8 SERVINGS

BARBECUED ZUCCHINI IN YOGURT WITH SAUTÉED MUSTARD SEEDS

RYE VALA BHUNI ZUCCHINI KA RAITA

In the summer months, when faced with a plethora of garden-grown zucchini, this recipe paves your way to a new and exciting use of this common vegetable. It is perfect as a side dish or dip, or just by itself.

1 large zucchini or 2 or 3 smaller ones (2 pounds or more)
3 cups nonfat plain yogurt, whisked until smooth
½ cup loosely packed finely chopped cilantro (fresh coriander), soft stems included
½ cup finely chopped scallions (white and green parts included)
½ teaspoon salt, or to taste
Freshly ground black pepper to taste
1 tablespoon mustard or peanut oil
1 teaspoon black mustard seeds
Minced fresh dill for garnish
½ teaspoon paprika for garnish

Over hot coals, grill the zucchini until the skin is charred and the pulp soft. Set aside until cool. Alternately, bake in a preheated 350° F oven until soft, 25 to 30 minutes. Remove the skin and discard. Mash the pulp and set aside. There should be about 1 ½ cups of pulp.

Mix the zucchini pulp with the yogurt and stir in the cilantro, scallions, salt, and pepper. Refrigerate.

Prior to serving, heat the oil in a small saucepan over moderately high heat and fry the mustard seeds until they pop. Cover the pan as soon as they pop to avoid splattering. Immediately add to the yogurt. Garnish with the dill and paprika and serve as a side dish or dip.

This raita can be prepared up to 2 days in advance. The zucchini can be barbecued and stored in the refrigerator for 5 to 6 days or frozen for 2 to 3 months.

MAKES 8 SERVINGS

VARIATION: Steam a few small zucchinis until tender-crisp. Dice finely, then add to the whisked yogurt. Or you can grate the zucchini and steam it, then squeeze out the excess liquid and add it to the yogurt with the rest of the ingredients.

YOGURT WITH SPINACH, SCALLIONS, AND ROASTED CORIANDER

PALAK AUR HARÉ PYAZ KA RAITA

An Indian dip, this thick and creamy raita is ideal to serve with your favorite crackers or vegetables. As a side dish, it works perfectly as a refresher to balance the stronger and more flavorful Indian entrées.

For a change in flavor, try making it with watercress or Swiss chard and ground roasted cumin (see page 16) or pan-toasted (page 181) sesame seeds.

1 bunch fresh spinach or one 10-ounce package frozen chopped spinach, thawed
3 cups nonfat plain yogurt, whisked until smooth
½ cup finely sliced scallions (white and green parts included)
¼ cup loosely packed finely chopped cilantro (fresh coriander), soft stems included
2 teaspoons ground roasted coriander (see page 15)
½ teaspoon salt, or to taste
½ teaspoon freshly ground black pepper, or to taste
½ teaspoon paprika or ground cayenne pepper for garnish
Several cilantro leaves for garnish

Remove the hard stems from the fresh spinach, then wash the leaves and chop them finely. Place in a medium-size pan and cook over moderately high heat until wilted, 3 to 4 minutes. Cool the cooked spinach, squeeze out the excess water, and set aside. (This can be done 3 to 4 days ahead of time.) If you are using frozen spinach, squeeze out the excess water.

Place the yogurt in a serving bowl and mix in the spinach, scallions, cilantro, coriander, salt, and pepper. Cover and refrigerate until needed. Garnish with the paprika and cilantro leaves and serve. This dish stays fresh in the refrigerator for 2 to 3 days, though the color of the spinach turns darker. If you want to prepare it ahead of time, keep all the ingredients ready separately and combine them 3 to 4 hours before serving.

MAKES 8 SERVINGS

YOGURT WITH POTATOES AND CHAAT MASALA

ALU KA RAITA

As a child, my brother Rakesh loved his potato raita, whereas the rest of the family enjoyed variety in their raitas. To accommodate him, my mother would boil a couple of small potatoes by throwing them in the saucepan with her lentils and use them to make an individual serving of this raita for him.

3 cups nonfat plain yogurt
½ cup low-fat milk
3 large potatoes, boiled until tender, peeled, and finely diced
½ cup loosely packed finely chopped cilantro (fresh coriander), soft stems included
3 tablespoons finely chopped fresh mint
1 teaspoon chaat masala (see page 26; optional)
½ teaspoon salt, or to taste
½ teaspoon freshly ground black pepper, or to taste
½ teaspoon paprika for garnish
Chopped cilantro and mint leaves for garnish

Place the yogurt and milk in a serving bowl and whisk until smooth. Add the potatoes, cilantro, mint, chaat masala, salt, and pepper. Garnish with the paprika, cilantro, and mint and serve as a side dish with any meal.

This raita can be made 5 to 6 hours in advance and refrigerated.

MAKES 8 SERVINGS

VARIATIONS: To make a "no frills" version of this raita, add the diced potatoes to whisked yogurt along with salt and pepper to taste.

Cooked sweet potatoes, purple potatoes, and yams are also wonderful in this recipe.

GARBANZO BEAN DROPLETS IN YOGURT

BOONDI OR PAKODI KA RAITA

Crispy fried droplets of garbanzo bean flour batter called *boondi* are soaked in boiling water to remove all their oil and then added to silky smooth yogurt. Packaged boondi are sold at most Indian markets. Some people add Rice Krispies cereal instead of boondi to their raita.

Though not generally made on a daily basis, this raita is reserved for those special occasions when a little extra work is rewarded with mega compliments.

2 cups nonfat plain yogurt
½ cup low-fat milk
2 ½ cups *boondi*
Boiling water for soaking
½ teaspoon salt, or to taste
½ teaspoon freshly ground black pepper, or to taste
1 teaspoon ground roasted cumin (see page 16) or 2 teaspoons toasted (page 76)
    sesame seeds
½ teaspoon paprika for garnish
1 teaspoon finely chopped scallion greens for garnish

Whisk the yogurt and the milk together until smooth. Transfer to a serving bowl.

Soak the *boondi* in boiling water to cover for about 1 minute, then drain. Press on the *boondi* to squeeze out all the excess water. (This process also removes all the oil.) Add the *boondi* to the yogurt, then stir in the salt, pepper, and cumin. Garnish with the paprika and scallions and serve.

This raita can be made 5 to 6 hours ahead of time and refrigerated. If it seems too thick, stir in some more milk.

MAKES 8 SERVINGS

VARIATION: *Boondi* can also be added to the whisked yogurt without soaking and draining. The flavor will stay the same, but the raita will have a welcome crunch.

Add to Classic Curry Sauce (see page 123) to make a simple main dish.

Yellow Mung Bean Puffs in Yogurt

MUNG DAL KE LADOO KA RAITA

This slightly involved and time consuming recipe is generally reserved for special occasions. Topped with Mango or Tamarind and Ginger Chutney (see page 96 or 100), this raita enters the *chaat* (see page 26) category and can be served as a savory snack.

3 cups nonfat plain yogurt
½ cup lowfat milk
½ teaspoon salt
½ teaspoon freshly ground black pepper, or to taste
2 tablespoons finely chopped fresh mint
1 recipe Mung Bean Puffs for Yogurt (see page 68)
Boiling water for soaking
1 teaspoon ground roasted cumin (see page 16) for garnish
½ teaspoon paprika for garnish

Whisk the yogurt and milk together until smooth. Stir in the salt, pepper, and mint and refrigerate until needed. (This can be done 5 to 6 hours ahead of time.)

Soak the mung bean puffs in boiling water to cover until they become soft, 2 to 3 minutes. (Press lightly to see if the center is soft; if not, then add some more boiling water, or put them on the stove and bring them to a boil.) Drain out the water, wait until cool enough to handle, then squeeze out the excess water from each puff by pressing it between the palms of your hands. Set aside to cool.

Place the puffs in a serving casserole and top with the yogurt. Garnish with the cumin and paprika and serve with any meal.

MAKES 8 SERVINGS

LENTIL DUMPLINGS IN CREAMY YOGURT

DAHI BHALLÉ OR BADÉ

This is one of the most labor-intensive recipes in the raita category but it is worth the effort. When paired with Mango Powder and Ginger Chutney, this highly nutritious, savory delight is almost like a meal in itself.

Indians regard this as a party dish par excellence and it is no coincidence when it shows up, dressed in white and brown with specks of red paprika, as a part of more formal and impressive lunch, afternoon tea, or dinner menus.

Bhalle are made with a fermented, pastelike ground bean batter. These deep-fried dumplings are sometimes shaped like disks or doughnuts, and sometimes contain a ground nut-and-raisin filling.

FOR THE BHALLÉ
1 cup dried split yellow urad beans (see page 254), picked over
2 ¼ cups water
One 1 ½-inch piece fresh ginger, peeled
2 serrano peppers, stemmed (optional)
1 teaspoon roasted (see page 13) cumin seeds
½ teaspoon asafetida (see page 13)
¼ teaspoon baking soda
1 teaspoon salt, or to taste
3 to 4 cups peanut oil for deep-frying

FOR THE RAITA
3 ½ cups nonfat plain yogurt
½ cup low-fat milk
1 teaspoon salt, or to taste
1 teaspoon freshly ground black pepper
2 teaspoons ground roasted cumin (see page 16), plus extra for garnish
Boiling water for soaking
1 teaspoon paprika for garnish
Chopped cilantro (fresh coriander) for garnish
¼ cup Mango Powder and Ginger Chutney (see page 100), or to taste, for garnish

Wash the urad beans, then soak them overnight in 2 cups of the water. Drain, rinse, and set aside.

In a food processor fitted with the metal S-blade, mince the ginger and peppers together. Add the beans and the remaining water and process until it turns into a thick, smooth paste, about 1 minute. (You may have to scrape the sides of the work bowl a few times and add more water.) Add the cumin seeds, asafetida, baking soda, and salt and process once again until smooth, 45 seconds. (The batter will be smooth but slightly grainy. If it seems too thin, add some garbanzo bean flour [see page 254] to it.)

Transfer to a bowl, cover, and keep in a warm and draft-free place for 8 to 10 hours to ferment slightly. Stir occasionally.

Heat the oil in a wok or skillet to 375° to 400° F. (Drop a little of the mixture into the hot oil, and if it bubbles and rises to the top immediately, then the oil is ready to be used.)

Form the batter into 1 ½-inch disks, and deep-fry them (in three to four batches), turning occasionally, until golden, 3 to 4 minutes. Drain the *bhallé* on paper towels and set aside until cold. (If making disks seems difficult, then drop about 1 teaspoon of the batter into the hot oil with your fingers or a spoon, until all of it is used up.) These deep-fried *bhallé* can be stored in the refrigerator for 5 to 6 days, or frozen for 3 to 4 months.

Whisk the yogurt and milk together until smooth. Stir in the salt, pepper, and cumin and set aside.

An hour before serving, soak the dumplings in boiling water to cover until they become soft, 3 to 4 minutes. Place each dumpling between the palms of your hands and squeeze out the excess water. Arrange on a serving dish or platter.

Pour the yogurt on top, ensuring that each dumpling is well covered. Garnish with the paprika, cumin, and cilantro. Drizzle the chutney on top and serve by itself as a snack or as a part of a larger menu. (Chopped serrano peppers or ground hot chilies are a welcome addition to this dish.)

MAKES 8 SERVINGS

AVOCADO YOGURT WITH TOASTED ALMOND SLIVERS

AVOCADO AUR BADAAM KA RAITA

My observation that adding yogurt to guacamole prevents the natural discoloring that usually occurs prompted me to try various avocado-and-yogurt combinations. These experiments led to the birth of this nontraditional pale green dish which, though unusual, can still be called a raita.

Besides being a soothing side dish, this can be served as a sauce with grilled or barbe-cued chicken and seafood. It is great as a creamy salad dressing also.

3 cups nonfat plain yogurt, whisked until smooth
1 large ripe avocado, peeled, pitted, and mashed until smooth
¼ cup finely chopped scallion greens
¼ cup finely chopped fresh tomato
¼ cup loosely packed finely chopped cilantro (fresh coriander), soft stems included
2 tablespoons fresh lemon juice
1 teaspoon curry powder (see page 21)
½ teaspoon salt, or to taste
Freshly ground black pepper to taste
½ teaspoon paprika for garnish
2 to 3 tablespoons toasted (see page 76) blanched almond slivers for garnish

Place the yogurt in a medium-size serving bowl and stir in the mashed avocado, scallions, tomato, cilantro, lemon juice, curry powder, salt and pepper. Garnish with the paprika and almond slivers and serve.

MAKES 8 SERVINGS

In Love with Vegetables

India is an agriculture-based culture. Remember that half the population strictly observes the Hindu principle of a meatless diet. With an enormous vegetarian population, the demand for variety and quality of produce is constant. The vegetable carts that make their daily journey from the farms to cities offer the cook the freshest fruits and vegetables at the peak of their flavors. In the United States, I have found the variety of vegetables marvelous, but sometimes the flavors haven't ripened to their fullest. To meet this challenge I use my "little bag of tricks," spice and herb combinations and the pairing of vegetables in unusual ways to achieve maximum palate pleasure.

It appears that America has been moving to a more vegetarian-based diet in the form of pastas, salads, and other nonmeat entrées. However, the cooking methods seemed to have stayed pretty much the same until recently. With the advent of stove-top grills and sautéing methods not dependent upon heavy oils or deep-fat frying, the ways of preparing vegetables are expanding daily.

The American Heart Association recommends "borrowing from some exotic cuisines: use spices to create the tastes of foods from India." This reaffirms my belief that Indian cuisine is a beneficial addition to the American diet. The replacement of salt with traditional Indian spices not only conforms to the AHA's guidelines but opens up whole new avenues of exciting and nutritionally sound cooking. In India salt is used in cooking, but its constant inclusion in food preparation stems from necessity. The temperature and humidity in India cause a daily loss of body salts and water. The population must replace the salt to prevent dehydration. This is not the case in most of America. We do not sweat as much and consequently do not need to replenish our body's salt on such a daily basis. America has depended too heavily upon salt as a flavor enhancer, conditioning our taste buds to a very narrow definition of seasoning. Now is a good time to change our traditional cooking and consumption habits. In my recipes I use very little salt, but rely on the spices for flavor.

The preparation of vegetables truly excites me as much as anything else I cook. Fresh and slightly cooked vegetables add the brightest splashes of color to the table, which I deem crucial for stimulating the appetite. As supermarkets expand their range of produce, and farmers' markets gain in popularity and number, I fervently hope that more and more Americans will be adventuresome in their food repertoire. Like the proverbial "choco-holic" who looks for ways to sneak chocolate into everything, I experiment with new and nontraditional uses of fruits and vegetables. I will try anything twice; once according to the recommended usage of the vegetable and then according to my own intuition. In this way cooking is always a challenge and not a chore.

My generation in India did not have the choice of junk foods or "foreign" cuisines. Variety came from the innovative methods of preparing the vegetables with ever-changing herbs and spices. So, although everything was inherently "Indian," the perception of a changing diet came from the spontaneous and creative approach of the cook. It is this liberating approach that enables the cook to bring forth a new dish to the table every time.

SAUTÉED JAPANESE EGGPLANT WITH MANGO POWDER

AMCHUR VALÉ LAMBÉ BAINGAN

Japanese eggplants are sweeter than their larger oval or round cousins, and they also cook much faster.

Choose eggplants that have a shiny and smooth skin. Brown spots or wrinkles suggest that the eggplants have surpassed their shelf life and peak flavor. This recipe calls for eggplants that are 6 to 7 inches long and about 1 inch in diameter. If you find smaller ones, allow four instead of three per person. The 10- to 12-inch-long ones work well also, provided they are not more than 1 ½ inches in diameter, because the fatter ones have more seeds. (Adjust the cooking time according to size.)

As a variation, try using the white Japanese eggplants or the light purple Chinese variety. To stretch this dish, add lightly sautéed boiled potato wedges before you sprinkle the left-over spice mixture. (You could add some extra spices also.)

1 tablespoon ground coriander

1 teaspoon ground cumin

1 teaspoon mango powder (see page 18)

½ teaspoon garam masala (see page 23)

½ teaspoon turmeric

½ teaspoon ground cayenne pepper (optional)

1 teaspoon salt, or to taste

3 tablespoons peanut oil

24 Japanese eggplants (3 pounds total), slit lengthwise up to the stem, leaving the stem intact

Tomato wedges or cherry tomatoes for garnish

3 tablespoons chopped cilantro (fresh coriander) for garnish

Combine the coriander, cumin, mango powder, garam masala, turmeric, cayenne, and salt in a small bowl and set aside.

Heat the oil over high heat in a large nonstick skillet and place the eggplants in it in a single layer. (Use two skillets if one is not large enough to hold them, or cook them in two batches.) Cover and cook until slightly done on the bottom side, 3 to 4 minutes. Remove the skillet from the heat.

Leaving the eggplants in the skillet, use kitchen tongs (or your fingers) to turn each eggplant over, one by one. Working with each eggplant separately, lift the cooked top side gently, and sprinkle about ½ teaspoon of the spice mixture inside the uncooked bottom side (as if you were stuffing the eggplants with the spices). Set aside the unused spice mixture.

Return the skillet to the stove and cook the eggplants again over medium to high heat until the second side of the eggplant is almost done, 3 to 4 minutes. Sprinkle the leftover spices on the top and cook for another 3 to 4 minutes. Transfer to a serving platter, garnish with tomato wedges and cilantro, and serve as a side dish. If you make this dish ahead of time, let the cooked eggplant remain in the skillet. Reheat in the skillet, initially over high heat, then over medium heat, until heated through and completely dry. Turn over one time only. Too much handling will cause the eggplants to break.

MAKES 8 SERVINGS

VARIATION: For a special touch, place 15 to 20 red and/or yellow cherry tomatoes in the skillet after removing the eggplants and sauté them until they are lightly glazed with the spices remaining in the skillet, 3 to 4 minutes. Shake the skillet a few times to stir. Transfer the tomatoes to the platter with the eggplants and serve.

Japanese Eggplant with Potato Wedges

LAMBÉ BAINGAN AUR ALU

In this recipe you can use any eggplant variety, so long as you stick to one kind only. The dark and light purple ones are sweet, with a soft skin that cooks fast. The white ones, though sweet, have a skin that takes longer to cook, and the green ones are not as sweet but their skin is soft and cooks quickly. All are a delight to eat.

  3 tablespoons safflower oil
  1 teaspoon cumin seeds
  3 small russet potatoes, boiled until tender, peeled, and cut into 8 wedges each
  1 ½ pounds Japanese eggplant, cut into ½- by 4-inch sticks
  1 tablespoon ground coriander
  1 teaspoon ground cumin
  ½ teaspoon turmeric
  ½ teaspoon ground cayenne pepper (optional)
  1 teaspoon salt, or to taste
  1 teaspoon mango powder (see page 18) for garnish
  3 tablespoons chopped cilantro (fresh coriander) for garnish
  10 red cherry tomatoes, cut in half, for garnish

Heat the oil in a large nonstick skillet over moderately high heat and cook, stirring, the cumin seeds, until they sizzle, about 10 seconds. Add the potatoes in a single layer, and cook, turning them as necessary until they turn golden on all sides, 5 to 7 minutes. Remove from the skillet and set aside.

Add the eggplant pieces to the skillet over the same heat and cook until soft, 7 to 10 minutes. Turn the pieces with a spatula as necessary.

Return the potatoes to the skillet, then stir in the coriander, cumin, turmeric, cayenne, and salt. Cook for another 3 to 4 minutes to blend the flavors, stirring occasionally.

Transfer to a serving dish, garnish with the mango powder, chopped cilantro, and cherry tomatoes, and serve as a side dish with any vegetable or bean entrée. If this dish is prepared a few hours ahead of time, let it remain in the skillet in which it is cooked until needed. Reheat, transfer to a serving dish, garnish, and serve.

MAKES 8 SERVINGS

OVAL EGGPLANT WITH DICED POTATOES

BAINGAN ALU

Even though they sound the same, this recipe is very different from the preceding Japanese Eggplant with Potato Wedges. In this dish, the eggplant and potatoes are cooked together right from the start and the result is a complete blend of these two vegetables.

My mother always cooked this dish in a cast-iron wok, which, according to her, enriched the dish by adding traces of iron. She also used generous amounts of clarified butter (*ghee*) instead of oil to enhance the flavor, and it is no wonder that everyone thought that she cooked the best eggplant.

This dish has a rustic aroma when cooked in mustard oil and is reminiscent of my trip to Kathmandu, Nepal. While we studied the topographical changes in the countryside, we also sampled the authentic country cuisine and noticed how the flavor of foods changed as we traveled farther away from New Delhi.

3 tablespoons mustard or peanut oil or clarified butter (see page 30)
2 teaspoons cumin seeds
2 tablespoons ground coriander
½ teaspoon turmeric
1 ½ teaspoons salt, or to taste
2 medium-size eggplants (¾ pound each), cut into 1-inch cubes
2 large russet potatoes, peeled and cut into ½-inch cubes
1 teaspoon mango powder (see page 18)
1 teaspoon garam masala (see page 23) for garnish
Chopped cilantro (fresh coriander) or parsley for garnish

Heat the oil in a large cast-iron wok or a nonstick saucepan over moderately high heat and cook the cumin seeds, stirring until they sizzle, about 10 seconds. Stir in the coriander, turmeric, and salt, then add the eggplants and potatoes. Cover the pan and cook over high heat until heated through, 3 to 4 minutes. Reduce the heat to medium-low and continue to cook until the potatoes are tender and the eggplant is very soft, 20 to 25 minutes. Stir every 3 to 4 minutes. Add the mango powder and cook for another minute.

Transfer to a serving dish, garnish with the garam masala and cilantro, and serve as a side dish with any vegetable or lentil main dish. This dish stays fresh in the refrigerator for 4 to 5 days.

MAKES 8 SERVINGS

Barbecued Eggplant with Onion and Tomatoes

BAINGAN BHARTHA

Eggplant, a universally popular vegetable, is a staple in Middle Eastern, Eastern, and Mediterranean cooking. It is now appearing regularly on American menus also. I think eggplant is as natural a companion to meat and nonmeat dishes as potatoes are, just less filling.

Baingan bhartha literally means "eggplant mush." This traditional dish has a special place in the hearts of most Indians. Each one of us has fond memories of how it was prepared in our family, and wonders why no one else is ever able to make it quite the same. The answer is relatively simple. Every family actually does makes it in a different manner. Each recipe varies with the amount of onions, tomatoes, and spices that are added and to which stage (transparent, golden, or brown) the onion and tomatoes are cooked.

Look for eggplants that seem light for their size; the lighter they are, the fewer seeds they contain.

As a colorful variation, try adding about 2 cups thawed petite green peas. This is a lovely way to stretch this dish, especially in the advent of unexpected company. If there are any leftovers, try using them as a filling to make unique vegetarian sandwiches or as a dip for your favorite crackers. I love *baingan bhartha* on toasted sourdough bread.

2 medium-large eggplants (1 pound each)
3 tablespoons vegetable oil
5 serrano peppers, skin punctured to prevent them from bursting
1 ½ cups finely chopped onion
2 cups finely chopped fresh tomatoes
1 cup loosely packed finely chopped cilantro (fresh coriander), soft stems included
1 ½ teaspoons salt, or to taste
1 teaspoon paprika
1 tablespoon clarified (see page 30) or regular butter (optional)
3 tablespoons chopped cilantro for garnish

Lightly oil your hands and rub them over the surface of the eggplants. Get a hot charcoal fire going. Remove the metal grill and barbecue the eggplants by placing them directly over the hot coals. (This is the best way to barbecue them, because the eggplants become tender very quickly, absorb the smoky aroma, and the pulp remains white.) The eggplants can also be grilled over a gas flame. Turn every 4 to 5 minutes, until the skin is charred and the eggplants are tender, 10 to 15 minutes.

Alternately, puncture the skin of the eggplants in a few places with the tip of a knife, place on an aluminum foil–covered cookie sheet and grill 6 inches (on the middle rack) under a broiler, turning three or four times. They can also be baked in a preheated 400° F oven for 30 to 40 minutes.

Cool the eggplants and peel off the charred skin and discard. Mash the pulp with a fork or in a food processor until smooth. Set aside until needed. (Barbecued eggplant pulp stays fresh in the refrigerator for 4 to 5 days and can be frozen successfully for 3 to 4 months.)

Heat the oil in a large wok or saucepan over moderately high heat and cook the serrano peppers and onion, stirring, until the onion turns golden, 5 to 7 minutes. Add the tomatoes and cilantro and continue to cook, stirring occasionally, until all the liquid from the tomatoes evaporates, 10 to 12 minutes. Then add the mashed eggplant and season with the salt and paprika. Reduce the heat to medium-low and continue to cook, stirring occasionally, for another 10 to 15 minutes to blend flavors. Toward the end of the cooking time, add the butter to enhance the flavor. (This really does make a difference.)

Transfer to a serving dish, garnish with the chopped cilantro, and serve hot as a side dish. To serve as a dip, refrigerate and serve cold with your favorite crackers or with freshly chopped vegetables.

Bhartha stays fresh in the refrigerator for 4 to 5 days. It can also be frozen for 3 to 4 months.

MAKES 8 SERVINGS

VARIATION: Make this recipe with barbecued large zucchini or the smooth pale green opo squash.

ROYAL EGGPLANT WITH GARLIC AND SPICES

SHAHI BAINGAN BHARTHA

The difference between the preceding simple version of *Baingan Bhartha* and this more glamorous entrée is the addition of a few magical ingredients. The combination of the earthy, smoky barbecue flavor and garlic, ginger, and fresh cream creates a dish to die for.

2 medium-large eggplants (1 pound each)
3 tablespoons vegetable oil or clarified butter (see page 30)
1 teaspoon cumin seeds (see page 16)
1 teaspoon minced garlic

1 tablespoon peeled and minced fresh ginger

1 ½ cups finely chopped onion

1 ½ cups finely chopped fresh tomatoes

1 cup loosely packed finely chopped cilantro (fresh coriander), soft stems included

4 jalapeño peppers, whole, split, or finely chopped

1 teaspoon paprika

1 teaspoon dried fenugreek leaves (see page 17)

½ teaspoon turmeric

¼ teaspoon ground cinnamon

¼ teaspoon ground cloves

¼ teaspoon freshly grated nutmeg

1 teaspoon salt, or to taste

¼ cup light cream

2 tablespoons chopped cilantro for garnish

Barbecue, grill or bake and mash the eggplants according to the directions on page 165.

Heat the oil in a large wok or saucepan over moderately high heat and fry the cumin seeds until they sizzle, 10 seconds. Stir in the garlic and ginger, then add the onion and cook, stirring occasionally, until the onions are golden, 5 to 7 minutes. Add the tomatoes, cilantro, and peppers and cook until all the liquid from the tomatoes evaporates, 5 to 7 minutes. Mix in the spices, then add the mashed eggplant pulp. Reduce the heat to medium-low and continue to cook for 15 to 20 minutes, stirring occasionally. Finally, add the cream and cook another 5 minutes to blend the flavors.

Transfer to a serving dish, garnish with the chopped cilantro, and serve hot as a side dish with any vegetable or meat preparation. *Bhartha* stays fresh in the refrigerator for 4 to 5 days. It can also be frozen.

MAKES 8 SERVINGS

VARIATION: Make this dish with barbecued zucchini or opo squash.

MARINATED EGGPLANT "FINGERS"

NIMBOO AUR JEERA BAINGAN

Roasted peppercorns and cumin seeds are the main flavorings of this marinated and lightly cooked eggplant specialty.

Serve on a bed of sautéed greens with slices of Oven-Dried Tomatoes (see page 207)

placed as a garnish around the edges of a platter. For a light brunch, make open-face sandwiches by brushing the bread with Yogurt Mint Chutney (see page 88) and topping it with shredded radicchio and and these fingers. Sprinkle some Hot Pepper Chutney with Ginger and Lemon Juice (see page 92) on top for long-lasting flavor. Serve Vanilla and Mango Ice Cream (see page 372) on the side as a refreshing cooler.

1 or 2 eggplants (1 ½ pounds total)
One 1 ½-inch piece fresh ginger, peeled
2 large cloves garlic, peeled
¼ cup fresh lemon juice
2 teaspoons ground roasted peppercorns (see page 13)
2 teaspoons ground roasted cumin (see page 16)
1 teaspoon crushed carom seeds (see page 14)
¾ teaspoon salt, or to taste
2 to 3 tablespoons peanut or vegetable oil

Wash and dry the eggplants, then cut into ½- by 4-inch sticks. (Do not peel.)

Pound the ginger and garlic with a mortar and pestle until it becomes pastelike, or process in a small food processor. Add the lemon juice, peppercorns, cumin, carom seeds, and salt and grind to incorporate. Marinate the eggplant sticks in this marinade for 6 to 8 hours in the refrigerator.

Heat the oil in a large nonstick skillet over moderately high heat. Add the eggplant sticks in a single layer (in two batches or two skillets, if need be) and cook undisturbed for 2 to 3 minutes. Reduce the heat to medium-low, turn once, cover the pan, and continue to cook, carefully turning the sticks as necessary, until they become soft, 10 to 15 minutes. They should not break.

Serve as suggested above. This dish is best when served fresh.

MAKES 8 SERVINGS

CUT OKRA WITH SAUTÉED BABY PEAR TOMATOES

TAMATAR VALI CUTTI HUI BHINDI

Young and tender okra and baby red and yellow pear tomatoes are at their prime during the hot summer months and this traditional recipe capitalizes on their flavors. I remember being served this dish at least two or three times a week during the summer months.

The trick to cooking okra is to stir it as little as possible (too much stirring will cause the okra to break and turn starchy) and when you do, to lift the pieces with a spatula and gently turn them over, almost like folding beaten egg whites into cake batter.

2 pounds young okra
3 tablespoons plus 1 teaspoon vegetable oil
1 small onion, cut in half lengthwise and thinly sliced
1 tablespoon ground coriander
1 teaspoon ground cumin
1 teaspoon mango powder (see page 18)
½ teaspoon turmeric (see page 21)
1 teaspoon salt, or to taste
20 to 25 baby pear tomatoes or colorful cherry tomatoes
½ cup loosely packed finely chopped cilantro (fresh coriander), soft stems included

Wash and wipe dry each okra. Cut off the stems and then slice each okra into ½-inch pieces. Discard the tips if they look too brown.

Heat the 3 tablespoons of oil in a large nonstick skillet over moderately high heat and cook the okra, stirring occasionally, until it starts to turn golden, 5 to 7 minutes. Stir in the onion and continue to cook, stirring occasionally, until the onion turns brown, 5 to 7 minutes. Add the coriander, cumin, mango powder, turmeric, and salt, reduce the heat to low, and cook until the okra turns brown and crisp, 5 to 7 minutes. Transfer to a serving dish and keep warm.

Heat the remaining oil in the same skillet over medium heat, then cook the tomatoes until they are lightly glazed with the spices remaining in the skillet, 3 to 4 minutes. Shake the skillet a few times to stir. Top the tomatoes with the chopped cilantro and transfer them to the okra dish.

Serve hot as a side dish with Yogurt Sauce with Garbanzo Bean Flour Dumplings (see page 222) or any other entrée. I like it with paranthas (see page 322) also.

MAKES 8 SERVINGS

OKRA STUFFED WITH SPICES

SABUT MASALA BHINDI

The transformation of okra from a slimy and starchy vegetable into a sautéed crispy side dish is one of India's priceless contributions to cooking. This dish will truly change your opinion of this sometimes unpopular vegetable. After you sample this dish, and try the other okra recipes, I'm sure you will incorporate this "squash" into your regular vegetable repertoire.

Choose young, tender okra, not more than 3 inches long. If you can locate only larger okra, try to snap the tip with your fingers. If the tip snaps and breaks off, then the okra is fine, but if it just bends and does not break, then the okra is too fibrous and should not be purchased.

75 to 80 medium-size young okra
1 tablespoon ground coriander
1 teaspoon ground cumin
1 teaspoon mango powder (see page 18)
½ teaspoon paprika
½ teaspoon turmeric
½ teaspoon garam masala (see page 23)
1 teaspoon salt, or to taste
3 to 4 tablespoons peanut oil
1 large onion, cut in half lengthwise and thinly sliced
Several cherry tomatoes or tomato wedges for garnish

Wash and wipe dry the okra. Working with each okra separately, cut off the stem and make a long slit, from the stem side, stopping ¾ inch from the tip. The slit should not cut the okra into two parts, but should make a pocket to hold the spice mixture.

In a small bowl, mix together all the dry spices. Using a small spoon, stuff each okra with this mixture. Save any left over.

Heat 2 or 3 tablespoons of the oil in a large skillet over high heat and cook the okra until medium brown on all sides (as the okra begins to brown, reduce the heat to medium), turning each okra individually and removing it from the skillet as it browns, about 15 to 20 minutes. Set aside.

Add the remaining oil to the skillet and cook the onion, stirring, over medium to high heat until golden, about 5 minutes. Transfer the cooked okra back to the skillet and stir gently to mix. Reduce the heat to medium-low, top with any leftover spice mixture, and continue to cook until crisp, another 4 to 5 minutes.

Remove to a serving dish. Garnish with the tomatoes and serve hot as a side dish with any vegetarian or nonvegetarian "curry." The okra can be cooked a few hours in advance. Reheat, preferably in the skillet in which it was cooked, or in a microwave oven.

MAKES 8 SERVINGS

VARIATION: This dish can also be made by baking the okra instead of sautéing it. With a sharp knife, cut each okra vertically, from the stem end, stopping ½ inch from the tip; do not cut the okra in half.

Lightly oil your hands and rub them over each okra. Place the oiled okra on a cookie sheet in a single layer and bake in a preheated 400° F oven until they turn medium brown, about 20 to 30 minutes. Reposition and remove the okra as they brown. (This can be done up to 3 days ahead of time.)

Heat 1 tablespoon oil in a large skillet and cook, stirring, the onion until golden. Mix in the baked okra and spices and cook until crisp, 4 to 5 minutes.

MAKES 8 SERVINGS

BABY ZUCCHINI WITH SPICES

ZUCCHINI MASALA

As the popularity of farmers' markets rises, so does the variety of their produce. How can one resist tempting baby yellow and green zucchini that look as if they were grown specially for you? This recipe uses zucchini that are not more than 4 inches long and about ½ to ¾ inch in diameter.

    25 to 30 baby green and yellow zucchini (2 pounds)
    1 tablespoon ground coriander
    1 teaspoon ground cumin
    1 teaspoon mango powder (see page 18)
    1 teaspoon dried mint leaves
    ½ teaspoon paprika
    ½ teaspoon ground cayenne pepper (optional)
    1 teaspoon salt, or to taste
    2 tablespoons vegetable oil
    2 cups 2-inch julienne strips red and yellow bell peppers
    3 tablespoons chopped cilantro (fresh coriander), soft stems included

Wash and dry each zucchini. With a sharp knife slit each zucchini vertically, from the "tip" end, stopping ½ inch from the stem, and leaving the stem intact. Do not cut the zucchini into two parts. In a small bowl, mix together the coriander, cumin, mango powder, mint, paprika, cayenne pepper, and salt. Set aside.

Heat the oil in a large nonstick skillet over moderately high heat and cook the zucchini, gently turning each one with kitchen tongs, until they turn lightly brown on all sides. (You may have to cook the zucchini in two batches if the skillet is not big enough to hold all of them at one time.) Top with three quarters of the spice mixture and cook, shaking the pan, for 2 minutes.

Remove the zucchini to a serving platter, cover lightly, and keep them warm. Place the julienned peppers in the same skillet and cook them over moderately high heat until they are barely tender, 2 to 3 minutes. Stir in the remaining spice mixture and the cilantro and garnish the zucchini platter with these peppers. Serve immediately as a side dish. This dish is best when served fresh.

MAKES 8 SERVINGS

ZUCCHINI BOATS WITH PINK LENTILS

DAL VALI ZUCCHINI

In this recipe, the zucchini and lentils are cooked separately and combined before serving. The lentils can be cooked and stored in the refrigerator for up to 3 days. Cooked zucchini, on the other hand, generally tends to "sweat" and become limp if refrigerated and reheated. For that reason, cook the zucchini as close to serving time as possible. However, if you need to cook it a few hours ahead of time, cool it uncovered until it reaches room temperature. At this point just cover and set it aside.

To assemble, place the zucchini boats in an ungreased ovenproof dish, fill them with reheated lentils, and bake in a preheated 400° F oven until heated through, 4 to 5 minutes.

3 tablespoons vegetable oil
1 cup finely chopped onion
1 teaspoon cumin seeds
½ teaspoon turmeric
1 teaspoon salt, or to taste
1 cup dried pink lentils (see page 254), picked over and washed
1 cup water
1 tablespoon peeled and minced fresh ginger
½ cup loosely packed finely chopped cilantro (fresh coriander), soft stems included

½ teaspoon mango powder (see page 18)
½ teaspoon garam masala (see page 23)
12 medium-size zucchini (5 to 6 inches long)
2 small tomatoes, cut into 8 wedges each, for garnish

Heat 2 tablespoons of the oil in a small nonstick saucepan over moderately high heat and cook the onion, stirring, until medium-brown, 5 to 7 minutes. Stir in the cumin seeds, turmeric, and ½ teaspoon of the salt, then add the lentils and water and bring to a boil, uncovered. Reduce the heat to low, cover partially (to let the steam escape and prevent the froth from spilling over), and cook until all the water is absorbed and the lentils are tender, 10 to 12 minutes. Gently fork in the fresh ginger, cilantro, mango powder, and garam masala and set aside.

While the lentils are cooking, prepare the zucchini. Cut each zucchini in half lengthwise and scoop out the pulp, leaving a ¼-inch "boat." Place each boat in a large nonstick skillet, cut side down. Drizzle the remaining oil over the zucchini and cook over moderately high heat until the edges turn golden, 4 to 5 minutes. (Reposition each zucchini to ensure even cooking.) Turn each boat over and lightly cook the other side. Sprinkle a little of the remaining salt on each zucchini (this is optional). Arrange the boats on a platter and fill with the cooked lentils. Garnish with tomato wedges and serve as a side dish.

MAKES 8 SERVINGS

CAULIFLOWER, POTATOES, AND RED BELL PEPPER

SUKHA GOBI ALU AUR MIRCH

This popular cauliflower dish from northern India is bursting with flavor. The serrano peppers do not make it spicy hot, but add an aromatic distinction. The specks of finely diced red bell peppers make this otherwise traditional recipe sparkle and stand out as a new invention.

3 tablespoons vegetable oil
6 serrano peppers, skin punctured to prevent them from bursting
1 ½ teaspoons cumin seeds
2 tablespoons ground coriander
2 teaspoons ground cumin
¾ teaspoon turmeric
1 ½ teaspoons salt, or to taste
2 cauliflowers (about 1 ¼ pounds each), cut into small florets
2 medium-size potatoes, peeled and cut into ½-inch dice
1 cup seeded and finely diced red bell pepper
2 tablespoons peeled and minced fresh ginger
1 cup loosely packed finely chopped cilantro (fresh coriander), soft stems included
¼ cup water
½ teaspoon garam masala (see page 23) for garnish
2 tablespoons chopped cilantro for garnish

Heat the oil in a large wok or saucepan over medium-high heat, then cook the peppers, stirring, for 1 minute. Stir in the cumin seeds, ground coriander, cumin, turmeric, and salt. Then add the cauliflower, potatoes, bell pepper, ginger, cilantro, and water. Cover the pan and cook 4 to 5 minutes, then reduce the heat to medium-low and continue cooking until the potatoes are soft, 30 to 40 minutes. Stir gently as necessary. Transfer the vegetables to a serving dish, garnish with the garam masala and cilantro, and serve hot as a side dish.

This dish can be prepared up to 3 days in advance.

MAKES 8 SERVINGS

MINTY CAULIFLOWER, BROCCOLI, AND CHERRY TOMATOES

GOBI HARI GOBI AUR CHOTÉ TAMATAR

Most Indian menus tend to focus on the high-protein lentils and beans that are the main attraction, around which the other dishes are chosen. Let's make an exception and select an entrée that will complement this predominantly mint-flavored cauliflower-and-broccoli preparation. Opt for simple tasting dishes like Lentils and Yellow Mung Beans (see page 256), Yogurt with Potatoes and Chaat Masala (page 154), and Steamed Basmati Rice (page 286).

For an exotic touch, add 2 teaspoons mint masala to the steamed rice (while cooking it), then garnish it with some fresh mint leaves and sliced scallion greens.

1 medium-size cauliflower (1 ¼ pounds)
1 large broccoli (1 pound)
2 to 3 tablespoons vegetable oil
2 teaspoons cumin seeds
1 cup sliced scallions (white and green parts included)
½ cup loosely packed finely chopped fresh mint
1 tablespoon peeled and minced fresh ginger
1 teaspoon minced garlic
1 tablespoon ground coriander
¼ teaspoon turmeric
1 teaspoon salt, or to taste
1½ cups finely chopped fresh tomatoes
3 to 4 tablespoons water
20 to 25 cherry tomatoes
1 teaspoon mint masala (see page 28) for garnish

Place the cauliflower upside down on a cutting board. Separate the tiny flower heads on the sides by cutting off the branches from the main stem. (You will get eight to ten heads that look like individual baby cauliflowers.) Set aside. Repeat this procedure with the broccoli.

Heat the oil in a large nonstick wok or saucepan over moderately high heat and cook the cumin seeds, stirring, until they sizzle, 10 seconds. Add the scallions, mint, ginger, and garlic and cook, stirring gently, until the ginger turns golden, 1 to 2 minutes. Stir in the coriander, turmeric, and salt, then add the tomatoes, water, and cauliflower. Reduce the heat to medium-low, cover the pan, and cook the cauliflower, turning each piece over occasionally, until they are tender-crisp, 15 to 20 minutes, and most of the water evapo-rates.

Add the broccoli, cover the pan, and continue to cook until the broccoli is tender-crisp, 5 to 7 minutes. Turn the pieces over carefully and try to keep the florets intact, as it adds to the visual presentation of the dish.

Arrange artistically on a serving platter and keep warm. Add the cherry tomatoes to the pot in which the cauliflower and broccoli were cooked and stir gently to glaze with what-ever remains in the pan. Cook over high heat for 2 to 3 minutes, then transfer to the cauli-flower platter. Garnish with the mint masala and serve. This dish can be made 5 to 6 hours ahead of time. Do not freeze.

MAKES 8 SERVINGS

DOUGH-WRAPPED CAULIFLOWER FLORETS

ATTÉ KI PUDIA MEIN GOBI

I'm sure you have heard of fish wrapped in aluminum foil and broiled or barbecued, and the Chinese style of paper-wrapped chicken or pork appetizers, but have you heard of veg-etables wrapped in dough and then baked? Probably not. Even I was unaware of this pop-ular Indian practice. Vegetables are wrapped in rolled out whole-wheat dough and placed in dying ashes for a few hours (or overnight) until the outside dough turns into a hard brown shell; nestled inside it is the most succulent vegetable.

My husband's cousin, who we fondly call Sanjokta Bhanji (sister), informed me of this practice. She even brought me some pattypan squash to try out with this recipe. I also tried cauliflower and broccoli florets and potatoes at the same time. All were equally deli-cious.

I apply a touch of oil and spices to the dough, and these delicate flavors penetrate into the vegetables. The cooked dough itself becomes so flavorful that I always end up eating some of it. The moisture released by the vegetables is absorbed by the dough, so they don't become watery like ones cooked in aluminum foil do.

3 cloves garlic, peeled
One 1 ½-inch piece fresh ginger, peeled
Basic Whole-Wheat Dough made with 4 cups whole-wheat flour (see page 319)
1 teaspoon vegetable oil
1 teaspoon coarsely crushed carom seeds (see page 14)

Salt and freshly ground black pepper to taste
1 medium-size cauliflower, cut into 3-inch florets

Puree the garlic and ginger together in a food processor or with a mortar and pestle until it develops the consistency of a paste. (The food processor will only mince the garlic and ginger, not make it into a paste.)

Divide the dough into the same number of pieces as there are cauliflower florets. Form each piece of dough into a ball and roll it on a lightly floured surface into a 6- to 7-inch circle. Apply a scant brushing of oil (with your fingers or a pastry brush) and then top with ¼ teaspoon of the garlic-ginger paste and a touch of the carom seed, salt, and pepper. Wrap and pinch to seal it around each cauliflower floret.

Baste lightly with oil and place on an ungreased cookie sheet and bake in a preheated 375° F oven until the outside becomes golden and hard like a shell, 35 to 40 minutes.

Serve as a side dish or snack. The shell can be cut with a knife before the vegetables are served, or it can be done right at the table by the guests themselves.

MAKES 8 SERVINGS

CUMIN-SMOKED CAULIFLOWER FLORETS

DHUANDAR JEERA GOBI

The natural sweetness of cauliflower really shines through when it is treated in this simple yet uncommon manner. A squeeze of fresh lime is all that is required before serving it as a side dish or a salad on a bed of mixed baby greens.

Keep the lid handy and allow the least amount of smoke from the spices to escape. It is this smoke, plus the roasted spices, that imparts a rare flavor to this everyday vegetable. The black peppercorns do not give any heat unless you bite on them.

1 tablespoon cumin seeds (see page 16)
2 teaspoons black peppercorns, or to taste
1 teaspoon melted clarified butter (see page 30)
1 small cauliflower, cut into florets
¼ cup loosely packed finely chopped fresh parsley
Salt to taste (optional)
1 tablespoon fresh lime juice, or to taste
Fresh sprigs parsley for garnish

Place the cumin and peppercorns in a large saucepan and toast over medium to high heat until they turn dark brown and smoky, 1 to 2 minutes. Immediately, as quickly as you can, add the butter, then the cauliflower florets and parsley to the pan. Quickly cover the pan to retain all the smoke. Reduce the heat to low and smoke the cauliflower until it turns light brown and tender-crisp, 15 to 20 minutes. (Turn gently two or three times only.) Midway through the smoking, increase the heat to high for 1 to 2 minutes. Uncover the pan and quickly stir the cauliflower. Cover the pan once again, reduce the heat to low, and continue to smoke until done.

Season with salt, sprinkle the lime juice on top, garnish with parsley sprigs, and serve. This dish is best when served fresh, though it can be made a few hours in advance and reheated in the pan in which it was smoked.

MAKES 4 SERVINGS

CABBAGE WITH YELLOW MUNG BEANS

BUND GOBI AUR PEELI MUNG DAL

Cabbage, a member of the cruciferous family (which also includes cauliflower, broccoli, and brussels sprouts), is gaining recognition in the culinary world because of its nutritional and health-promoting qualities. As a child, cabbage was never one of my favorite vegetables (though we still had to eat it), yet this recipe, given to me by my mother-in-law, I really enjoy. It erases the image of soggy cabbage dishes completely. The yellow mung beans absorb all the extra juices and enable you to enjoy the cabbage at its best.

3 tablespoons vegetable oil
2 tablespoons peeled and finely chopped fresh ginger
1 teaspoon finely chopped garlic
1 cup finely chopped scallion greens
5 jalapeño peppers, skin punctured to prevent bursting
1 cup loosely packed finely chopped cilantro (fresh coriander), soft stems included
1 tablespoon ground coriander
1 teaspoon ground cumin
½ teaspoon turmeric
1 teaspoon salt, or to taste
1 cup finely chopped fresh tomato

1 medium-size head green cabbage (1 ½ pounds), finely shredded
½ cup dried yellow mung beans (see page 254), picked over and washed
Freshly ground black pepper to taste
3 tablespoons chopped cilantro for garnish

Heat the oil in a large wok or saucepan over moderately high heat and cook the ginger and garlic, stirring, until golden, 1 to 2 minutes. Add and cook the scallion greens, jalapeño peppers, and cilantro for 1 to 2 minutes, then stir in the coriander, cumin, turmeric, and salt. Cook for a few seconds and add the tomato, cabbage, and mung beans. Reduce the heat to medium and cook, stirring, until the cabbage wilts, 3 to 4 minutes. Cover the pan, reduce the heat to low, and cook until the *dal* is tender, 25 to 30 minutes. Stir occasionally.

Transfer to a serving dish, season with black pepper, garnish with cilantro, and serve hot as a side dish. This dish stays fresh in the refrigerator for 4 to 5 days.

MAKES 8 SERVINGS

WHOLE CAULIFLOWER BAKED IN CLASSIC CURRY SAUCE

SABUT MASALA GOBI

Traditionally this recipe calls for the cauliflower to be deep-fried before being baked in the curry sauce, but I find that the microwave produces just as flavorful a cauliflower as deep-frying does and, more importantly, reduces the fat and calorie count. This dish works best with small cauliflowers because they absorb the seasonings much better than their larger counterparts, thus making the dish more flavorful. Purchase cauliflowers that are white and "tight" looking. Yellow coloring and brown spots suggest that the cauliflower has passed its shelf life. Cauliflowers with "open" heads were harvested too late and tend to be slightly bitter.

2 small cauliflowers (about 1 pound each)
2 tablespoons peeled and minced fresh ginger
3 tablespoons finely chopped fresh mint
1 teaspoon salt, or to taste
1 teaspoon garam masala (see page 23)
4 cups Classic Curry Sauce (see page 123)
3 tablespoons chopped cilantro (fresh coriander) for garnish

Wash and place the cauliflowers in a microwave-proof dish. Smear the tops with the ginger, mint, salt, and garam masala. Cover and microwave on full power until the cauliflower is tender-crisp, 3 to 4 minutes.

Remove the cauliflowers from the microwave and place them in an ovenproof casserole. Top with the curry sauce. Cover the casserole and bake in a preheated 375° F oven until they become tender, 20 to 25 minutes. Spoon the sauce over the cauliflower while it is baking. Uncover and broil until the tops turn golden, 2 to 3 minutes.

Garnish with the chopped cilantro and serve with any meat or lentil preparation.

MAKES 8 SERVINGS

VARIATIONS: Starting with a large cauliflower (1 ¾ to 2 pounds), place it upside down on a cutting board. Separate the tiny "flower heads" on the sides by cutting off the "branches" from the main stem. (You will get four or five heads that look like individual baby cauliflowers.) Cut the rest of the cauliflower to make similar heads. Use these individual heads to make this dish.

This dish can also be made with the light green broccoflower, which, in California at least, is widely available in the winter months. The flavor of this vegetable is almost like that of the cauliflower, and the two can be used interchangeably. Make your decision according to your color preference.

To give the dish a different flavor, use Tomato Cream Sauce (see page 128 or 129) instead of the curry sauce.

GREEN AND YELLOW BEANS WITH RED BELL PEPPERS

PHALLI AUR LAL MIRCH

My visits to the farmers' markets have introduced me to a large variety of tender green and yellow stringless beans that are loaded with flavor. They look so inviting that it is impossible for me to leave the market without buying them. When presented at the table, this dish looks like a mosaic work of art.

2 tablespoons mustard or walnut oil
1 teaspoon garlic slivers
1 teaspoon cumin seeds
1 tablespoon ground coriander

1 teaspoon ground ginger
1 cup loosely packed finely chopped cilantro (fresh coriander), soft stems included
1 teaspoon salt, or to taste
6 cups mixed green and yellow stringless beans, cut into diagonal 1-inch pieces (1 ½ pounds)
1 cup seeded and finely diced red bell pepper or red Swiss Chard stems
1 teaspoon mango powder (see page 18)
Freshly ground black pepper to taste
1 tablespoon Crispy Fried Fresh Ginger (see page 11), or to taste, for garnish

Heat the oil in a large nonstick skillet over moderately high heat and fry the garlic slivers and cumin seeds until they sizzle, 10 seconds. Quickly stir in the ground coriander, ginger, cilantro, and salt. Add the beans and red peppers, cover the skillet, and cook over high heat for 2 to 3 minutes. Reduce the heat to low, stir, and continue to cook until the beans are tender-crisp, 10 minutes. Stir occasionally.

Transfer to a serving dish and gently mix in the mango powder. Season with pepper, garnish with the fried ginger, and serve as an elegant side dish with any entrée.

This dish is best when served fresh. To partially prepare ahead of time, cook the garlic and spices, then add the beans and the red peppers to the skillet. Set aside for 3 to 4 hours. Do not cover the skillet while it is still warm. Finish cooking just prior to serving.

MAKES 8 SERVINGS

VARIATION: Add ½ cup or more pan-toasted sliced almonds, chopped walnuts, or pine nuts instead of (or in addition to) the fried ginger. (To pan toast, place the nuts in a small nonstick skillet or pan and stir lightly over medium-high heat until they become golden and highly fragrant.)

Peas, Carrots, and Potatoes

MATTAR GAJJAR AUR ALU

Try this dish in the summer months, when the vegetables are at the peak of their flavors. Although shelling fresh peas is quite a tedious process, it is time well invested. My mother always says, "The results are only as good as the raw materials used."

2 tablespoons vegetable oil
4 jalapeño peppers, skin punctured to prevent them from bursting
1 tablespoon peeled and finely chopped fresh ginger
1 teaspoon cumin seeds
1 tablespoon ground coriander
1 teaspoon ground cumin
½ teaspoon turmeric
1 teaspoon salt, or to taste
½ cup finely chopped fresh tomatoes
1 cup loosely packed finely chopped cilantro (fresh coriander), soft stems included
3 cups shelled fresh peas
2 cups young carrots, cut into ½-inch slices
3 small red or white potatoes, cut into 6 wedges each
1 teaspoon mango powder (see page 18)
½ teaspoon garam masala (see page 23) for garnish
3 tablespoons chopped cilantro for garnish

Heat the oil in a large nonstick wok or saucepan over moderately high heat and cook the jalapeños and ginger, stirring, until golden, 1 minute. Add the cumin seeds, then stir in the coriander, cumin, turmeric, and salt. Mix in the tomatoes, cilantro, peas, carrots, and potatoes. Cover the pan and cook over high heat about 3 to 4 minutes. Reduce the heat to medium-low and continue to cook, stirring occasionally, until the vegetables are tender, 15 minutes. Gently stir in the mango powder, ensuring that the potatoes do not break.

Transfer to a serving dish, garnish with the garam masala and cilantro, and serve hot as a side dish with any entrée. This dish, though best when served fresh, stays good refrigerated for 3 to 4 days.

MAKES 8 SERVINGS

Fresh Peas with Sautéed Onion

SUKHÉ PYAZ VALÉ MATTAR

I grew up in a country where raw vegetables were available only in their true and natural form. The concept of cooking with commercially available frozen vegetables was quite foreign to most of us, although we were aware that this was a common practice in the Western world. We also knew that freezing would never be part of our natural Indian routine.

Cleaning, shelling, chopping, grating, and even grinding were (and to a large extent still are) all done manually. Nobody seemed to think twice about the work that went into the preparation of the vegetables. Today, modern conveniences have found their way into a lot of affluent Indian kitchens, but the majority of food preparation is still done "the old-fashioned way."

I recall bags full of fresh pea pods that were brought to the house and shelled about an hour before they were to be used. Sometimes my brother and I would pretend to lend a hand, but we ended up eating more peas than we put in the bowl to be cooked. I smile to myself when I see my daughters do the same.

3 tablespoons peanut oil
1 large onion, cut in half lengthwise and thinly sliced
One 1 ½- by 1-inch piece fresh ginger, peeled and cut into julienne strips
5 serrano peppers, skin punctured to prevent them from bursting
2 teaspoons cumin seeds
1 tablespoon ground coriander
½ teaspoon turmeric
1 teaspoon salt, or to taste
5 cups freshly shelled peas (3 ½ pounds in the pod)
3 to 4 tablespoons water
½ cup loosely packed finely chopped cilantro (fresh coriander), soft stems included
½ teaspoon mango powder (see page 18) for garnish
½ teaspoon garam masala (see page 23) for garnish

Heat the oil in a large wok or saucepan over moderately high heat and cook the onion, ginger, and peppers, stirring, until the onion turns medium brown, 8 to 10 minutes. Add the cumin seeds, then stir in the coriander, turmeric, and salt. Add the shelled peas and water and cook over high heat for 3 to 4 minutes. Reduce the heat to medium-low, cover the pan, and cook, stirring occasionally, until the peas are soft, 12 to 15 minutes. Stir in the cilantro, cover the pan, and cook another 2 to 3 minutes.

Transfer to a serving dish, garnish with the mango powder and garam masala, and serve as a side dish. This dish is delicious with Lentils and Yellow Mung Beans (see page 256) or Kidney Beans in a Curry Sauce (page 266). A simple yogurt raita (see page 147) and some bread or rice will complete the meal.

MAKES 8 SERVINGS

VARIATION: Add 1 cup seeded and finely chopped red bell peppers or chopped red Swiss chard stems when you add the cilantro and serve on a bed of lightly sautéed chopped spinach.

Even though fresh peas are the best in this recipe, you could use thawed frozen peas instead, adjusting the cooking times as needed.

BELL PEPPERS STUFFED WITH RICOTTA CHEESE

RICOTTA CHEESE SE BHARI HUI SIMLA MIRCH

Bell peppers can be prepared in endless ways just by themselves, or can be added to other dishes to enhance their flavor. The variety of colors adds a sparkle to every dish in which they are included or when they are used just as a garnish. In this recipe, I cross continents, stuffing peppers with Italian ricotta cheese and flavoring them with a hint of New Delhi. This preparation is a perfect addition to any snack, lunch, or dinner menu.

The smaller bell peppers are more flavorful. These are generally available in the farmers' markets or at the greengrocers. Try using three or four different colors if you can find them. This dish can be assembled a day in advance and baked an hour before serving.

2 tablespoons vegetable oil
2 teaspoons cumin seeds
½ teaspoon fennel seeds
1 cup finely chopped onion
1 cup finely chopped fresh tomatoes
1 cup loosely packed finely chopped cilantro (fresh coriander), soft stems included
2 cups part-skim ricotta cheese
1 tablespoon ground coriander
½ teaspoon paprika
1 teaspoon salt, or to taste

Freshly ground black pepper to taste
10 to 12 small bell peppers, cut in half lengthwise and seeded
½ cup grated mild cheddar or jack cheese
Tomato wedges for garnish
½ teaspoon garam masala (see page 23) for garnish

Heat the oil in a medium-size saucepan over moderately high heat and cook the cumin and fennel seeds, stirring, until they sizzle, 10 seconds. Add the onion and continue to cook, stirring occasionally, until it turns medium brown, 5 to 7 minutes. Add the tomatoes and cilantro and continue cooking until all the liquid from the tomato evaporates, 5 to 7 minutes. Mix in the ricotta cheese, coriander, paprika, salt, and pepper. Reduce the heat to medium and cook, stirring occasionally, until all the liquid from the ricotta cheese evaporates, 7 to 10 minutes.

Fill each bell pepper half with this stuffing and top with the grated cheese. Arrange in a single layer in a lightly greased ovenproof casserole and bake in a preheated 375° F oven until lightly browned on top, 25 to 30 minutes.

Garnish with tomato wedges and garam masala and serve hot as an appetizer or side dish.

MAKES 8 SERVINGS

VARIATION: This stuffing can also be used for tomatoes, zucchini boats, and baked potatoes. I often make a platter with all four vegetables combined and let the guests make their own choice.

COLORFUL BELL PEPPERS AND POTATO WEDGES

RANG VALI SIMLA MIRCH AUR ALU

A delicious aroma fills the house as you cook the potatoes and bell peppers on the stove. Through open windows, the smell escapes to the homes of our neighbors, who wish they could join us for dinner. They can only smell what we see—colorful bell peppers that both increase the visual presentation of this dish and give it a lovely flavor. Served with whole-wheat chapatis (see page 320) and Yogurt Mint Chutney (page 88), this dish parallels Mexican-style *fajitas*.

3 tablespoons vegetable oil
1 teaspoon black mustard seeds
1 teaspoon cumin seeds
2 tablespoons ground coriander
2 teaspoons ground cumin
½ teaspoon turmeric
1 teaspoon salt, or to taste
6 medium-size potatoes, peeled and cut into 8 wedges each
¼ cup water
6 medium-size mixed red, green, and yellow bell peppers (about 1 ½ pounds), seeded
    and cut into 2-inch julienne strips
2 tablespoons chopped cilantro (fresh coriander) for garnish
1 teaspoon garam masala (see page 23) for garnish
1 teaspoon mango powder (see page 18) for garnish

Heat the oil in a large skillet over high heat and fry the mustard and cumin seeds until they sizzle, 10 seconds. Quickly stir in the coriander, cumin, turmeric, and salt, then add the potatoes and water. Reduce the heat to medium, cover the skillet, and cook the potatoes until they are tender-crisp, 10 to 12 minutes. Stir occasionally.

Add the peppers and continue to cook, covered, until the potatoes are tender, 5 to 7 minutes. Stir carefully or the potatoes will break.

Garnish with the cilantro, garam masala, and mango powder and serve hot as a side dish with any meat or vegetable preparation.

This dish tastes best when served fresh. The potatoes can be partially cooked and kept for 5 to 6 hours. Add the peppers and finish the cooking closer to serving time. If completely cooked and kept for a few hours, the peppers become limp and dull and the real charm of the dish will be lost.

MAKES 8 SERVINGS

DICED POTATOES WITH BELL PEPPERS

ALU AUR SIMLA MIRCH KI SABZI

This traditional way of making bell peppers and potatoes is completely different from Colorful Bell Peppers and Potato Wedges (above).

Indian bell peppers are small, about two inches in size, but extremely flavorful, with a touch of peppery hotness. As a result, a few of them can go a long way. They are used as a vegetable to make side dishes, and as a seasoning to enhance the flavor of other vegetables. The taste of the long Anaheim peppers comes the closest to the ones in India.

In comparison, the oversized bell peppers in America contain large amounts of water and not enough flavor. These bell peppers are adequate as a seasoning and a garnish, but are not distinct enough to be used as a separate side dish. I often dice them finely and stir them into other dishes to add color and a flavor boost. It would be well worth your effort to try to find the smaller and more flavorful vine-ripened bell peppers at your local farmers' or organic produce market.

3 tablespoons vegetable oil
2 teaspoons cumin seeds
½ teaspoon crushed carom seeds (see page 14)
3 serrano peppers, finely chopped (optional)
2 tablespoons ground coriander
½ teaspoon turmeric
1 ½ teaspoons salt, or to taste
5 to 6 large potatoes, boiled until tender, peeled, and cut into 1 ½-inch dice
5 small red or green bell peppers, seeded and cut into ¾-inch dice
1 cup finely diced scallion greens
½ cup firmly packed finely chopped cilantro (fresh coriander), soft stems included
2 tablespoons fresh lemon juice
1 teaspoon mango powder (see page 18) for garnish
1 teaspoon garam masala (see page 23) for garnish

Heat the oil in a large nonstick skillet over moderately high heat, then fry the cumin and carom seeds until they sizzle, 10 seconds. Add the serrano peppers, coriander, turmeric, and salt, then the diced potatoes. Reduce the heat to medium, cover, and cook the potatoes, turning as necessary (carefully, with a spatula) until they get slightly crusty, 10 to 15 minutes. Stir in the bell peppers, cover the pan, and continue to cook, turning the potatoes with a spatula, until the bell peppers become slightly soft, about 10 minutes.

Stir in the scallion greens, cilantro, and lemon juice and continue to cook over medium to high heat for another 5 to 7 minutes.

Transfer to a serving platter, garnish with the mango powder and garam masala, and serve as a side dish with any lentil or bean dish that has a sauce. This dish is best served fresh.

MAKES 8 SERVINGS

NEW POTATOES WITH GINGER AND CILANTRO

ADRAK AUR DHANIÉ VALÉ SUKHÉ ALU

Ginger, cilantro (also called fresh coriander), and ground coriander are the predominant flavors in this savory side dish that can also be served as an appetizer. Make sure you have a few extra potatoes when you start, because some will disappear as you are cooking them. The seductive aroma that rises when you add the cilantro and ground coriander can cause havoc and a stampede to the kitchen.

    24 to 30 baby (1-inch) new white potatoes (1 ¾ to 2 pounds)
    3 to 4 tablespoons vegetable oil
    2 tablespoons peeled and grated or julienned fresh ginger
    2 tablespoons ground coriander
    1 teaspoon salt, or to taste
    1 cup loosely packed finely chopped cilantro (fresh coriander), soft stems included
    ¼ cup fresh lemon juice, or to taste
    3 tablespoons finely chopped cilantro for garnish
    ⅓ cup fresh pomegranate seeds for garnish (optional)

Boil the potatoes in lightly salted water to cover until they are tender (not broken). Let cool, then peel and cut in half. Cover and set aside. (This can be done up to 24 hours ahead of time.)

Heat the oil in a small saucepan or skillet over medium heat and stir-fry the ginger until golden, 2 to 3 minutes. Remove to paper towels to drain. Reserve for garnish.

Transfer the oil remaining in the pan (without straining it) to a large nonstick skillet. Place the skillet over medium heat and stir in the ground coriander and salt, then add the potatoes one at a time so that each piece lies flat in the skillet. (Use two skillets if one is not large enough, or cook in two batches.) Add the cilantro, increase the heat to high, and cook, turning the potatoes as necessary, until golden on both sides, 8 to 10 minutes. Top with lemon juice, and cook for another minute. Transfer to a platter, garnish with the reserved stir-fried ginger, cilantro, and pomegranate seeds, and serve as a side dish or an appetizer with Green Mint Chutney (see page 85) or Yogurt Mint Chutney (page 88).

This dish can be made a few hours ahead of time and reheated, preferably in the skillet in which it was cooked.

MAKES 8 SERVINGS

CILANTRO MASHED POTATOES

DHANIÉ VALÉ MASSLÉ HUÉ ALU

"Sounds like cilantro-flavored mashed potatoes—you could eat this on its own, couldn't you?" was my editor Pam Hoenig's reaction, when she read this potato preparation as a part of Spinach and Cheese Casserole (see page 218). At her request, I am including it as a separate recipe in this chapter.

Though mashed potatoes are a favorite dish in the Western world, Indians almost never serve them as such. They mash potatoes only as a preparatory step leading to their incorporation in other recipes.

3 large potatoes (1 ½ pounds)
2 tablespoons butter, melted
1 cup nonfat plain yogurt, whisked until smooth
½ cup firmly packed finely chopped cilantro (fresh coriander), soft stems included
1 teaspoon freshly ground black pepper, or to taste
½ teaspoon salt, or to taste
Cilantro sprigs for garnish
2 tablespoons finely chopped chives for garnish
2 to 5 serrano peppers, halved lengthwise, for garnish

In a saucepan with water to cover, boil the potatoes until tender, then peel and mash (or grate) them. While the potatoes are still warm, mix in the butter, yogurt, cilantro, pepper, and salt.

Transfer to a serving bowl, garnish with the cilantro sprigs, chives, and peppers and serve as a side dish whenever baked or mashed potatoes are called for. This dish can be made 2 to 3 days in advance. Additional yogurt may be required in the reheating.

MAKES ABOUT 4 CUPS

SAUTÉED PURPLE AND GOLD POTATOES

RANG BIRANGÉ ALU

I had never seen the truly gold and the rich and sweet-tasting purple potatoes before in my life. (In truth, I had never even heard about them.) When they started to appear in my local supermarkets, my curiosity prompted an immediate purchase, especially of the purple variety. When I unpacked and displayed my newly found "treasures," my daughters, Sumita and Supriya, looked at me rather strangely. Their "eeew!" was enough to warn me what I was up against.

- 3 large purple potatoes
- 2 large Yukon gold potatoes
- 3 tablespoons walnut, almond, or peanut oil
- 1 teaspoon salt, or to taste
- ½ cup loosely packed coarsely chopped fresh baby dill or finely chopped cilantro (fresh coriander), soft stems included
- 1 teaspoon freshly ground white or black pepper, or to taste
- 2 to 3 tablespoons fresh lemon juice
- Sprigs fresh dill or cilantro for garnish

With water to cover, boil the potatoes in their jackets until they are tender. (You can do this in a pressure cooker or a regular saucepan.) When they are cool enough to handle, peel and cut each potato in half lengthwise. With the cut side down, slice each half into ¼-inch wedges.

Heat the oil in a large nonstick skillet over moderately high heat, then place the potato wedges in it in a single layer. (Use two skillets if one is not large enough or cook in two batches.) Turn each piece over when the bottom side is lightly golden, 4 to 5 minutes. (Move the pieces around by sliding them to ensure that each one gets an equal amount of heat.) When the second side becomes lightly golden, sprinkle with ½ teaspoon of the salt and ¼ cup of the chopped dill, then turn the pieces over. Sprinkle with the remaining salt and chopped dill. Cook, shaking the pan lightly, for another 3 to 4 minutes, then top with the pepper and lemon juice.

Transfer to a serving platter, garnish with fresh dill sprigs and serve as a side dish. These potatoes can also be served as appetizers. This dish can be made a few hours ahead of time and reheated in the skillet in which it was cooked, or in a conventional oven. Do not reheat in a microwave oven. The potatoes should be slightly crisp and a microwave destroys that quality.

MAKES 8 SERVINGS

Potatoes with Onion and Mustard Seeds

PYAZ AUR RYE VALÉ ALU

This is loaded with flavors from southern India. The creative culinary skills of these people prompted them to include dried lentils and beans (whole or ground) as spices in selected dishes. When added whole, they lend a distinct crunch and flavor, as is manifested in this recipe.

This dish is typically made spicy and hot, but that is entirely up to your personal preference. To render this recipe milder, reduce or completely omit the jalapeño peppers.

3 tablespoons peanut oil
2 teaspoons black mustard seeds
1 tablespoon dried yellow urad beans (see page 254)
1 tablespoon dried split yellow garbanzo beans (see page 253)
1 tablespoon dried split yellow pigeon peas (see page 255)
1 large onion, cut in half lengthwise and thinly sliced
¾ teaspoon asafetida (see page 13)
1 tablespoon ground coriander
½ teaspoon turmeric
3 tablespoons unsweetened finely grated fresh or dried coconut
½ cup firmly packed finely chopped cilantro (fresh coriander), soft stems included
3 jalapeño peppers, whole or chopped (optional)
7 large russet potatoes, boiled until tender, peeled, and cut into 1-inch cubes
¼ cup water
1 teaspoon salt, or to taste
3 tablespoons finely chopped cilantro for garnish

Heat the oil in a large saucepan over moderately high heat and fry the mustard seeds until they pop, about 30 seconds. (You may need to cover the pan to prevent the seeds from flying off.) Immediately stir in the beans and fry until they turn golden, 1 to 2 minutes. Add the onion and cook, stirring, until it turns golden, 7 to 8 minutes. Mix in the asafetida, coriander, turmeric, and coconut. Cook another 2 to 3 minutes, then stir in the cilantro and jalapeños. Add the potatoes, water, and salt. Cover and cook over medium-low heat until the potatoes absorb all the water and become tender, 7 to 10 minutes. Stir occasionally.

Transfer to a serving dish, garnish with cilantro and serve as a side dish with South Indian-Style Lentil Soup (see page 264) and Steamed Basmati Rice (see page 286). This dish stays fresh in the refrigerator for 5 to 6 days.

MAKES 8 SERVINGS

FRESH FENUGREEK AND POTATOES

TAZI METHI AUR ALU

The slightly bitter and highly fragrant fresh fenugreek leaves are traditionally paired with potatoes (somewhat like the dill-and-potatoes combination) to make this "dry" dish. The Indians love this recipe and enjoy it on the side or just by itself with paranthas (see page 322). This is another dish that benefits from being cooked in a cast-iron wok.

Today I am able to find fresh fenugreek leaves in my farmer's market and also in Indian markets, but when I came to this country, my only source was my garden.

4 to 5 bunches fresh fenugreek leaves (1 ½ pounds total) (see page 17)
3 tablespoons vegetable oil
3 large russet potatoes, peeled and cut into ½-inch dice
½ to ¾ cup water
1 teaspoon salt, or to taste
2 tablespoons chopped cilantro (fresh coriander) for garnish

Separate the fenugreek leaves and tender stems from the hard stalks. Discard them and wash the leaves and tender stems. Then puree them in a food processor or chop finely by hand.

Heat the oil in a large cast-iron wok or nonstick saucepan over medium to low heat and cook, stirring, the fenugreek leaves until they turn dark green, 20 to 25 minutes. Then add the potatoes, water, and salt and cook over high heat until heated through, 3 to 4 minutes. Cover the pan, reduce the heat to low, and cook, gently stirring the potatoes occasionally until they are tender, 25 to 30 minutes. (By now there should be no water left in the pan and the fenugreek leaves should be very dark.)

Transfer to a serving dish, garnish with the chopped cilantro, and serve as a side dish with any curry or lentil preparation. This dish stays fresh in the refrigerator for 5 to 6 days and can be made ahead of time. Leftovers can be mashed and used as a stuffing for paranthas (see page 334).

MAKES 8 SERVINGS

VARIATIONS: To make this dish with dried fenugreek leaves, heat the oil and add the potatoes, ½ cup dried fenugreek leaves, the water, and salt and cook according to the directions above.

FRESH DILL AND POTATOES (*Sowa Alu*): Use fresh dill leaves instead of fresh fenugreek.

KALE WITH DICED POTATOES

KALE KA SAAG AUR ALU

Kale, a member of the cruciferous cabbage family and sharing its anti-cancer benefits, is also rich in beta carotene, vitamin C, and calcium. I have seen three types of kale in the markets, the regular green-leaved type, the flowering purple, and the flowering white and green. (The edible flowering varieties make magnificent centerpieces and garnishes also.)

The leaves of kale are slightly tough, and though they are often added to salads raw, they have to be cooked when presented as a dish. They have a distinctive flavor reminiscent of that of mustard greens.

2 bunches green, white, or purple kale (¾ pound each)
3 tablespoons mustard or vegetable oil
1 teaspoon coarsely ground fenugreek seeds (see page 16)
2 large cloves garlic, cut into thin slivers
1 tablespoon peeled and finely chopped fresh ginger
1 cup finely chopped onion
1 cup finely chopped fresh tomatoes
1 teaspoon garam masala (see page 23)
¼ cup nonfat plain yogurt, whisked until smooth
¼ cup water or more
2 large potatoes, peeled and cut into 1-inch dice
¼ cup finely sliced scallion whites for garnish
Freshly ground black pepper for garnish

Wash and trim the kale leaves, then chop them finely. (This can be done in a food processor.) Set aside.

Heat the oil in a large nonstick saucepan over moderately high heat and fry the fenugreek seeds, garlic, and ginger, stirring, until golden, 30 to 40 seconds. Add the onions and cook, stirring occasionally, until they turn golden, 4 to 5 minutes. Add the tomatoes and cook until all the liquid evaporates, 4 to 5 minutes. Stir in the garam masala, then add the yogurt and stir until it is absorbed into the tomatoes.

Add the water, then stir in the potatoes and chopped kale, cover the pan, and cook over high heat until the kale is wilted, 3 to 4 minutes Reduce the heat to medium-low and cook until the potatoes are tender, 15 to 20 minutes.

Transfer to a serving dish, garnish with the scallion whites and black pepper, and serve with any curry or legume dish. This dish stays fresh in the refrigerator for 4 to 5 days.

MAKES 8 SERVINGS

Diced Potatoes with Onion and Tomatoes

SUKHA ALU TAMATAR AUR PYAZ

I can't help but remember our lunch breaks during college days when my friends and I would sit around in a circle and unpack what our mothers had given us for lunch. All eyes would be glued to my paper bag as I pulled out paranthas (Indian bread) topped with these sumptuous potatoes which my friends fondly referred to as *Neelam valé alu*, or Neelam's potatoes. The flavors and juices that penetrated into the paranthas made them so soft and inviting that our hungry stomachs could not wait to devour them. Thank goodness my mother always packed enough to share!

3 tablespoons peanut oil
5 jalapeño peppers, whole or chopped (if using whole, puncture the skin to prevent bursting)
1 ½ cups finely chopped onion
2 cups finely chopped fresh tomatoes
1 cup loosely packed finely chopped cilantro (fresh coriander), soft stems included
2 tablespoons ground coriander
1 teaspoon ground cumin
½ teaspoon paprika
1 teaspoon salt, or to taste
Freshly ground black pepper to taste
3 large potatoes, boiled until tender, peeled, and cut into ½-inch dice (about 5 cups)
½ teaspoon garam masala (see page 23) for garnish
3 tablespoons chopped cilantro for garnish

Heat the oil in a medium-size nonstick pan over moderately high heat and cook the peppers, stirring, for 30 seconds. Add the onion and continue to cook, stirring, until the onion turns medium brown, 8 to 10 minutes. Add the tomatoes and cilantro and cook, stirring occasionally, until most of the liquid from the tomatoes evaporates, 7 to 10 minutes.

Add the coriander, cumin, paprika, salt, and pepper, then add the potatoes. Reduce the heat to medium-low and continue to cook until the potatoes absorb all the flavors and become almost a part of the cooked onion and tomatoes, another 10 to 15 minutes. Stir occasionally. Transfer to a serving dish, garnish with the garam masala and cilantro, and serve hot as a side dish with your choice of a vegetarian or nonvegetarian main dish.

This dish is delightful with freshly cooked paranthas or rolled in whole-wheat tortillas to make an Indian-style burrito.

MAKES 8 SERVINGS

CURRIED BABY POTATOES

DUM ALU

Tender 1-inch "baby" new red, white, or gold potatoes, smothered with thick gravy, are as irresistible as they sound. This vibrantly flavored dish is fit for any occasion. Serve with a vegetable side dish, and whole-wheat chapati (see page 320), or a vegetable rice pullao. Throw in a few hot chili peppers for added flavor.

If using potatoes in their jackets, prick holes all over each potato so the juices can penetrate and flavor them from the inside as well as from the outside. If you are unable to locate new potatoes, cut the larger ones into 1-inch pieces and proceed with the recipe.

The addition of fresh mint leaves in this traditional recipe is here courtesy of Veena Dua, my sister-in-law in India.

3 tablespoons vegetable oil
10 green or 5 black cardamom pods, pounded lightly to break the skin
1 teaspoon cumin seeds
2 tablespoons ground coriander
2 teaspoons ground cumin
½ teaspoon turmeric
3 cups finely chopped or pureed fresh tomatoes
2 tablespoons peeled and minced fresh ginger
2 teaspoons minced garlic
5 jalapeño peppers, whole or finely chopped (optional)
½ cup loosely packed finely chopped fresh mint leaves
½ cup loosely packed finely chopped cilantro (fresh coriander), soft stems included
1 ½ teaspoons salt, or to taste
1 cup nonfat plain yogurt, whisked until smooth
30 to 35 baby new red, white, or gold potatoes (about 2 ½ pounds)
½ teaspoon garam masala (see page 23) for garnish
Chopped cilantro for garnish

Heat the oil in a pressure cooker or a large saucepan over high heat and fry the cardamom pods and cumin seeds until they sizzle, 30 to 40 seconds. Stir in the coriander, cumin, and turmeric, then quickly add the tomatoes, ginger, garlic, jalapeños, mint, cilantro, and salt. Continue to cook, stirring occasionally, over high heat until all the liquid from the tomatoes evaporates, 5 to 7 minutes.

Add the whisked yogurt, a little at a time, stirring constantly to prevent the yogurt from curdling, until all the yogurt is absorbed into the tomatoes. Stir in the potatoes, reduce the heat to medium-low and simmer, uncovered, for 5 to 7 minutes, stirring occasionally.

Secure the lid on the pressure cooker and cook the potatoes until the pressure regulator starts rocking. Remove from the heat and let it cool until the pressure drops, 5 to 7 minutes, then remove the lid. If the potatoes are not completely done, add ½ cup water, place the pressure cooker over medium heat and cook, stirring carefully, until the potatoes are done and the gravy is thick. (Do not pressure cook again.)

If using a saucepan, add 1 cup water, cover the pan, and simmer on medium to high heat for the first 5 to 7 minutes, then reduce the heat to medium-low and continue to simmer until the potatoes are tender, 40 to 45 minutes.

Transfer to a serving dish, garnish with the garam masala and cilantro, and serve as a main dish.

This dish can be made 2 to 3 days ahead of time. If it looks too dry, add some water or whisked yogurt and reheat in a microwave oven or over moderately high heat.

MAKES 8 SERVINGS

DICED POTATOES IN GRAVY

ALU KI SABZI

Today in India, as in the yesterdays of hundreds of years ago, it is the custom and unquestioned tradition to visit friends and relatives unannounced. Indian families regard these spontaneous visits as an honor bestowed upon them. The belief that God always visits homes in the guise of guests prompts the host family to entertain visitors in the truest spirit of graciousness. Naturally, one of the easiest ways to please the guests is to feed them and prepare these instant meals in such a way as to make them seem effortless.

Our home always seemed full of people dropping by for just a brief hello or staying for hours. My mother was the perfect hostess and never let anyone leave the house hungry. One of her "quickie" recipes that could be prepared without fuss was this potato dish that she served during morning visitations. I remember her saying that the hardest step in this recipe was the peeling and dicing of the potatoes. She always served them with traditional pooris, the deep-fried whole-wheat puffy bread.

3 tablespoons vegetable oil
1 teaspoon cumin seeds
2 teaspoons dried fenugreek leaves (see page 17)
2 tablespoons ground coriander
2 teaspoons ground cumin

½ teaspoon paprika
½ teaspoon turmeric
1 teaspoon salt, or to taste
3 cups finely chopped fresh tomatoes
2 serrano peppers, whole or finely chopped (optional)
1 cup loosely packed finely chopped cilantro (fresh coriander), soft stems included
5 large russet potatoes (2 ½ to 3 pounds), peeled and cut into ¾-inch dice
3 to 3 ½ cups water
½ teaspoon garam masala (see page 23) for garnish
Chopped cilantro for garnish

Heat the oil in a pressure cooker over moderately high heat and fry the cumin seeds until they sizzle, 10 seconds, then add all the dry spices. Add the tomatoes, peppers, and cilantro and cook, stirring occasionally, until all the liquid from the tomatoes evaporates, 10 to 15 minutes. Reduce the heat to low, add the diced potatoes and cook, stirring occasionally, for 5 minutes. Finally, add the water and secure the lid of the pressure cooker. Cook on high heat for about 1 minute after the pressure regulator starts rocking. Remove from the heat and let it cool until the pressure drops, 5 to 7 minutes.

Open the lid of the pressure cooker and cook the potatoes another 5 minutes over low heat, stirring occasionally. Mash a few potatoes as you stir to thicken the gravy, or add more water if you prefer a thinner sauce.

Garnish with the garam masala and cilantro and serve with poori.

MAKES 8 SERVINGS

VARIATION: This dish is very simple to make without a pressure cooker also. Just add an additional 1 cup of water and simmer, covered, until the potatoes are tender, 25 to 30 minutes.

You could also make the sauce, add previously boiled, peeled, and diced potatoes and simmer for 5 to 7 minutes to blend the flavors.

ASPARAGUS WITH TOMATOES

TAMATAR VALI DUSSAN

My mother still remembers her father bringing home bunches of freshly picked asparagus when he returned from his morning walks. Those young and tender stalks were transformed into a delicate side dish in a matter of minutes by her mother.

When buying asparagus, choose firm, thick or thin spears with closed tips. Bend to snap off the woody end and save it for soup or stock. Use the tender portions for this delicious side dish, compliments of my grandmother.

2 to 3 tablespoons peanut oil
1 cup finely chopped onion
1 cup finely chopped fresh tomatoes
1 cup loosely packed finely chopped cilantro (fresh coriander), soft stems included
1 teaspoon white poppyseeds
1 tablespoon ground coriander
1 teaspoon ground cumin
1 teaspoon salt, or to taste
Freshly ground black pepper to taste
2 pounds asparagus, tough stems snapped off and cut into ½-inch pieces
½ teaspoon garam masala (see page 23) for garnish
2 tablespoons chopped cilantro for garnish

Heat the oil in a medium-size saucepan over moderately high heat and cook the onion, stirring, until golden, 5 minutes. Add the tomatoes and cilantro and cook, stirring occasionally, until all the liquid from the tomatoes evaporates, 3 to 5 minutes. Mix in the poppyseeds, coriander, cumin, salt, and pepper, then add the asparagus. Reduce the heat to medium-low, cover the pan, and cook the asparagus for 2 to 3 minutes. Uncover the pan, increase the heat to high, and cook until the asparagus is tender, 4 to 5 minutes.

Transfer to a serving dish, garnish with the garam masala and cilantro, and serve hot as a side dish with any meal. This dish is best when served fresh.

MAKES 8 SERVINGS

VARIATION: Steam the asparagus spears whole until they are tender-crisp, 3 to 4 minutes. Cook the onion, tomatoes, and the spices, then add about ½ cup nonfat plain yogurt or light cream that has been whipped until smooth to make it into a sauce. To serve, place the asparagus spears on a serving dish, and drizzle the onion-and-tomato sauce over it.

Stir-Fried Asparagus, Mushrooms, and Yellow Bell Peppers

DUSSAN KHUMB AUR PEELI MIRCH KI SABZI

At a friend's house I was challenged to create something unusual with whatever was in the refrigerator. The dish had to be quick-cooking and not contain more than three different spices. My reputation was at stake.

Hesitatingly, I opened the refrigerator, and all I could see was a bunch of asparagus, a few mushrooms, and yellow bell peppers (exotic vegetables for one who doesn't cook, I thought). So I put on my thinking cap, crossed my fingers, and took them out. As I washed and chopped them into 1-inch pieces, this delicious recipe was born. I hope you will like it too. (I found out much later that those vegetables had purposely been planted in the refrigerator.)

    2 tablespoons mustard or walnut oil
    1 tablespoon black mustard seeds
    1 tablespoon peeled and minced fresh ginger
    2 bunches asparagus, the tough stems snapped off and cut into 1-inch pieces
    2 large yellow bell peppers, seeded and cut into 1-inch pieces
    8 large mushrooms, each cut into 8 pieces
    ½ teaspoon freshly ground black pepper, or to taste
    1 teaspoon salt, or to taste
    ½ cup loosely packed finely chopped cilantro (fresh coriander), soft stems included

Heat the oil in a large nonstick skillet over moderately high heat for at least 1 minute, then add the mustard seeds and fry, shaking the skillet, until they sizzle, 30 to 40 seconds. (Cover the skillet as soon as the mustard seeds start popping, or they will fly out.)

When the popping subsides, add the ginger, stir for 1 minute, then add the asparagus, peppers, mushrooms, black pepper, and salt. Stir for 1 to 2 minutes on high heat, then reduce the heat to medium-low, cover the skillet, and cook the vegetables until they are tender-crisp, 5 to 7 minutes. Uncover the pan, increase the heat to high again, add the cilantro and cook, stirring occasionally, until all the juices from the vegetables evaporate, 4 to 5 minutes.

Transfer to a platter and serve as a side dish with any meal. This dish goes very well with cooked pasta that has been lightly sautéed in mustard or olive oil and fresh garlic.

MAKES 8 SERVINGS

MUSHROOMS WITH PEAS AND TOMATOES

KHUMB MATTAR AUR TAMATAR

There is practically an infinite variety of dishes that one can prepare with these three basic ingredients and just a pinch of one spice or another to give it a distinct taste. Here is a recipe full of character—a standout, not just a mere side dish. I like to sauté the mushrooms separately before adding them to the pan with the other ingredients, as they have a tendency to "sweat" when they are cooked. Adding raw mushrooms makes the dish too watery and causes it to lose its character. By sautéing them separately we get rid of all the extra liquid and are able to enjoy the delicate flavor of this traditional specialty.

1 ½ pounds medium-size mushrooms, quartered
3 tablespoons vegetable oil
1 cup finely chopped onion
1 cup finely chopped fresh tomatoes
½ cup firmly packed finely chopped cilantro (fresh coriander), soft stems included
1 tablespoon ground coriander
1 teaspoon ground cumin
3 cups frozen peas, thawed
1 teaspoon salt, or to taste
Freshly ground black pepper to taste
½ teaspoon garam masala (see page 23) for garnish
3 tablespoons chopped cilantro for garnish

Cook the mushrooms, without oil, in a medium-size nonstick skillet, initially on high heat and then over medium, until all the water from the mushrooms evaporates and they turn golden, 5 to 7 minutes. Stir frequently. Set aside.

Heat the oil in a medium-size saucepan over moderately high heat and cook the onion, stirring, until it turns medium brown, 5 to 7 minutes. Stir in the tomatoes and cilantro and continue to cook until all the liquid from the tomatoes evaporates, 3 to 4 minutes. Add the coriander and cumin, then stir in the peas, salt, and pepper. Cook over high heat until all the liquid from the peas evaporates, 4 to 5 minutes.

Add the reserved mushrooms and cook another 3 to 4 minutes to blend the flavors. Transfer to a serving dish, garnish with the garam masala and cilantro, and serve as a side dish.

This dish can be made a few hours ahead of time, though it is best when served fresh.

MAKES 8 SERVINGS

STIR-FRIED PORTOBELLO MUSHROOMS

BHUNI HUI KHUMB KI SABZI

This dish is another one of my farmers' market–inspired recipes. My fascination with different types of mushrooms led me to bring home a huge portobello mushroom, which I was told had a lot of flavor. It sat in my refrigerator for a good 4 to 5 days before I figured out how to use it.

My first bite acquainted me with its "meaty" texture. This quick and easy stir-fry is great over pasta, rice, orzo, risotto, or just by itself.

Look for the freshest mushrooms, with smooth tops and unbroken unshriveled edges. Other mushroom varieties can be substituted if portobellos are not available.

2 tablespoons peanut oil or clarified butter (see page 30)
5 bay leaves
1 teaspoon minced garlic
1 teaspoon peeled and minced fresh ginger
3 large portobello mushrooms (about ½ pound each), cut into 16 to 20 wedges each
½ cup firmly packed finely chopped cilantro (fresh coriander), soft stems included
1 teaspoon coarsely crushed roasted peppercorns (see page 13)
½ teaspoon salt, or to taste
2 small vine-ripe, very firm tomatoes, cut into wedges

Heat the oil in a large nonstick skillet over moderately high heat and cook the bay leaves, garlic, and ginger, stirring, until golden, 1 to 2 minutes. Add the mushroom wedges and cook, stirring gently, until golden, 5 to 6 minutes. Add the cilantro, peppercorns, and salt and cook another 2 to 3 minutes. Add the tomatoes, stirring gently to coat. Cook 2 to 3 minutes, then serve immediately.

The mushrooms can be cooked a few hours in advance and reheated in the skillet in which they were cooked. Add the tomatoes almost at the last minute and finish cooking.

MAKES 8 SERVINGS

MUSHROOMS IN CASHEW NUT SAUCE

KHUMB KAJU MASALA

Elaborate-sounding yet easy to assemble, this mushroom dish is packed with enticing ingredients that guarantee oohs and aahs at any party. Its flavors seem to simulate those of chicken, and that is one of the reasons why it is so popular among Indian vegetarians.

¾ cup cashew pieces

4 cups water

3 tablespoons vegetable oil

3 black cardamom pods, pounded lightly to break the skin

One 1-inch piece cinnamon

5 serrano peppers, skin punctured to prevent them from bursting

1 cup finely chopped onion

½ cup nonfat plain yogurt, whisked until smooth

1 teaspoon salt, or to taste

1 pound small mushrooms, trimmed

2 large potatoes, boiled until tender, peeled, and cut into ¾-inch dice

½ teaspoon garam masala (see page 23) for garnish

3 tablespoons chopped cilantro (fresh coriander) for garnish

Soak the cashews in 1 cup of the water for 1 hour or longer. Drain and puree in a blender until smooth. Set aside.

Heat the oil in a medium to large nonstick saucepan over moderately high heat and cook the cardamom pods, cinnamon, and serrano peppers, stirring, until they sizzle, 30 to 40 seconds. Add the onion and cook, stirring occasionally, until it turns medium to dark brown, 8 to 10 minutes. Add the pureed cashews and continue to cook, stirring, until they turn brown, 5 to 7 minutes.

Stir in the yogurt a little at a time to prevent it from curdling, then add the salt and mushrooms. Cook, stirring, for 3 to 4 minutes, then add the potatoes and remaining water and bring to a boil. Reduce the heat to medium and simmer until the sauce becomes thick and creamy, another 5 minutes.

Transfer to a serving dish, garnish with the garam masala and cilantro, and serve with Black Urad Beans in Fragrant Butter Sauce (see page 263) and Fresh Spinach Bread (page 327).

MAKES 8 SERVINGS

SPICY TARO ROOT

Available in Asian and Indian markets, this hairy brown starchy root vegetable has a distinct place in Indian cuisine. It is used to make special salads (see variation), appetizers, curries, and side dishes. Its leaves are also considered quite a delicacy and are used in various preparations.

When buying this vegetable, make sure that you pick even-sized, firm, and fresh-looking pieces, with no sign of decay. Ideally, you should try to find the pieces that are 1 inch by 2 to 3 inches. This ensures even cooking. If you buy larger taro root, boil it until tender, then cut it into small pieces. (Be aware that the boiled taro root is very starchy, but it will not remain that way after you finish making this dish.)

16 medium-size pieces taro root (1 ½ to 1 ¾ pounds)
3 tablespoons vegetable oil
1 cup sliced scallion greens
1 teaspoon crushed carom seeds (see page 14)
1 tablespoon ground coriander
1 teaspoon ground cumin
1 teaspoon mango powder (see page 18)
1 teaspoon salt, or to taste
2 cups finely chopped fresh tomatoes
½ cup loosely packed finely chopped cilantro (fresh coriander), soft stems included
Freshly ground black pepper to taste
3 tablespoons chopped cilantro for garnish

Wash and place the taro root in a medium-size pot and boil until tender like a potato, 25 to 30 minutes. Remove from the pot, cool, peel, and cut each piece in half (or quarter it if large) lengthwise.

Heat 2 tablespoons of the oil in a large nonstick skillet over moderately high heat and place the taro root in it in a single layer. (Cook in two batches if the skillet is not big enough to hold all the pieces.) Cook, shaking the skillet and moving the pieces around, until the undersides become golden, 5 to 7 minutes, then turn each piece over. (Add the remaining 1 tablespoon oil if needed.) When both sides are golden, remove them to a bowl.

Reduce the heat to medium and add the scallion greens to the same skillet. Cook, stirring, for 1 minute, then add the carom seeds, coriander, cumin, mango powder, and salt. Stir in the tomatoes and cilantro and cook for 2 to 3 minutes. Return the cooked taro root to the skillet and cook another 3 to 4 minutes to blend the flavors.

Remove to a serving dish, season with pepper, garnish with the cilantro, and serve with any lentil or curry preparation. This dish can be made a few hours in advance. Reheat, preferably in the skillet in which it was cooked or in a microwave oven. Boiled taro root can be refrigerated for 4 to 5 days.

MAKES 8 SERVINGS

VARIATION: Boiled taro root can be peeled, diced, and then topped with chaat masala (see page 26) and fresh lemon juice to make a quick and savory appetizer-snack. It can also be added to Potato and Sweet Potato Salad (page 108).

LOTUS ROOT

KAMAL KAKDI (BHAIN) KI SABZI

This exotic root vegetable is the rhizome of the lotus plant (also known as the water lily). It looks like a smooth, beige rod about 10 to 12 inches long and 1 to 1 ½ inches in diameter. Upon cutting it, you notice ten holes that run the length of the lotus root. When sliced, these holes give it a natural lacy appearance (somewhat like pasta wheels). Slicing the lotus roots at an angle accentuates this feature.

The lotus root retains its crunch and shape even after prolonged cooking (unless it breaks due to excessive stirring). It is available fresh at Oriental and Indian markets. Canned lotus root is a good substitute if fresh is not available. I am using canned lotus root to make this recipe more easily accessible.

2 tablespoons peanut oil
1 small onion, cut in half lengthwise and thinly sliced
1 cup finely chopped fresh tomatoes
2 serrano peppers, finely chopped (optional)
1 tablespoon ground coriander
¼ teaspoon turmeric
¼ teaspoon salt, or to taste
One 14-ounce can lotus root, rinsed, drained, and cut into ¼-inch slices
½ cup water
¼ cup firmly packed finely chopped cilantro (fresh coriander), soft stems included
¼ teaspoon garam masala (see page 23) for garnish

Heat the oil in a small skillet or saucepan over moderately high heat and cook the onion, stirring, until golden, 5 to 7 minutes. Add the tomatoes and peppers and cook until most of the liquid from the tomatoes evaporates, 3 to 4 minutes. Add the coriander, turmeric, and salt, then add the sliced lotus root and water, cover the pan, and bring to a boil. Reduce the heat to medium-low and continue to cook, stirring occasionally, until the lotus root becomes tender-crisp and most of the water evaporates, 5 to 7 minutes. (While it is cooking, the lotus root may seem starchy, but it will not stay that way.) Stir in the cilantro.

Transfer to a serving dish, garnish with the garam masala, and serve as a side dish. This dish stays fresh in the refrigerator for 4 to 5 days.

MAKES 4 SERVINGS

VARIATION: Add some diced boiled potato, diced cooked or frozen carrots, or some frozen peas along with the lotus root.

SAUTÉED BITTER MELON WITH PICKLING SPICES

MASALEDAR KARELA

Bitter melon is a green, oval vegetable with pointy tips. Its skin is bumpy and uneven and the Indian variety is generally 3 to 5 inches long and 1 to 1 ¼ inches in diameter. In America, I have seen ones that are much larger and plumper (and very seedy and tough as a result) and another variety that is 12 to 14 inches long and about 1 inch in diameter (almost seedless and tender). As a general rule, the thinner bitter melons contain fewer seeds. When selecting them, look for the firm, bright green, young, and tender ones (the length is not important). The older ones contain hard seeds that have to be removed before you cook them.

A familiar vegetable to most Asian communities, the bitter melon has a special place in the hearts of the Indian people. Its name rightly warns you about the taste, but in spite of this, the bitter melon is very popular, particularly among the people of Punjab. It is frequently cooked in Punjabi homes, and even the children develop a taste for it. (It's a cultivated taste, like that of bitter almonds in desserts.) My little nieces and nephews in India like bitter melons, though my own children do not.

According to Indian folk medicine, bitter melon has tremendous therapeutic value. It is listed as being a blood purifier that also prevents acne, acts as a mosquito repellent, and is recommended to diabetic patients because it contains plant insulin, which helps to lower the blood sugar.

Most recipes advocate peeling and using salt to drain the bitter juices from this melon, but I don't find it necessary. I simply wash the melons and use them as required in my cooking. Another way in which I vary from traditional cooking is that I bake it instead of deep-frying it. Baked slices or whole slit bitter melon freezes well, ready to be transformed into a dish at a moment's notice.

Ten to fourteen 3- to 4-inch-long bitter melons (about 2 pounds)
3 tablespoons mustard or vegetable oil
1 tablespoon coriander seeds
1 teaspoon cumin seeds
1 teaspoon fennel seeds
1 teaspoon fenugreek seeds (see page 16)
½ teaspoon nigella seeds (see page 19)
2 small onions, cut in half lengthwise and thinly sliced
⅓ teaspoon turmeric
4 small potatoes, peeled and cut into 6 wedges each
¾ plus ½ teaspoon salt, or to taste
½ cup water (plus 1 tablespoon, if needed)
1 teaspoon tamarind powder (see page 21) for garnish
Tomato wedges and chopped cilantro (fresh coriander) for garnish

Wash the bitter melons and cut them into ¼-inch-thick round slices. Drizzle 1 teaspoon of the oil over the slices and toss to mix. Place on a cookie sheet in a single layer and bake in a preheated 400° F oven until golden, 15 to 20 minutes. Reposition the slices on the cookie sheet to promote even cooking and remove them as they turn golden. Set aside.

Place the seeds in a spice or coffee grinder and grind until reduced to a coarse powder. Remove to a bowl and set aside.

Heat the remaining oil in a large nonstick wok or skillet over high heat and cook the onion, stirring, until it turns medium brown, 10 to 12 minutes. Add the seed mixture and turmeric and cook, stirring, until it becomes fragrant, about 1 minute. Add the potato wedges, ¾ teaspoon salt, and water. Cover and cook, stirring carefully as necessary, initially over medium, then over low heat until the potatoes become tender and all the water evaporates, 10 to 15 minutes.

Add the baked melon slices and the remaining salt. Cook, stirring gently, for 2 to 3 minutes, then cover and cook for another 5 minutes to blend the flavors.

Remove to a platter, garnish with tamarind powder, tomato wedges, and chopped cilantro, and serve as a side dish.

MAKES 8 SERVINGS

VARIATION: POTATOES IN PICKLING SPICES: Grind the spices and cook them in exactly the same way with 8 potatoes cut into wedges until the potatoes are tender. Garnish and serve.

OVEN-DRIED TOMATOES

SUKHÉ HUÉ TAMATAR

Starting with thick slices of firm, Italian plum tomatoes (they have more pulp and less liquid), basting them with a lemon juice, garlic, and roasted peppercorn marinade, and then baking them very slowly in a warm oven is one of the best ways of preparing a tomato.

8 large fresh Italian plum tomatoes (about 3 ounces each) or 4 medium to large
   tomatoes
2 nickel-size slices fresh ginger, peeled
2 medium-size cloves garlic, peeled
2 teaspoons fresh lemon juice
1 ½ teaspoons coarsely ground roasted peppercorns (see page 13)
¼ teaspoon salt, or to taste
Fresh mint leaves for garnish

Wash and dry the tomatoes, then cut them into ⅓-inch-thick slices. Place on cookie sheets lined with aluminum foil.

Pound the ginger and garlic together with a mortar and pestle until it becomes pastelike or process in a small food processor. Add the lemon juice and then the roasted peppercorns and salt and stir to incorporate.

Rub each slice of tomato with this marinade, taking care that each slice gets an equal amount.

Preheat the oven to 200° F, then place the cookie sheet on the center rack. Bake for 3 to 6 hours, depending on how dry you want your tomatoes. The slices baked for 3 to 4 hours can be presented as an exciting side dish. Top with fresh mint leaves and serve. Prolonged baking dries the slices and makes them perfect as a topping for pasta, pizza, or grilled seafood. They are lovely as a savory snack also.

MAKES 8 SERVINGS

Nine Jewel Vegetables

SABZ NAVRATTAN

Navrattan, or "nine jewels," is a term that is used to describe one particular style of traditional Indian jewelry that has nine sparkling precious and semiprecious stones all set together in an exquisite 22-karat gold setting. Every Indian girl hopes to get at least one piece of *navrattan* jewelry in her trousseau.

Likewise, the term *navrattan* is used to describe exquisite dishes that contain nine or more exotic ingredients. This recipe, a vegetable preparation, contains nine distinct nuts and vegetables and is served with a creamy saffron sauce, making it a culinary pièce de résistance.

    2 tablespoons vegetable oil
    1 cup mixed unsalted nuts (cashews, almonds, pistachios)
    2 tablespoons golden or black raisins
    2 teaspoons cumin seeds
    1 teaspoon fennel seeds
    1 teaspoon white poppyseeds
    2 tablespoons peeled and minced fresh ginger
    5 cups mixed fresh vegetables, cut into ¾-inch pieces (beans, bell peppers, potatoes,
        carrots, cauliflower, broccoli, mushrooms)
    1 cup finely chopped fresh tomato
    1 teaspoon salt, or to taste
    Freshly ground black pepper to taste
    2 cups Creamy Saffron Sauce (see page 135)
    ½ teaspoon garam masala (see page 23) for garnish

Heat 1 tablespoon of the oil in a large skillet over moderately high heat and cook the nuts and raisins, stirring, until golden, 1 to 2 minutes. Drain on paper towels.

Heat the remaining oil in the same skillet over moderately high heat and cook the cumin, fennel, and poppyseeds and the ginger, stirring, for 30 to 40 seconds. Add the vegetables, tomatoes, salt, and pepper, and cook, stirring, for 3 to 4 minutes. Reduce the heat to medium-low, cover the skillet, and continue cooking until the vegetables are tender-crisp, 10 to 15 minutes. Stir occasionally.

Remove the vegetables to a serving platter, drizzle 1 cup saffron sauce over the vegetables and top with the reserved sautéed nuts and raisins. Garnish with the garam masala and serve with more saffron sauce on the side. This dish is best when served fresh.

MAKES 8 SERVINGS

Baked Mixed Vegetable Casserole

SAFAID SAUCE VALI BAKED SABZIAN

This British-inspired, unconventional way of treating vegetables has become a part of traditional Indian cooking. Indian families turn to this variation whenever they want a change or to create an impression. (In America we are exposed to cuisines from all over the world, but to many Indians, simple variations like this one mean a lot.) This "traditional" sauce with a dash of Indian herbs and spices is an offshoot of the basic roux.

It is an excellent party dish, because it can be assembled 2 to 3 days ahead of time and simply baked when needed. I love to serve this casserole with my Thanksgiving turkey.

⅓ cup cornstarch
3 ½ cups low-fat milk
½ cup grated Monterey Jack cheese
1 tablespoon butter
1 tablespoon peeled and minced fresh ginger
1 teaspoon dried mint or basil
½ teaspoon garam masala (see page 23)
½ teaspoon freshly ground black pepper
½ teaspoon salt, or to taste
4 to 5 cups frozen mixed vegetables, thawed
1 large potato, boiled until tender, peeled, and diced
½ cup finely chopped scallion greens
1 tablespoon butter, at room temperature
1 cup grated mild cheddar or Monterey Jack cheese
¾ to 1 cup plain bread crumbs

Combine the cornstarch and ½ cup of the milk and stir until mixed. Set aside.

Place the remaining milk in a medium-size, heavy nonstick saucepan (not Teflon coated) and bring to a boil, stirring occasionally, over moderately high heat. Add the cornstarch mixture and stir until thick and smooth, 30 to 40 seconds. Add the jack cheese, butter, ginger, mint, garam masala, pepper, and salt. Set aside. (This sauce can be refrigerated for 4 to 5 days.)

Place the thawed vegetables, potatoes, and scallion greens in a large nonstick skillet and stir over moderately high heat until completely dry. Transfer to a shallow, wide casserole dish and mix in the sauce. Dot with the butter, and then spread the cheddar cheese and bread crumbs on top.

Bake, uncovered, in a preheated 375° F oven until the top becomes crispy, 40 to 50 minutes. Place under a broiler to brown if desired. Serve hot as a main dish with Garlic Naan (see page 347) and a green salad. Hot Pepper Chutney with Ginger and Lemon Juice (see page 92) is a delightful accompaniment for daring taste buds.

MAKES 8 SERVINGS

SAUTÉED VEGETABLES WITH FRESH MANGO SAUCE

MILLI JULLI SABZIAN

A summertime special, make this dish as often as you can when an array of vibrantly colorful vegetables are at the peak of their flavors. This multicolored dish is so decorative it could be a party centerpiece. Use a platter so it is not condensed into a small area, and watch the colors explode.

The pureed mango sauce adds a delicate sweet and sour touch to the vegetables. In the house of Harish and Madhu Seth, in New Delhi, this dish is often served with a creamy tomato sauce or a sauce made with yogurt, nuts, and saffron.

2 tablespoons vegetable oil
2 teaspoons cumin seeds
1 tablespoon peeled and minced fresh ginger
1 teaspoon minced garlic
1 teaspoon salt, or to taste
1 teaspoon freshly ground black pepper, or to taste
1 cup loosely packed finely chopped cilantro (fresh coriander), soft stems included
5 cups fresh mixed vegetables (baby yellow and green zucchini or pattypan squash, cauliflower and broccoli florets, red, yellow, and green bell peppers, green beans, mushrooms, and carrots), cut into ¾-inch pieces or left whole
1 cup Fresh Mango and Ginger Sauce (see page 141)

Heat the oil in a large skillet or wok over moderately high heat and cook the cumin seeds until they sizzle, 10 seconds. Stir in the ginger, garlic, salt, pepper, and cilantro and then the vegetables. Cook, stirring, 2 to 3 minutes. Reduce the heat to medium, cover the pan, and cook until the vegetables are tender-crisp, 10 to 15 minutes. Stir occasionally.

Remove to a serving platter, drizzle ½ to 1 cup of the mango sauce on top, and serve with any chicken or meat preparation. (Additional sauce can be served on the side.) This dish is best when served fresh.

MAKES 8 SERVINGS

PUMPKIN WITH FENUGREEK SEEDS

PETHÉ KI SABZI

This often neglected vegetable, packed with beta carotene (which is good for the heart and for fighting cancer in the body), has not found its rightful place at the dinner table. It makes an appearance in just a few recipes around Halloween time and then is forgotten. Let's make a combined effort to welcome it into our menus more often.

The subtle flavor of pumpkin is greatly enhanced when it is combined with the appropriate spices. Pumpkin has a natural affinity for sautéed fenugreek seeds, and together they are transformed into a charming side dish. The fenugreek seeds should not be allowed to become too brown or they will turn bitter.

> 3 tablespoons vegetable oil
> 1 large onion, cut in half lengthwise and thinly sliced
> 2 teaspoons coarsely ground fenugreek seeds (see page 16)
> 1 teaspoon ground cayenne pepper, or to taste (optional)
> ½ teaspoon turmeric
> 1 teaspoon salt, or to taste
> 2 pounds pumpkin or any other orange squash, peeled and diced
> About 1 cup water
> Chopped cilantro (fresh coriander) for garnish
> ½ teaspoon garam masala (see page 23) for garnish

Heat the oil in a large nonstick saucepan over moderately high heat and cook, stirring, the onion until golden, 7 to 8 minutes. Stir in the fenugreek seeds, then add the cayenne, turmeric, and salt. Add the pumpkin and water, cover the pan, and cook for 5 minutes. Stir the pumpkin, reduce the heat to medium-low, and continue to cook until the pumpkin becomes soft, 15 to 20 minutes. Puree the cooked pumpkin by mashing it with the back of a ladle and stirring vigorously.

Transfer to a serving dish, garnish with the cilantro and garam masala, and serve hot as a side dish. This dish stays fresh in the refrigerator for 4 to 5 days and can also be frozen.

MAKES 8 SERVINGS

SPICY KOHLRABI

GANTH GOBI KI SABZI

Ganth means "knot" and *gobi* is cauliflower. This knotted relative of the cauliflower is a fine addition to your vegetable list. Its texture is somewhat like that of a turnip, the taste like that of cauliflower and cabbage, and it contains all the beneficial nutrients of the cruciferous family.

Choose young and tender bulbs, as the larger ones tend to be fibrous. In this recipe they are peeled, diced, and cooked with their greens to make a delicious side dish.

4 to 5 medium-size kohlrabi with their greens, washed (about 2 pounds)
3 tablespoons vegetable oil
4 bay leaves, crushed
1 teaspoon finely chopped garlic
2 serrano peppers, finely chopped (optional)
½ teaspoon crushed carom seeds (see page 14)
1 tablespoon ground coriander
½ teaspoon cracked black peppercorns, or to taste
½ teaspoon turmeric
1 ½ to 2 cups water
2 tablespoons fresh lemon juice
½ teaspoon garam masala (see page 23) for garnish

Peel and dice the kohlrabi into ½-inch pieces. Shred the greens or mince them.

Heat the oil in a medium-size nonstick saucepan over moderately high heat and fry the bay leaves for 15 to 20 seconds. Stir in the garlic, peppers, carom seeds, coriander, peppercorns, and turmeric, then add the kohlrabi greens. Cook, stirring occasionally, 5 to 7 minutes, then add the diced kohlrabi and continue to cook, stirring occasionally, for 2 to 3 minutes.

Add the water and bring to a boil over high heat. Cover and continue to boil for about 5 minutes, then reduce the heat to medium-low and simmer until the kohlrabi is tender, 35 to 40 minutes. Stir occasionally. (If the dish looks too dry before it gets cooked, add some more water.) Uncover the pan, add the lemon juice, and cook until most of the liquid evaporates and the dish is almost dry, about 5 minutes.

Transfer to a serving dish, garnish with the garam masala, and serve as a side dish with any lentil or curry preparation and rice or bread. It stays fresh in the refrigerator for 4 to 5 days.

MAKES 8 SERVINGS

Swiss Chard with Vegetables and Green Garlic

LAL SAAG, SABZIAN AUR HARA LASUN

Whenever I buy extra greens (and that happens very often), I cook them partially and refrigerate or freeze them. This way I can use them when I will. I also don't have to plan all my menus ahead of time and can create surprise dishes when the need arises.

Green garlic looks like a large and coarse green onion (somewhat between a scallion and leek). Its flavor is milder than that of a regular garlic bulb. Both the green and white parts are edible.

1 bunch red Swiss chard or any other green (½ pound)
2 tablespoons walnut or almond oil
½ cup finely chopped green garlic (green and white parts included) or 1 teaspoon minced garlic
½ cup finely chopped scallions (green and white parts included; use this only if you're using regular garlic)
2 teaspoons cumin seeds
½ teaspoon ground paprika
½ teaspoon ground cayenne pepper (optional)
¾ teaspoon salt, or to taste
4 cups frozen mixed vegetables, thawed
Tomato wedges for garnish
½ teaspoon roasted ground cumin (see page 16) for garnish

Wash the Swiss chard and separate the leaves from the red stems. Chop the leaves finely and save the stems for another purpose.

Heat 1 tablespoon of the oil in a medium-size nonstick skillet over moderately high heat and cook the chard, stirring, until it wilts. Reduce the heat to medium-low, cover the pan, and continue to cook until the chard looks completely dry and shiny, 20 to 25 minutes. Remove from the skillet. (At this point the chard can be cooled and refrigerated or frozen.)

Heat the remaining oil in the same skillet over moderately high heat and cook the green garlic (or garlic and scallion), stirring, until golden, 1 to 2 minutes. Stir in the cumin, paprika, cayenne, and salt. Add the mixed vegetables and stir-fry until all the water evaporates, 2 to 3 minutes. Reduce the heat to low and add the cooked chard. Cover the pan and cook, stirring occasionally, until the vegetables become tender, 4 to 5 minutes. (Add 1 or 2 tablespoons of water if the dish looks too dry.)

Transfer to a serving dish, garnish with tomato wedges and roasted ground cumin, and serve as a main or a side dish. A dollop of whipped butter adds an extra flavor to this dish. This dish looks very attractive when served over a bed of Steamed Turmeric Rice (see page 286).

MAKES 8 SERVINGS

RED SWISS CHARD WITH CAULIFLOWER

LAL SAAG AUR GOBI

This recipe is a variation of a dish made by Lalit Pant at his restaurant Nawab of India in Santa Monica. At the restaurant they make this dish with spinach, but my ongoing search for innovative ways of including an assortment of healthful greens in my family's diet inspired me to replace the spinach with red Swiss chard, and the results were marvelous. The delicate flavor of the pureed leaves and finely diced rhubarblike stems adds a brand-new dimension to this popular recipe. The diced stem pieces are mixed in when the dish is almost ready so that, besides adding a crunch, they also serve the purpose of a garnish.

Try this dish with different types of greens and other vegetables like boiled potatoes, yams, mushrooms, or with pieces of paneer cheese (see page 230).

3 bunches fresh red Swiss chard (½ pound each)
¾ cup water
½ cup nonfat plain yogurt
3 tablespoons vegetable oil
3 large cloves garlic, cut into thin slivers
½ cup finely chopped onion
1 tablespoon peeled and minced fresh ginger

1 teaspoon garam masala (see page 23)
1 teaspoon paprika
½ teaspoon ground nutmeg
1 teaspoon salt, or to taste
½ teaspoon freshly ground black pepper, or to taste
1 small cauliflower (about 1 pound), cut into 1 ½-inch florets
Tomato wedges and chopped cilantro (fresh coriander) for garnish

Wash the chard. Remove the rhubarblike stems, chop them finely, and reserve. Coarsely chop the leaves and place them in a large nonstick saucepan with ½ cup of the water. Cover and bring to a boil over high heat. Reduce the heat to medium and simmer until wilted, 4 to 5 minutes. Cool and puree in a food processor until smooth.

Combine the yogurt and remaining water and whisk until smooth. Set aside.

Heat the oil in another large saucepan over moderately high heat and cook the garlic and onion, stirring, until golden, 4 to 5 minutes. Add the ginger and cook, stirring for 2 to 3 minutes. Mix in the garam masala, paprika, nutmeg, salt, and pepper, then add the cauliflower, pureed chard, and whisked yogurt. Reduce the heat to medium-low, cover the pan, and simmer until the cauliflower is tender, 10 to 15 minutes. Stir occasionally.

Add the diced chard stems and cook another 3 to 4 minutes to blend the flavors.

Transfer to a serving bowl, garnish with the tomato wedges and cilantro, and serve as a main dish with any Indian bread. This dish stays fresh in the refrigerator for 4 to 5 days. The processed red Swiss chard can be frozen very successfully for 2 to 3 months.

Makes 8 servings

Mustard Greens with Turnips

Sarsoon Aur Shalgam

A dish for mustard lovers. Mustard greens have a strong "mustardy" flavor when cooked by themselves. To really enjoy them, they should be combined with spinach or some other mild green that can provide a balance. Turnips add a delicate sweet touch that enhances this flavor.

1 bunch fresh mustard greens (¾ pound)
1 bunch fresh spinach (¾ pound)
2 large turnips (1 pound), peeled and cut into ¾-inch pieces
1 tablespoon peeled and minced fresh ginger
1 teaspoon minced garlic
½ teaspoon turmeric
1 teaspoon salt, or to taste
½ teaspoon freshly ground black pepper, or to taste
3 tablespoons vegetable oil
1 cup finely chopped onion
1 teaspoon cumin seeds
2 tablespoons ground coriander
2 teaspoons ground cumin
1 cup finely chopped fresh tomatoes
1 teaspoon garam masala (see page 23) for garnish

Remove the hard stems from the mustard and spinach, then wash the leaves thoroughly and chop finely.

Place the chopped mustard, spinach, and turnips in a large nonstick saucepan and cook over high heat, stirring occasionally, until wilted, 3 to 4 minutes. Stir in the ginger, garlic, turmeric, salt, and pepper. Reduce the heat to medium, cover the pan, and simmer until the turnips are soft, 5 to 7 minutes. Transfer to a serving dish, cover, and keep warm.

Heat the oil in a small saucepan over high heat and cook the onion, stirring, until golden, 3 to 4 minutes. Stir in the cumin seeds, then add the ground coriander and cumin. Mix in the tomatoes and cook until all the liquid from the tomatoes evaporates, 4 to 5 minutes.

Top the cooked greens and turnips with the cooked onion and tomatoes. Garnish with the garam masala and serve hot as a side dish with any meal. This dish stays fresh in the refrigerator for 4 to 5 days.

MAKES 8 SERVINGS

PUNJABI MUSTARD GREENS

PUNJABI SARSOON KA SAAG

Springtime in rural Punjab, with its endless fields of mustard greens topped in brilliant, deep yellow blossoms, is a feast for hungry eyes. This is the time when the farmers eagerly anticipate reaping the fruit of their intense labor. Celebrations are held with a lot of sumptuous foods, and the villages are alive with folk music and dance as the earth's bounty of wheat, lentils, and beans reaches its peak.

This traditional dish is delicious when topped with a dollop of homemade whipped butter (commercial whipped butter is a good substitute) and served with Punjabi Corn Flatbread (see page 333) and a tall glass of ice-cold Yogurt Cooler (page 38).

2 bunches mustard greens (¾ pound each)
1 bunch spinach (¾ pound)
2 large cloves garlic, peeled
1 tablespoon whole-wheat flour
½ cup water
1 teaspoon salt, or to taste
3 tablespoons vegetable oil or clarified butter (see page 30)
2 tablespoons peeled and finely chopped fresh ginger
2 tablespoons ground coriander
1 tablespoon dried fenugreek leaves (see page 17)
1 teaspoon ground cumin
1 teaspoon paprika
Whipped butter for garnish

Remove the hard stems from the mustard and spinach, then wash the leaves well and place them (with the water clinging to the leaves) in a large nonstick saucepan. Add the garlic, cover the pan, and cook over moderately high heat, stirring occasionally, until the leaves are wilted, 4 to 5 minutes. Remove from the heat and set aside for 5 to 10 minutes to cool. Then place in a food processor and puree until smooth.

Return the pureed greens to the pan and bring to a boil over high heat. Stir the flour into the water and add it to the greens. Add the salt, cover the pan, and simmer over medium heat, stirring occasionally, to blend the flavors, 15 to 20 minutes. Transfer to a serving dish and keep warm.

(The authentic recipe starts with chopped greens and simmers them on low heat until everything turns into a smooth puree, 1 to 3 hours. Slow cooking adds an unusual flavor to the greens.)

Heat the oil in a small saucepan, and cook the ginger, stirring, until golden, 1 to 2 minutes. Stir in the coriander, fenugreek, and cumin, then add the paprika and immediately pour it over the cooked greens. Garnish with dollops of whipped butter and serve as a main dish.

This dish stays fresh in the refrigerator for 5 to 6 days. It can also be frozen for 2 to 3 months. Additional water may be required when reheating.

Makes 8 servings

SPINACH AND CHEESE CASSEROLE

BAKED SAAG AUR PANEER

My brother-in-law Raj Puri lived in Cardiff, Wales, during his student days. There he developed a great fondness for shepherd's pie, and actually began making his own. At first he baked it according to the traditional English recipe, but then he experimented with different spices and herbs, like black peppercorns, coriander, cilantro, and mint, to satisfy his Indian taste buds. They worked beautifully, and today Raj continues to make his unbelievable Indian shepherd's pie.

Inspired by him, I went a step further. I decided to use spinach and paneer cheese, along with some authentic Indian seasonings to make a vegetarian variation. It turned out to be equally delicious.

Double recipe Basic Paneer Cheese (see page 230)
2 tablespoons vegetable oil or clarified butter (see page 30)
1 cup finely chopped onion
2 tablespoons peeled and minced fresh ginger
1 tablespoon ground coriander
2 teaspoons ground cumin
1 teaspoon paprika
2 teaspoons dried fenugreek leaves (see page 17)
1 teaspoon salt, or to taste
Freshly ground black pepper to taste
Two 1-pound packages frozen cut spinach, thawed and any excess liquid squeezed out
1 large red bell pepper, seeded and finely diced
1 recipe Cilantro Mashed Potatoes (see page 189)
1 cup grated mild cheddar or Montery Jack cheese
1 tablespoon butter
Several sprigs fresh parsley or cilantro (fresh coriander) for garnish

Crumble the paneer cheese by hand until it is smooth but still grainy. Set aside.

Heat the oil in a large saucepan over high heat and cook the onion, stirring, until golden, 4 to 5 minutes. Add the ginger, coriander, cumin, paprika, fenugreek, salt, and pepper, then stir in the paneer, spinach, and bell pepper. Reduce the heat to medium, and cook, stirring occasionally, for 4 to 5 minutes. Set aside.

Grease a shallow ovenproof casserole and spread the cooked spinach and cheese on it. Cover with a layer of Cilantro Mashed Potatoes. Top with the cheddar and dot with the butter.

Bake in a preheated 400° F oven until lightly golden, 35 to 40 minutes. Garnish with the parsley and serve hot with salad and bread.

MAKES 8 SERVINGS

VARIATIONS: Use one 2-pound container of part-skim ricotta cheese in place of the paneer to make an easier version of this dish.

Other greens can be used instead of the spinach.

SPINACH AND PORTOBELLO MUSHROOMS

PALAK AUR KHUMB KI SABZI

The process of sautéing the spinach makes this dish very fragrant, and you need only some salt and pepper to enhance the flavors. The sorrel leaves and yogurt provide a subtle tang, and the portobello mushrooms lend a "meaty" bite to this quixotic quartet of flavors.

If the large (5- to 6-inch) portobello mushrooms are not easily available, use fresh or reconstituted morels, chanterelles, or the common supermarket variety.

1 large green bell pepper, seeded and coarsely chopped
2 small bunches fresh sorrel leaves (¼ pound each), well washed and any tough stems
    removed
2 bunches fresh spinach (¾ pound each), well washed and any tough stems removed
1 cup nonfat plain yogurt
1 cup water
¼ cup olive oil
1 tablespoon minced garlic
2 large portobello mushrooms (about ½ pound each), cut into 1-inch-thick slices
1 cup loosely packed finely chopped cilantro (fresh coriander), soft stems included
¾ teaspoon salt, or to taste
½ teaspoon freshly ground black pepper, or to taste
2 tablespoons finely chopped scallion whites

In a food processor fitted with the metal S-blade, process the bell pepper until minced. Add the sorrel leaves and pulse until minced. Remove the mixture to a bowl. Add the spinach to the food processor a little at a time and pulse until all of it is minced. (You will have to stop the motor and scrape the sides with a spatula, or do it in two or three batches.) Remove to the bowl with the sorrel.

Place the yogurt and water in the food processor and pulse until smooth. Set aside.

Heat 3 tablespoons of the oil in a large cast-iron wok or nonstick skillet over moderately high heat and fry the garlic until golden, 30 to 40 seconds. Add the minced peppers, sorrel, and spinach and cook, stirring with a large slotted spatula, until it starts to gather and is reduced to about 1 ½ cups, 20 to 25 minutes. Remove to a bowl and set aside.

Heat the remaining oil in the same pan over medium heat and cook the mushrooms, stirring, until they become golden, 5 to 7 minutes. Stir in the cilantro, salt, and pepper, then return the cooked spinach mixture to the pan. Add the yogurt and water mixture and cook, stirring, over high heat until it comes to a boil. Reduce the heat to low and simmer for 5 to 7 minutes.

Transfer to a serving dish, garnish with the scallion whites, and serve as a main entrée. This dish stays fresh in the refrigerator for 4 to 5 days and can be prepared ahead of time.

MAKES 8 SERVINGS

VARIATION: To make a this dish more "mushroomy," make it with 2 bunches of sorrel, 3 to 4 portobello mushrooms, and ¼ cup yogurt. Add some seeded and diced red bell peppers also.

SPINACH WITH BABY POTATOES

PALAK AUR CHOTÉ ALU

This superb spinach preparation uses "baby" new potatoes, which are about 1 inch in size. I love this dish with baby Yukon Gold or red and white potatoes. If these are not available, I often cut the large baking-size russet potatoes into 1 ½-inch pieces and then round off the sharp corners with a vegetable peeler to make my own "baby" potatoes.

The amount of spinach and potatoes used in this recipe can vary, depending upon the rest of the menu. (Poke a few holes in the potatoes, especially if you are not peeling them.)

2 bunches fresh spinach (¾ pound each), trimmed of tough stems and well washed
¼ cup water
3 tablespoons vegetable oil
1 cup finely chopped onion
3 cups finely chopped fresh tomatoes
2 tablespoons peeled and minced fresh ginger
1 teaspoon minced garlic
1 cup loosely packed finely chopped cilantro (fresh coriander), soft stems included

1 cup loosely packed finely chopped fresh fenugreek leaves (see page 17) or 3 tablespoons dried
2 tablespoons ground coriander
2 teaspoons ground cumin
1 teaspoon paprika
1 teaspoon salt, or to taste
¾ cup nonfat plain yogurt, whisked until smooth
15 to 20 peeled or unpeeled baby potatoes (1 to 1 ½ pounds)
Tomato wedges and chopped cilantro for garnish

Place the spinach and water in a large nonstick saucepan. Cover and bring to a boil over high heat. Reduce the heat to medium and simmer until wilted, 4 to 5 minutes. Cool and process in a food processor until smooth, then set aside.

Heat the oil in another large saucepan over moderately high heat and cook the onion, stirring, until medium brown, 8 to 10 minutes. Add the tomatoes, ginger, garlic, cilantro, and fenugreek leaves, and cook until all the liquid from the tomatoes evaporates, 10 to 12 minutes. Mix in the coriander, cumin, paprika, and salt, then add the yogurt a little at a time to prevent it from curdling, until all of it is used up.

Add the potatoes, cover the pan, and bring to a boil over high heat. Reduce the heat to medium-low and simmer, stirring occasionally, until the potatoes are tender, 25 to 30 minutes. (If the dish looks too dry, add a little water.) Stir in the pureed spinach and cook for another 5 to 7 minutes to blend the flavors.

Garnish with tomato wedges and cilantro and serve as a main dish with any Indian bread. This dish stays fresh in the refrigerator for 4 to 5 days. Pureed spinach can be frozen very successfully for about 2 to 3 months. Reheat in a microwave oven, then combine with the cooked potatoes.

MAKES 8 SERVINGS

YOGURT SAUCE WITH GARBANZO BEAN FLOUR DUMPLINGS

PUNJABI KADHI

This dish is a staple in every Punjabi household, with each family adding their own special touch to it. The family recipe is as sacred as an heirloom, mother passing it down to her daughters and ensuring its continuity. I think it is the same in Italian or Jewish households when it comes to Mama's sauce or Mama's chicken soup. Every family feels that their recipe is the best and none other comes close to it. My daughters also feel that their "Nani-Mama" (maternal grandmother) makes the best-tasting *kadhi*. Maybe this onion-and-potato dumpling dish with its striking yellow sauce will become one of your family favorites, too!

In this recipe, the yogurt sauce and dumplings are made separately, then simmered together for a short time. The yogurt sauce itself must be simmered for about 45 to 50 minutes to obtain the smooth and silky texture that is commonly associated with this dish. Before serving, the *kadhi* is garnished with sautéed dried red peppers and paprika, which provide a perfect color contrast with the tangy yellow sauce and add the desired amount of piquancy to the dish.

3 cups nonfat plain yogurt
5 cups water
½ cup garbanzo bean flour (see page 254)
2 tablespoons plus 2 teaspoons ground coriander
¾ teaspoon turmeric
1 teaspoon salt, or to taste
¼ cup vegetable oil
5 serrano peppers, skin punctured to prevent them from bursting
¼ cup minced onion
1 tablespoon peeled and minced fresh ginger
1 teaspoon minced garlic
1 teaspoon dried fenugreek leaves (see page 17)
25 Garbanzo Bean Flour Dumplings for Kadhi (see page 50)
5 to 7 dried hot red peppers
½ teaspoon paprika

Process together the yogurt, water, flour, 2 tablespoons of the coriander, the turmeric, and salt in a blender in two batches (because of the volume). Set aside. (It is essential to blend the yogurt thoroughly, or it will curdle while cooking.)

Heat 2 tablespoons of the oil in a large wok or a saucepan over moderately high heat and cook the serrano peppers, stirring, until they sizzle and start getting white spots on them, 30 to 45 seconds. (Stand away from the pan until you add the onion as the peppers may burst and fly to your eyes.) Add the onion, ginger, and garlic and cook, stirring, until the onion turns golden, 2 minutes. Slowly add the yogurt mixture and stir until it comes to a boil, 4 to 5 minutes. (Constant slow stirring is essential for the first 2 minutes or the yogurt will curdle. You can reduce the amount of stirring after that. Keep a watch on the wok and reduce the heat if the sauce starts to boil over.)

Once the sauce comes to a boil, reduce the heat to medium and simmer, uncovered, stirring occasionally, until the sauce looks smooth and silky, and traces of oil are visible on the top surface and the sides, 45 to 50 minutes. (Remember that the sauce will thicken after you add the dumplings.) This can be made up to 2 days ahead of time.

Stir in the fenugreek, then add the dumplings and simmer for about 5 minutes more. (Add ¼ to ½ cup water if you prefer a thinner sauce and bring it to a boil.) Transfer to a serving casserole and keep warm.

Heat the remaining oil in a small saucepan over moderately high heat and cook the dried peppers, stirring, for 30 seconds. Stir in the remaining coriander and remove the pan from the heat. Add the paprika and immediately pour the contents over the *kadhi*. (You have to be fast when doing this or the paprika will burn and make the dish bitter.) Serve with Steamed Basmati Rice (see page 286) and Cut Okra with Sautéed Baby Pear Tomatoes (see page 168).

MAKES 8 SERVINGS

VARIATION: Make a delicious spinach *kadhi* by adding 4 to 5 cups of finely chopped fresh spinach in place of the dumplings. Other type of greens (mustard, amaranth, chicory, dandelion, etc.) can also be used.

Sautéed thinly sliced onion also makes a wonderful addition.

Turnips in a Light Curry Sauce

TARI VALÉ SHALGAM

Of late, I have noticed a surge in the popularity of turnips. This is a vegetable that most people are visually familiar with, but they are at a loss when faced with actually cooking it (other than steaming or pureeing it).

Though not as popular as potatoes, turnips have a noticeable presence in Indian cuisine. They are offered as main dishes, side dishes, chutneys, pickles, and are even dried in the sun (like tomatoes) and then used to make side dishes or to flavor other foods.

Here is a recipe that transforms the ordinary turnip into an elegant entrée; it pairs well with Spinach and Sweet Pepper Rice (see page 294). You can serve it with any dry style vegetable dish and chapatis (see page 320).

Generally, this dish is made with diced turnips, but I am using young and tender baby turnips instead. (If you use larger turnips, peel them.)

1 ½ pounds baby turnips (about 1 inch wide)
One 1-inch piece fresh ginger, peeled
1 clove garlic, peeled
1 small onion, peeled
1 to 3 serrano peppers, stemmed (optional)
2 to 3 tablespoons corn oil
2 teaspoons ground coriander
½ teaspoon turmeric
1 teaspoon salt, or to taste
1 large tomato, cut into 1-inch dice
3 cups water
Chopped cilantro (fresh coriander) for garnish
½ teaspoon garam masala (see page 23) for garnish

Cut off a very thin slice from the stem and root of each turnip, then wash and set aside. (Do not peel.)

In a food processor fitted with the metal S-blade, process the ginger, garlic, onion, and serrano peppers until they turn into a smooth paste. (You will have to scrape the sides of the work bowl down with a spatula.)

Heat the oil in a large nonstick pan over moderately high heat and cook the onion paste, stirring as necessary, until it browns, 5 to 7 minutes. Reduce the heat to medium-low, add the coriander, turmeric, and salt, then the tomatoes, and cook until the tomato become soft, 3 to 4 minutes.

Add the turnips and cook, stirring, for 3 to 4 minutes, then add the water. Cover the pan, increase the heat to high, and bring to a boil. Reduce the heat to medium and simmer until the turnips become tender and the gravy is slightly thick, 10 to 15 minutes.

Transfer to a serving dish, garnish with chopped cilantro and the garam masala, and serve as a main dish.

MAKES 8 SERVINGS

ANAHEIM PEPPERS IN A TAMARIND-FENUGREEK SAUCE

IMLI AUR DAANA METHI VALI MIRCH

Try this dish once and you'll be addicted to it forever. My friend Reita Bhalla introduced me to this dynamic preparation, which uses the highly fragrant fenugreek and cumin seeds and pairs them with dried red chili peppers and tamarind paste to make an exceptional sauce that is something to die for. Attempt this recipe only if you have a strong heart.

Don't shortchange the soaking time for the tamarind; it facilitates the extraction of the pulp from the fiber. Shelled seedless tamarind is available in packets in Indian markets.

5 ounces shelled seedless tamarind
3 cups boiling water
8 to 10 Anaheim peppers (1 pound or more)
2 tablespoons fenugreek seeds (see page 16)
1 tablespoon cumin seeds
5 to 8 dried hot red peppers
10 large cloves garlic, peeled
1 large onion, cut into 8 to 10 pieces
1/4 cup peanut oil
1 1/2 teaspoons salt, or to taste
1/2 teaspoon turmeric
5 to 8 dried hot red peppers for garnish
Chopped cilantro (fresh coriander) for garnish

Soak the tamarind in the boiling water for 3 to 4 hours or longer. Stir it a few times during soaking. Then pass it through a food mill or a sieve to extract all the pulp. Add 1/4 cup water to the leftover fibrous parts and extract some more pulp. Set aside the pulp. This can be done up to a week in advance and refrigerated. (The pulp can also be frozen up to 6 months.)

Leaving the stems on, wash and dry the Anaheim peppers. Make a 3-inch slit in the center of each one. Set aside.

Place the fenugreek and cumin seeds in a small nonstick skillet and roast over moderately high heat, stirring until fragrant and lightly golden, 1 to 2 minutes. Cool and grind coarsely with the dried red peppers in a spice grinder. Set aside.

In a food processor fitted with a metal S-blade, process the garlic and onion until finely minced but not too watery. Remove from the food processor and set aside.

Heat the oil in a medium-size nonstick saucepan over moderately high heat and cook the roasted spices, stirring, for about 1 minute, then add the garlic-and-onion mixture. Cook, stirring, for 2 to 3 minutes, reduce the heat to medium for 3 to 4 minutes and then to low, and continue to cook, stirring occasionally, until the mixture turns dark brown and highly fragrant, 15 to 20 minutes.

Increase the heat to high, stir in the salt and turmeric, then add the tamarind pulp and bring to a boil.

Place the peppers in a large nonstick skillet in a single layer and pour the tamarind sauce over them, scraping up whatever is left in the pan (with additional water if needed). Cover the skillet and cook the peppers over medium heat until the peppers are fork tender and juicy (some of the spice mixture should find its way into the peppers through the slits) and the sauce is very thick, 45 minutes to 1 hour. Add more water if needed.

Transfer to a platter, garnish with the chili peppers and cilantro, and serve with a mild lentil or bean dish like Yellow Urad Beans with Minced Ginger (see page 260) and whole-wheat chapatis (page 320) or Mexican-style tortillas. As a soother, serve plain homemade yogurt or a raita (see page 147).

When served as part of a larger menu, this dish makes enough to serve 15 to 20 people. Make a few diagonal cuts on each pepper to make smaller servings. (It's like slicing a long loaf of bread, people serve themselves smaller pieces instead of whole peppers.)

This dish can be made 2 to 3 days ahead of time and be frozen for 2 to 3 months.

MAKES 8 SERVINGS

VEGETABLE BALLS IN CLASSIC CURRY SAUCE

SABZ KOFTA KI CURRY

The term *kofta* refers to deep-fried meat or vegetable balls. This preparation is instantly transformed into a sophisticated entrée when served in Classic Curry Sauce (see page 123). Vegetable koftas are a clever alternative to meatballs, especially since the vast majority of India's population is vegetarian. For the nonvegetarians, this dish is an elegant addition to any party table.

The koftas and curry sauce are prepared separately, then combined almost at the last minute. This is an excellent choice for a party dish because the koftas can be made up to 2 months ahead of time and frozen. Just make fresh curry sauce and you have an impressive main dish in no time. Remember, once the koftas are added to the sauce, they become soft, and excess handling will cause them to disintegrate.

1 ½ cups grated potatoes

1 cup grated cauliflower

1 cup grated carrot

1 cup grated zucchini

1 cup finely chopped onion

½ cup loosely packed finely chopped cilantro (fresh coriander), soft stems included

2 tablespoons peeled and minced fresh ginger

1 ½ to 2 cups garbanzo bean flour (see page 254)

2 tablespoons ground coriander

2 teaspoons ground cumin

1 teaspoon salt, or to taste

¼ teaspoon baking soda

3 to 4 cups peanut oil for deep-frying

4 cups Classic Curry Sauce (see page 123)

3 tablespoons finely chopped cilantro for garnish

½ teaspoon garam masala (see page 23) for garnish

Combine the potatoes, cauliflower, carrot, zucchini, onion, cilantro, and ginger in a medium-size bowl. Mix in the flour, coriander, cumin, salt, and baking soda. (If the mixture is too soft, add a little extra garbanzo flour.) Make thirty-two to thirty-five 1 ½-inch balls and set aside.

Heat the oil in a wok or a skillet to 350° to 375° F. (Drop ½ teaspoon of the mixture into the hot oil and if it bubbles and rises to the top immediately, the oil is ready to be used.) Deep-fry the koftas, a few at a time, until they turn medium brown. Using a slotted spoon, remove to paper towels and set aside to drain. Meanwhile, prepare the curry sauce.

Place the koftas in a serving dish. Top with boiling hot curry sauce, cover, and keep in a warm oven (300° F) for 5 to 10 minutes. Remove from the oven, garnish with the cilantro and garam masala, and serve as a main dish.

To freeze koftas, place them individually on a cookie sheet in the freezer until they are completely frozen. Then transfer to plastic freezer bags. Always make enough for two or three meals. To assemble, place the frozen koftas in a serving dish, top with boiling hot curry sauce, and place in a hot oven (400° F) for 25 to 30 minutes. Koftas can be served as appetizers also.

MAKES 8 SERVINGS

Today's Guilt-Free Cheese

If you love cheese as most people do, and don't want to feel guilty with each bite, note that the majority of the recipes in this chapter make use of an Indian cheese called paneer that is virtually cholesterol-free. Made with 1 or 2 percent low-fat milk, this cheese can reward those midnight raids on the fridge.

Paneer is a type of farmer's cheese and is made by curdling milk and then separating the curds from the whey by passing everything through cheesecloth. (The cheese remains in the cheesecloth and the liquid whey drains out.)

Like the Chinese bean curd (tofu), this delicate cheese absorbs the flavors of various spices, and can be used to create numerous appetizers, main dishes, side dishes, breads, rice dishes, and desserts. Its uses in Indian cuisine are endless, as it can be cut into any shape or size, or can be mashed coarsely or finely to suit the occasion. Its main advantage is that it maintains its shape and texture even after prolonged cooking.

In rural India it is commonplace for families to keep cows and water buffaloes. In fact, water-buffalo milk is by far the most popular source of dairy products. The vegetarian population relies on milk as its main source of protein, so creative cooks over the centuries have found infinite uses for dairy products to keep the cuisine varied and appetizing.

Understanding the Basics of Making Paneer

Here are a few pointers that can facilitate the paneer-making process in your home.

The most important thing to remember is that the milk must actually boil before any souring agent can be added, but we all know how easily milk burns when it is boiled. To minimize the possibility of this problem and its effects, I thoroughly recommend the use of heavy aluminum or nonstick metal pans. The Silverstone-coated ones can be quite a disaster because burned milk forms a thin film on the bottom of the pan and, as you stir, it gets lifted from the bottom and is added to the milk, giving it a distinct burned odor and an unwanted marbling effect. Rinsing the pan you are going to use, adding 1 to 2 table-spoons of water prior to adding the milk, and stirring often, especially after it becomes hot, will prevent the milk from burning.

Regular homogenized milk is the more popular choice for most people, though I prefer to make my paneer cheese with low-fat milk for obvious health reasons. Nonfat milk does not work well; it burns in the pan too easily, and the resulting cheese is quite tough and chewy.

As a souring agent, nonfat yogurt is my first preference. Since yogurt is a dairy product, it melds superbly with the milk to make the softest and best-tasting paneer that will pos-sess no extra flavors that could clash with other ingredients when you cook with it. Also, when you add yogurt to the milk, the quantity of the paneer it yields increases substantial-ly (the result of the milk solids in the yogurt), giving you more paneer in the same amount of time.

Lemon (or lime) juice is my second preference. This makes very good quality paneer and the flavor is quite harmonious in most preparations, with the exception of desserts.

Buttermilk is very good, but it contains too much liquid, so you have to use it in large quantities, unless it is very sour. Ordinary white vinegar imparts a distinct flavor which has to be camouflaged with various spices. I love to use flavored vinegars to make specialty paneer cheeses (see page 232), but this is definitely not the best bet when you're looking to make everyday cooking paneer. Finally, citric acid can be used.

BASIC PANEER CHEESE

PANEER BANAO

½ gallon low-fat milk
2 cups nonfat plain yogurt, whisked until smooth
One 2-foot-square piece fine muslin or 4 layers cheesecloth

Rinse a heavy-bottomed saucepan, place the milk in it, and bring to a boil, stirring, over high heat. Before the milk bubbles rise and spill over, add the yogurt and continue to stir over high heat, until the milk curdles and separates into curds and whey, 2 to 3 minutes. (Whey is a dull green, semitransparent liquid.) Remove from the heat.

Drape the muslin or cheesecloth over a large pan and pour the curdled milk over it. As you do this, the whey will drain through the muslin into the pan, and the cheese will remain in the muslin.

With the cheese still in the muslin, bring the four corners of the muslin together, pick it up from the pan and tie it to the kitchen faucet to drain further, 4 to 5 minutes.

Remove from the faucet and gently twist the muslin to extract as much whey as possible from the cheese. With the muslin still twisted, place the cheese between two flat surfaces (salad-size plates work well), with the twisted muslin on one side. (Keep the muslin twisted, as that will result in the formation of a compressed chunk of cheese.) Place a heavy object on the top plate (like a pan of water) and let the cheese drain further for 10 to 12 minutes.

Remove the heavy object and let the cheese remain undisturbed until it is cool enough to handle. When cool, cut into desired shapes and sizes and use as needed.

This cheese can be stored in airtight containers in the refrigerator for 4 to 5 days, or it can be frozen. I recommend cutting the cheese before it is refrigerated or frozen (cold paneer is harder to cut).

To freeze the cheese, place the pieces on a plate in a single layer and freeze. When frozen, transfer the pieces to plastic freezer bags and freeze; it will keep for 3 to 4 months. This way you can remove and use only the number of pieces that are needed for a recipe. I often make cheese using 2 gallons of milk at one time, cut them into pieces (some big and some small), and then freeze them. Cooking with cheese has never been easier.

MAKES 8 OUNCES OR ABOUT THIRTY 1- BY ¼-INCH PIECES

VARIATION: To curdle the milk you could, in the place of the yogurt, add ¼ cup fresh or bottled lemon or lime juice (start with ¼ cup, and add ½ to 1 tablespoon more only if needed), 3 to 4 tablespoons white vinegar, or 1 quart buttermilk. Lemon juice and vinegar will yield about 6 ½ ounces of paneer cheese, and the buttermilk about 8 ounces.

FLAVORED PANEER CHEESE

PANEER KE NAYÉ ZAYEKÉ

Authentic paneer cheese is mild tasting. The fact that it is a sponge ready to absorb a multitude of flavors prompted me to add different herbs, spices, and vinegars to it before the actual curdling process.

Paneer cheese made this way is lovely to eat just by itself, or it can be added to light salads (instead of cooked seafood or chicken). It is wonderful on pizza and pasta, and in stir-fried dishes, too.

Use the basic paneer recipe above. Bring the milk to a boil over high heat, stir in the spices and herbs of your choice (see the combinations suggested below), then add the souring agent of your choice (the citrus juices and vinegars listed in the combinations function as the souring agent, so don't add the agent asked for in the basic recipe). Drain and press according to the directions on page 231. The whey from this paneer cheese should not be discarded, but used as a base for soups, the cooking liquid for various dishes, or to make whole-wheat or other flour doughs. Breads made with whey-enriched dough are softer and more flavorful.

Try any of the following combinations, or create your own as you become adept at making this cheese. Be aware that ground dried herbs work very well, but the heavier seeds tend to settle at the bottom, making the flavor distribution slightly different.

Version 1
½ teaspoon ground dried oregano
1 teaspoon ground ginger
¼ teaspoon salt, or to taste
¼ cup Italian herb vinegar, or more if needed

Version 2
1 tablespoon walnut oil
1 teaspoon crushed celery seeds
¼ teaspoon salt, or to taste
¼ cup balsamic vinegar, or more if needed

Version 3
1 tablespoon avocado oil
½ teaspoon garlic juice
½ teaspoon ground dried mint
¼ cup fresh lemon juice, or more if needed

Version 4
1 teaspoon extra virgin olive oil
1 teaspoon minced garlic
½ teaspoon ground dried basil
½ teaspoon salt, or to taste
¼ cup basil or other Italian herb vinegar, or more if needed

Version 5
1 teaspoon Chinese sesame oil
1 tablespoon soy sauce

- 1 teaspoon peeled and minced fresh ginger
1 ½ teaspoons sesame seeds, toasted (see page 76)
¼ cup white or red rice vinegar, or more if needed

Version 6
½ or 1 teaspoon ground white pepper
1 tablespoon roasted cumin seeds (see page 16)
½ teaspoon salt
¼ cup fresh lemon juice, or more if needed

Version 7
⅛ teaspoon turmeric
1 teaspoon minced serrano peppers (mince in a food processor, not by hand; optional)
½ teaspoon garam masala (see page 23)
½ teaspoon salt, or to taste
¼ cup fresh lemon or lime juice, or more if needed

Version 8
½ teaspoon ground carom seeds (see page 14)
½ teaspoon coarsely ground roasted black peppercorns (see page 13)
½ teaspoon salt, or to taste
1 to 4 serrano peppers, minced, or 1 tablespoon Hot Pepper Chutney with Ginger and
    Lemon Juice (see page 92; optional)
¼ cup fresh lime or lemon juice, or more if needed

Version 9
Add any of the blended mint or yogurt chutneys for variety, or try the hot chili chutneys (see pages 91–92). Use the leftover spicy vinegar from pickle jars or try a combination of orange and lemon juice or apple cider. All of these make delicious paneer cheese. Now it's your turn to experiment!

SAUTÉED SPICY PANEER CHEESE WITH CHAAT MASALA

CHAAT MASALA PANEER

Even before it's sautéed, this paneer cheese has a terrific flavor and a hot bite. It can be eaten as is or used as a salad, pasta, pizza, or taco topping, or it can be cut into thick chunks, sautéed lightly in butter or oil, and instantly transformed into an elegant side dish. It can also be marinated and then barbecued.

>   1 recipe Flavored Paneer Cheese, Version 8 (see page 233)
>   2 to 3 tablespoons walnut or peanut oil
>   3 tablespoons finely chopped cilantro (fresh coriander), soft stems included
>   2 to 3 tablespoons fresh lemon juice
>   1 teaspoon chaat masala (see page 26)
>   Chopped cilantro for garnish

Cut the paneer cheese into twenty to thirty equal-size pieces. Heat the oil in a large skillet over moderately high heat, then add the paneer in a single layer. Turn the pieces over when they become light golden on the bottom. Sprinkle the cilantro on top and continue to cook until the other side is also slightly golden (reduce the heat if necessary; the pieces should not become brown). Add the lemon juice, then sprinkle the chaat masala on top. Transfer to a serving platter, garnish with chopped cilantro, and serve as an appetizer or side dish.

MAKES 8 SERVINGS

PANEER CHEESE, PEA, AND POTATO CURRY

TARI VALÉ MATTAR ALU PANEER

In this conventional recipe, pieces of paneer cheese are first deep-fried and then combined with a classic onion and tomato–based sauce to make one of the most basic curries of Indian cuisine. This recipe can be paired with almost any "dry" vegetable dish and served with rice or bread (or both).

This recipe can be made without a pressure cooker. All you need to do is add about ½ cup extra water, cover the pan, and simmer over medium to low heat until the potatoes are tender, 20 to 30 minutes.

>   1 to 2 cups peanut oil for deep-frying
>   1 recipe Basic Paneer Cheese (see page 230), cut into 1- by ¼-inch pieces
>   1 large clove garlic, peeled
>   One 1-inch piece fresh ginger, peeled
>   1 small onion, cut into 4 to 6 pieces
>   1 large ripe tomato, cut into 6 to 8 wedges

1 cup loosely packed cilantro (fresh coriander), soft stems included
3 tablespoons peanut oil
5 jalapeño peppers, skin punctured to prevent them from bursting
1 tablespoon ground coriander
2 teaspoons ground cumin
½ teaspoon paprika
½ teaspoon turmeric
1 teaspoon salt, or to taste
1 large potato, peeled and cut into ¾-inch dice
2 ½ cups shelled peas, preferably fresh (1 ½ pounds in pods)
3 cups water (or more if required)
1 teaspoon dried fenugreek leaves (see page 17)
½ teaspoon garam masala (see page 23) for garnish
Finely chopped cilantro for garnish

Heat the oil for deep-frying in a wok or skillet over moderately high heat until it reaches 325° to 350° F, until a small piece of paneer cheese added to the oil immediately bubbles and rises to the top. Add the paneer pieces in two or three batches and fry, turning once with a large slotted spoon, until barely golden, about 1 minute or less. Drain on paper towels and set aside. (The paneer can be deep-fried and refrigerated for 4 to 5 days or frozen for 3 to 4 months.)

In a food processor fitted with the metal S-blade and the motor running, process the garlic, ginger, and onion until smooth. Remove to a bowl. Add the tomato and cilantro to the food processor and process until smooth. Remove to another bowl and set aside.

Heat the oil in a pressure cooker over moderately high heat and add the onion mixture. Cook, stirring, for 2 to 3 minutes, then reduce the heat to medium and continue to cook, stirring, until the onions turn brown, 5 to 6 minutes. Add the tomato mixture and jalapeños, increase the heat to high and cook, stirring, until all the liquid from the tomatoes evaporates, 5 to 7 minutes. Stir in the coriander, cumin, paprika, turmeric, and salt, then add the potato, peas, paneer cheese, and water.

Secure the lid of the pressure cooker and cook over high heat for 1 minute after the pressure regulator starts rocking. Remove from the heat and let the pressure drop by itself, 15 to 20 minutes. Open the pressure cooker, add the fenugreek, stir the contents carefully, and mash a few potatoes to thicken the gravy. (Add more water if you desire a thinner gravy.)

Transfer to a serving bowl, garnish with the garam masala and cilantro, and serve hot as a main dish with a vegetable side dish, yogurt, and bread.

This dish stays fresh in the refrigerator for 4 to 5 days.

MAKES 8 SERVINGS

PANEER CHEESE AND PEA CURRY

Why did this traditional curry taste so different at my friend Neelam Malhotra's house? I loved the taste but could not figure out the difference until one day it was pointed out to me that it didn't contain any onion. I had always thought that onion was the most important ingredient in a curry.

Much to my delight and amazement, when I got married I noticed that my mother-in-law cooked her paneer curry in exactly the same way. No matter how often I make it, this dish remains my family's favorite.

> 2 tablespoons clarified butter (see page 30) or vegetable oil
> 1 teaspoon cumin seeds
> 1 tablespoon ground coriander
> 1 teaspoon ground cumin
> 1 teaspoon dried fenugreek leaves (see page 17)
> ½ teaspoon paprika
> ½ teaspoon turmeric
> 1 teaspoon salt, or to taste
> 2 cups finely chopped fresh tomatoes
> 5 jalapeño peppers, whole (stemmed and skin punctured to prevent bursting) or chopped
> 1 cup loosely packed finely chopped cilantro (fresh coriander), soft stems included
> 1 tablespoon peeled and minced fresh ginger
> 1 large potato, peeled and cut into ¾-inch dice
> 2 ½ cups shelled peas, preferably fresh (1 ½ pounds in pods)
> 3 to 4 cups water
> 1 recipe Basic Paneer Cheese (see page 230), cut into 1- by ¼-inch squares
> ½ teaspoon garam masala (see page 23) for garnish
> 3 tablespoons chopped cilantro for garnish

Heat the butter in a large nonstick saucepan over moderately high heat and cook the cumin seeds, stirring, until they sizzle, 10 seconds. Stir in the coriander, ground cumin, fenugreek, paprika, turmeric, and salt, then add the tomatoes, jalapeños, cilantro, and ginger and cook until most of the liquid from the tomatoes evaporates, 7 to 10 minutes. Add the potatoes and cook, stirring, until all the liquid from the tomatoes evaporates, 3 to 4 minutes, then add the fresh peas and water. Cover the pot and cook, first over high heat for 3 to 4 minutes, then over medium-low, until the potatoes are tender, 20 to 25 minutes. (If using frozen peas, add them after the potatoes are cooked.) Stir occasionally.

Mash a few potatoes to thicken the gravy. Add the paneer and simmer for 4 to 5 minutes, stirring carefully. Add ½ cup additional water if the gravy gets too thick.

Transfer to a serving casserole, garnish with the garam masala and cilantro, and serve hot as a main dish with a vegetable side dish, yogurt, and bread. This dish stays fresh in the refrigerator for 4 to 5 days.

MAKES 8 SERVINGS

VARIATION: This is a perfect dish to make in a pressure cooker. Using a pressure cooker instead of a nonstick pot, proceed with the recipe until you add the fresh peas and water. (You will need 1 cup less water.) Then secure the lid of the pressure cooker and cook until the pressure regulator starts rocking. Remove from the heat, let it cool, open, add the paneer, and finish cooking on the stovetop.

FRESH SPINACH WITH PANEER CHEESE

PALAK PANEER

I vividly remember bunches of fresh spinach being set in front of my grandmother while she sat on a *pidi*, a traditional low wooden stool with a hand-woven jute seat. She would methodically pick off the leaves, break off the hard stems, and set them aside. It was then be taken to the kitchen to be washed, after which it was brought back to her. Her job now was to shred the washed spinach and get it ready for cooking.

Cooking the spinach was another story. It was put in a large cast-iron *kadahi*, an Indian wok, and then set on an *angithi*, a coal-burning clay stove that was kept alive by adding fresh coal every few hours. The spinach would sit on this stove for hours over low heat, until it became smooth and silky. A wood churner, *madhani*, was used to ensure the smoothness.

Pieces of fresh paneer and dollops of freshly churned butter would be added to this. Hours of simmering probably destroyed half the nutrients, but it surely added that "something special" to its flavor.

To make my recipe richer, stir in about ½ cup heavy cream before adding the paneer pieces.

3 bunches fresh spinach, trimmed of tough stems and washed
1 bunch mustard greens, trimmed of tough stems and washed
1 small turnip, peeled and chopped
¼ cup water
3 tablespoons vegetable oil
One 3-inch stick cinnamon
8 green cardamom pods, pounded lightly to break the skin
One 1 ½- by 1-inch piece fresh ginger, peeled and cut into julienne strips
1 ½ cups finely chopped onion
1 teaspoon minced garlic
1 cup finely chopped fresh tomatoes
¼ cup nonfat plain yogurt, whisked until smooth
2 tablespoons ground coriander
1 teaspoon garam masala (see page 23)
1 teaspoon paprika
1 teaspoon salt, or to taste
1 recipe Basic Paneer Cheese made with whole milk (see page 230), cut into 1- by ¼-
    inch squares
10 to 15 cherry tomatoes for garnish

Place the spinach, mustard greens, turnip, and water in a large nonstick saucepan. Cover
and bring to a boil over high heat. Reduce the heat to medium and continue to simmer
until the turnip is tender, 5 to 7 minutes. Cool, then process in a food processor until
smooth. Return to the pot and set aside.

Heat the oil in a small saucepan over moderately high heat and cook the cinnamon, cardamom pods, onion, and ginger, stirring, until the onion turns medium brown, 8 to 10
minutes. Add the garlic and tomatoes and cook until all the liquid from the tomatoes
evaporates, 2 to 3 minutes. Stir in the yogurt a little at a time to prevent curdling, then add
the coriander, garam masala, paprika, and salt.

Immediately transfer the contents to the pan with the blended spinach, cover, and simmer over medium heat for 7 to 10 minutes. Add paneer and stir gently to mix (do not
break the pieces). Simmer another 5 to 7 minutes to blend the flavors.

Transfer to a serving dish, garnish with the cherry tomatoes, and serve as a main dish
with any Indian bread. *Palak paneer* stays fresh in the refrigerator for 4 to 5 days.

MAKES 8 SERVINGS

PANEER CHEESE WITH TOMATOES AND ONION

PANEER BHURJI

When you make the paneer cheese for this dish, it is not essential to press it into a chunk. Just let it drain for an extra 10 minutes suspended from the kitchen faucet, then crumble it coarsely with your fingers.

This recipe also works well with Pressed Ricotta Paneer Cheese (see page248). Cooked in this manner, the paneer makes a great filling for hot grilled sandwiches, especially Tasty Toast (see page 82) made in a sandwich grill.

This "dry" side dish should be served with any sauced lentil, bean, or chicken preparation. To complete the meal, serve a yogurt raita (see page 147) and whole-wheat chapatis (page 320).

3 tablespoons vegetable oil
5 serrano peppers, skin punctured to prevent them from bursting
5 green cardamom pods, pounded lightly to break the skin
1 teaspoon cumin seeds
2 cups finely chopped onion
2 cups finely chopped fresh tomatoes
1 cup loosely packed finely chopped cilantro (fresh coriander), soft stems included
2 tablespoons ground coriander
¾ teaspoon paprika
1 teaspoon salt, or to taste
Double recipe Basic Paneer Cheese (see page 230), crumbled
2 cups frozen peas, thawed
Freshly ground black pepper for garnish

Heat the oil in a large nonstick saucepan or wok over moderately high heat and fry the peppers, cardamom pods, and cumin seeds until they sizzle, 10 seconds. Add the onion and cook, stirring, until it turns medium brown, 7 to 10 minutes. Add the tomatoes and cilantro and continue to cook, stirring, until most of the liquid from the tomatoes evaporates, 7 to 10 minutes. Stir in the coriander, paprika, and salt, then add the paneer and peas. Reduce the heat to medium and continue to cook, stirring occasionally, for another 10 minutes to blend the flavors.

Transfer to a serving dish, garnish with freshly ground black pepper, and serve.

MAKES 8 SERVINGS

PANEER CHEESE "FAJITAS"

PANEER AUR SIMLA MIRCH

Five years ago, I was faced with the task of feeding a group of vegetarian guests who had recently arrived from India and wanted to try something different yet "Indian." I developed this mouth-watering dish and served it with warmed corn and flour tortillas and Yogurt Mint Chutney. Tofu can replace paneer for convenience or variation.

3 tablespoons peanut or almond oil
2 large cloves garlic, cut into slivers
1 medium-size onion, cut in half lengthwise and thinly sliced
Double recipe Basic Paneer Cheese (see page 230), cut into thick ½- by 1 ½-inch
    rectangles
3 large bell peppers, 1 each red, yellow, and green, seeded and cut into 2-inch-long
    julienne strips
1 tablespoon ground roasted cumin (see page 16)
1 tablespoon ground roasted coriander (see page 15)
½ teaspoon paprika
1 teaspoon salt, or to taste
¼ cup fresh lemon juice
¼ cup finely chopped cilantro (fresh coriander) for garnish

Heat the oil in a large nonstick skillet or a griddle over moderately high heat and cook the garlic and onion, stirring, until golden, 4 to 5 minutes. Add the paneer cheese in a single layer and continue to cook, turning them once or twice, until golden, 4 to 5 minutes. Add the bell peppers, stir for 3 to 4 minutes, then add the roasted cumin, coriander, paprika, salt, and lemon juice. Cook until the bell peppers are tender-crisp, 4 to 5 minutes.

Transfer to a serving platter (or let it remain in the skillet), garnish with the cilantro, and serve as a main or side dish. This dish is best when served fresh. To save last-minute hassles, cook until the paneer is golden, cover, and set aside for 4 to 5 hours. (If the paneer seems too dry after reheating, add ½ cup water, cover, and simmer until all the water is absorbed.) Then add the peppers and finish the cooking closer to serving time.

MAKES 8 SERVINGS

Paneer Cheese with Sautéed Onion and Colorful Pear Tomatoes

PANEER PYAZ AUR CHOTÉ TAMATAR

Perfect for a light meal, this ingenious mélange proves to be a winner every time.

3 tablespoons safflower oil
2 cups finely chopped onion
1 tablespoon ground coriander
1 teaspoon garam masala (see page 23)
1 cup loosely packed chopped fresh dill, cilantro (fresh coriander), or fresh fenugreek leaves (see page 17)
Double recipe Flavored Paneer Cheese, Version 8 (see page 233), cut into ½-inch cubes
1 teaspoon salt, or to taste
¼ cup water
20 to 25 pear or cherry tomatoes
½ cup finely chopped scallion greens for garnish
Freshly ground black pepper for garnish

Heat the oil in a large nonstick skillet over moderately high heat and cook the onion, stirring, until golden, 7 to 10 minutes. Add the coriander, garam masala, and fresh herbs, stir for 2 to 3 minutes (a little longer if you add fenugreek), then add the paneer cheese, salt, and water, reduce the heat to medium, cover the pan, and cook until the water is absorbed by the paneer cheese, 5 to 7 minutes.

Transfer to a platter and keep warm. Add the tomatoes to the same skillet and cook, shaking the skillet, until they turn slightly soft, 1 to 2 minutes. Transfer to the platter with the paneer. Garnish with the scallion greens and freshly ground black pepper and serve as a side dish with a gravied vegetable or bean preparation.

MAKES 8 SERVINGS

VARIATION: Sauté 2 cups thawed frozen peas or thinly sliced mushrooms and add to the dish after it is cooked.

Paneer Cheese Cubes with Jalapeño Peppers and Carom Seeds

HARI MIRCH AUR AJWAIN VALA PANEER

In this dish, the paneer cheese gets most of its piquancy from the chopped jalapeño peppers, and its flavor from the crushed carom seeds. Carom seeds are similar in appearance to celery seeds, but they have an assertive taste. They are known to relieve flatulence and, for that reason, are popularly served with the hard-to-digest legumes and beans. Thus it is appropriate to serve this dish with any garbanzo, kidney bean, or black-eyed pea preparation.

I often use the leftovers as a filling for either Mexican-style tacos or Italian pasta shells.

3 tablespoons safflower oil or clarified butter (see page 30)
5 jalapeño peppers, skin punctured to prevent them from bursting
1 teaspoon crushed carom seeds (see page 14)
1 teaspoon cumin seeds
2 jalapeño peppers, finely chopped (optional)
1 tablespoon peeled and minced fresh ginger
2 cups finely chopped fresh tomatoes
1 tablespoon curry powder (see page 21) or 1 teaspoon garam masala (page 23)
¼ cup fresh lemon juice
Double recipe Basic Paneer Cheese (see page 230), cut into ½-inch cubes
2 large potatoes, boiled until tender, peeled, and cut into ¾-inch pieces
¼ cup water
1 cup loosely packed finely chopped cilantro (fresh coriander), soft stems included
Freshly ground black pepper for garnish

Heat the oil in a large nonstick saucepan over moderately high heat and cook the whole jalapeños, stirring, for about 1 minute. Then add the carom and cumin seeds and the chopped jalapeños. Stir for 30 seconds, add the ginger and tomatoes, and cook until most of the liquid from the tomatoes evaporates, 10 to 15 minutes. Add the curry powder and lemon juice, then stir in the paneer cubes and potatoes. Add the water and cook, stirring very carefully a few times, until all the water is absorbed by the paneer, about 5 minutes.

Stir in the chopped cilantro and transfer to a serving dish. Garnish with freshly ground black pepper and serve as a side dish. This dish is best when served fresh.

MAKES 8 SERVINGS

PAN-FRIED PANEER
CHEESE BALLS

PANEER KE KOFTÉ

Paneer koftas are to Indian vegetarians what meatballs are to the rest of the world. As is true for meatballs, paneer koftas are made and served in a number of ways, starting with appetizers and ending at desserts.

Once the cheese balls are made, they can be served as is, in a sauce, or with rice. They combine well with most types of cooked sauces, so I vary my choice in accordance with the other recipes and colors in the menu.

To team them with rice, choose a dish like Simple Cumin-Flavored Rice (see page 287) and fork them in when the rice is almost done. Koftas are supposed to be deep-fried, but I've found that pan-frying yields very good results.

1 recipe Basic Paneer Cheese (see page 230)
1 medium-size potato, boiled until tender, peeled, and grated
½ teaspoon turmeric
½ teaspoon garam masala (see page 23)
1 teaspoon salt, or to taste
¼ cup loosely packed finely chopped cilantro (fresh coriander), soft stems included
2 to 3 tablespoons peanut oil

Puree the paneer in a food processor until it is soft and smooth and starts to gather like dough. Remove to a bowl and add the grated potato, turmeric, garam masala, salt, and cilantro. Mix with your hands or a large spoon until the mixture resembles a soft dough. Make forty-five to fifty 1-inch or smaller round balls and set aside.

Heat the oil in a large nonstick skillet over moderately high heat and cook the koftas, turning as necessary, until they are lightly golden on all sides. You may have to do this in several batches. Cool and refrigerate for 4 to 5 days or freeze for 3 to 4 months.

To serve the koftas as a main dish in a sauce, place freshly made, refrigerated, or frozen koftas in a serving casserole and pour 3 to 4 cups of boiling sauce of your choice over them. Then place the casserole in a preheated 375° F oven for 7 to 10 minutes or longer. (Adjust the time according to the temperature of the koftas.)

Do not stir the koftas after they have been added to the sauce or they will disintegrate.

MAKES 45 TO 50 ONE-INCH KOFTAS

PANEER CHEESE IN FRESH TOMATO SAUCE

SHAHI PANEER

This majestic recipe is made with pieces of fresh paneer cheese, and an astonishingly fragrant fresh tomato-and-cream sauce. The addition of pistachios and raisins lends an exotic touch and makes this dish a magnificent choice for entertaining.

I often cook pureed tomatoes and cilantro (over medium-high heat until all the liquid evaporates) ahead of time, and freeze them in ice cube trays. The cheese can also be made in advance, cut into pieces, and frozen. This makes the last-minute assembly of this dish very simple.

8 large ripe tomatoes, cut into 8 wedges each
½ cup loosely packed cilantro (fresh coriander), soft stems included
3 tablespoons peanut oil or clarified butter (see page 30)
½ cup raw pistachios
½ cup golden raisins
5 serrano peppers, skin punctured to prevent them from bursting
3 tablespoons peeled and finely chopped fresh ginger
3 tablespoons ground coriander
1 tablespoon ground cumin
2 teaspoons dried fenugreek leaves (see page 17)
1 teaspoon paprika
1 ½ teaspoons garam masala (see page 23)
1 ½ teaspoons salt, or to taste
½ cup nonfat plain yogurt, whisked until smooth
1 cup water or whey reserved from making the paneer
1 cup heavy cream or milk
Double recipe Basic Paneer Cheese (see page 230), cut into thick 1- inch squares
Chopped cilantro for garnish

Puree the tomatoes and cilantro in a food processor and set aside. Heat the oil in a large nonstick saucepan over moderately high heat and fry the pistachios and raisins, stirring, until the raisins start to puff up, 1 to 2 minutes. Remove to a plate lined with paper towels and reserve for garnish.

Add the peppers and ginger and cook, stirring, until the ginger turns golden, about 1 minute. Add the pureed tomato mixture and cook over high heat for 3 to 4 minutes, then reduce the heat to medium and cook until all the liquid evaporates, 25 to 30 minutes.

Stir in the coriander, cumin, fenugreek, paprika, 1 teaspoon of the garam masala, and the salt, then add the yogurt a little at a time, stirring constantly to prevent it from curdling, until all of it is absorbed into the tomatoes.

Increase the heat to high, add the water, and bring to a boil. Then add the cream and simmer over medium heat for 7 to 10 minutes to blend the flavors. (At this point, the sauce should be of medium consistency because some of the liquid will be absorbed by the cheese, making it thicker.)

Mix in the cheese and simmer for 5 to 7 minutes. Transfer to a serving dish, garnish with the remaining garam masala, cilantro, and reserved pistachios and raisins, and serve as a main dish with any Indian bread or rice. This dish stays fresh in the refrigerator for 4 to 5 days. The sauce stays fresh longer if it is kept separately. Combine with the cheese when ready to serve.

MAKES 8 SERVINGS

PANEER CHEESE WITH BAY LEAVES AND SORREL

TEJ PATTA AUR SORREL SAAG VALA PANEER

The tangy, yet delicate sorrel leaves, so popular in the Western world, are not available in India. Their addition, however, adds a surprising and unusual flavor to traditional paneer cheese dishes.

This recipe is quick to prepare especially if you have paneer cheese in the freezer.

3 tablespoons canola oil
5 large bay leaves, crushed
1 cup finely chopped onion
1 teaspoon coarsely chopped garlic
1 cup finely chopped fresh tomatoes
1 tablespoon ground coriander
1 teaspoon salt, or to taste
Double recipe Basic Paneer Cheese (see page 230), cut into ¾-inch cubes
3 cups loosely packed trimmed and finely shredded fresh sorrel
2 cups water
Shredded sorrel for garnish

Heat the oil in a large nonstick skillet over moderately high heat and fry the bay leaves for 30 seconds. Add the onion and garlic and cook, stirring, until they turn golden, 4 to 5 minutes. Add the tomatoes and cook until all the water evaporates, 4 to 5 minutes. Stir in the coriander and salt, then add the paneer. Cook, turning the pieces once or twice, until the they are lightly golden. Add the sorrel and cook, stirring, until wilted, 2 to 3 minutes. Continue to cook, stirring as necessary, for 3 to 4 minutes, then add the water. Cover and cook until the water is absorbed into the paneer and the sorrel sauce becomes thick, 5 to 7 minutes.

Transfer to a serving dish, garnish with shredded sorrel, and serve as an entrée with any meal.

MAKES 8 SERVINGS

BARBECUED PANEER CHEESE AND VEGETABLE SKEWERS

PANEER SHASLIK

This recipe was given to me by my friend Sunil Vora, the owner of The Clay Pit, a prestigious Indian restaurant in Los Angeles. Not just an owner, Sunil is also an ardent and innovative cook. His recipes are always a source of inspiration to me.

In this recipe, the vegetables and paneer cheese are first marinated and then barbecued in the intense heat of a tandoor, an Indian clay oven. At home, we have to use the barbecue to get similar results. Sunil adds some garbanzo bean flour to the marinade to help the seasonings adhere to the vegetables.

FOR THE MARINADE
1 cup nonfat plain yogurt, whisked until smooth
2 tablespoons fresh lemon juice
2 tablespoons peanut oil
1 tablespoon garbanzo bean flour (see page 254)
4 cloves garlic, minced
½ teaspoon peeled and minced fresh ginger
1 teaspoon ground cumin
½ teaspoon garam masala (see page 23)
1 teaspoon salt, or to taste

FOR THE SKEWERS

Four 1-inch-wide yellow summer squash, each cut in half
Four 1-inch-wide green squash, each cut in half
8 small mushrooms
2 medium-size ripe tomatoes, each cut into 4 wedges
1 small green bell pepper, seeded and cut into eight 1-inch pieces
Eight 2-inch-wide cauliflower florets
1 ½ recipes Basic Paneer Cheese (see page 230), cut into twenty-four 1- by ½-inch
   squares
8 wooden skewers soaked in ¼ cup orange juice or water for 1 hour or longer

Combine the marinade ingredients in a large bowl. Add all the vegetables and the cheese and let marinate for 4 to 6 hours or longer.

Thread the marinated vegetables and paneer cheese on the moist skewers and barbecue over a medium-hot fire until tender-crisp, 7 to 10 minutes. Baste occasionally with the marinade.

Transfer to a serving platter and serve immediately as appetizers or with a basmati or wild rice pullao. Serve a sauced lentil dish, a chutney, and a yogurt raita (see page 147) on the side. These vegetables are great over pasta also.

MAKES 8 SERVINGS

ABOUT RICOTTA CHEESE

Ricotta cheese is not a true cheese, but a by-product of the cheese-making process. It is made from the whey that is left over after the cheese has been made. Its texture and taste are very similar to those of paneer cheese, and it looks like curdled milk that has not been completely drained or pressed into a chunk.

Upon pressing ricotta cheese under a heavy weight, I found that it emerged looking exactly like paneer cheese. It is a little more crumbly than paneer and has to be handled very carefully, especially if the shape and the size of the pieces have to be preserved. But otherwise I find that the two cheeses are quite alike. Like paneer, ricotta cheese can be used in all sorts of appetizers, side and main dishes, and desserts.

If you are pressed for time, or making paneer seems like an ordeal, by all means use this excellent substitute.

Tofu can also replace paneer cheese in most of the recipes, but it retains its subtle taste, whereas ricotta can easily pass as the real thing.

PRESSED RICOTTA PANEER CHEESE

RICOTTA KA PANEER

One 2-pound container part-skim ricotta cheese
One 2-foot-square piece fine muslin or 4 layers cheesecloth

Place the ricotta cheese in the muslin. Gently twist the muslin around the cheese, forming a ball. Then place the cheese (while still in the muslin) between two flat surfaces (dinner plates work well). (Keep the muslin twisted, as that will result in the formation of a compressed chunk of cheese.) Place a heavy object on the top plate (a large pan of water works well) and let the cheese drain for 8 to 10 hours or overnight at room temperature.

Remove the heavy object and cut the cheese into desired shapes and sizes and use as required. This cheese can be stored in airtight containers in the refrigerator for 5 to 6 days or can be frozen for 2 to 3 months. Frozen cheese becomes even more crumbly, so it should be pan- or deep-fried before freezing. (It can go straight from the freezer to the dish.)

To use in curries, sauté ½-inch-thick pieces in 1 to 2 tablespons oil in a heavy nonstick skillet over medium heat. Then simmer in the sauce for 4 to 5 minutes. Don't stir too much or too vigorously or the cheese will crumble.

MAKES THIRTY TO THIRTY-FIVE 1-INCH PIECES OR 1 ½ POUNDS

SILKY RICOTTA CHEESE BALLS

RICOTTA CHEESE KE MALAI KOFTÉ

My research with ricotta cheese led to this almost effortless and time-saving *kofta* recipe. Authentically made with paneer cheese, these silky smooth balls are customarily served in a curry or a tomato-based sauce. They can just as easily be served as a snack with a green chutney, added to pita bread to make pocket sandwiches, or broken coarsely and served over pasta or pizza.

1 recipe Pressed Ricotta Paneer Cheese (see above)
½ cup or more garbanzo bean flour (see page 254)
1 tablespoon ground coriander
1 teaspoon ground cumin

½ teaspoon salt, or to taste

¼ cup loosely packed finely chopped cilantro (fresh coriander), soft stems included

2 to 3 cups peanut oil for deep-frying

Place the ricotta cheese in a bowl and mash it with your fingers until smooth. Add the flour, coriander, cumin, salt, and cilantro and mix with your fingers until smooth. Form into forty 1-inch balls and set aside.

Heat the oil in a wok or skillet over moderately high heat until it reaches 350° to 375° F, until a piece of cheese dropped into the oil bubbles and rises to the top immediately. Add the koftas in two to three batches (don't crowd them) and fry until they become golden brown. Remove to paper towels to drain.

To serve, follow the directions as explained for Pan-Fried Paneer Cheese Balls (see page 243).

MAKES 40 KOFTAS

RICOTTA CHEESE WITH ANAHEIM PEPPERS

RICOTTA PANEER AUR HARI MIRCH

Press the ricotta cheese ahead of time, and this dish can be ready in a snap. Ideal for summer brunches and lunches, especially when served with a sauced bean or vegetable main dish.

Sautéed mushrooms, pan-toasted raw pistachios or almond slivers, and raisins make an ornate garnish on this yellow side dish.

3 tablespoons safflower oil

1 large onion, cut in half lengthwise and thinly sliced

4 Anaheim peppers, seeded and cut into ¼-inch slices

2 cups Pressed Ricotta Paneer Cheese (see page 248)

2 teaspoons ground coriander

½ teaspoon ground cumin

½ teaspoon turmeric

½ teaspoon paprika

¾ teaspoon salt, or to taste

½ cup firmly packed finely chopped cilantro (fresh coriander), soft stems included

½ teaspoon garam masala (see page 23) for garnish

Heat the oil in a heavy medium-size saucepan over moderately high heat and cook the onion, stirring, until it turns golden, 7 to 10 minutes. Add the peppers and stir for 1 to 2 minutes. Stir in the ricotta cheese, then add the coriander, cumin, turmeric, paprika, and salt. Reduce the heat to medium-low and cook, stirring occasionally, until all the liquid (from the peppers and the cheese) dries up and the cheese starts to turn golden, 7 to 10 minutes. Mix in the chopped cilantro, transfer to a serving dish, garnish with the garam masala, and serve.

MAKES 4 SERVINGS

YOGURT CHEESE

DAHI KA PANEER

Made by draining the water from yogurt and then pressing it under a heavy weight, this soft cheese has a distinctly tangy flavor, especially if it is made with commercial yogurt. The practice of draining the water from yogurt is very common among Indians. They resort to this method especially when they want to sweeten their sour yogurt. (When you remove excess water from the yogurt and then reconstitute it with cold milk, you end up with a naturally sweet yogurt.) With the water drained and some milk added, it can then be treated as normal homemade yogurt and served as is or transformed into a raita (see page 147). Because its texture is comparable to that of cream cheese, this cheese can actually replace it in many Western recipes. It stays fresh in the refrigerator for 5 to 7 days.

Yogurt cheese can be combined with garbanzo bean flour and made into koftas or may be crumbled over green salads. It is wonderful when spiced up with various chutneys, spices, and herbs and served as a dip or a sandwich spread, especially on toasted bagels and muffins. Added to sautéed onions and tomatoes, it makes a lovely side dish. Add sugar and saffron and you have a mousselike dessert.

To make yogurt cheese, place nonfat (or any other) plain yogurt in a 2-foot-square piece of muslin or four layers of cheesecloth and tie it to the kitchen faucet for 8 to 10 hours or longer, or drain it in a colander or sieve lined with muslin or cheesecloth. You will be left with very thick curds. These curds can now be placed between two flat surfaces and pressed under a heavy weight to make a chunk of cheese as directed for Pressed Ricotta Paneer Cheese (see page 248). One 32-ounce container of plain nonfat yogurt will yield about 2 cups of thick yogurt cheese.

To sweeten sour yogurt, drain the 2 cups yogurt as directed above for 1 to 2 hours. Transfer to a dish and add ½ cup cold milk. (You should get to the same consistency of yogurt as you started with.)

To serve over salad, add salt and coarsely ground black pepper or roasted cumin (see page 16) to the yogurt. Then drain as directed above and set under a heavy weight. When set, sauté the whole piece lightly in 1 tablespoon olive or peanut oil in a nonstick skillet over medium heat. Cool and crumble it over a tossed green or any vegetable salad. It can be added to salad without sautéing, if you like.

Lentils, Beans, and Peas, Oh My!

"What should we make today?" is a worldwide dilemma in every household, but for most Indian families the answer is invariably a legume dish. Lentils and beans are prepared in some form or other for every meal and are mostly served with whole-wheat breads or rice and vegetables. However much we might enjoy eating all the wonderful foods of the world, there is a special comfort derived from eating our basic "*dal* and *roti*" (lentils and flatbreads).

In America, beans, as a general rule, are more popular in the winter months, the obvious preference of "heavier" or more substantial dishes belonging to that time of year as opposed to the lighter menus of the summer.

In India, however, they are served year round, and are eaten almost as a staple, like Americans eat potatoes. These powerhouses of nourishment are packed with protein, complex carbohydrates, B vitamins, iron, calcium, and some other minerals. The protein found in dried beans lacks some of the essential amino acids that would make it complete, but this deficiency is overcome when they are served with bread or rice.

The smaller lentils and peas generally cook faster than the larger beans. Within the various groups, the skinless and split varieties are the fastest to prepare. They require no presoaking, and can be made in an hour or less. (These include the yellow mung, yellow urad, and pink lentils, pigeon peas, etc.) Whole black urad lentils take the longest time, and these should be treated like beans and not lentils.

Beans require about 5 to 6 hours of cooking unless they have been soaked overnight or are cooked in a pressure cooker. Presoaking combined with pressure cooking gives the fastest results. Of all the beans, I find garbanzos take the longest, even when you soak and pressure cook them. (In my recipes, these are the only ones I use in their precooked canned form, though you could use the others also.)

You have four choices when cooking dried beans:

1. Boil them continuously until tender;
2. Soak them overnight, then boil them until tender (this will now take less time);
3. Bring them to a boil over high heat, turn off the heat and let them soak undisturbed for 1 hour, then repeat the process;
4. Pressure cook the dried or presoaked beans.

Most lentils are boiled (with or without spices), then topped with a special flavor-enhancing butter or oil called *tarka* (or *chaunk* or *bhagar*). *Tarka* is made by quickly frying chopped onion, ginger, garlic, tomatoes, and fragrant herbs and spices. The ingredients vary according to personal preferences. Beans, on the other hand, are boiled, then simmered with the *tarka* to blend the flavors.

Paprika adds tremendously to the flavor and the visual presentation of *dal*s. One very important fact to remember is to add paprika (or ground cayenne pepper) after removing the *tarka* from the heat or it will burn and make the whole dish bitter.

Cooked beans and lentils stay fresh in the refrigerator for 4 to 5 days. Reheat (with additional water if needed) in the microwave oven or over medium heat. Add fresh *tarka* to hot *dal* when ready to serve for maximum flavor and presentation. Fresh *tarka* should be added to reheated bean dishes also. If you like a thinner sauce in your dish, add some water and bring to a boil; if you'd like it creamier, reduce by boiling over high heat. Generally, thinner-sauced dishes accompany rice preparations and the creamier ones are served with breads.

Use leftover beans and lentils to make paranthas (see page 322).

Here is an introduction to some of the lesser known beans and lentils that are called for in this book.

GARBANZO BEANS (CHICKPEAS, CECI BEANS, *CHANNE,* OR *CHOLE*) are about ⅓-inch spheres with pointed tips and wrinkled skin. India grows two types of garbanzo beans, the popular pale yellow-white variety (called *kabuli* or *safaid channe*) and the dark brown ones (called *kale channe*). Both these varieties are rich in protein and minerals and are a staple in all Indian homes. As a main dish both are paired with special breads (pooris, bhaturas, or kulchas; see pages 344 and 348) and served as party fare. This combination is also very popular in Indian restaurants.

Unlike most beans, each garbanzo bean grows enclosed in an individual pod. The immature dark green garbanzo beans (known as *cholia*) are soft and tender and can be used as a vegetable like fresh peas to make rice pullaos, curries, and vegetable side dishes. They are occasionally available in farmers' markets.

Dried pale garbanzo beans are available in most American and ethnic markets but the black ones are found only in Indian markets. Both these varieties are delicious when sprouted (see page 255).

Garbanzo bean flour (also called chick-pea flour, gram flour, or *besan*) is a pale yellow, high-protein flour made from hulled and split black garbanzo beans. It contains almost no gluten and thus cannot be used to make breads and cakes. It is, however, invaluable when made into a batter for fritters (pakoras; see page 42), used as a thickener for curry sauces, and as a binding agent for koftas. *Besan* is a staple in homes all over India and is available in Indian markets and some health food stores.

Split yellow chick peas (*channe* or *chole ki dal*) are deep yellow and ¼-inch in diameter and are made from hulled and split black garbanzo beans. They resemble the commonly available yellow split peas. Even though the flavor of both these "peas" is different, they can in most cases be used interchangeably. Besides being used to create various main dishes, *channe ki dal* is ground to make garbanzo bean flour or used as a spice in certain spice blends and vegetables.

LENTILS (MASOOR OR MASSAR KI DAL) are brown-green ¼-inch or smaller lens-shaped discs. The Indian variety is smaller than the ones available in America, but both have a similar flavor and can be changed interchangeably. This *dal* is found in two forms, the whole brown-green discs (*sabut masoor ki dal*) and the hulled pink variety (*masoor ki dhulli dal*). The pink variety can be found whole or split in half. Both are available in most American and ethnic markets.

Masoor ki dal is used to prepare various soups, entrées, and side dishes. The whole variety can be sprouted at home (see page 255).

MUNG BEANS (MOONG, MUNGI KI DAL, OR GREEN GRAM) are tiny green kidney-shaped seeds. These dried beans are available as whole green beans (*sabut mungi ki dal*), split in half with the skin intact (*mungi ki chilke vali dal*), or in the skinless rectangular yellow split form (*mungi ki dhulli dal*). All the forms of this *dal* are very easy to digest and are cooked on a regular basis in most Indian homes. They are also ground into a powder and used to make a variety of dumplings, fritters, and desserts.

Green mung beans are often sprouted (see page 255) and served as a salad or a side dish. They are available in some American and in all Indian and Oriental markets.

URAD BEANS (URAD OR MAHN KI DAL OR BLACK GRAM) are dull black and similar in shape and size to green mung beans. Like the mung beans, they are available in their whole form (*sabut urad ki dal*), split in half with the skin intact (*urad ki chilke vali dal*), and in the pale creamy yellow skinless and split version (*urad ki dhulli dal*).

This *dal* is generally considered harder to digest, so ginger, garlic, and asafetida are customarily added while it is cooking to facilitate its digestion. This is especially true when cooking whole black beans. (Out of all the *dal*s, this one takes the longest time to cook, and it is advisable to soak it before it is cooked.)

Flour made from this *dal* is invaluable in making special appetizers and batter crepes.

Urad ki dal is available in Indian and Middle Eastern markets. The whole dried bean can be sprouted (below).

PIGEON PEAS (TOOR, TOVAR, OR ARHAR KI DAL) are yellow-gold and similar in shape and size to the split yellow chick-peas and American split peas. (It is often difficult to differentiate between them.) Tastewise however, this dal is slightly sweeter, and is popularly used to prepare special soups with the flavors of southern India.

Two types of *toor dal* are found in the Indian markets, the plain yellow and the oil-coated (to prevent insect infestation). Both these can be used interchangeably (after washing the oily *dal* in three or four changes of warm water to remove the oil).

Kidney beans, pinto beans, lima beans, soybeans, yellow peas, and black-eyed peas are all readily available in American markets.

BEAN SPROUTS AND LENTILS

PHOOTI HUI SABUT DALEIN

This is a basic recipe that can be used for sprouting various beans and lentils at home.

1 cup whole beans, picked over and washed
4 cups water

Place the beans in a medium-size bowl. Add the water, cover with cheesecloth, and place in a dark closet for 12 to 24 hours. Drain and rinse the beans. Then cover them with damp cheesecloth and place them back in the closet. Keep the cheesecloth damp at all times. The beans will sprout in 2 to 3 days. If you need longer sprouts, let the beans remain in the closet for an extra 1 to 2 days.

Remove from the closet and refrigerate. Sprouted beans stay fresh for 7 to 10 days.

Sprouts can be made with whole dried lentils, peas, mung beans, soybeans, garbanzo beans, fenugreek seeds, sunflower seeds, whole wheat, and various other beans and seeds in a similar manner.

MAKES ABOUT 4 TO 5 CUPS

LENTILS AND YELLOW MUNG BEANS

DHULLI MASOOR AUR MUNG KI DAL

Considered light and easy to digest, this *dal* was a favorite in my family when I was grow-ing up. My father is particularly fond of it, especially when served with a side of Cut Okra with Sautéed Baby Pear Tomatoes (see page 168) and Yogurt with Potatoes and Chaat Masala (page 154).

1 cup dried pink lentils (see page 254), picked over and washed
1 cup dried yellow mung beans (see page 254), picked over and washed
6 cups water
5 fresh serrano or dried red peppers
½ teaspoon turmeric
1 teaspoon salt, or to taste
1 tablespoon peeled and minced fresh ginger
½ cup loosely packed finely chopped cilantro (fresh coriander), soft stems included

FOR THE TARKA TOPPING
3 tablespoons vegetable oil or clarified butter (see page 30)
½ cup finely chopped onion
2 teaspoons cumin seeds
1 tablespoon ground coriander
½ teaspoon paprika
2 small tomatoes, cut into 6 to 8 wedges each
3 tablespoons chopped cilantro for garnish

Place the beans, water, peppers, turmeric, and salt in a large saucepan and bring to a boil, uncovered, over high heat. Reduce the heat to low, cover the pan partially (this is essential because this *dal* produces a froth that rises to the top and spills over if covered, creating a mess that has to be cleaned), and simmer until creamy, 20 to 25 minutes. Stir a few times during the simmering process.

Transfer to a serving dish, gently stir in the ginger and cilantro, and keep hot.

Heat the oil in a small saucepan over high heat and cook the onion, stirring, until medi-um brown, 4 to 5 minutes. Add the cumin seeds, coriander, and paprika, then add the tomato wedges, and cook until they become slightly soft, 2 to 3 minutes. Immediately pour over the hot *dal* and mix lightly with the back of a spoon. (This topping also serves the purpose of a garnish.)

Garnish with the chopped cilantro and serve as a main dish with any vegetable side dish, yogurt raita, and rice or bread.

MAKES 8 SERVINGS

YELLOW MUNG BEANS WITH ZUCCHINI

MUNG DAL AUR GHIA

This is a high-protein vegetarian main dish that is quick and easy to prepare. Although this recipe calls for cooking the *dal* in a pressure cooker, it can be made just as easily without one. Cook it uncovered, over high heat, with an additional ½ cup water until it boils. Then reduce the heat to low, partially cover, and cook until creamy, 20 to 25 minutes. Stir gently and mix in the froth as it rises to the top.

2 cups dried yellow mung beans (see page 254), picked over and washed
4 to 5 small zucchini, cut into 1-inch rounds (about 1 pound)
5 ½ cups water
½ teaspoon turmeric
1 ½ teaspoons salt, or to taste
5 jalapeño peppers, whole or chopped (optional)
2 tablespoons peeled and minced fresh ginger
½ cup firmly packed finely chopped cilantro (fresh coriander), soft stems included

FOR THE TARKA TOPPING
3 tablespoons peanut oil or clarified butter (see page 30)
½ cup finely chopped onion
1 ½ teaspoons cumin seeds
1 tablespoon ground coriander
2 teaspoons ground cumin
½ teaspoon paprika
3 tablespoons chopped cilantro for garnish

Place the beans, zucchini, water, turmeric, salt, and jalapeños in a pressure cooker. Cover and cook over high heat until the pressure regulator starts rocking. Immediately remove the pressure cooker from the heat and let it cool until the pressure drops, about 10 minutes.

Open the lid, transfer the mixture to a serving dish and gently stir in the ginger and cilantro. Cover and keep hot.

Heat the oil in a small saucepan over high heat and cook the onion, stirring, until medium brown, 4 to 5 minutes. Stir in the cumin seeds, then the ground coriander and cumin. Remove the pot from the heat and stir in the paprika. Immediately pour over the hot *dal* and stir lightly. Garnish with the chopped cilantro and serve hot as a main dish.

MAKES 8 SERVINGS

VARIATION: Try using other types of squashes instead of zucchini. Baby green pattypan and some of the other round varieties can be added whole.

PILAF-STYLE YELLOW MUNG BEANS WITH CURRY POWDER

SUKHI MUNG KI DAL

A short soaking of the beans allows them to cook in a few minutes. If you make this recipe with packaged curry powder, add half the amount. This is wonderful hot or cold.

1 cup dried split yellow mung beans (see page 254), picked over
2 ¼ cups water
1 tablespoon vegetable oil
One 1-inch piece fresh ginger, peeled and cut into julienne strips
1 large clove garlic, cut into julienne strips
1 teaspoon cumin seeds
2 teaspoons curry powder (see page 21)
1 teaspoon salt, or to taste
½ teaspoon paprika
¼ cup loosely packed finely chopped cilantro (fresh coriander), soft stems included
2 tablespoons fresh lime juice, or to taste

Wash the mung beans in three to four changes of water, stirring lightly with your fingers until the water runs almost clear. Then soak them in 2 cups of the water for 1 to 2 hours or more. Drain and set aside.

Heat the oil in a large nonstick skillet over moderately high heat and cook the ginger and garlic, stirring, until they turn golden, 1 to 2 minutes. Stir in the cumin seeds, curry powder, and salt, then add the drained beans and remaining water. Cook over high heat for 3 to 4 minutes. Add the paprika, reduce the heat to medium, cover the skillet, and cook, stirring occasionally and very lightly with a spatula until the beans are tender, 10 to

12 minutes. Add a sprinkling of water if the beans stick to the skillet. The finished dish should look like a yellow pullao.

Stir in the cilantro and lime juice and serve.

Makes 4 servings

VARIATION: When the dish is done, stir in some finely diced boiled potatoes, raw onion, chopped cilantro, and mint. Stir in 2 teaspoons of chaat masala (see page 26)and additional fresh lemon juice and and cilantro and serve as a cold appetizer salad.

GREEN MUNG BEANS

SABUT MUNG KI DAL

These "skin-on" green mung beans take more time to cook than the skinless and split yellow ones, but are a more nutritious variation. This recipe can also be made with whole brown lentils (*sabut masoor ki dal*; see page 254).

1 ½ cups dried green mung beans (see page 254), picked over and washed
7 cups water
1 teaspoon salt, or to taste
½ teaspoon turmeric
4 serrano peppers
2 tablespoons peeled and minced fresh ginger

FOR THE TARKA TOPPING
3 tablespoons canola oil or clarified butter (see page 30)
2 teaspoons cumin seeds
1 tablespoon ground coriander
½ teaspoon garam masala (see page 23)
½ teaspoon paprika

Place the mung beans, water, salt, turmeric, and peppers in a pressure cooker. Secure the lid and cook over high heat for 2 to 2 ½ minutes after the pressure regulator starts rocking. Remove from the heat and let the pressure drop by itself, 15 to 20 minutes. Stir in the ginger, then transfer the *dal* to a serving bowl.

Heat the oil in a small saucepan over moderately high heat and cook the cumin seeds, stirring, until they sizzle, 10 seconds. Remove the pan from the heat and stir in the coriander, garam masala, and paprika, then immediately add everything to the cooked *dal*. Stir very gently, allowing part of the *tarka* to mix in the *dal* and the rest to show on the top and sides. Serve as a main dish with any "dry" vegetable preparation on the side.

MAKES 8 SERVINGS

YELLOW URAD BEANS WITH MINCED GINGER

URAD KI DHULLI DAL

These pale yellow beans are the shelled and split version of the familiar whole black urad beans (see page 254) that are popularly served in a fragrant butter sauce (pages 31 and 263). Even though they remain in the shadow of the black variety, the yellow ones have carved out their own niche in Indian cuisine. They are used in a multitude of ways to prepare dishes from appetizers to desserts.

A word of caution: excessive, vigorous stirring will cause the beans to disintegrate and become too starchy, and the dish will lose its appeal.

2 cups dried yellow urad beans (see page 254), picked over and washed
7 cups water
1 tablespoon peeled and minced fresh ginger
5 serrano or jalapeño peppers, skin punctured to prevent them from bursting
¾ teaspoon turmeric
1 ½ teaspoons salt or to taste
½ cup loosely packed finely chopped cilantro (fresh coriander), soft stems included

FOR THE TARKA TOPPING
3 tablespoons clarified butter (see page 30) or safflower oil
1 teaspoon black mustard seeds
½ cup finely chopped onion
1 tablespoon peeled and minced fresh ginger
1 tablespoon ground coriander
½ teaspoon coarsely ground black pepper
½ teaspoon asafetida (see page 13)
2 small firm tomatoes, cut into 6 wedges each
1 teaspoon paprika

Place the beans, water, ginger, peppers, turmeric, and salt in a large saucepan and bring to a boil over high heat, uncovered. Stir in the froth that rises to the top, cover the pot partially (leaving a ½-inch opening to enable the steam to escape), and continue to boil for 4 to 5 minutes. Watch for the rising froth and stir occasionally.

Reduce the heat to medium-low, cover the pan completely, and simmer until the *dal* becomes soft but still maintains its texture, 45 to 50 minutes. (It should not disintegrate completely and become soupy.) Stir occasionally, and add ½ cup more water if it looks too dry.

Transfer to a serving casserole and stir in the cilantro. Cover and keep warm.

Heat the butter in a medium-size saucepan over high heat for about 1 minute, then fry the mustard seeds until they pop, 30 to 40 seconds. (Cover the pan as soon as this happens, or the seeds will fly out.) When the popping subsides, add the onion, reduce the heat to medium, and cook, uncovered, stirring as necessary, until the onion turns golden, 3 to 4 minutes. Add the ginger and stir for another minute, until everything turns a few shades darker. Then stir in the coriander, pepper, asafetida, and tomatoes (in that sequence). When the tomatoes look slightly softened, about 1 minute, remove the pan from the heat and stir in the paprika. Immediately pour over the *dal* and serve as hot as possible. This dish is quite substantial, and can be served just with whole-wheat chapatis (see page 320) and a yogurt salad. I generally like to add a dry vegetable dish like Barbecued Eggplant with Onion and Tomatoes (see page 165) or Baby Zucchini with Spices (page 171) to the menu also.

MAKES 8 SERVINGS

VARIATION: To make this dish in the pressure cooker, use only 6 cups water and cook for 1 ½ to 2 minutes after the pressure regulator starts rocking. Then add the cilantro and *tarka*.

SPLIT BLACK URAD BEANS WITH SPINACH

URAD DAL AUR SAAG

This popular bean main dish can be made 2 to 3 days ahead of time. Remember to refrigerate it as soon as it cools. It will thicken as it cools and will require additional water when reheating. My sister-in-law Asha Puri often serves this dish with a simple rice pullao and a yogurt raita and combines the leftover dal with whole-wheat flour and transforms it into paranthas.

1 cup dried split black urad beans (see page 254), picked over and washed

½ cup dried split yellow chick-peas (see page 255), picked over and washed

6 cups water

5 jalapeño peppers

½ teaspoon turmeric

1 teaspoon salt, or to taste

1 bunch fresh spinach, trimmed of tough stems, washed, and finely chopped (¾ pound)

1 cup firmly packed chopped cilantro (fresh coriander), soft stems included

FOR THE TARKA TOPPING

3 tablespoons vegetable oil

1 cup finely chopped onion

2 tablespoons peeled and minced fresh ginger

1 teaspoon minced garlic

1 cup finely chopped fresh tomatoes

3 tablespoons nonfat plain yogurt, whisked until smooth

2 tablespoons ground coriander

2 teaspoons ground cumin

1 teaspoon paprika

½ teaspoon garam masala (see page 23) for garnish

3 tablespoons chopped cilantro for garnish

Place the beans, water, jalapeños, turmeric, and salt in a pressure cooker. Secure the lid and cook over high heat for 3 minutes after the pressure regulator starts rocking. Remove from the heat and let the pressure drop, 10 to 15 minutes.

Open the lid, stir the beans, and simmer, stirring occasionally, over low heat until the *dal* becomes creamy, another 5 to 10 minutes. Add the chopped spinach and cilantro and cook 2 to 3 minutes more, transfer to a serving dish, and keep warm.

Heat the oil in a medium-size saucepan over moderately high heat and cook the onion, stirring, until golden, 4 to 5 minutes. Add the ginger and garlic, then the tomatoes, and cook, stirring, until all the liquid from the tomatoes evaporates, 3 to 4 minutes. Stir in the yogurt and cook until all liquid evaporates again, 1 to 2 minutes. Immediately pour over the *dal* and mix it in. Garnish with the garam masala and cilantro and serve as a main dish.

MAKES 8 SERVINGS

VARIATION: To make without a pressure cooker, simmer the lentils with about 1 cup extra water until they become thick and creamy, about an hour or longer.

Black Urad Beans in Fragrant Butter Sauce

DAL MAKHANI

Dal is lentils and *makhani* means containing butter. This dish, traditionally made with black urad *dal* and clarified butter (see page 30) is one of the most favored *dal* preparations in many northern Indian homes and restaurants. Popularly presented as a main dish in vegetarian menus, it shares equal limelight with nonvegetarian entrées. I have yet to meet someone who does not like it.

Don't be scared by the long list of ingredients. Once you get everything together, this *dal* does not take much time. It is not essential to soak the beans; it just shortens the cooking time. Add 3 to 4 cups extra water if the beans have not been soaked.

1 cup dried black urad beans (see page 254), picked over
2 tablespoons dried pinto beans, picked over
3 cups water
¼ cup dried split yellow chickpeas (see page 255), picked over and washed
2 tablespoons mustard or peanut oil
10 small dried hot red peppers
1 tablespoon coarsely chopped garlic
1 teaspoon cumin seeds
2 tablespoons ground coriander
1 teaspoon ground cumin
½ teaspoon asafetida (see page 13)
2 tablespoons peeled and minced fresh ginger
1 cup lightly packed finely chopped cilantro (fresh coriander), soft stems included
6 to 7 cups water
1 teaspoon salt, or to taste
1 15-ounce can tomato sauce
½ cup low-fat milk or light cream
2 to 4 tablespoons butter (optional)
3 tablespoons chopped cilantro for garnish
½ teaspoon garam masala (see page 23) for garnish

Wash the urad and pinto beans and soak overnight in the 3 cups of water. Drain, rinse, and set aside. Mix in the chickpeas.

Heat the oil in a pressure cooker over high heat, add the red peppers and garlic, and fry, stirring, until the garlic turns golden, 30 to 40 seconds. Stir in the cumin seeds, coriander, cumin, asafetida, ginger, and cilantro and fry, stirring, for another minute. Add the beans, reduce the heat to medium, and cook, stirring constantly, for 5 to 6 minutes. Add 6 cups of the water and the salt. Increase the heat to high, secure the lid of the pressure cooker, and cook for 5 to 7 minutes after the pressure regulator starts rocking. (Cook for 10 to 15 minutes under pressure if the beans have not been soaked overnight.)

Remove from the heat and let the pressure drop, 20 to 25 minutes. Open the lid, remove the peppers (they might break when you stir and make the dish spicy hot), stir the beans, cover loosely, and simmer over medium heat for 25 to 30 minutes, or longer. (Add more water if the *dal* seems too thick and sticks to the bottom of the pan.) Stir occasionally.

Reduce the heat to low, add the tomato sauce and the milk, cover loosely, and simmer until the *dal* is creamy, another 30 to 40 minutes. Stir occasionally. (At this point, the butter can be added to enhance the flavor.)

Transfer to a serving casserole, garnish with the chopped cilantro and garam masala, and serve. The flavor of this dish improves with the passage of time, so it can be prepared 2 to 3 days in advance. Just remember that it will thicken as time goes by, and additional water will be required when reheating.

Serve with any paneer cheese preparation, a dry vegetable side dish and *Tandoori Naan* (see page 346) or paranthas (see page 322).

MAKES 8 SERVINGS

VARIATIONS: If you hesitate to use a pressure cooker, cook these beans in a large saucepan, cooking initially over high heat for about 10 minutes, then over medium to low until the *dal* becomes creamy, 4 to 6 hours.

The beans can also be placed over very low heat for 8 to 10 hours and allowed to cook slowly. A slow cooker (crockpot) works very well also. The only thing to watch for is the water. There should always be enough water in the pot or the beans will burn before they cook.

SOUTH INDIAN-STYLE LENTIL SOUP

SAMBAR

Of all the lentil dishes included in this chapter, this is the only one that qualifies as a soup (though in India it is served as a main dish). Made with *toor dal* and flavored with sambar masala and fresh coconut, this typical South Indian preparation comes loaded with delicious vegetables and intricate flavors and is best when served with plain Steamed Basmati

Rice (see page 286). Generally, it is made hot and spicy, but that is entirely up to individual choice.

In spite of its origin, this dish has become a part of normal North Indian home cooking.

1 ½ cups dried split yellow pigeon peas (see page 255), picked over and washed
7 cups water
6 jalapeño peppers
8 to 10 curry leaves, preferably fresh (see page 16; optional)
½ teaspoon turmeric
1 teaspoon salt, or to taste
4 cups mixed vegetables (okra, beans, eggplant, potatoes, squash) cut into 1-inch
   pieces
2 tablespoons fresh lemon juice
3 to 4 tablespoons tamarind powder (see page 21)
3 to 4 tablespoons sambar masala (see page 28)
1 tablespoon ground coriander
1 cup loosely packed finely chopped cilantro (fresh coriander), soft stems included

FOR THE TARKA TOPPING
3 tablespoons peanut oil
8 to 10 dried hot red peppers
5 to 7 curry leaves, preferably fresh (see page 16; optional)
1 medium-size onion, cut in half lengthwise and thinly sliced
1 tablespoon peeled and minced fresh ginger
½ teaspoon asafetida (see page 13)
2 teaspoons black mustard seeds
3 tablespoons finely grated fresh or dried coconut (optional)
Chopped cilantro and freshly ground black pepper for garnish

Place the pigeon peas, water, peppers, curry leaves, turmeric, and salt in a pressure cooker. Secure the lid and cook over high heat for 2 to 3 minutes after the pressure regulator starts rocking. Remove from the flame and let the pressure drop by itself, 15 to 20 minutes. Open the lid, stir in the vegetables, lemon juice, tamarind powder, sambar masala, coriander, and cilantro. Secure the lid, and cook once again over high heat until the pressure regulator starts rocking. Remove from the heat and set aside until the pressure drops. Transfer to a serving bowl and keep warm.

Heat the oil in a medium-size saucepan over moderately high heat and fry the peppers and curry leaves, stirring, for 30 seconds. Add the onion and ginger and cook, stirring, until it turns medium brown, 4 to 5 minutes. Add the asafetida and the black mustard seeds and cook until they pop, 30 to 40 seconds. (Cover the pan as soon as this happens, or the seeds will fly out.) When the popping subsides, open the lid, stir in the coconut, and immediately add the *tarka* to the cooked sambar. Garnish with the chopped cilantro and black pepper and serve hot.

Sambar will thicken as it cools. Add ½ to 1 cup additional water while reheating.

MAKES 8 SERVINGS

KIDNEY BEANS IN A CURRY SAUCE

RASEDAR RAJMA

These deep red beans are among the most favored in India. They are traditionally paired with steamed basmati rice and are generally served at lunchtime. I love them with chapatis (see page 320) and paranthas (see page 322).

Rajma aur chaval, kidney beans and rice (like the Mexican rice and beans), is one of the most popular "combination" foods served. To complete the meal, add a side dish of okra or cauliflower and serve with slices of freshly cut mangoes.

Keep the sauce thin if you plan to serve this dish with rice, or make it thick to serve with breads.

2 cups dried kidney beans, picked over
1 tablespoon peeled and minced fresh ginger
½ cup firmly packed finely chopped cilantro (fresh coriander), soft stems included
1 teaspoon salt, or to taste
8 cups water
2 tablespoons vegetable oil
1 teaspoon minced fresh garlic
½ teaspoon carom seeds (see page 14)
2 cups finely chopped fresh tomatoes
¼ cup nonfat plain yogurt, whisked until smooth
2 tablespoons ground coriander
2 teaspoons dried fenugreek leaves (see page 17)
¾ teaspoon turmeric
3 tablespoons chopped cilantro for garnish
½ teaspoon garam masala (see page 23) for garnish

Place the kidney beans, ginger, cilantro, salt, and 6 cups of the water in a medium-size saucepan. Cover and bring to a boil over high heat. Turn off the heat, stir the beans, cover the pan, and let them soak undisturbed for about 1 hour. (You may stir once or twice.) Bring to a boil again and set them aside for another hour. Bring to a boil once again and then let boil until the kidney beans are tender, 20 to 25 minutes, or use any of the other methods mentioned on page 253.

Heat the oil in a small saucepan over high heat and fry the garlic and carom seeds for a few seconds. Add the tomatoes and cook, stirring occasionally, until all their liquid evaporates, 8 to 10 minutes. Add the yogurt, a little at a time, stirring constantly to prevent it from curdling. Stir in the coriander, fenugreek, and turmeric, then add the remaining water and bring to a boil. Add this gravy to the cooked kidney beans and simmer, stirring occasionally, over low heat for another 15 to 20 minutes. Transfer to a serving casserole, garnish with the cilantro and the garam masala and serve as a main dish with Steamed Basmati Rice (see page 286).

MAKES 8 SERVINGS

VARIATION: PINTO BEANS IN CLASSIC CURRY SAUCE (*chittree valé rajma*): Pinto beans are very similar to kidney beans in texture, taste, and cooking time. The two can be used interchangeably in all the recipes.

Start with 2 cups dried pinto beans and cook them until tender as instructed above. Then make Classic Curry Sauce (see page 123) and simmer the beans in it over high heat for 5 to 7 minutes, then over low until the gravy becomes thick, 20 to 30 minutes. Garnish with chopped cilantro and garam masala and serve.

MAKES 8 SERVINGS

BLACK-EYED PEAS WITH GARLIC AND SCALLIONS

SUKHA LOBIA OR RONGI

"Oh no! Not black-eyed peas again," said my husband, Pradeep, when he saw me with a bowl full of dried black-eyed peas. He was remembering the countless times his cousin Vikram Budhraja had cooked them, and how he, as a bachelor, politely ate them, pretended to love every bite, and after the meal correctly praised his cousin on his culinary expertise.

Even though these are not his favorite beans, Pradeep does enjoy them now. I urge you to try this recipe.

2 cups dried black-eyed peas
5 or more serrano peppers
1 tablespoon peeled and minced fresh ginger
4 cups water
1 teaspoon salt, or to taste
2 tablespoons vegetable oil or clarified butter (see page 30)
1 cup finely sliced scallions, (white and light green parts only)
2 teaspoons minced garlic
½ teaspoon turmeric
2 tablespoons ground coriander
2 cups finely chopped fresh tomatoes
1 cup loosely packed finely chopped cilantro (fresh coriander), soft stems included
1 tablespoon fresh lemon juice
2 to 3 cups shredded lettuce, any variety
½ teaspoon garam masala (see page 23) for garnish

Place the peas, peppers, ginger, water, and salt in a medium-size saucepan. Cover and bring to a boil over high heat. Turn off the heat and let the peas soak undisturbed for 1 hour or longer. Stir and repeat the procedure once more. Check to see if the peas are tender; if not, add ¼ cup more water and simmer over medium heat until done. (Alternatively, soak the peas overnight in 4 cups water, then add the peppers, ginger and salt, and boil them over high heat for 2 to 3 minutes, then cook over low heat until tender, about 20 to 25 minutes.)

Heat the oil in a large nonstick skillet or wok over moderately high heat, then cook the scallions and garlic, stirring, until golden, 1 to 2 minutes. Stir in the turmeric and coriander, then the tomatoes. Cook, stirring, until most of the liquid evaporates, 2 to 3 minutes. Add the peas and cilantro and cook, stirring occasionally, until the dish is almost dry, 5 to 7 minutes. Stir in the lemon juice.

Transfer to a serving platter lined with the shredded lettuce, garnish with the garam masala, and serve as a main dish with Sautéed Japanese Eggplant with Mango Powder (see page 161), a yogurt raita, and any plain parantha (page 322).

MAKES 8 SERVINGS

Fresh Black-Eyed Peas in Tomato-Fenugreek Sauce

TARI VALA TAZA LOBIA

During one of my weekly trips to my favorite farmers' market in Santa Monica, I saw a farmer shelling something that looked like black-eyed peas, and to my surprise that's exactly what they were. I had never seen them fresh. Some were pale green, others pale yellow, and some were half and half. I could not resist purchasing them and trying them out. My first effort turned out to be delicious.

3 tablespoons safflower oil
6 to 8 serrano peppers, skin punctured to prevent them from bursting
3 large tomatoes, pureed
1 cup loosely packed finely chopped cilantro (fresh coriander), soft stems included
1 tablespoon ground coriander
1 teaspoon ground cumin
1 teaspoon salt, or to taste
1 tablespoon dried fenugreek leaves (see page 17)
½ teaspoon turmeric
1 tablespoon peeled and minced fresh ginger
2 pounds shelled fresh black-eyed peas
1 large russet potato, peeled and cut into ½-inch dice
3 cups water
1 teaspoon garam masala (see page 23) for garnish
3 tablespoons finely chopped cilantro for garnish

Heat the oil in a large nonstick saucepan over moderately high heat and cook, stirring, the peppers for 1 minute. (Stand as far away as possible from the pan, just in case the peppers burst.) Stir in the tomatoes and cilantro and cook, stirring occasionally, until most of the liquid from the tomatoes evaporates, 10 to 12 minutes. Add the coriander, cumin, salt, fenugreek, turmeric, and ginger and cook, stirring, for 1 minute, then add the peas and potatoes and continue to cook, stirring, for 3 to 4 minutes. Add the water, cover the pan, and bring to a boil. Reduce the heat to medium-low and simmer until the gravy is thick and the peas are tender, 20 to 25 minutes.

Transfer to a serving bowl, garnish with the garam masala and cilantro, and serve as a main dish with a vegetable and bread on the side.

MAKES 8 SERVINGS

VARIATION: Try this recipe with freshly shelled cranberry or fava beans.

SPLIT YELLOW CHICKPEAS WITH JAPANESE EGGPLANT

CHANNA DAL AUR LAMBÉ BAINGAN

This is a perfect example of how beans and lentils can be cooked with vegetables to create truly unusual dishes. This rare combination from Reita and Virender's kitchen is very different from anything I've tasted. The beans are cooked separately until soft and the eggplants are prepared in a tangy tamarind "curry" sauce that is spiked with hot peppers. This dish is perfect with Steamed Basmati Rice (see page 286) and a simple yogurt raita (page 147).

Remember to soak the tamarind in boiling water for at least 3 to 4 hours or longer. This facilitates the extraction of the pulp from the fiber. Seedless shelled tamarind is available in compressed packets in Indian markets.

One 2-inch-square piece seedless shelled tamarind pods (3 ounces)
¾ cup boiling water
1 ½ cups dried split yellow chickpeas (see page 255), picked over
4 ½ cups water
8 large cloves garlic, peeled
5 serrano peppers, or to taste (optional)
1 medium-size onion, cut into 6 to 8 wedges
2 large tomatoes, cut into 8 wedges each
1 cup loosely packed finely chopped cilantro (fresh coriander), soft stems included
2 to 3 tablespoons vegetable oil
½ teaspoon paprika
¼ teaspoon turmeric
¾ teaspoon salt, or to taste
3 to 4 long Japanese or Chinese eggplants, cut into ½- by 3-inch sticks or ¾-inch
    rounds (about 1 pound)
3 tablespoons chopped cilantro for garnish

Break the tamarind in small pieces and soak it in the boiling water for 3 to 4 hours or longer. Stir it a few times during soaking. Then pass it through a food mill or sieve to extract all the pulp. Add ¼ cup water to the leftover fibrous parts and extract some more pulp. Set aside. This can be done up to a week in advance. (This pulp can also be frozen for 5 to 6 months.)

Wash and soak the chickpeas in the 4 ½ cups water for about 1 hour or longer.

In a food processor fitted with the metal S-blade, process the garlic, peppers, and onion until smooth. (Stop the motor to scrape the sides with a spatula a few times.) Remove to a bowl and set aside. Then process the tomatoes and cilantro in the same manner.

Heat the oil in a medium-size nonstick saucepan over moderately high heat and cook the pureed onion mixture, stirring, until it turns dark brown, 12 to 15 minutes. (Turn the heat down as the puree starts to brown.) Add the pureed tomatoes and cook over high heat for 3 to 4 minutes, then over medium-low heat, stirring as necessary, until all the liquid evaporates, 12 to 15 minutes. Stir in the paprika, turmeric, and salt, then add the eggplant, cover the pan, and cook over medium-low heat, stirring occasionally, until the eggplant becomes slightly soft, 10 to 12 minutes. Add the reserved tamarind pulp and continue to cook, stirring occasionally, until the eggplant is soft. (Do not break the eggplant when stirring.) (At this point, the eggplant can also be served as a separate side dish.)

While the eggplant is cooking, place the chickpeas and their soaking water in a pressure cooker. Secure the lid and cook over high heat for 2 minutes after the pressure regulator starts rocking. Let the pressure drop by itself, 10 to 12 minutes, then open the lid and transfer the beans to the pan with the eggplant. (The chickpeas can also be cooked in a saucepan over high to medium heat until they become just soft, about 30 to 40 minutes. An additional ½ cup water may be required.)

Simmer for 10 to 12 minutes to blend the flavors. This dish should have a thick sauce. (If most of the liquid dries up during cooking, add an extra ½ cup of water and bring to a boil.) Transfer to a serving dish, garnish with the cilantro, and serve.

If you make this dish ahead of time, remember that the sauce will thicken, so additional water will be required when you reheat it.

Makes 8 servings

Variation: Instead of the compressed tamarind pods, you can substitute 3 to 4 tablespoons of tamarind powder (see page 21) and omit the boiling water.

Curried Garbanzo Beans with Onion and Garlic

RASEDAR CHANNÉ

These pale round beans with pointy tips are available dried or in cans. Dried garbanzo beans need to be soaked overnight and then boiled for a long time before they are recipe ready. Using canned garbanzo beans eliminates this tedious process.

You can also make this dish with Classic Curry Sauce (see page 123).

4 large cloves garlic, peeled
One 1-inch piece fresh ginger, peeled
1 small onion, quartered
1 large tomato, cut into 6 to 8 wedges
1 cup firmly packed cilantro (fresh coriander), soft stems included
3 tablespoons vegetable oil
1 teaspoon carom seeds (see page 14)
3 jalapeño peppers, with skin punctured to prevent bursting or sliced (optional)
¼ cup nonfat plain yogurt, whisked until smooth
2 tablespoons curry powder (see page 21)
Four 15 ½-ounce cans garbanzo beans, drained and rinsed
2 cups water
½ teaspoon garam masala (see page 23) and chopped cilantro for garnish

In a food processor process the garlic, ginger, and onion until smooth. Remove to a bowl and set aside. In the same work bowl, process the tomatoes and cilantro until smooth and set aside also.

Heat the oil in a large nonstick saucepan over moderately high heat and fry the carom seeds, stirring, for 30 seconds. Add the processed onion mixture and cook, stirring, until it turns brown, 5 to 7 minutes. (Cook initially over high heat for 2 to 3 minutes, then over low.) Mix in the tomato puree and jalapeños and cook until all the liquid evaporates, 5 to 7 minutes. Add the yogurt, a little at a time, stirring constantly to prevent it from curdling, then stir in the curry powder. Cook for another minute and mix in the garbanzo beans and water.

Cover and bring to a boil over high heat, then reduce the heat to medium-low. Simmer for 10 to 15 minutes or longer, depending upon how much gravy is required. (The longer you cook, the less gravy you will have.)

Transfer to a serving dish, garnish with the garam masala and cilantro, and serve hot as an entrée with a vegetable side dish and any Indian bread.

MAKES 8 SERVINGS

GARBANZO BEANS WITH ROASTED POMEGRANATE SEEDS

CHANNA MASALA

Sometimes referred to as *Pindi channé* (Pindi is now a city in Pakistan, but it used to be a part of India before the partition of India and Pakistan in 1947) or *Kwality valé channé*

(Kwality is a famous chain of restaurants that made this dish popular all over India), this distinctive preparation of garbanzo beans is characterized by its dark brown color and savory taste. The color is obtained by dry-roasting part of the spices before adding them to the dish. (Some recipes call for adding tea bags for color, but I don't see why you should add caffeine to this perfectly nutritious dish.)

This dish is often made for large gatherings. It makes an appearance on all types of menus, be it brunch, lunch, tea or dinner. Deep-fried bhaturas or pooris (see page 340) are traditionally served with it, but if you are watching your diet, serve it with naan (see page 346), kulchas, or toasted sourdough bread.

Do not add any salt, because the canned garbanzo beans already contain enough.

1 tablespoon ground pomegranate seeds (see page 20)
2 tablespoons ground coriander
1 tablespoon ground cumin
3 tablespoons peanut oil
6 serrano peppers, skin punctured to prevent them from bursting
1 ½ cups finely chopped onion
2 teaspoons minced fresh garlic
1 tablespoon peeled and minced fresh ginger
1 tablespoon dried fenugreek leaves (see page 17)
1 tablespoon mango powder (see page 18)
½ teaspoon ground cinnamon
½ teaspoon ground cloves
½ teaspoon black salt (see page 14; optional)
1 cup loosely packed finely chopped cilantro (fresh coriander), soft stems included
Four 15 ½-ounce cans garbanzo beans, drained and rinsed
1 to 1 ½ cups water
Tomato wedges, sliced scallions, and chopped cilantro for garnish

Place the pomegranate, 1 tablespoon of the coriander, and the cumin in a small skillet and roast, stirring constantly, over medium-high heat until they turn to an "instant coffee" color, 2 to 3 minutes. Transfer to a bowl and set aside until needed.

Heat the oil in a large nonstick wok or skillet over moderately high heat and cook the peppers, stirring, for 30 seconds. (Stand as far as possible from the pan just in case the peppers burst.) Add the onion and cook, stirring, until it turns dark brown, 10 to 12 minutes (reduce the heat if it starts to burn). Stir in the garlic, ginger, the remaining coriander, the fenugreek, mango powder, cinnamon, cloves, and black salt, then add the cilantro and roasted spices.

Add the beans and water and bring to a boil over high heat. Reduce the heat to medium, cover, and continue to cook until the beans are tender and almost all the water is absorbed, 10 to 12 minutes. Stir occasionally.

Transfer to a serving dish, garnish with the tomato wedges, scallions, and cilantro, and serve with Yogurt Mint Chutney (see page 88) and Tamarind and Ginger Chutney (page 100).

MAKES 8 SERVINGS

VARIATION: Use 3 tablespoons of homemade channa masala (see page 25) instead of dry-roasting the spices separately.

GARBANZO BEANS IN TOMATO-SPINACH SAUCE

TAMATAR AUR PALAK VALÉ CHANNÉ

This is a very fast and easy recipe, especially if your channa masala blend is already made. Use prepackaged channa masala with caution, as it contains a lot of hot peppers.

As an alternative, add some other spices from your spice box and 2 to 3 tablespoons of fresh lemon juice.

¾ cup nonfat plain yogurt
¼ cup water
3 tablespoons peanut oil
2 teaspoons cumin seeds
1 tablespoon finely chopped garlic
2 cups finely chopped fresh tomatoes
4 cups loosely packed finely chopped spinach (tough stems removed)
1 tablespoon peeled and minced fresh ginger
2 tablespoons ground coriander
3 tablespoons homemade channa masala (see page 25) or 1 to 2 tablespoons store-bought
Two 15 ½-ounce cans garbanzo beans, drained and rinsed
½ cup firmly packed finely chopped cilantro (fresh coriander), soft stems included
½ cup thinly sliced scallion whites for garnish
Tomato wedges for garnish

Whisk the yogurt and water together until smooth. Set aside.

Heat the oil in a medium-size nonstick skillet over moderately high heat and fry the cumin seeds until they sizzle, 10 seconds. Add the garlic and cook, stirring, until golden, 1 to 2 minutes. Add the tomatoes and cook, stirring occasionally, until all the liquid evaporates, 5 to 7 minutes. Stir in the spinach and cook until it is wilted, 3 to 4 minutes, then add the ginger, coriander, and channa masala. Cook, stirring, for 1 to 2 minutes, then add the whisked yogurt, a little at a time to prevent it from curdling. Add the beans, cover the pan, and cook, stirring as necessary, over high heat for 3 to 4 minutes, then over medium to low heat until the beans are tender and the sauce thick, 10 to 15 minutes. Stir in the cilantro and transfer to a serving bowl. Garnish with the scallions and tomato wedges and serve as a main dish with paranthas (see page 322). Any dry vegetable dish can be presented on the side.

MAKES 8 SERVINGS

BLACK GARBANZO BEANS

KALÉ CHANNÉ

This recipe is an inspiration from Renu Bhatla, my sister-in-law. Renu uses prepackaged channa masala, but I prefer to use my homemade version.

The black garbanzo beans are only available dried and therefore have to be cooked until soft enough to be usable. (They can be made recipe-ready up to 4 days ahead of time and stored in the refrigerator.) Then they are simmered, preferably in a cast-iron wok, which enriches these highly nutritious beans and also adds the deep brown color associated with this authentic recipe.

Choose contrasting-color vegetable dishes to serve on the side: for example, Cauliflower, Potatoes, and Red Bell Pepper (see page 174) or Nine Jewel Vegetables (page 208). Remember to serve Green Mint Chutney (see page 85) and yogurt also.

3 cups dried black garbanzo beans, picked over

11 cups water

1 ½ teaspoons salt, or to taste

1 tablespoon peeled and minced fresh ginger

2 serrano peppers, finely chopped (optional)

½ teaspoon black salt (see page 14; optional)

3 to 4 tablespoons homemade channa masala (see page 25) or 1 to 2 tablespoons store-
  bought

2 to 3 tablespoons fresh lemon juice

3 small firm tomatoes, cut into 6 wedges each

½ cup thickly sliced scallion whites or thin slices red onion

½ cup firmly packed finely chopped cilantro (fresh coriander), soft stems included

2 to 3 tablespoons peanut oil or clarified butter (see page 30)

One 1 ½-inch piece fresh ginger, peeled and cut into julienne strips

2 teaspoons cumin seeds

Wash the beans and soak them in 5 cups of the water for 12 to 24 hours at room temperature. Drain and place them in a pressure cooker with the remaining 6 cups of water. Stir in
the salt, ginger, and peppers. Secure the lid and cook over high heat for 2 to 3 minutes
after the pressure regulator starts rocking. Turn off the heat and let the pressure drop by
itself, 15 to 20 minutes. Open the pressure cooker and check to see if the beans are tender. If not completely soft, cook them in the pressure cooker for another 1 to 2 minutes
after the pressure regulator starts rocking. (The beans can also be cooked in a saucepan,
simmering them over medium heat with 7 to 8 cups water until tender, 1 to 1 ½ hours.)

Place the cooked beans in a cast-iron wok (or any other nonstick wok or saucepan).
Add the black salt and cook, stirring as necessary, over high for 3 to 4 minutes, then medium heat until most of the water evaporates, 15 to 20 minutes. (Stop at this point if you are
making the beans ahead of time.)

Transfer to a serving platter and gently mix in the channa masala, lemon juice, tomato
wedges, scallions, and cilantro. Cover and keep warm.

Before serving, heat the oil in a small saucepan over high heat and fry the julienned ginger until it turns golden, 30 to 40 seconds. Add the cumin seeds and immediately drizzle
everything over the warm beans, stir lightly to mix, and serve as a main dish. This dish can
also be served as a savory snack any time of the day.

MAKES 8 SERVINGS

Sun-Dried Urad Bean Nuggets

URAD DAL KI BADIAN

Known as *vadian* among the Punjabis in northern India and *badian* among the Hindi-speaking population, these spicy hot, uneven, sun-dried lentil nuggets come in all shapes and sizes. The homemade ones generally tend to be about 1 to 2 inches and the commercial varieties 3 to 4. (The larger ones are generally broken into smaller pieces before cooking.)

In India they are dried by placing them on portable cots lined with fine muslin and drying them in the hot summer sun.

These highly flavorful nuggets are first deep-fried or sautéed in oil and then cooked with rice, dried beans, lentils, or vegetables to make delicious curries and side dishes. If they are to be added to a dry dish, they should be softened by simmering them in spices and water, then added to the dish. In dishes that have a sauce, the nuggets are cooked along with the other ingredients.

2 cups dried yellow urad beans (see page 254), picked over
4 ½ cups water
2 tablespoons black peppercorns, or to taste
1 tablespoon cumin seeds
1 tablespoon black cumin seeds (see page 16)
2 teaspoons fenugreek seeds (see page 16)
3 large cloves garlic, peeled
One 2-inch piece fresh ginger, peeled and cut into 3 to 4 pieces
5 jalapeño or serrano peppers, stemmed (optional)
1 cup firmly packed fresh fenugreek leaves or 1 tablespoon dried (see page 17)
1 teaspoon ground asafetida (see page 13)
½ teaspoon baking soda
1 ½ teaspoons salt, or to taste
1 ½ cups grated and squeezed cucumber or zucchini

Wash the urad *dal* and then soak it overnight in 4 cups of the water. Drain, rinse, and set aside.

Place the peppercorns, cumin and fenugreek seeds in a small nonstick skillet and roast over medium to high heat until they start popping, 2 to 3 minutes. Remove from the heat and set aside for about 5 minutes to cool.

Transfer the roasted spices to a food processor fitted with the metal S-blade and process until they are coarsely ground. Add the garlic, ginger, and peppers and process until smooth. Add the rinsed *dal* and water and process until it turns into a thick, smooth paste, about 1 minute. (You may have to stop the motor and scrape down the sides of the work bowl.) Add the fenugreek leaves, asafetida, baking soda, and salt and process once again until smooth, 45 seconds. (The batter will be smooth but slightly textured.)

Transfer to a bowl, cover, and keep in a warm, draft-free place for 6 to 8 hours or longer to ferment. Stir occasionally. The fermented batter will feel light and starchy when it is ready.

Before making the nuggets, mix in the grated cucumber. Coat a cookie sheet or tray lightly with oil and drop the lentil batter on it with a spoon or with your fingers, making about 1-inch nuggets. Set the tray out in the sun and let them dry until they turn as hard as rocks. This may take 3 to 4 days or longer, depending upon their size. (Keep them in the sun during the day and inside at night.) Once they start to firm up, turn them over to expose the bottom side.

This drying can also be done in a dehydrator or oven. Preheat the oven to 200° F, turn off the heat, and then place the tray in the oven. After 6 to 8 hours, reheat the oven to 200° F again and turn it off. Keep repeating this until the pieces are dry. Ovens with pilot lights do not require any reheating.

Once the nuggets are completely dried, they should be stored in an airtight container. Their shelf life at room temperature is between 4 to 5 months and in the refrigerator about 1 year.

MAKES EIGHTEEN TO TWENTY 1-INCH NUGGETS

DRIED YELLOW PEAS WITH URAD BEAN NUGGETS

SUKHÉ PEELÉ MATTAR AUR BADIAN

Dried yellow peas look like pearls, and our aim in this recipe is to make sure they maintain their appearance even after they have been softened. Gentle back-and-forth motions with the back of a ladle is my preferred method of moving these "pearls" around in the pot.

The dark brown urad bean nuggets seen against yellow pearls studded with cilantro greens and sweet red pepper confetti make this a picture perfect dish. A complementary menu might include Sautéed Japanese Eggplant with Mango Powder (see page 161), Scallion and Mint Raita (page 148) and Plain Layered Griddle-fried Bread (page 325). Round off the meal with Layered Vanilla and Chocolate Fudge (see page 363).

2 cups dried whole yellow peas (see page 255), picked over
10 cups water
3 tablespoons peanut oil
20 Sun-Dried Urad Bean Nuggets (see page 277)
1 cup finely chopped onion
1 tablespoon peeled and finely chopped fresh ginger
2 large cloves garlic, cut into thin slivers
5 serrano peppers, skin punctured to prevent them from bursting
1 cup finely chopped fresh tomatoes
2 tablespoons ground coriander
1 teaspoon ground cumin
1 teaspoon dried fenugreek leaves (see page 17)
1 teaspoon garam masala (see page 23)
½ teaspoon turmeric
1 teaspoon salt, or to taste
½ cup firmly packed finely chopped cilantro (fresh coriander) for garnish
½ cup seeded and finely diced red bell pepper for garnish
Freshly ground black pepper for garnish

Wash and soak the peas in 4 cups of the water overnight. Drain, rinse, and set aside. (These soaked peas can be stored in the refrigerator for 6 to 7 days.)

Heat the oil in a large wok or nonstick saucepan over moderately high heat and fry the bean nuggets until they turn dark brown, turning to brown them evenly. Remove from the pan and set aside.

Add the onion, ginger, garlic, and peppers to the same pan and cook, stirring, until the onion turns medium brown, 5 to 7 minutes. Add the tomatoes and cook, stirring, until all the liquid evaporates, 3 to 4 minutes. Stir in the coriander, cumin, fenugreek, garam masala, turmeric, and salt, then add the peas, fried nuggets, and the remaining water. Cover and cook over high heat for 5 to 7 minutes, then medium heat until the peas and nuggets become fork-tender, 30 to 40 minutes. (Add more water if necessary.) Stir occasionally. When it is ready, this dish should contain very little gravy.

Transfer to a serving dish, garnish with the cilantro (stir some into the dish), red pepper, and freshly ground black pepper, and serve as a main dish.

MAKES 8 SERVINGS

VARIATION: To serve as an appetizer or a salad, the softened peas can be sprinkled with 1 to 2 teaspoons chaat masala (see page 26) and some freshly squeezed lime or lemon juice and served in "bowls" of radicchio or endive.

Soybeans in Curry Sauce

SOYA BEAN KI KARI

Dried soybeans look almost like dried yellow peas, but after cooking they more closely resemble black-eyed peas without the black part. They are quite easy to prepare, and can be transformed into main entrées or side dishes with the help of fragrant herbs and spices or can be added to other dishes to give them a nutritional boost.

2 cups dried soybeans, picked over
12 cups water
1 ½ teaspoons salt, or to taste
½ teaspoon turmeric
2 large cloves garlic, peeled
One 1-inch piece fresh ginger, peeled
1 small onion, peeled and cut into 4 to 5 pieces
2 large tomatoes, cut into 5 to 6 pieces each
3 tablespoons vegetable oil
2 tablespoons ground coriander
1 teaspoon ground cumin
½ teaspoon paprika
½ teaspoon garam masala (see page 23) for garnish
Chopped cilantro (fresh coriander) for garnish

Wash the soybeans and soak them overnight in 5 cups of the water. Drain and rinse the beans and place them in a pressure cooker with the remaining water, the salt, and turmeric. Secure the lid and cook over high heat for 3 to 4 minutes after the pressure regulator starts rocking. Remove from the heat and let the pressure drop by itself, 10 to 15 minutes. Open the lid and check to see if the beans are tender. If they are, proceed with the recipe, if not pressure cook for another 1 to 2 minutes after the regulator starts rocking. (Add more water if the beans look too dry.)

In a food processor fitted with the metal S-blade, process the garlic, ginger, and onion (stopping to scrape the sides down once or twice) until smooth. Remove to a bowl and set aside. Process the tomatoes in the same work bowl and set aside.

Heat the oil in a small saucepan over medium heat and cook, the onion mixture, stirring until it turns brown, 15 to 20 minutes. Add the coriander, cumin, and paprika, then stir in the pureed tomatoes. Cook until all the liquid evaporates, 7 to 10 minutes. Transfer the cooked onion and tomatoes to the pressure cooker containing the softened soybeans and bring to a boil over high heat. Reduce the heat to medium and simmer for 3 to 4 minutes to blend the flavors.

Transfer to a serving dish, garnish with the garam masala and cilantro, and serve as a main dish with Steamed Basmati Rice (see page 286) and a dry vegetable side dish.

MAKES 8 SERVINGS

VARIATION: To make this dish without a pressure cooker, boil the soaked beans in 7 cups water with the turmeric and salt for 5 minutes, then turn off the heat and let them soak another 1 to 2 hours. Boil once again, reduce the heat to low, and continue to simmer until they become tender, about 1 hour. Then proceed with the recipe.

LIMA BEANS WITH POTATO ROUNDS

SUKHÉ LIMA BEAN AUR ALU

This lima bean preparation from Reita Bhalla's kitchen is new even to most Indian people, mainly because lima beans are not readily available in India. Cooked with potatoes in a cilantro "pesto"-type sauce, this "New World" dish is loaded with mouth-watering flavors.

This "dry" bean entrée is best served with a "semi-dry" vegetable dish like Barbecued Eggplant with Onion and Tomatoes (see page 165) or Fresh Spinach with Paneer Cheese (page 237), a yogurt raita, and paranthas (page 322).

5 large cloves garlic, peeled
5 serrano peppers, stemmed (optional)
1 medium-size onion, cut into 6 to 8 wedges
1 cup firmly packed cilantro (fresh coriander), soft stems included
3 tablespoons peanut oil
One 3-inch stick cinnamon
5 black cardamom pods, pounded lightly to break the skin
1 teaspoon salt, or to taste
½ teaspoon freshly ground black pepper, or to taste
3 medium-size russet potatoes, peeled and cut into ¼-inch rounds
¾ to 1 cup water (as necessary)
One 16-ounce package frozen lima beans, thawed
1 cup seeded and finely chopped red bell peppers for garnish
Toasted (see page 76) almond slivers for garnish

In a food processor fitted with the metal S-blade, process the garlic, peppers, and onion. Stop the motor, scrape the sides, add the cilantro, and process again until everything turns into a smooth puree.

Heat the oil in a large nonstick skillet over moderately high heat and stir-fry the cinnamon and cardamom for about 1 minute. Add the onion mixture, reduce the heat to medium, and cook, stirring as necessary, until it turns light golden, 8 to 10 minutes. Add the salt, pepper, and potatoes and continue to cook, stirring as necessary with a spatula, until the potatoes are partially cooked, 8 to 10 minutes. Add the water and lima beans, cover the pan, and simmer over low heat until the potatoes and lima beans are tender and all the water evaporates, 25 to 30 minutes. Stir very carefully to avoid breaking the potatoes.

Transfer to a serving platter, surround with the diced red peppers and lemon curls, top with the almond slivers, and serve.

MAKES 8 SERVINGS

A Grain of Rice

Rice—the one grain most familiar to the whole world—really needs no introduction. Its versatility is unlimited, whether used as a side dish or the main ingredient of a casserole. It can cleverly be transformed into fashionable fare ranging from appetizers to desserts.

Rice can be combined with all types of vegetables. Its soft texture works well with crispy sautéed vegetables and blends smoothly with the less crunchy legumes, beans, and potatoes. A favorite addition of mine in most rice recipes is cardamom pods. Rice constitutes a large part of a vegetarian diet. In northern India wheat is the dominant carbohydrate staple; throughout the rest of India, however, rice is the center of each meal.

Though various types of rice are available in India, India is renowned for its aromatic long-grain basmati rice, which is grown at the foothills of the Himalayan mountain ranges. It is this rare variety of rice that scores far above all the others in the world. Various countries have tried to duplicate the production of Indian basmati rice, but so far have not fully succeeded. The climatic conditions and soil components of India are unique in producing this special fragrant and flavor-laden rice.

In America rice is considered second cousin to, or the poor relation of, the potato. In India the status of rice is much more elevated. It is as important a component of the meal as you make it. To emphasize this point I always present the rice dish in the most attractive way possible, served in a colorful bowl or adorned with brightly colored vegetables or with assorted sautéed nuts on top.

Rice in all its forms can be a wonderful alternative to salads and sandwiches for lunch. In convenient plastic containers, rice travels well to work or picnics or even school. It is always satisfying and the nutritional value increases with each additional healthful food mixed in.

Another convenient feature of rice is that it can be served hot or at room temperature.

When heating leftover rice, I add a few teaspoons of water to restore the moisture. Cooked rice can be kept in the refrigerator up to 5 days.

GENERAL COOKING INSTRUCTIONS FOR BASMATI RICE

- Wash it in three to four changes of water to remove the excess starch.
- Soak the rice for at least 30 minutes before cooking. This causes the grains to absorb moisture and swell up and also decreases the actual cooking time, resulting in perfectly cooked fluffy rice every time.
- Use less than twice the amount of water as you have rice, especially if the rice has been soaked.
- Cook the rice in the soaking liquid. This minimizes the loss of the water-soluble B vitamins.
- Cook, uncovered, over high heat until it boils, then reduce the heat to a minimum, cover the pan, and finish cooking.
- Do not stir the rice once it is cooked. Stirring causes the rice grains to break and lose their characteristic appeal.
- Let the rice rest for 5 to 7 minutes after it has been cooked. This gives the grains a chance to firm up. (At this point you will notice that some of the grains on top will stand up erect, almost as though they were informing you that they are ready to be served.)
- Each cup of uncooked rice yields approximately 3 cups of cooked rice.

ABOUT PRECOOKING BASMATI RICE

Contrary to popular belief among the Indians, I find that basmati can indeed be cooked ahead of time. Fully cooked rice reheats very well (with a sprinkling of water) in a microwave or conventional oven. Exercise caution when handling cooked rice, as it breaks very easily.

For a "right off of the stove" look, cook any rice recipe partially (until the water gets absorbed but the grain is not completely soft). To finish cooking, follow any of these methods:

- Transfer to a microwave-proof dish and set aside. Cover and reheat in the microwave for 2 to 3 minutes on high power.
- Transfer to an ovenproof dish. Cover and reheat in a preheated 300° F oven for 20 to 25 minutes.
- Let the rice remain in the pan in which it was cooked, cover and reheat on the lowest stovetop setting for 15 to 20 minutes.

Another method I often rely on is to follow the recipe to the point when the water and rice are added to the pan. The pan can then be set aside for 5 to 6 hours or longer. Finish cooking 30 minutes prior to serving.

SPICE-FLAVORED BROTH FOR RICE

MASALÉ VALA PANI

Made with a blend of health-promoting herbs and spices, this highly aromatic broth imparts a subtle flavor to basmati rice, making it taste absolutely divine. Try adding it to soups, sauces, casseroles, and vegetables. Half a cup is enough to flavor 2 cups of uncooked rice.

    1 teaspoon peanut oil
    15 cloves
    10 green cardamom pods, pounded to break open
    4 black cardamom pods, pounded to break open
    4 bay leaves, crumbled
    4 sprigs fresh mint leaves
    2 large cloves garlic, crushed
    One 3-inch stick cinnamon
    1 teaspoon black peppercorns, coarsely crushed
    4 cups water

Place the oil, cloves, cardamom pods, bay leaves, mint, garlic, cinnamon, and peppercorns in a medium-size saucepan and cook over high heat, stirring continuously, until the seeds start popping and the garlic becomes golden, 1 to 2 minutes. Add the water, cover the pan, and boil over moderately high heat for 4 to 5 minutes. Reduce the heat to medium-low and continue to simmer until reduced to about 2 cups, 15 to 20 minutes.

Cool and store in the refrigerator for 10 to 15 days or freeze in ice cube trays, transfer to freezer bags, and keep frozen for 2 to 3 months. If storing in the refrigerator, let the spices remain in the water; they will continue to enhance the flavor of this broth.

MAKES ABOUT 2 CUPS

STEAMED BASMATI RICE

UBLÉ HUÉ CHAVAL

Plain steamed basmati rice has a splendid flavor that is complementary to the other dishes served with it. It makes a simple yet distinctive addition to meals.

While cooking this rice, it is essential, initially, to cover the pan in part only, or the rising foam will spill, making an extra mess that has to be cleaned. Once the foam subsides, the lid should be placed snugly on the pan.

2 ½ cups basmati rice, picked over
4 ¾ cups water

Wash the rice in three to four changes of water, stirring gently with your fingertips, until the water runs almost clear. Then soak it in the water for 30 minutes or longer.

Place the rice and water in a large nonstick pan and bring to a boil over high heat. Reduce the heat to a minimum, cover the pan (partially for the first 2 to 3 minutes and then snugly), and cook the rice until done, 10 to 15 minutes.

Let the rice rest for about 5 minutes, transfer to a platter, and serve with any meal. It is especially favored with Kidney Beans in a Curry Sauce (see page 266) and Yogurt Sauce with Garbanzo Bean Flour Dumplings (page 222).

MAKES 8 SERVINGS

STEAMED TURMERIC RICE

UBLÉ HUÉ HALDI CHAVAL

This is a slightly more elaborate version of regular steamed rice. In this dish we will add some turmeric (which according to Indian Aryurvedic medicine is believed to be a blood purifier and have natural antiseptic and anti-inflammatory properties) and some whole cloves and dried red peppers. (These peppers do not make the dish hot unless you break them.)

2 ½ cups basmati rice
4 ¾ cups water
2 tablespoons fresh lemon juice
½ teaspoon turmeric

5 dried hot red peppers
½ teaspoon whole cloves
½ teaspoon black peppercorns
1 teaspoon salt, or to taste
½ cup finely sliced scallion greens

Wash the rice in three to four changes of water, stirring lightly with your fingertips, until the water runs almost clear. Soak it in the water for 30 minutes or longer.

Place the rice, water, lemon juice, turmeric, peppers, cloves, peppercorns, and salt in a large saucepan. Bring to a boil over high heat, then reduce the heat to a minimum. Cover the pan (partially at first, until the foam subsides, then snugly) and cook the rice until done, 10 to 15 minutes.

Transfer to a serving platter, garnish with the scallion greens, and serve with any meal.

MAKES 8 SERVINGS

VARIATION: Add 1 cup frozen chopped mixed vegetables or peas when you begin cooking the rice.

SIMPLE CUMIN-FLAVORED RICE

JEERA CHAVAL

My mother wakes up in the morning, and the first thing she hears is the sound of a crow. She rushes outside, and sees it on the wall of our house, looking straight into the veranda and crowing loudly, as if to warn her that visitors will soon be arriving. (She had secretly hoped that the sound came from the neighbor's house.) She immediately takes heed of this warning, and while she goes about her morning chores, in her mind she is already planning the lunch menu. The "crowing" has proved right too many times, and so she takes it quite seriously.

This is a common belief among the superstitious Indians, who feel very strongly that if a crow serenades you, there is a good chance that someone will visit you. You can choose whether or not to heed its call but here is a simple recipe in case you do.

2 ½ cups basmati rice, picked over
4 ¾ cups water
2 tablespoons clarified butter (see page 30) or vegetable oil
2 teaspoons cumin seeds
½ teaspoon ground green or black cardamom seeds
¼ teaspoon ground cinnamon
¼ teaspoon ground cloves
1 teaspoon salt, or to taste
1 teaspoon ground roasted cumin (see page 16)

Wash the rice in three to four changes of water, stirring lightly with your fingertips, until the water runs almost clear. Soak it in the water for 30 minutes or longer.

Heat the butter in a large saucepan over moderately high heat and cook the cumin seeds, stirring, until they sizzle, 10 seconds. Immediately add the cardamom, cinnamon, and cloves, then stir in the rice and water. Add the salt and bring to a boil over high heat. Reduce the heat to a minimum, cover the pan (partially at first, until the foam subsides, then snugly), and cook until the rice is done, 10 to 15 minutes.

Transfer to a serving platter, garnish with the ground cumin, and serve with any curry or lentil preparation.

MAKES 8 SERVINGS

RICE WITH PEAS AND CHERRY TOMATOES

MATTAR AUR TAMATAR KA PULLAO

Fresh green peas, cherry tomatoes, and cumin seeds provide a perfect contrast in color to the fluffy white rice. This dish is simple enough to be cooked for everyday meals and festive enough to be served as part of a more elaborate menu.

2 cups basmati rice, picked over
3 ¾ cups water
2 tablespoons clarified butter (see page 30) or vegetable oil
1 small onion, cut in half lengthwise and thinly sliced
2 teaspoons cumin seeds
5 black cardamom pods, pounded lightly to break the skin
One 3-inch stick cinnamon

1 teaspoon salt, or to taste
2 cups shelled peas (preferably fresh)
1 teaspoon vegetable oil
15 to 20 red or yellow cherry tomatoes
2 tablespoons finely chopped fresh mint leaves

Wash the rice in three to four changes of water, stirring lightly with your fingertips, until the water runs almost clear. Then soak it in the water for 30 minutes or longer.

Heat the butter in a large saucepan over moderately high heat and cook the onion, stirring, until golden, 4 to 5 minutes. Add the cumin, cardamom, cinnamon, and salt and stir for 30 to 40 seconds, then add the peas, rice, and water. Bring to a boil over high heat, then reduce the heat to a minimum, cover the pan (partially at first, until the foam subsides, then snugly), and cook the rice until done, 10 to 15 minutes. Do not stir.

Heat the vegetable oil in a small nonstick skillet over medium-high heat and cook the tomatoes, stirring, until heated through, 1 to 2 minutes. Sprinkle the mint leaves on top and stir the tomatoes by shaking the skillet. Remove from the heat. Transfer the rice to a serving platter, fluff with a fork, garnish with the tomatoes, and serve.

MAKES 8 SERVINGS

VARIATION: Garnish with steamed peas, broccoli, and carrots, or with sautéed mushrooms, raisins, and nuts.

RICE WITH POTATOES, PEAS, AND CARROTS

ALU AUR GAJJAR KE CHAVAL

As a child it seemed to me that our kitchen was always well stocked with potatoes, peas, and carrots. Why else did my mother make this dish every time my father walked in with his friends 30 minutes before dinner? Little did I realize there was another reason behind it. This is one of those fast-cooking dishes that looks "glamorous." (She made it even faster by using a pressure cooker.) The use of black cumin seeds (a rare variety of cumin) and the "saffron added" look from the grated carrots makes the whole meal seem festive.

Small russet potatoes work best in this recipe. Choose potatoes that are about 3 inches long.

1 ½ cups basmati rice, picked over

2 ¾ cups water

3 tablespoons vegetable oil

2 teaspoons black cumin seeds (see page 16)

One 3-inch stick cinnamon

5 bay leaves

5 black cardamom pods, pounded lightly to break the skin

4 small russet potatoes, peeled and cut into 6 to 8 wedges each

1 cup shelled peas (preferably fresh)

1 cup grated carrots

1 teaspoon salt, or to taste

2 tablespoons chopped cilantro (fresh coriander) or parsley for garnish

1 teaspoon garam masala (see page 23) for garnish

Wash the rice in three to four changes of water, stirring lightly with your fingertips, until the water runs almost clear. Then soak it in the water for 30 minutes or longer.

Heat the oil in a large saucepan over high heat and cook the cumin, cinnamon, bay leaves, and cardamom, stirring, until they sizzle, 30 to 45 seconds. Add the potato wedges and continue to cook, stirring, for another 2 to 3 minutes. Mix in the peas, carrots, rice, and water. Add the salt and bring to a boil. Reduce the heat to a minimum, cover the pan (partially at first, until the foam subsides, then snugly), and cook the rice until done, 10 to 15 minutes.

Transfer the rice to a serving platter, fluff with a fork, garnish with the cilantro and garam masala, and serve hot with any meal.

MAKES 8 SERVINGS

RICE WITH PEAS AND TOMATOES

MATTAR AUR TAMATAR KE CHAVAL

Inspired by my favorite pasta recipe, this innovative dish is influenced by the Western style of cooking. Substitute cooked tortellini or ravioli for the rice and create a new dish with Indian flavors.

Baby "pear" tomatoes are available in the gourmet produce section of most supermarkets.

1 tablespoon olive oil

3 cups coarsely chopped fresh tomatoes

1 teaspoon minced garlic

1 tablespoon peeled and minced fresh ginger

2 tablespoons ground coriander

1 teaspoon freshly ground black pepper, or to taste

1 tablespoon dried fenugreek leaves (see page 17)

1 teaspoon salt, or to taste

½ cup loosely packed finely chopped cilantro (fresh coriander), soft stems included

2 cups frozen peas, thawed

20 yellow or red baby pear or cherry tomatoes

8 cups Steamed Basmati Rice (see page 286)

3 tablespoon minced scallion greens for garnish

½ teaspoon garam masala (see page 23) for garnish

Heat the oil in a large nonstick skillet over high heat and cook the tomatoes, stirring, for about 2 minutes. Add the garlic, ginger, coriander, pepper, fenugreek, salt, cilantro, peas, and pear tomatoes. Cook, stirring gently, for 3 to 4 minutes, then stir in the steamed rice. Cover the skillet, reduce the heat to medium, and cook another 3 to 4 minutes to blend the flavors.

Transfer to a platter, garnish with the scallion greens and garam masala, and serve hot or at room temperature.

MAKES 8 SERVINGS

RICE WITH GARBANZO BEANS AND SCALLIONS

CHANNÉ AUR HARÉ PYAZ KE CHAVAL

I have used canned garbanzo beans in this recipe because cooking garbanzos from scratch is quite time-consuming. Rinsing the canned beans eliminates the preservatives and leaves perfectly cooked garbanzo beans that are quick and easy to use.

1 ½ cups basmati rice, picked over
2 ¾ cups water
3 tablespoons vegetable oil
4 bay leaves, crumbled
½ cup sliced scallion whites
5 dried hot red peppers
1 teaspoon minced garlic
2 teaspoons cumin seeds
1 teaspoon carom seeds (see page 14)
1 teaspoon black peppercorns (optional)
½ cup firmly packed finely chopped cilantro (fresh coriander), soft stems included
1 teaspoon salt, or to taste
One 15 ½-ounce can garbanzo beans, drained and rinsed
3 medium-size potatoes, peeled and cut into ½-inch dice
½ cup sliced scallion greens for garnish
½ cup finely diced red radishes for garnish
Few sprigs cilantro for garnish

Wash the rice in three to four changes of water, stirring lightly with your fingertips, until the water runs almost clear. Then soak it in the water for 30 minutes or longer.

Heat the oil in a large saucepan over high heat and cook the bay leaves, scallion whites, and red peppers, stirring, until the scallions turn golden, 2 to 3 minutes. Add the garlic, cumin, carom seeds, peppercorns, cilantro, and salt, then stir in the beans and potatoes. Add the rice and water and bring to a boil. Reduce the heat to a minimum, cover the pan (partially at first, until the foam subsides, then snugly), and cook the rice until done, 10 to 15 minutes. Do not stir.

Transfer the rice to a serving platter, garnish with the scallion greens, radishes, and cilantro and serve hot with any meal.

MAKES 8 SERVINGS

RICE WITH GARBANZO AND KIDNEY BEANS

CHANNÉ AUR RAJMA KE CHAVAL

Using the Chinese stir-fry technique of preparing rice, this recipe calls for steamed basmati rice to be stir-fried with precooked garbanzo and kidney beans. Serve with a sauced vegetable or paneer cheese dish and a yogurt raita of your choice.

The white peppercorns produce a "hot" bite and should be added with caution. They provide welcome bursts of heat for the adventuresome, but could catch others unguarded. A good alternative is to disperse the heat evenly by coarsely grinding and then adding the peppercorns to the dish.

1 ½ cups basmati rice, picked over
2 ¾ cups water
2 tablespoons vegetable oil
1 cup finely chopped onion
1 teaspoon cumin seeds
½ teaspoon white peppercorns (optional)
2 teaspoons minced garlic
2 tablespoons ground coriander
1 tablespoon ground ginger
2 teaspoons garam masala (see page 23)
1 cup loosely packed chopped cilantro (fresh coriander), soft stems included
1 ½ cups cooked or canned (drained and rinsed) garbanzo beans
1 ½ cups cooked or canned (drained and rinsed) kidney beans
2 cups quartered small mushrooms
½ cup fresh lemon or lime juice
1 teaspoon salt, or to taste
½ cup sliced scallion greens for garnish
½ cup seeded and finely diced colorful bell peppers for garnish

Wash the rice in three to four changes of water, stirring lightly with your fingertips, until the water runs almost clear. Soak the rice in the water for 30 minutes or longer.

Place the rice and water in a large nonstick saucepan and bring to a boil over high heat, uncovered. Reduce the heat to a minimum, cover the pan (partially at first, until the foam subsides, then snugly), and cook the rice until done, 10 to 15 minutes.

Heat the oil in a large nonstick skillet or wok and cook the onion, stirring, until golden, 5 to 7 minutes. Stir in the cumin, peppercorns, garlic, coriander, ginger, garam masala, and cilantro, then add the beans and mushrooms. Cook, stirring, for 2 to 3 minutes, then add the steamed rice. Stir gently to mix, add the lemon juice and salt, and cook 2 to 3 minutes more to blend the flavors.

Transfer to a serving platter, garnish with the scallion greens and peppers, and serve.

MAKES 8 SERVINGS

Spinach and Sweet Pepper Rice

SAAG AUR MIRCH PULLAO

This enticing dish, embellished with splashes of red, yellow, and green, is delicious by itself but incredible when served with Black Urad Beans in Fragrant Butter Sauce (see page 263) and a yogurt raita (page 147). This is a great recipe to choose when you want to call attention to your culinary skills. My cousins, Billoo and Poonam Bhatla, often add Italian seasonings to give this rice dish a new character.

2 cups basmati rice, picked over
3 ¾ cups water
3 tablespoons vegetable oil
1 teaspoon cumin seeds
1 teaspoon fennel seeds
10 green cardamom pods, pounded lightly to break the skin
One 3-inch stick cinnamon
2 small bunches fresh spinach, washed, tough stems removed, and finely chopped
   (1 pound)
2 cups seeded and finely diced red and yellow bell peppers
1 tablespoon peeled and minced fresh ginger
1 teaspoon salt, or to taste

Wash the rice in three to four changes of water, stirring lightly with your fingertips, until the water runs almost clear. Then soak it in the water for 30 minutes or longer.

Heat the oil in a large saucepan over high heat and cook the cumin, fennel, cardamom, and cinnamon, stirring, for about 1 minute. Stir in the spinach and peppers and continue to cook until the spinach is wilted, about 2 minutes. Remove the spinach and peppers to a bowl and set aside until needed. Leave the cardamom pods and cinnamon in the pan.

Stir in the rice and water. Add the ginger and salt and bring to a boil over high heat. Reduce the heat to a minimum, cover the pan (partially at first, until the foam subsides, then snugly), and cook the rice until done, 10 to 15 minutes.

Transfer the rice to a serving platter, gently mix in the reserved spinach and peppers, and serve hot.

MAKES 8 SERVINGS

SAFFRON AND SPINACH RICE WITH RAISINS AND PINE NUTS

KESAR AUR SAAG PULLAO

Perfect for entertaining, this easy-to-prepare dish uses some of the world's most exotic spices—saffron, cardamom, and black cumin seeds. These exquisite flavors complement both Indian and Western menus alike.

2 cups basmati rice, picked over
3 ¾ cups water
½ teaspoon saffron threads
3 tablespoons milk, at room temperature
3 tablespoons vegetable oil
1 medium-size onion, cut in half lengthwise and thinly sliced
5 black cardamom pods, pounded lightly to break the skin
One 3-inch stick cinnamon
2 teaspoons black cumin seeds (see page 16)
1 cup golden raisins
½ cup pine nuts or chopped walnuts
2 large bunches spinach, washed, tough stems removed, and finely chopped
1 ½ teaspoons salt, or to taste
Chopped cilantro (fresh coriander) for garnish
2 medium-size tomatoes, cut into wedges, for garnish

Wash the rice in three to four changes of the water, stirring lightly with your fingertips, until the water runs almost clear. Then soak it in the water for 30 minutes or longer. Soak the saffron in the milk for 30 minutes or longer.

Heat the oil in a large saucepan over medium-high heat and cook the onion, stirring, until dark brown and crisp, about 5 minutes. Remove to paper towels to drain and reserve for garnish.

In the same oil cook, stirring, the cardamom, cinnamon, and cumin until they sizzle, 10 seconds. Stir in the raisins and pine nuts and continue to cook, stirring, until the raisins puff up and the nuts become golden, 3 to 4 minutes; be careful not to burn the raisins. Mix in the spinach and salt and cook, stirring, for another minute.

Add the rice and water. Bring to boil over high heat, then reduce the heat to a minimum. Cover (partially at first, until the foam subsides, then snugly) and cook the rice until done, 10 to 15 minutes. Remove from the heat. Gently fork in the saffron milk and let it sit undisturbed for about 5 minutes.

Transfer to a serving platter, garnish with the reserved onion, the cilantro, and tomato wedges and serve.

Makes 8 servings

Rice with Red Swiss Chard

LAL SAAG KE CHAVAL

Swiss chard belongs to the beet family and is cultivated for its leaves and stems only. The large, dark green leaves with deep red veins and rhubarblike stems are similar to beet leaves, and contain generous amounts of calcium and vitamin C.

The pureed greens and diced deep red stems combine superbly with the long and tender grains of basmati rice to make this rice dish, which comes to you highly recommended by Sumita and Supriya, my teenage daughters.

2 ½ cups basmati rice, picked over
4 ⅔ cups water, plus ¼ cup
1 large bunch Swiss chard (¾ pound)
2 tablespoons vegetable oil
1 teaspoon cumin seeds
3 large cloves garlic, cut into thin slivers
1 cup finely sliced scallions (greens included)
1 ½ teaspoons garam masala (see page 23)
1 teaspoon salt, or to taste
Freshly ground black pepper to taste

Wash the rice in three to four changes of water, stirring lightly with your fingertips, until the water runs almost clear. Soak it in 4 ⅔ cups of the water for 30 minutes or longer.

Wash the Swiss chard. Remove the stems and chop finely. Set aside. Coarsely chop the leaves and place them in a large nonstick saucepan with the remaining ¼ cup water. Cover and bring to a boil over high heat. Reduce the heat to medium and simmer until wilted, 4 to 5 minutes. Cool and process in a food processor until smooth. Set aside.

Heat the oil in a large saucepan over high heat and fry the cumin seeds until they sizzle, 10 seconds. Add the garlic and scallions and cook, stirring, until the scallions are golden, 2 to 3 minutes. Add the garam masala and salt, then stir in the rice and water. Bring to a boil, then reduce the heat to a minimum, cover the pan (partially at first, until the foam subsides, then snugly), and cook until the rice is almost done, 8 to 10 minutes. Uncover the pan and gently fork in the pureed leaves with their liquid. (Do not stir, or the rice will break.) Cover the pan and cook for 2 to 3 minutes on low heat.

Gently fork in the reserved diced stems, cover the pan, and cook over low heat for 4 to 5 minutes. (The greens and stems are added separately so each will retain its distinct character.)

Let the rice rest for a few minutes, then transfer to a serving platter, garnish with pepper, and serve with your favorite curry or lentil preparation.

MAKES 8 SERVINGS

RICE WITH GREENS AND BAY LEAVES

SAAG PULLAO

Ever since I discovered the distinct lemony fragrance of the fresh bay leaves that grow in my backyard, I've been hooked on them. Their perfume had an immediate effect on me, and my food underwent an instant transformation. From being an occasional user of dried bay leaves, I became an avid fan of these leaves. Today, I like both the fresh and dried ones. Just remember to crush them before using and to add them early on to obtain maximum flavor.

Seasoned with bay leaves and garlic and enriched with different types of greens, this pullao recipe enables you to bring a creative dish to the table every time. Use kale, collards, sorrel, chicory, Swiss chard, daikon, turnip, beet, or mustard greens.

2 cups basmati rice, picked over
3 ¾ cups water
2 tablespoons peanut oil
8 to 10 bay leaves (preferably fresh), crushed
2 teaspoons finely chopped garlic
2 teaspoons cumin seeds
1 cup finely chopped red onion
2 cups minced greens (do this in a food processor)
1 teaspoon salt, or to taste
1 teaspoon dried mint leaves for garnish
Chopped Red Swiss chard stems or cooked beets for garnish (optional)

Wash the rice in three to four changes of water, stirring lightly with your fingertips, until the water runs almost clear. Soak it in the water for at least 30 minutes or longer.

Heat the oil in a large nonstick saucepan over moderately high heat and fry the bay leaves for 15 to 20 seconds. Add the garlic and cook, stirring, until it turns golden, 1 to 2 minutes. Stir in the cumin seeds, then add the onion and cook, stirring, until it turns brown, 4 to 5 minutes. Add the greens and cook, stirring, for 4 to 5 minutes.

Stir in the rice, water, and salt and bring to a boil over high heat. Reduce the heat to a minimum, cover the pan (partially at first, until the foam subsides, then snugly), and cook until the rice is done, 10 to 15 minutes.

Transfer to a serving platter, garnish with the mint and chard, and serve as a side dish with any meal.

Makes 8 servings

RICE WITH TWO COLORS

DO RANGA CHAVAL

This pretty dish calls for precooked white and yellow grains of rice, with color accents provided by cumin, fresh green garlic, and red chili peppers. It is essential to cool the cooked rice completely, because the grains of freshly cooked rice are soft and delicate and too much handling causes them to break, thus destroying the visual presentation of this dish. This recipe is a good way to use leftover steamed rice.

Fresh green garlic looks like a slightly coarser and larger version of the scallion but has a mild yet distinct garlic flavor.

2 ½ cups basmati rice, picked over
4 ½ cups water

FOR RICE 1
1 tablespoon peanut oil
1 teaspoon black cumin seeds (see page 16)
½ cup finely chopped fresh green garlic or ½ teaspoon minced garlic and ½ cup finely chopped scallions
½ teaspoon salt

FOR RICE 2
¼ teaspoon turmeric

1 teaspoon peeled and minced fresh ginger
6 dried hot red peppers

¼ cup loosely packed chopped cilantro for garnish

Divide the rice evenly in half. Wash the two batches separately in three to four changes of water each, stirring gently with your fingertips, until the water runs almost clear. Then soak them separately, each in 2 ¼ cups of the water for 30 minutes or longer.

For the first batch, heat the oil in a medium-size saucepan over moderately high heat and fry the cumin seeds until they sizzle, 10 seconds. Then add the fresh garlic and cook, stirring gently, for 1 minute. Add one batch of the rice with its water and the salt and bring to a boil over high heat. Reduce the heat to a minimum, cover the pan (partially at first, until the foam subsides, then snugly), and cook the rice until done, 8 to 10 minutes. Remove from the heat and set aside until cool, 3 to 4 hours at least.

For the second batch, place the rice and its water, turmeric, ginger, and peppers in a medium-size saucepan and bring to a boil over high heat. Reduce the heat to a minimum, cover the pan (partially at first, then snugly), and cook the rice until done, 8 to 10 minutes. Remove from the heat and set aside until cool.

Combine the rices and place in a microwave-proof casserole. Cover and reheat for 2 to 3 minutes on full power. Stir in the chopped cilantro and serve. It can also be reheated in a preheated 400° F oven.

Makes 8 servings

VARIATIONS: To make green-colored rice, add pureed spinach or any other greens.

To make brown-colored rice, sauté sliced onion over moderately high heat until almost caramel-colored, then add the washed rice and continue to sauté until it turns golden. Then add the water and cook.

Another lovely variation is to combine any of the above prepared rice dishes with cooked wild rice.

RICE WITH FRESH
FENUGREEK LEAVES

TAZI METHI KE CHAVAL

Fresh fenugreek leaves are slightly bitter but extremely fragrant. They are considered quite a delicacy (much like radicchio), and are used in a number specialty dishes. One such dish is this rice preparation. The tantalizing aroma of this lovely green rice draws everybody to the dinner table, so let it be the last dish to be brought out.

If you are unable to find fresh fenugreek leaves, spinach or watercress leaves in combination with ¼ cup dried fenugreek leaves are acceptable substitutes. Fresh fenugreek leaves are available at Indian and Middle Eastern markets.

2 ½ cups basmati rice, picked over
4 ¾ cups water
2 tablespoons mustard or vegetable oil
1 ½ teaspoons cumin seeds
1 cup finely chopped onion
1 teaspoon minced garlic
2 cups firmly packed minced fresh fenugreek leaves
1 ½ teaspoons salt, or to taste
½ cup seeded and diced red bell peppers for garnish
Chopped fresh green herbs for garnish

Wash the rice in three to four changes of water, stirring gently with your fingertips, until the water runs almost clear. Then soak it in the water for 30 minutes or longer.

Heat the oil in a large saucepan over high heat and cook the cumin seeds, stirring, until they sizzle, 10 seconds. Add the onion and cook, stirring occasionally, until it turns medium brown, 5 to 7 minutes. Stir in the garlic and fenugreek leaves, reduce the heat to medium-low, and cook, stirring, until the fenugreek wilts and becomes darker in color, 7 to 10 minutes. Add the rice, water, and salt. Increase the heat to high and bring to a boil. Immediately reduce the heat to a minimum, cover the pan (partially at first, until the foam subsides, then snugly), and cook the rice until done, 10 to 15 minutes.

Transfer to a serving platter and fluff the rice with a fork. Garnish with the red peppers and herbs and serve hot with any meal.

MAKES 8 SERVINGS

BROCCOLI AND RED PEPPER RICE

HARI GOBI AUR LAL MIRCH KE CHAVAL

I like to leave the cardamom and cinnamon in the rice when I serve this dish because they add an exotic touch to this colorful preparation. But do inform the uninitiated to "just look but don't crunch." To those who like them, they are a fragrant delight.

2 cups basmati rice, picked over

3 ¾ cups water

2 tablespoons peanut oil

8 green cardamom pods, pounded lightly to break the skin

One 3-inch stick cinnamon

1 teaspoon cumin seeds

1 small onion, cut in half lengthwise and thinly sliced

35 to 40 two-inch broccoli florets

1 ½ cups seeded and finely diced red bell peppers

1 teaspoon salt, or to taste

3 tablespoons toasted (see page 76) blanched almond slivers for garnish

1 teaspoon garam masala (see page 23) for garnish

Wash the rice in three to four changes of water, stirring lightly with your fingertips, until the water runs almost clear. Then soak it in the water for 30 minutes or longer.

Heat the oil in a large saucepan over high heat and cook the cardamom and cinnamon, stirring, for a few seconds. Stir in the cumin seeds, then add the onion and cook, stirring, until the onion turns medium brown, 5 to 6 minutes. Add the broccoli, red peppers, and salt. Cook for another 3 to 4 minutes, then mix in the rice and water. Bring to a boil over high heat, reduce the heat to a minimum, cover the pan (partially at first, until the foam subsides, then snugly), and continue to cook until the rice is done, 10 to 15 minutes.

Transfer to a platter, fluff with a fork, garnish with the almonds and garam masala, and serve hot with any meal.

MAKES 8 SERVINGS

RICE WITH BASIL AND SUN-DRIED TOMATOES

TULSI AUR TAMATAR KE CHAVAL

Though the concept of drying vegetables and fruits in the sun is quite popular in India, I have never seen any form of dried tomatoes used in Indian cuisine. I don't see why it has to remain that way. Their delicate flavor adds an exotic touch to even the most ordinary dishes.

2 cups basmati rice, picked over
3 ¾ cups water
3 tablespoons olive oil
1 small onion, cut in half lengthwise and thinly sliced
1 cup dry-packed sun-dried tomatoes, cut into ½-inch pieces
2 tablespoons golden raisins
One 3-inch stick cinnamon
¼ cup loosely packed coarsely chopped fresh basil
1 teaspoon salt, or to taste
Freshly ground black pepper for garnish
½ cup finely sliced scallion greens for garnish

Wash the rice in three to four changes of water, stirring lightly with your fingertips, until the water runs almost clear. Then soak it in the water for 30 minutes or longer.

Heat the oil in a large saucepan over moderately high heat and cook the onion, stirring, until it becomes golden, 4 to 5 minutes. Add the tomatoes, raisins, and cinnamon and cook, stirring, until the raisins start to puff up, 1 to 2 minutes; be careful not to let the raisins burn. Add the basil and salt, then stir in the rice and water. Bring to a boil. Reduce the heat to a minimum, cover the pan (partially at first, until the foam subsides, then snugly), and cook the rice until done, 10 to 15 minutes. Do not stir.

Transfer to a serving platter, garnish with the pepper and scallion greens, and serve.

MAKES 8 SERVINGS

THREE MUSHROOM RICE

TEEN KHUMBI PULLAO

The combination of three distinct varieties of mushrooms with cumin and cardamom makes this dish a real palate pleaser.

Dried and fresh mushrooms should be treated similarly. Sauté them lightly, then add the rice and cook everything together. It is not necessary to reconstitute the dried mushrooms because they plump up as they cook with the rice. Their delicate flavors (which are lost if you soak the mushrooms prior to cooking) remain in the dish and are absorbed by the rice. (Make sure, though, that the mushrooms are clean.)

2 cups basmati rice, picked over
3 ⅔ cups water

3 tablespoons peanut oil

2 teaspoons cumin seeds

10 green cardamom pods, pounded lightly to break the skin

One 3-inch stick cinnamon

1 medium-size onion, cut in half lengthwise and thinly sliced

10 to 12 one-inch dried morel mushrooms, whole or sliced

8 medium-size dried shiitake mushrooms, sliced into 6 pieces each

8 large fresh mushrooms, cut into 8 pieces each

1 ½ teaspoons salt, or to taste

3 tablespoons minced scallion greens for garnish

Several cherry tomatoes or tomato wedges for garnish

Wash the rice in three to four changes of water, stirring lightly with your fingertips, until the water runs almost clear. Then soak it in the water for 30 minutes or longer.

Heat the oil in a large saucepan over high heat and cook the cumin, cardamom, and cinnamon, stirring, until they sizzle, 30 seconds. Then add the onion and cook, stirring, until golden, 4 to 5 minutes. Stir in all the mushrooms and cook for another minute. Add the rice and water. Stir in the salt and bring to a boil. Reduce the heat to a minimum, cover the pan (partially at first, until the foam subsides, then snugly), and cook until the rice is done, 20 to 25 minutes. Do not stir.

Transfer the rice to a serving platter, fluff with a fork, garnish with the scallions and tomatoes, and serve hot with any meal.

MAKES 8 SERVINGS

RICE WITH STIR-FRIED CAPERS AND FRESH MOREL MUSHROOMS

GUCCHI PULLAO

Brine-packed capers add an international twist to this stir-fried rice preparation. The flavor of capers is not too foreign to the Indians; they actually remind me of a particular variety of pickled berries, which in India are called *dahlé*.

This recipe calls for fresh morel mushrooms, but you can use any type of wild mushroom. A combination of steamed basmati and wild rice would add a new dimension to this recipe.

2 tablespoons olive oil

1 small onion, thinly sliced

1 teaspoon black cumin seeds (see page 16)

1 tablespoon peeled and minced fresh ginger

15 to 20 small fresh morel mushrooms, sliced

1 tablespoon brine-packed capers, drained

6 cups Steamed Basmati Rice (see page 286), cold or at room temperature

2 to 3 tablespoons fresh lemon juice

¼ cup loosely packed finely chopped cilantro (fresh coriander), soft stems included

½ teaspoon garam masala (see page 23) for garnish

Heat the oil in a large skillet over moderately high heat and cook the onion, stirring, until it becomes golden, 4 to 5 minutes. Add the cumin and stir until it sizzles, 10 seconds. Add the ginger, mushrooms, and capers and cook, stirring, for 2 to 3 minutes. Mix in the rice, then add the lemon juice. Cover the skillet, reduce the heat to medium-low, and cook, stirring as necessary, with a spatula, for 5 to 7 minutes to blend the flavors.

Transfer to a serving platter and lightly mix in the cilantro. Garnish with the garam masala and serve.

MAKES 6 SERVINGS

RICE WITH SPROUTED MUNG BEANS

MUNG DAL KE CHAVAL

The flavors of mung beans and rice are perfectly complementary, and when served together, they form a complete protein. The Indians often cook mung beans and rice as separate dishes and then serve them side by side at one meal. In this recipe, they are cooked together, creating a wholesome and highly nutritious one-dish meal.

Mung beans are relatively easy to sprout at home (see page 255), and presprouted mung beans are also available at most local health food markets. Make sure that the sprouts are about ½ inch or smaller. (Do not buy the Oriental type of bean sprouts.)

2 cups basmati rice, picked over

3 ¾ cups water

2 tablespoons vegetable oil

1 cup finely chopped onion

2 teaspoons cumin seeds

5 black cardamom pods, pounded lightly to break the skin

1 teaspoon salt, or to taste

½ cup seeded and finely diced red bell pepper

½ cup seeded and finely diced yellow bell pepper

2 teaspoons minced garlic

1 cup loosely packed finely chopped cilantro (fresh coriander), soft stems included

4 cups sprouted mung beans

1 teaspoon chaat masala (see page 26) for garnish (optional)

Wash the rice in three to four changes of water, stirring lightly with your fingertips, until the water runs almost clear. Then soak it in the water for 30 minutes or longer.

Heat the oil in a large saucepan over high heat and cook the onion, stirring, until golden, 4 to 5 minutes. Stir in the cumin, cardamom, and salt. Then add the bell peppers, garlic, and cilantro and cook for another minute. Mix in the rice and water and bring to a boil. Reduce the heat to a minimum, cover the pan (partially at first, until the foam subsides, then snugly), and cook until all the water is absorbed, 7 to 10 minutes. Gently fork in the mung beans, cover the pan once again, and cook over low heat until the rice is cooked and the sprouted mung beans have lost their raw taste, 5 to 7 minutes.

Transfer to a serving platter and garnish with the chaat masala. Serve hot or at room temperature with any yogurt raita.

MAKES 8 SERVINGS

NINE JEWEL RICE

NAVRATTAN PULLAO

This definitely is a party dish that elicits rave reviews. *Nav* means "nine," and *rattan* means "jewels." *Navrattan* is a term used in reference to Indian jewelry, but in this instance can appropriately be used to describe this treasure, which is loaded with health-promoting ingredients and delicious nuts.

Serve it as a one-dish meal with a yogurt on the side or pair it with a chicken or lamb entrée.

1 ½ cups basmati rice, picked over
2 ⅔ cups water
3 tablespoons vegetable oil
½ cup blanched almonds, split into halves
½ cup raw pistachios
½ cup cashews, split into halves
½ cup golden raisins
1 cup finely chopped onion
2 teaspoons finely chopped garlic
1 tablespoon peeled and finely chopped fresh ginger
8 green cardamom pods, pounded lightly to break the skin
One 3-inch stick cinnamon
2 teaspoons black peppercorns, or to taste (optional)
1 cup 1-inch or smaller cauliflower florets
1 cup 1-inch or smaller broccoli florets
1 cup seeded and finely diced red bell pepper
1 cup ½-inch pieces yellow squash
½ cup fresh or frozen peas
1 ½ teaspoons salt, or to taste

Wash the rice in three to four changes of water, stirring lightly with your fingertips, until the water runs almost clear. Then soak it in the water for at least 30 minutes or longer.

Heat the oil in a large nonstick saucepan over high heat and cook the nuts, stirring, until lightly golden, 1 to 2 minutes. Remove to paper towels to drain. Add the raisins and cook until they start to puff up, 30 to 45 seconds, then remove to paper towels also. Set aside for garnish.

In the same oil over moderately high heat, cook, stirring, the onion, garlic, ginger, cardamom, cinnamon, and peppercorns until the onion turns golden, 3 to 4 minutes. Stir in the vegetables and cook, stirring, for another 2 minutes. Then add the rice and water. Stir in the salt and bring to a boil over high heat. Reduce the heat to a minimum, cover the pan (partially at first, until the foam subsides, then snugly), and cook the rice until done, 10 to 15 minutes.

Transfer the rice to a serving platter. Garnish with the sautéed nuts and raisins and serve with Yogurt Mint Chutney (see page 88) or any yogurt raita (page 147). This dish is best when served fresh.

MAKES 8 SERVINGS

Fragrant Vegetable Rice

SABZ BIRYANI

The term *biryani* is used to define fancy rice preparations that form the focal point of the dinner table. They are traditionally served as one-dish meals with flavor-laden mint- or cilantro-based chutneys and plain yogurt. Occasionally, they are included on a festive menu. Whichever way they are presented, they are always a standout.

Although preparation of this highly elaborate dish involves cooking the vegetables and rice separately and layering them together in a dish, it can be assembled 8 to 10 hours in advance. Simply reheat in the oven or in the microwave and serve.

FOR THE VEGETABLES
2 tablespoons vegetable oil
1 medium-size onion, cut in half lengthwise and thinly sliced
1 teaspoon minced garlic
1 tablespoon peeled and minced fresh ginger
½ cup firmly packed finely chopped cilantro (fresh coriander), soft stems included
1 teaspoon garam masala (see page 23)
1 tablespoon ground coriander
1 teaspoon ground cumin
1 teaspoon ground cayenne pepper, or to taste (optional)
1 teaspoon salt, or to taste
5 cups mixed fresh vegetables, cut into 1-inch pieces (broccoli, cauliflower, carrots, beans, mushrooms, colorful bell peppers, and peas)

FOR THE RICE
2 ½ cups basmati rice, picked over
4 ¾ cups water
1 tablespoon vegetable oil
5 black cardamom pods, pounded lightly to break the skin
1 teaspoon black peppercorns (optional)
One 3-inch stick cinnamon
1 ½ teaspoons cumin seeds
1 teaspoon salt, or to taste

½ teaspoon garam masala for garnish

Heat the oil in a large skillet or saucepan over high heat and cook the onion, stirring, until golden, 4 to 5 minutes. Stir in the garlic, ginger, and cilantro, then add the garam masala, coriander, cumin, cayenne, and salt. Stir in the vegetables. Cover and cook for 2 to 3 minutes over high heat, then reduce the heat to medium and continue to cook until the vegetables are tender-crisp, 4 to 5 minutes. Stir occasionally.

Wash the rice in 3 to 4 changes of water, stirring lightly with your fingertips, until the water runs almost clear. Then soak it in the water for 30 minutes or longer.

Heat the oil in a large nonstick saucepan over high heat and cook the cardamom, peppercorns, cinnamon, and cumin, stirring, until they sizzle, 30 to 40 seconds. Add the salt, stir in the rice and water, and bring to a boil. Reduce the heat to a minimum, cover the pan (partially at first, until the foam subsides, then snugly), and cook the rice until all the water is absorbed, 5 to 7 minutes. Remove from the heat.

Preheat the oven to 300° F. Line a large ovenproof casserole with a 1-inch layer of the rice and top with a layer of cooked vegetables. Cover with rice and repeat until all the vegetables and rice are used up. Cover the casserole and bake for 10 to 15 minutes. (The rice can stay in the oven for 30 to 40 minutes if need be.)

Garnish with the garam masala and serve as a main dish or as a part of a festive menu.

MAKES 8 SERVINGS

RICE WITH CURRIED RED POTATOES

CHOTÉ LAL ALU KI BIRYANI

This combination dish of curried potatoes and rice is a perfect example of how various curries and rice can be combined to create one-dish meals. Rice cooked in the curry sauce (from the potatoes) takes on a wonderful fragrance. The cooked potatoes can also be served separately as a main dish.

2 cups basmati rice, picked over
4 ½ to 4 ¾ cups water
3 tablespoons vegetable oil
1 cup finely chopped onion
1 tablespoon peeled and minced fresh ginger
1 teaspoon minced garlic
1 cup finely chopped fresh tomatoes
4 ½ teaspoons curry powder (see page 21)

1 ½ teaspoons salt, or to taste
½ cup nonfat plain yogurt, whisked until smooth
12 to 15 baby new red potatoes, washed and cut in half
1 teaspoon dried fenugreek leaves (see page 17)
¼ cup finely chopped cilantro (fresh coriander) for garnish

Wash the rice in three to four changes of water, stirring lightly with your fingertips, until the water runs almost clear. Soak it in 3 cups of the water for 30 minutes or longer.

Heat the oil in a large nonstick saucepan over high heat and cook the onion, stirring, until it turns medium brown, 5 to 7 minutes. Add the ginger, garlic, and tomatoes and cook, stirring occasionally, for 3 to 4 minutes. Stir in the curry powder and 1 teaspoon of the salt, then add the yogurt a little at a time to prevent it from curdling. Cook, stirring, for 1 minute, then add the potatoes. Reduce the heat to low, cover the pan, and cook, stirring occasionally, for 7 to 10 minutes. (If the potatoes get stuck to the bottom of the pan, add ¼ cup water.)

Increase the heat to high, add the remaining 1 ½ cups of water, cover the pan, and cook, stirring occasionally, for 5 to 7 minutes. Reduce the heat to medium-low and cook until the potatoes are soft and the gravy is very thick, 10 to 12 minutes. Remove the cooked potatoes to a bowl, leaving the curry sauce in the pan.

Add the rice and its water to the pan with the curry sauce, stir in the remaining salt and the fenugreek, and bring to a boil over high heat. Reduce the heat to a minimum, cover the pan (partially at first, until the foam subsides, then snugly), and cook until the rice is almost done, 7 to 10 minutes. Uncover the pan, stir the rice lightly with the back of a ladle, and carefully mix in the cooked potatoes. Cover the pan again and cook the rice and potatoes for another 5 minutes.

Transfer to a serving platter, garnish with the chopped cilantro, and serve hot.

MAKES 8 SERVINGS

SOFT RICE WITH LENTILS

KHITCHREE

You've spent a whole day at an amusement park, and all you've eaten is junk food. Your stomach is complaining, and what you want is a light, home-cooked dish that will soothe it. Try making this easy to digest (and cook), creamy rice preparation. This dish has a reputation for providing the body with the right nutrients, especially when it is served with plain yogurt and Sun-Cooked Lime Pickle (see page 102).

Yellow mung beans and pink lentils also work well in this recipe.

2 cups basmati rice, picked over
1 cup dried split green mung beans (see page 254), picked over
10 cups water
4 black cardamom pods, pounded lightly to break the skin
1 teaspoon black peppercorns
1 teaspoon salt, or to taste

FOR THE TARKA TOPPING
3 tablespoons clarified butter (see page 30) or vegetable oil
1 tablespoon cumin seeds

Wash the rice in three to four changes of water, stirring lightly with your fingertips, until the water runs almost clear. Wash the mung beans.

Place all the ingredients in a pressure cooker. Secure the lid and cook over high heat for 1 minute after the pressure regulator starts rocking. Remove from the heat and let the pressure drop by itself, 10 to 15 minutes. Open the lid, stir the rice a few times to make it creamy, then transfer it to a serving bowl. Alternatively, cook in a large saucepan over high heat until it boils. Reduce the heat to medium, cover the pan (partially at first, until the foam subsides, then snugly), and cook, stirring occasionally, until it becomes soft and creamy, 30 to 40 minutes.

Heat the butter in a small saucepan over moderately high heat and fry the cumin seeds until they sizzle, 10 seconds. Immediately pour the *tarka* over the hot *khitchree* and serve. *Khitchree* can be made 2 to 3 days ahead of time. It will thicken as it cools, and additional water will be required to reheat it.

MAKES 8 SERVINGS

SOFT RICE WITH SUN-DRIED LENTIL NUGGETS

BADIAN VALI KHITCHREE

My mother reserves this recipe for our immediate family. The beauty of it is that it looks more like a curry (a dish with gravy) than a rice preparation and can sometimes be presented as such. For maximum flavor, make this dish as spicy-hot as you can tolerate.

3 tablespoons vegetable oil

Eighteen to twenty 1-inch Sun-Dried Urad Bean Nuggets (see page 277)

One 1 ½-inch piece fresh ginger, peeled and cut into julienne strips

½ cup finely chopped onion

2 tablespoons ground coriander

1 teaspoon coarsely ground black pepper, or to taste (optional)

¾ teaspoon turmeric

1 ½ teaspoons salt, or to taste

1 teaspoon ground cayenne pepper (optional)

2 cups basmati rice, picked over and washed in several changes of water until the water runs almost clear

5 serrano peppers, whole or chopped (optional)

11 cups water

1 cup loosely packed finely chopped cilantro (fresh coriander), soft stems included

1 teaspoon garam masala (see page 23) for garnish

Heat 1 ½ tablespoons of the oil in a large saucepan over moderately high heat and cook the nuggets, stirring, until they turn brown, 2 to 3 minutes. Remove to a small bowl and set aside until needed.

Increase the heat to high and add the remaining oil to the same pan and cook the ginger, stirring, for 1 minute, then add the onion. Cook, stirring, until it turns golden, 2 to 3 minutes. Stir in the coriander, black pepper, turmeric, salt, and cayenne, then add the rice, serrano peppers, and water.

Bring to a boil, uncovered, and continue to boil for 3 to 4 minutes. Cover the pan (partially at first, until the foam subsides, then snugly), reduce the heat to medium-low, and cook, stirring often until the rice is soft and creamy, 20 to 25 minutes.

Transfer to a serving casserole, stir in the chopped cilantro, garnish with the garam masala, and serve hot with plain yogurt on the side.

MAKES 8 SERVINGS

VARIATION: This is a perfect recipe to cook in a pressure cooker. Add 10 cups water, and cook for 1 to 1 ½ minutes after the pressure regulator starts rocking. Let the pressure drop by itself, then open the lid.

SAVORY POUNDED RICE PILAF

POOHA

Pounded rice is made by pounding partially cooked grains of husked rice until they look like tiny oblong flakes with ragged edges. They soften very quickly and should be stirred very gently to avoid breaking them. Two varieties (thick and thin) of pounded rice are available in Indian markets. This recipe uses the thick kind.

This dish is served as a savory snack or a light meal. Top with toasted peanut or almond slivers to add a welcome crunch.

3 cups thick pounded rice
3 tablespoons vegetable oil
2 teaspoons black mustard seeds
½ teaspoon asafetida (see page 13)
5 serrano peppers, skin punctured to prevent bursting, or cut in half lengthwise
1 small onion, cut in half lengthwise and thinly sliced
2 ½ cups frozen peas, thawed
4 small potatoes, boiled until tender, peeled, and cut into wedges
½ teaspoon turmeric
1 tablespoon ground coriander
1 ½ teaspoons salt, or to taste
1 cup loosely packed finely chopped cilantro (fresh coriander), soft stems included
½ cup fresh lime or lemon juice, or to taste
Lime or lemon slices for garnish

Place the pounded rice in a sieve and wash it under running water. Then soak it (while still in the sieve) in a large bowl of water for about 2 minutes. Drain well and set aside until needed.

Heat the oil in a large nonstick skillet over moderately high heat for at least 1 minute. Add the mustard seeds and fry, shaking the skillet, until they start to pop, 30 seconds. (Cover the skillet when they pop to prevent them from flying out.) When the popping subsides, add the asafetida, peppers, and onion and cook, stirring, until the onion turns golden, 3 to 4 minutes. Add the peas and potatoes and cook, stirring as necessary with a spatula, until the potatoes turn golden, 3 to 4 minutes, then mix in the turmeric, coriander, and salt.

Add the pounded rice and stir gently to mix. Cover and cook over medium-low heat until fluffy and yellow, 4 to 5 minutes. Stir occasionally.

Stir in the cilantro and lime juice. Transfer to a platter, garnish with lemon slices, and serve hot, cold, or at room temperature. This savory dish is popularly served as a snack. If you want to present it as a salad, serve it on a bed of shredded red oak or bronze leaf lettuce that has been spiked up with lime juice, salt, and black or cayenne pepper.

MAKES 8 SERVINGS

RICE WITH PEANUTS AND LEMON JUICE

MOONGPHALLI AUR NIMBOO KE CHAVAL

I first tasted this dish at a picnic luncheon. It was made by my friend Prabha, who is from southern India. The uncommon spice combinations in this slightly tangy preparation tasted divine, and I requested the recipe from her. She willingly parted with it, and advised me to make it with leftover steamed rice.

This dish can be an innovative addition to your picnic list. Chop the serrano peppers if you wish to make it peppery-hot.

3 tablespoons peanut oil
1 tablespoon black mustard seeds
½ teaspoon asafetida (see page 13)
1 teaspoon turmeric
6 serrano peppers, skin punctured to prevent them from bursting
½ cup shelled raw peanuts (with skin)
½ cup blanched almond slivers
½ cup shelled pistachios
6 cups Steamed Basmati Rice (see page 286)
1 teaspoon salt, or to taste
1 cup loosely packed chopped cilantro (fresh coriander), soft stems included
½ cup fresh lemon juice, or to taste

Heat the oil in a large nonstick saucepan over high heat and fry the mustard seeds until they pop, about 30 to 40 seconds. (Cover the pan as soon as you add them or the seeds will fly out.) When the popping subsides, stir in the asafetida, turmeric, and peppers, then add the nuts and cook, stirring, until they turn golden, 1 to 2 minutes. Add the steamed rice and salt and stir gently to mix with the nuts. Reduce the heat to low, add the cilantro and lemon juice, cover the pan, and cook 3 to 4 minutes longer to blend the flavors.

Transfer to a serving platter and serve by itself or with any Indian vegetable dish. It can be served hot or at room temperature.

MAKES 8 SERVINGS

WILD RICE WITH CARDAMOM PODS AND BAY LEAVES

ILLAICHI VALÉ KALÉ CHAVAL

Though wild rice is not a part of traditional Indian cuisine, I see no reason why it should remain that way. Its "wild" aroma is very receptive to Indian seasonings and its texture lends a firm bite to the customary soft-cooked Indian foods.

2 cups wild rice, picked over
5 cups water
1 tablespoon vegetable oil or clarified butter (see page 30)
1 teaspoon finely chopped garlic
4 to 6 bay leaves (preferably fresh), crushed
5 black cardamom pods, pounded lightly to break the skin
One 3-inch stick cinnamon
¾ teaspoon salt, or to taste
¼ cup finely sliced scallion greens for garnish
¼ cup loosely packed finely chopped cilantro (fresh coriander) for garnish

Wash the rice in three to four changes of water, stirring gently with your fingertips, until the water runs almost clear. Then soak it in the water for 1 to 2 hours. Drain and save the water.

Heat the oil in a medium-size nonstick saucepan over moderately high heat and cook the garlic, bay leaves, cardamom, and cinnamon, stirring, for about 1 minute. Add the drained rice, stir-fry for 2 to 4 minutes, then add the reserved water and salt. Cover the pot and boil over high heat for 3 to 4 minutes. Turn the heat to medium-low and cook until all the water is absorbed by the rice and it becomes soft, 45 to 50 minutes.

Transfer to a platter, garnish with the scallions and cilantro and serve with any meal.

MAKES 8 SERVINGS

Wild Rice with Capers and Lemon Juice

NIMBOO VALÉ KALÉ CHAVAL

At my request Carolyn Thacker, a prominent cooking teacher in Santa Monica, graciously cooked up this very special recipe. She does admit that this is an unusual combination, but it works very well. Grilled or barbecued chicken are excellent with it. Also good are Barbecued Paneer Cheese and Vegetable Skewers (see page 246) or Stir-Fried Asparagus, Mushrooms, and Yellow Bell Peppers (page 199).

2 ¼ cups water
¾ cup wild rice, picked over
¾ teaspoon minced garlic
2 tablespoons brine-packed capers, rinsed
¼ cup fresh lemon juice
1 tablespoon olive oil
3 tablespoons minced fresh parsley
½ teaspoon salt, or to taste
¼ teaspoon freshly ground black pepper, or to taste
Tomato wedges and fresh sprigs parsley for garnish

Place the water in a heavy saucepan and bring it to a boil over high heat. Place the rice in a strainer and wash it thoroughly by running cold water over it. Add it to the boiling water. Reduce the heat to medium-low, cover the pan, and simmer until the rice is cooked to the desired texture, 35 to 50 minutes. Drain any excess liquid.

In a food processor fitted with the metal S-blade, process the garlic, capers, lemon juice, olive oil, and parsley together until smooth. Fold the puree into the rice. Season with the salt and pepper. Let the rice rest for 5 to 10 minutes to blend the flavors. Transfer to a platter, garnish with the tomato wedges and parsley, and serve.

MAKES 4 SERVINGS

Upside-Down Basmati Rice Cake with Crispy Ginger and Onion

CHAVAL KA CHAKKA

This technique is adopted from the Middle Eastern way of making rice. The rice is cooked for a long time over very low heat until the bottom side becomes brown and crusty. As it cooks, the dish assumes the look of a cake. This cake is then inverted onto a platter and served.

To ensure that the rice doesn't stick at the bottom, use a heavy nonstick pan.

2 cups basmati rice, picked over
3 ¾ cups water
3 tablespoons peanut oil
One 1-inch piece fresh ginger, peeled and cut into thin julienne strips
½ small onion, thinly sliced
5 black cardamom pods, pounded lightly to break the skin
1 teaspoon black cumin seeds (see page 16)
¾ teaspoon salt, or to taste

Wash the rice in three to four changes of water, stirring lightly with your fingertips, until the water runs almost clear. Soak it in the water for about 10 minutes.

Heat 2 tablespoons of the oil in a large, heavy nonstick saucepan over moderately high heat, then stir-fry the ginger and onion until brown, 4 to 5 minutes. Drain on paper towels and set aside.

Heat the remaining oil in the same saucepan over moderately high heat and cook the cardamom and cumin, stirring, until they sizzle, 10 seconds. Add the rice and water, then stir in the salt and bring to a boil over high heat. Reduce the heat to a minimum, cover the pan (partially at first, until the foam subsides, then snugly), and cook for 40 to 45 minutes. Do not stir. By the end of this time, the bottom side will be crusty and have developed a rich brown color.

Remove from the heat and set aside for 5 to 15 minutes. Then invert onto a platter as you would an upside-down cake or flan. (If it breaks while turning, patch up the broken spots and cover them with the reserved ginger and onion.) Garnish with the ginger and onion and serve.

MAKES 8 SERVINGS

VARIATION: Garnish with steamed or lightly sautéed vegetables like cauliflower, broccoli, zucchini, summer squash, or shelled peas.

A Basket of Breads

Crunchy or meltingly soft, plain or stuffed, herbed or spiced, griddle-cooked, deep-fried, or baked, Indian flatbreads are loaded with exceptional flavor and mouth-watering ingredients. These highly nutritious breads form the backbone of Indian cuisine. Freshly made and served hot at every meal—breakfast, lunch, or dinner (or any time of the day)—they can be made part of a meal or be a complete meal by themselves. No Indian meal could ever be complete without them.

Flatbreads are simple to make, though some of them may be time-consuming. Most are made with unleavened, stone-ground whole-wheat flour. As a variation, other types of flour are also sometimes used.

Indian breads are authentically made on a 9- to 10-inch *tava*, a heavy and slightly concave cast-iron griddle. (*Tava*s are available in all Indian markets. Purchase one that has a wooden handle.) The shape of the *tava* is ideal for making all types of flatbreads, especially the griddle-fried paranthas. It actually allows you to use the minimum amount of oil while frying. (A pancake griddle or a skillet can replace the *tava*, but please be careful when using the skillet. The raised edge may burn your forearm if you accidentally touch it.)

Indian breads should authentically be made fresh at every meal, but today's lifestyle often does not allow us this luxury. So we have to find a way of making fresh breads without too much effort. To do this I often cook the breads lightly on both sides, spread them individually on cookie sheets (or any flat surface) to cool them completely, and stack them in plastic zipper bags. They stay fresh in the refrigerator for up to 5 days or in the freezer for up to 2 months.

To finish cooking, place them on an ungreased cookie sheet in a single layer and cook in the oven broiler, 4 to 5 inches from the heat. Or place each one on a hot *tava* and finish cooking. Turn them once or twice to ensure even cooking and to prevent them from burning. (It takes less than 1 ½ minutes to finish cooking one batch.) Brush the top surface with clarified butter (see page 30) or butter and serve.

Leftover breads can be reheated under the broiler, in a toaster, or on a *tava*. Never heat the breads in a microwave oven because they will become tough and chewy. They may be stacked, wrapped in aluminum foil, and reheated in a preheated 400° F oven, but the breads will not have the freshly cooked look.

About Whole-Wheat Flour

Whole-wheat flour is flour made by grinding the whole wheat kernel (including the bran, germ, and endosperm). A staple in most of northern India, whole-wheat flour is also very popular in the rest of India. It is commonly proclaimed by all in India that whole-wheat flour (*atta*) has a tremendous amount of strength (*takat*), and should be eaten every day. Today's modern nutritional analysis confirms what the Indians have always known instinctively—that whole-wheat flour is loaded with energy-promoting complex carbohydrates, protein, some vitamins, and minerals.

Wheat is the primary sustenance for a majority of the poor working-class population, who live almost solely on a diet consisting of whole-wheat breads, lentils, and raw onion from which the pungent juice has been extracted.

The whole-wheat flour used for making breads in India is very different from the packaged commercial whole-wheat flour available in American supermarkets. Made from the whole kernel of the light-colored, high-gluten "hard" wheat variety, it is ground in a *chakki*, a grinding mill made of two heavy rotating stones, one on top of the other. When ground finely, it looks similar to the western "pastry" flour, but is actually very different; pastry flour is made from the light-colored, low-gluten soft wheat. Although it can be used to make some Indian breads, it is not the best substitute.

American whole-wheat flour, made from a soft red wheat variety, contains less gluten than the Indian variety, is much too coarse, and, again, is not best suited for making Indian breads. It can be used, however, by adding one part all-purpose flour to two parts whole-wheat flour; unavoidably, though, breads made this way will tend to be heavier.

Whole-wheat flour sold in Indian markets as *atta* or chapati flour is the best choice. Made with stone-ground durum wheat, this flour is most similar to the flour available in India. A fact to remember about whole wheat is that the harder the wheat, the higher its protein (gluten) to starch ratio. This is what gives the flour its strength and elasticity. Durum wheat is the hardest white wheat of all and this is what Indians prefer above all others.

Basic Whole-Wheat Dough

GUNDHA HUA ATTA

The versatility of this basic dough knows no limits. It can used to make the everyday light chapatis or the fancier griddle-fried, plain, spiced, or stuffed paranthas.

This dough can be made up to 2 days in advance and stored in an airtight container in the refrigerator. I often make a large amount at one time, let it rest for about 1 hour, and then divide it into smaller batches and freeze it. Frozen dough needs to be thawed at room temperature before it can be used. Using the microwave to thaw frozen dough is not a good idea, because parts of it sometimes start to cook and that makes the dough lumpy and unusable.

4 cups stone-ground durum whole-wheat flour
About 1 ⅔ cups water

To make the dough in a food processor: Place the flour in a food processor fitted with the metal S-blade. Turn the machine on, pour the water in a thin stream through the feed tube, and continue to process until it gathers into a ball. Continue to process until the sides of the bowl look clean, 20 to 30 seconds. (Add 1 or 2 tablespoons extra flour if the dough sticks to the sides of the work bowl, or a touch of water if the dough looks too hard.) Stop the machine, remove the dough to a bowl, cover, and let rest for 1 to 4 hours. (If keeping for a longer period, refrigerate it.)

To make by hand: Place the flour in a bowl and add the water a little at a time, stirring with your fingers until it starts to gather. Add more water as necessary to make a medium-firm dough that does not stick to your fingers. (If the dough is too firm, the bread made from it will be hard; if it is too soft, it will stick to your fingers and you will not be able to use it.) Cover and let it rest for 1 to 4 hours.

Use or bake as directed in the recipes that follow.

MAKES 20 TO 25 CHAPATIS OR 16 TO 18 PARANTHAS

Unleavened Whole-Wheat Flatbread

CHAPATI, ROTI, OR PHULKA

Chapatis are unleavened flatbreads, very similar to Mexican tortillas. They are made with stone-ground whole-wheat flour and water. Freshly made chapatis are perfect round discs, grilled on a concave cast-iron griddle called a *tava* (see page 317 and below). No oil or shortening is used in the actual preparation, though they may be topped with a dollop of home-churned butter or clarified butter (see page 30) before they are served.

A staple in all north Indian households, chapatis are made fresh for every meal; there is always one person in the kitchen making them. They are brought to the table, one at a time, for each member of the family to enjoy while they are still hot and puffy. The highlight of my paternal grandmother's (Mataji) day was to make these for us.

1 recipe Basic Whole-Wheat Dough (see page 319)
3 to 4 tablespoons melted regular or clarified butter (see page 30)
1 cup whole-wheat flour for dusting

Heat a *tava* or griddle over moderately high heat. The *tava* is ready when a sprinkling of dry whole-wheat flour immediately turns brown (not black; if that happens, cool the *tava* before using it.)

While the *tava* is heating, lightly oil your hands with some of the butter (to prevent the dough from sticking) and divide the dough into 20 to 25 round balls. Cover and set aside. Working with each ball separately, flatten it with your fingertips, coat with some of the flour, and roll into a 6- to 7-inch circle of uniform thickness. (While rolling, if the dough sticks to the surface, dust with more flour. The rolling can be done on a lightly floured surface also.)

Place the rolled chapati on the hot *tava* and turn it over when it is slightly cooked and "dotted" with tiny golden spots on the bottom side. When the second side is covered with larger brown dots, turn it over once again. Press the top surface lightly with a dishcloth (crumpled into a ball) or a pot holder and guide the air to puff the chapati. (When you turn the chapati over the second time, it starts to puff up at certain points. Press lightly on these puffed areas and guide the air to the parts that have not puffed up.) Do not be disappointed if your initial attempts at puffing the chapatis are unsuccessful; their taste and texture will still be wonderful.

Check to see if edges are slightly golden, then remove the chapati to a sheet of aluminum foil. Brush with butter and serve hot with any meal.

Chapatis can be cooked, stacked one on top of the other, and kept in a warm oven if they are to be eaten within an hour or two. They can also be stored in the refrigerator for up to 5 days and in the freezer for as long as 2 months.

Allow at least two to three per person.

MAKES 20 TO 25 CHAPATIS

CHAPATI ROLLS WITH BROWN SUGAR

MITHI SHAKKAR KI ROTI

Shakkar rolls (the Indian version of crepe desserts) are often served as a quick and spontaneous dessert after the main meal is over. *Shakkar* is a granular, unrefined, soft light brown sugar made from sugarcane that is available in Indian markets. These rolls are enjoyed in all Punjabi households, mostly in the cold winter months when fresh *shakkar* and *gur* (solid, unrefined, dark brown sugar) flood the market. *Shakkar* and *gur* are generally believed to warm the body and are used extensively to make various paranthas and desserts that are popular only in the winter months.

½ recipe Basic Whole-Wheat Dough (see page 319)
¼ cup whipped butter
1 cup firmly packed Indian brown sugar (shakkar)

Divide the dough into 10 to 12 round balls and make the chapatis according to directions on page 320.

Working with each chapati as it gets made, top with 1 teaspoon of the whipped butter, then place 1 to 2 tablespoons of the *shakkar* over it.

The butter melts upon contact with the hot chapati, and the soft *shakkar* soaks up all this melted butter while still maintaining its soft, granular texture. Roll the chapati quickly and serve while it is still hot.

MAKES 10 ROLLS

GRIDDLE-FRIED BREAD

PARANTHA OR PARATHA

The word *parantha* refers to all types of leavened or unleavened flatbreads that are griddle-fried. Paranthas made in the *tandoor*—a cylindrical clay oven—appear later in this chapter. Though paranthas are made mostly with whole-wheat flour, other flours like barley (*jau*), millet (*bajra*), corn (*makki*), garbanzo bean (*besan*), all-purpose (*maida*), and semolina (*sooji*) can also be used.

There are five broad categories of paranthas, though there is a certain amount of overlap in all of them. What differentiates them are the spices, herbs, and vegetables used and their rolling techniques. They are:

1. Plain layered, with emphasis on creating layers while rolling.
2. Layered with herbs and/or spices, the paranthas being seasoned as you layer them.
3. Flaky, with some sort of oil or shortening, seasonings, and greens or cooked vegetables added to the flour before making the dough.
4. The dough is enriched, flaky, and layered.
5. The dough is rolled and stuffed with an array of cooked or raw vegetables.

ON MAKING PARANTHA DOUGH

The dough for paranthas can be made in a food processor or manually. In most of my recipes I have used the food processor. The only time I make an exception is when the finished paranthas demand a crunch or a fleck of color.

ON ROLLING THE PARANTHA

Rolling paranthas is an art in itself. They can be made into triangles, squares, or rounds. Triangles and squares are relatively easy to make; round paranthas can be made in a variety of ways.

Before you start to roll out and cook the paranthas, get out a rolling pin, a small flat bowl filled with whole-wheat flour, 3 to 4 tablespoons clarified butter (see page 30) or vegetable oil in a small bowl, and a basting brush.

TO MAKE A TRIANGLE, divide the dough into the required number of balls. Working with each ball separately, flatten into a disc with your fingertips, coat with flour, and roll it into a 5- to 6-inch circle. Brush the top surface lightly with oil, sprinkle on the spices, herbs, or vegetables, if you are using them, and fold in half, forming a semicircle. Brush the top of the semicircle with oil and fold in half once again, forming a triangle. Flatten this triangle into a larger triangle with your fingertips, coat it with flour, and roll it out into a 6- to 7-inch triangle, taking care to maintain its shape.

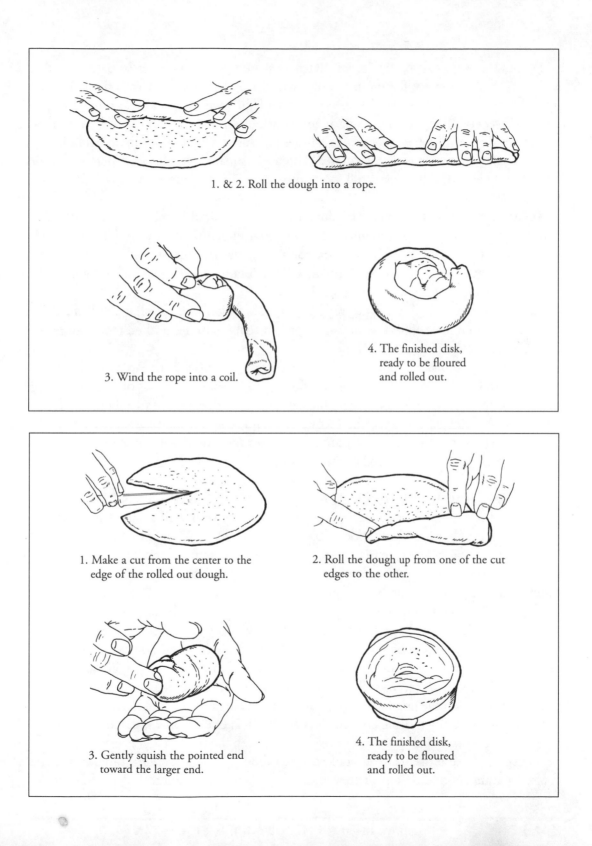

1. & 2. Roll the dough into a rope.

3. Wind the rope into a coil.

4. The finished disk, ready to be floured and rolled out.

1. Make a cut from the center to the edge of the rolled out dough.

2. Roll the dough up from one of the cut edges to the other.

3. Gently squish the pointed end toward the larger end.

4. The finished disk, ready to be floured and rolled out.

TO MAKE A SQUARE, divide the dough into the required number of balls. Working with each ball separately, flatten into a disk with your fingertips, coat with flour, and roll into a 5- to 6-inch circle. Brush the top surface lightly with oil, sprinkle on the spices, herbs, or vegetables, if you are using them, and fold the top and bottom edges into the center so they overlap one another. Brush the top surface with oil again and fold it into three parts again, making a small square. Flatten this square into a larger square with your fingertips, coat it with flour, and roll it out into a 6- to 7-inch square, taking care to maintain its shape.

TO MAKE A CIRCLE, divide the dough into the required number of balls. Working with each ball separately, flatten into a disc with your fingertips, coat with flour, and roll it into a 5- to 6-inch circle. Brush the top surface lightly with oil, sprinkle on the spices, herbs, or vegetables, if you are using them, and roll it into a rope 7 to 8 inches long and ½ inch in diameter. Brush the rope with oil.

Starting from one end, wind the rope in a spiral fashion into a coil, with all the sides touching. Flatten this coil with your fingertips and coat it with flour, then roll it out into a 6- to 7-inch circle.

Another way to make a round is to roll the dough out into a 5- to 6-inch circle. Brush the top with oil, then sprinkle 1 teaspoon flour (and any spices, herbs, or vegetables you may be using) over it. Make a cut from the center to the edge, then start rolling the dough up from the cut edge, ending at the second edge, forming a cone. Brush the cone lightly with oil, then pick it up and squish the pointy end toward the circular side to form a disc. Coat this disc with flour, then roll it into a 6- to 7-inch circle again.

ON COOKING AND GRIDDLE-FRYING PARANTHAS

Heat a *tava* or griddle over moderately high heat until a sprinkling of flour immediately turns brown (not black; if that happens, cool the *tava* slightly). Wipe off the browned flour.

While the *tava* is heating, lightly oil your hands with vegetable oil, melted butter, or clarified butter (see page 30) to prevent the dough from sticking to them, and divide the dough into the required number of round balls. Cover and set aside. Working with each ball separately, roll into a triangle, square, or round according to the above instructions.

Place the rolled parantha on the hot *tava*. Turn it over when it is slightly cooked and dotted with tiny golden spots on the bottom side. When the second side is covered with larger brown dots, turn it over and brush lightly with oil. Turn it over once again and fry the oiled side for about 30 seconds. Similarly, baste and fry the second side for about 30 seconds. Remove from the griddle and serve hot with any meal.

While one parantha is being cooked, prepare the next one. Keep a watch on both at the same time. This will save you a lot of time and will keep the rhythm going.

All types of paranthas can be cooked a few hours prior to serving time. Stack the cooked paranthas one on top of the other, wrap them in aluminum foil, and set aside.

Place in a preheated 350° F oven for 15 to 30 minutes to reheat the whole stack or place on a cookie sheet in a single layer and reheat 4 to 5 inches under the broiler for less than 1 minute. (This method gives the best results.)

Like the chapatis, paranthas can also be partially cooked, cooled, and frozen for 2 to 3 months (see introduction on page 319).

PLAIN LAYERED AND GRIDDLE-FRIED BREAD

LACHEDAR SAADA PARANTHA

Lachedar means "containing layers." This is the simplest and the most basic way of making paranthas. Starting with the basic flour-and-water dough, it is rolled into a triangle, square, or round, then rolled out again. This is then cooked and fried lightly on a griddle.

  1 recipe Basic Whole-Wheat Dough (see page 319)
  1 cup stone-ground whole-wheat flour for dusting
  ⅓ cup vegetable oil or melted regular or clarified butter (see page 30)

Heat a *tava*, pancake griddle, or skillet over moderately high heat until a sprinkling of flour immediately turns brown (if it turns black, let the *tava* cool down). Wipe off the browned flour.

While the *tava* is heating, lightly oil your hands to prevent the dough from sticking to them and divide the dough into sixteen to eighteen 1 ½-inch round balls. Cover and set aside. Working with each ball separately, roll into a triangle, square, or round according to the instructions on page 322.

Place on the hot *tava* and cook according to the directions on page 324.

MAKES 16 TO 18 PLAIN PARANTHAS

LAYERED BREAD WITH FRAGRANT SPICES

LACHEDAR MASALA PARANTHA

In this parantha, spices are added as the rolled dough is folded. To further enhance their flavor and visual appeal, I often sprinkle ground dried mint, basil, or dried fenugreek leaves over them while they are still hot.

These paranthas are a treat just by themselves or with mango pickle, Diced Potatoes with Onion and Tomatoes (see page 194), or scrambled eggs flavored with scallion and cilantro.

1 recipe Basic Whole-Wheat Dough (see page 319)
1 cup whole-wheat flour for dusting
⅓ cup oil or melted regular or clarified butter (see page 30)
2 to 3 teaspoons carom seeds (see page 14)
½ to 2 tablespoons ground dried mint leaves, or to taste
Salt and freshly ground black pepper to taste

Place the *tava* over moderately high heat and heat until a sprinkling of flour immediately turns brown (if it turns black, let the *tava* cool down). Wipe off the browned flour.

While the *tava* is heating, lightly oil your hands (to prevent the dough from sticking to them) and divide the dough into sixteen to eighteen 1 ½-inch round balls. Cover and set aside. Working with each ball separately, coat with flour and roll it into a 5- to 6-inch circle. Brush with oil and sprinkle each with ⅛ teaspoon of the carom seeds, ¼ teaspoon of the mint, and salt and pepper. Fold and roll into a triangle, square, or round according to the instructions on pages 322–324.

Place on the hot *tava* and cook according to the directions on page 324. Sprinkle some mint on the hot paranthas and serve.

MAKES 16 TO 18 PARANTHAS

VARIATIONS: Instead of carom seeds and dried mint, try using different spice and herb combinations like cumin and dried fenugreek, fennel and dried basil, garam masala (see page 23) and dried parsley, paprika and dill weed, celery seeds and dried oregano.

LAYERED BREAD WITH AROMATIC HERBS

LACHEDAR JADI BUTIYON KA PARANTHA

These paranthas are a major variation of the Plain Layered and Griddle-Fried Bread. Here we use 1 to 2 tablespoons of finely chopped fresh herbs and flavorful greens such as cilantro, mint, fenugreek, basil, dill, parsley, watercress, scallion, or chives. These herbs contribute specks of attractive green color along with flavor to these outstanding paranthas. Fresh herbs impart a different aroma each time, depending on how they have been used (individually or in combination). They also add a touch of moisture, which makes the paranthas even softer.

After brushing the top surface of the rolled dough with oil, sprinkle with any combination of the above-mentioned herbs, in the place of or with some spices. Minced peeled ginger, garlic, salt, and pepper also reinforce these flavor accents.

A light sprinkling of dried mint, basil, or dried fenugreek leaves over the cooked paranthas further enhances the flavor and visual appeal of these paranthas. This step is especially effective if you serve them hot, and one at a time, as they cook.

These paranthas are delicious alone or with plain homemade yogurt. They are excellent as a picnic food and in packed lunches particularly when paired with Pineapple or Mango Chutney (see pages 96–97) or Paneer Cheese with Tomatoes and Onion (page 239).

DOUGH-ENRICHED AND GRIDDLE-FRIED FLAKY BREAD

KHASTA PARANTHA

Khasta literally means "flaky" or "crumbly." These crispy, griddle-fried unleavened paranthas are made with whole-wheat flour that is first enriched with clarified butter, butter, or oil (much like pastry is) and various spice and herb combinations, or with raw or cooked greens, vegetables, lentils, and beans. To this is added some sort of flavorful liquid (such as yogurt, milk, buttermilk, or whey) or water to make the dough. (The more liberal you are with the butter, the flakier the bread will be.)

In my recipes I have tried very hard to use the minimum amount of clarified butter without making any compromises on taste, texture, and flavor. Serve these paranthas plain or with a side serving of spicy yogurt or vegetables. To serve as a finger food, place ½ cup or more cooked vegetables in the center and fold them over to make Indian-style sandwiches. Almost any "dry" type of vegetable dish goes well with them. Try Oval Eggplant with Diced Potatoes (see page 164), Fresh Peas with Sautéed Onion (page 183), or Lotus Root (page 204).

There is an infinite number of paranthas that can be made this way. The following are just a few examples.

FRESH SPINACH BREAD

SAAG KA PARANTHA

Green in color, this griddle-fried flatbread, made with pureed raw spinach and spices, is astonishingly delicious and easy to make.

1 bunch fresh spinach (¾ pound)
2 large cloves garlic, peeled
One 1 ½-inch piece fresh ginger, peeled
1 small onion, cut into 5 to 6 pieces
½ cup firmly packed cilantro (fresh coriander), soft stems included
3 tablespoons melted clarified butter (see page 30) or vegetable oil
1 teaspoon carom seeds (see page 14)
1 teaspoon garam masala (see page 23)
1 teaspoon salt, or to taste
4 cups stone-ground durum whole-wheat flour
1 to 2 tablespoons nonfat plain yogurt (if needed)

Remove the tough stems from the spinach, then wash the leaves and set aside to drain. Do not dry completely.

In a food processor fitted with the metal S-blade, process the garlic, ginger, onion, and cilantro until smooth. Add the spinach a little at a time and process (stopping to mix a few times) until the spinach is reduced to a smooth puree. Add the butter, carom seeds, garam masala, and salt, and process for 30 seconds. Add the flour and process until the dough gathers into a smooth ball and the sides of the work bowl look clean. (You may need to add a little yogurt if the dough looks too dry, or add extra flour if the dough is too wet.) Process for about 30 seconds.

Lightly oil your hands and transfer the dough to another bowl. Cover and let it rest for 1 to 4 hours.

Lightly oil your hands and divide the dough into 20 round balls. Cover and set aside. Working with each ball separately, roll into a simple round or a layered triangle, square, or round according to the instructions on page 322.

Cook according to the directions on page 324.

MAKES 20 PARANTHAS

VARIATION: To serve as appetizers, cut into wedges, place in a preheated 350° F oven till slightly crisp, 5 to 7 minutes, and serve with Yogurt with Spinach, Scallions, and Roasted Coriander (see page 153) and Mango Chutney (page 96).

FRESH FENUGREEK BREAD

METHI KA PARANTHA

Similar in color to the spinach bread, these green paranthas have a distinct flavor that it derives wholly from the fresh fenugreek leaves.

2 to 4 serrano peppers, stemmed (optional)
2 to 3 bunches fresh fenugreek leaves (see page 17), washed and trimmed (total
    ¾ pound)
4 cups stone-ground durum whole-wheat flour
3 tablespoons peanut oil
1 teaspoon salt, or to taste
½ to ¾ cup nonfat plain yogurt, whisked until smooth

In a food processor fitted with the metal S-blade, process the serrano peppers until minced. Add the fenugreek leaves and process until smooth (stop to scrape the sides a few times). Add the flour, oil, and salt and process until combined. With the motor running, add the yogurt through the feed tube in a slow stream until everything gathers into a ball and the sides of the work bowl look clean.

Lightly oil your hands, then transfer the dough to a bowl, cover, and let it rest for 1 to 4 hours.

Lightly oil your hands and divide the dough into twenty round balls. Cover and set aside. Working with each ball separately, roll into a simple round or a layered triangle, square, or round according to the instructions on page 322.

Cook according to the directions on page 324.

MAKES 20 PARANTHAS

CRISPY WHOLE-WHEAT GARLIC BREAD

KHASTA LASUN PARANTHA

These crispy, griddle-fried flatbreads, loaded with the goodness of whole-wheat and flavored with fresh garlic and hot serrano peppers, add a welcome zip to ordinary meals. Cut them into wedges and serve as appetizers, or top each wedge with a small steamed cauliflower or broccoli floret or asparagus spear and a drop of Hot Pepper Chutney with Ginger and Lemon Juice (see page 92) or any other chutney of your choice.

6 to 8 large cloves garlic, peeled
10 to 12 medium-size scallion whites
3 to 4 serrano peppers, stemmed (optional)
4 cups stone-ground durum whole-wheat flour
1 teaspoon cracked black peppercorns
1 teaspoon salt, or to taste
¼ cup vegetable oil
About 1 ½ cups buttermilk

In a food processor fitted with the metal S-blade, process the garlic, scallions, and peppers until minced. Add the flour, peppercorns, and salt and process for 15 seconds to mix, then add the oil and buttermilk in a slow, steady stream through the feed tube until the dough gathers into a smooth ball and cleans the sides of the work bowl. Continue to process for another 15 seconds.

Lightly oil your hands and transfer the dough to another bowl. Cover and let it rest for 1 to 4 hours. Lightly oil your hands and divide the dough into 16 to 18 round balls. Cover and set aside. Working with each ball separately, coat with dry flour and roll into a simple 7- to 8-inch round (not in layers) according to the instructions on page 322.

Cook according to the directions on page 324.

MAKES 16 TO 18 PARANTHAS

MINCED ONION AND PEPPER BREAD

PYAZ AUR MIRCH KA PARANTHA

The onion and pepper in this parantha provide a slight crunch and sudden bursts of flavor. To ensure the vegetables retain their crunch, this dough has to be made by hand only.

This is perfect as a light meal with a glass of Baked Mango Drink (see page 38) and slices of fresh tropical melons. Serve a sweet or green chutney on the side.

4 cups stone-ground durum whole-wheat flour
3 tablespoons vegetable oil or melted regular or clarified butter (see page 30)
1 cup minced red onion
½ cup seeded and minced red and/or green bell peppers
1 teaspoon minced jalapeño peppers (optional)
1 teaspoon coarsely ground roasted cumin (see page 16)

1 teaspoon salt, or to taste

½ teaspoon freshly ground black pepper, or to taste

1 ½ cups buttermilk, milk, or water (preferably at room temperature)

Place the flour and oil in a medium-size bowl and rub with your fingers to mix. Then add the onion, peppers, cumin, salt, and black pepper and mix once again with your fingertips. Add half the buttermilk a little at a time, stirring with your fingers until it starts to gather. Add more buttermilk as necessary to make a medium-firm dough. Knead for 1 to 2 minutes, then gather the dough into a ball, cover, and set aside for 1 to 4 hours.

Lightly oil your hands and divide the dough into 16 to 18 round balls. Cover and set aside. Working with each ball separately, coat with dry flour and roll into a simple 7- to 8-inch round (not in layers) according to the instructions on page 322.

Cook according to the directions on page 324.

MAKES 16 PARANTHAS

SEMOLINA AND GARBANZO BEAN BREAD

SOOJI AUR CHANNÉ KA PARANTHA

This is one bread that can be served just by itself, because when used in combination, the semolina, whole wheat, and garbanzo beans form a complete protein.

The use of canned garbanzo beans makes this bread easy. Leftover cooked lentils or beans can also be used. (Adjust the liquid if your leftovers have a sauce.)

2 large cloves garlic, peeled

One 1-inch piece fresh ginger, peeled

1 small onion, cut into 6 wedges

One 15 ½-ounce can garbanzo beans, rinsed and drained

1 teaspoon garam masala (see page 23)

1 teaspoon carom seeds (see page 14)

½ teaspoon salt, or to taste

1 cup fine semolina

1 ¼ cups stone-ground durum whole-wheat flour

½ cup (or more) nonfat plain yogurt, whisked until smooth

½ cup loosely packed finely chopped cilantro (fresh coriander), soft stems included

Ground dried mint leaves for garnish

In a food processor fitted with the metal S-blade, mince the garlic, ginger, and onion together. Scrape the sides of the work bowl with a spatula, add the garbanzo beans, garam masala, and carom seeds and process until smooth. Scrape the sides once again and add the semolina and whole-wheat flour. With the motor running, add the yogurt in a slow stream through the feed tube until the flour gathers into a ball and the sides of the work bowl look clean. (You may need 1 to 2 tablespoons additional yogurt.)

Lightly oil your hands, then remove the dough to a bowl and set aside to rest for 1 to 4 hours.

Lightly oil your hands and divide the dough into 16 to 18 round balls. Cover and set aside. Working with each ball separately, roll into a 7- to 8-inch layered square, triangle or round according to the instructions on page 322. As you roll, place some of the chopped cilantro between the layers for green highlights in a yellow-brown parantha.

Cook according to the directions on page 324.

Sprinkle some dried mint leaves on top and serve with plain homemade yogurt or as part of any meal.

MAKES 16 TO 18 PARANTHAS

Crispy Semolina and Flour Bread

SOOJI AUR MAIDA KA PARANTHA

The texture of this parantha is very different from all the others mentioned so far. Made with all-purpose flour and granular semolina, this bread is crispy on the outside and soft and moist on the inside. The trick is to roll it into a large, ¼-inch-thick circle and then cook it over medium heat until it is covered with golden brown spots and becomes crispy.

One 1-inch piece fresh ginger, peeled and cut into 3 slices
1 small onion, cut into 6 wedges
1 cup unbleached all-purpose flour
1 cup fine semolina
1 tablespoon vegetable oil
1 teaspoon carom seeds (see page 14)
1 teaspoon fennel seeds
½ teaspoon black peppercorns
½ teaspoon salt, or to taste
¼ teaspoon baking soda
¼ cup milk, nonfat plain yogurt, or water (preferably at room temperature)

2 tablespoons finely chopped cilantro (fresh coriander), soft stems included
Ground dried mint for garnish

In a food processor fitted with the metal S-blade, process the ginger and onion together until finely chopped. Add everything but the milk and process until combined. With the motor running, add the milk through the feed tube in a fine stream until the dough gathers into a smooth ball and the sides of the food processor look clean. (Add more milk or flour if too dry or too wet.)

Lightly oil your fingers, remove the dough to a bowl, and let set for 1 to 4 hours.

Lightly oil your hands and divide the dough into four round balls. Cover and set aside. Working with each ball separately, roll into a 7- to 8-inch layered triangle, square, or round according to the instructions on page 322. As you roll, place some of the chopped cilantro between the layers for green highlights in a pale yellow parantha.

Cook according to the directions on page 324.

Sprinkle some dried mint leaves on top, cut each parantha into four wedges, and serve as part of any meal. Cut into smaller pieces and serve as appetizers with Barbecued Eggplant with Onion and Tomatoes (see page 165) or Yogurt with Spinach, Scallions, and Roasted Coriander (page 153).

MAKES 4 PARANTHAS

PUNJABI CORN FLATBREAD

PUNJABI MAKKI KI ROTI

For people who have wheat allergies, this bread provides a welcome alternative. This robust, country-style flatbread, made with stone-ground corn, is the perfect partner to Punjabi Mustard Greens (see page 216). To really enjoy this specialty from the state of Punjab, eat it while it is still hot with a dollop of whipped butter.

Corn flour does not contain much gluten, so the bread cannot be rolled out with a rolling pin. Pure cornbread is traditionally rolled by gently transferring it back and forth between the hands. (This calls for some dexterity, especially if you make them large.)

2 cups yellow cornmeal
1 ½ cups yellow corn flour (this finely ground flour is available in Indian markets)
2 ½ cups boiling water
2 to 3 tablespoons corn oil
Whipped butter (optional)

Place the cornmeal and corn flour in a food processor fitted with the metal S-blade and process until mixed, 20 seconds. With the motor running, add the water in a thin stream through the feed tube until the dough becomes soft and starts to gather into a ball. Stop the motor and stir the flour with a spatula a few times. This dough can be made by hand also. (Heat the water only to a temperature you can tolerate comfortably.)

Heat a *tava* (see page 320), pancake griddle, or skillet over a moderately high flame. Divide the dough into ten to fifteen round balls. Working with each ball separately, flatten into a 4- to 5-inch circle by transferring the dough from one palm to the other, applying very gentle pressure as you go along. Alternatively, place the ball between two sheets of wax paper and spread it outward. (If the roti breaks in the process, just bring the dough together to seal, or add some extra dough and seal.)

Brush the *tava* lightly with oil and place the roti on it. Turn the roti over when it is slightly cooked on the bottom. When the second side is done, brush it with oil and fry until medium brown, about 1 minute. Turn over and fry the other side in the same manner. Serve hot with a dollop of whipped butter.

MAKES 10 TO 15 ROTIYAN

BASIC GRIDDLE-FRIED STUFFED BREAD

BHARA HUA PARANTHA

Stuffed with vegetables, greens, paneer cheese, or minced meats, these griddle-fried flatbreads are in a class by themselves. In India, some vegetables, like potatoes and cauliflower, are popularly used on a daily basis, whereas certain greens, paneer cheese, and cooked lentils are added on special occasions.

Served with plain or spicy homemade yogurt or with a yogurt raita (see page 147), stuffed paranthas can make a meal.

    1 recipe Basic Whole-Wheat Dough (see page 319)
    1 cup whole-wheat flour for dusting
    1 recipe any stuffing of your choice (see pages 335–340)
    ¼ cup vegetable oil or melted regular or clarified butter (see page 30)

Heat a *tava*, pancake griddle, or skillet over moderately high heat until a sprinkling of flour immediately turns brown (if it turns black, let the *tava* cool down). Wipe off the browned flour.

While the *tava* is heating, lightly oil your hands and divide the dough into twenty 1 ½-inch round balls. Cover and set aside. Working with each ball separately, flatten it with your fingertips, coat with flour, and roll it into a 4- to 5-inch circle. Place 2 ½ to 3 tablespoons of stuffing in the center. Bring the edges together, pinch to seal, then shape into a ball once again.

Flatten and coat this stuffed ball with flour and roll it out into a 7- to 8-inch circle of even thickness. Keep turning and dusting the parantha with flour while rolling or it may stick to the rolling surface. If the stuffing has excess moisture, the paranthas may develop tiny holes as you roll them. If that happens, seal the holes by putting a pinch of dry flour on them.

Place the rolled parantha on the hot *tava*. Turn it over when it is slightly cooked and dotted with tiny golden spots on the bottom. When the second side is covered with larger brown dots, turn it over and brush lightly with the oil. Turn it over once again and fry the brushed side for about 30 seconds. Repeat with the other side. Remove from the griddle and serve. They can be served warm or at room temperature.

MAKES 20 STUFFED PARANTHAS

SPICY MASHED POTATO STUFFING

PARANTHÉ MEIN BHARNÉ VALÉ ALU

This versatile stuffing can be used in a variety of ways. Mix in some garbanzo bean flour, shape into balls or disks, and deep-fry to make lovely appetizers; mix in some cheddar cheese, sandwich it between two pieces of bread, and grill in a sandwich grill or a skillet; or use as a stuffing for tomatoes, bell peppers, and zucchini.

7 to 8 large russet potatoes, boiled until tender, peeled, and grated or mashed
2 tablespoons peeled and minced fresh ginger
½ cup firmly packed finely chopped cilantro (fresh coriander), soft stems included
¼ cup finely chopped onion
2 serrano peppers, minced (optional)
2 tablespoons ground coriander
1 tablespoon mango powder (see page 18) or 2 tablespoons fresh lemon juice
2 teaspoons dried fenugreek leaves (see page 17)
1 teaspoon ground cumin
½ teaspoon garam masala (see page 23)
1 ½ teaspoons salt, or to taste

Place everything in a bowl and mix well. This stuffing can be made up to 2 days in advance.

MAKES ENOUGH FILLING FOR 20 PARANTHAS

SPICY CAULIFLOWER STUFFING

PARANTHÉ MEIN BHARNÉ VALI GOBI

This stuffing is wonderful in pooris (see page 340) and Vegetable Turnovers (page 57). Stir-fry with sautéed onion and garlic and serve as a side dish, or add some garbanzo bean flour and deep-fry to make delicious koftas (page 227) or fritters (page 42).

Adding salt to processed cauliflower causes it to sweat. I add whole-wheat flour to counter this effect and make the stuffing easier to use.

One 1-inch piece fresh ginger, peeled
2 serrano peppers, stemmed (optional)
½ cup firmly packed cilantro (fresh coriander), soft stems included
1 large cauliflower, cut into small pieces, soft stems included
¼ cup or more whole-wheat flour
2 tablespoons ground coriander
1 teaspoon ground cumin
1 teaspoon ground pomegranate seeds (see page 20; optional)
1 teaspoon crushed carom seeds (see page 14)
1 teaspoon mango powder (see page 18)
1 teaspoon salt, or to taste
½ teaspoon freshly ground black pepper
½ teaspoon paprika

In a food processor fitted with the metal S-blade, process the ginger, peppers, cilantro, and cauliflower until smooth. Remove to a bowl and mix in the remaining ingredients.

This stuffing can be made up to 2 days in advance.

MAKES ENOUGH FILLING FOR 20 PARANTHAS

VARIATION: Use broccoli or broccoflower instead of the cauliflower.

Spicy Daikon Radish Stuffing

PARANTHÉ MEIN BHARNÉ VALI MOOLI

This sharp-tasting, white root vegetable is akin in taste to that of prepared horseradish and is similar in shape to an over-sized carrot. It has a special place in the hearts of Indian people, who love it in its raw state, sprinkled with spices and fresh lime juice, or cut up with other vegetables and served as a salad. Occasionally it is made into a side dish. It is delicious as a stuffing for paranthas.

2 ½ to 3 pounds daikon radish
1 ½ teaspoons salt, or to taste
2 tablespoons peeled and minced fresh ginger
½ cup firmly packed finely chopped cilantro (fresh coriander), soft stems included
1 ½ teaspoons crushed carom seeds (see page 14)
½ teaspoon freshly ground black pepper
½ teaspoon garam masala (see page 23)

Grate the daikon in a food processor or by hand. Add the salt and set aside for 30 to 40 minutes, then squeeze out as much water as you can. (Sometimes I use this daikon water in place of regular water to make the dough for these paranthas.) Mix in the remaining ingredients until well combined.

This stuffing is best when freshly made.

MAKES ENOUGH FOR 20 PARANTHAS

GARLIC AND SPINACH STUFFING

PARANTHÉ MEIN BHARNÉ VALI PALAK

Try this parantha stuffing in Baked Potato Skins (see page 73) or mix with some Pressed Ricotta Paneer Cheese (page 248) and use to stuff bell peppers, tomatoes, or zucchini boats (see page 172).

2 bunches fresh spinach (¾ pound each)
2 tablespoons vegetable oil
2 teaspoons minced garlic
2 tablespoons peeled and minced fresh ginger
2 teaspoons dried fenugreek leaves (see page 17)
1 teaspoon crushed carom seeds (see page 14)
1 ½ teaspoons salt, or to taste
Freshly ground black pepper to taste

Remove the tough stems from the spinach, then wash and dry the leaves, and chop them finely. Heat the oil in a large skillet over high heat and cook the garlic, ginger, fenugreek leaves, and carom seeds, stirring, for about 1 minute. Stir in the chopped spinach, cover the skillet and cook, stirring as necessary, until the spinach is wilted, 3 to 4 minutes. Remove the cover, add the salt and pepper, and continue to cook over high heat until all the liquid evaporates. (This is very important, because liquid in the stuffing will cause the parantha dough to develop holes.) Set aside and let it cool uncovered, then use.

This stuffing can be made 5 to 6 days ahead of time. Reheat in an open skillet to ensure that all the moisture has dried up. Stir in some whole-wheat flour if the stuffing looks too moist. Then cool and use.

MAKES ENOUGH FOR 20 PARANTHAS

VARIATION: Use different greens like watercress, fenugreek, amaranth, or chicory instead of spinach to make paranthas with a different flavor.

YELLOW MUNG BEAN STUFFING

PARANTHÉ MEIN BHARNÉ VALI DAL

The fast-cooking yellow mung beans and pink lentils (which can be substituted in this recipe) are ideally suited to use as a stuffing for paranthas, pooris (see page 340), samosas

Making pooris is not as hard as it may seem. It is quite simple if you use the right ingredients and follow the tried and true technique. To make them light and crispy, use two parts stone-ground durum whole-wheat flour to one part all-purpose flour and fry them only when the oil reaches the desired temperature. If the oil is not hot enough, the poori will soak up too much oil and should be discarded. Pooris that do not puff up are still a delight to eat.

To really enjoy them, pooris should be eaten hot, though it is a common practice among Indian people to make them ahead of time and stack them one on top of the other. This, in my opinion, destroys their intrinsic appeal and makes them heavier and chewy.

2 cups stone-ground durum whole-wheat flour
1 cup all-purpose flour
1 teaspoon carom seeds (see page 14)
½ teaspoon freshly ground black pepper
½ teaspoon salt, or to taste
3 tablespoons peanut oil
¾ to 1 cup water
2 cups whole-wheat flour for coating
2 to 3 cups peanut oil for deep-frying

Place the stone-ground and all-purpose flours in a food processor fitted with the metal S-blade. Add the carom seeds, black pepper, and salt and process for 30 seconds to combine.

With the motor running, pour the oil and then the water in a thin stream through the feed tube until a ball is formed and the sides of the work bowl look clean. Transfer to a bowl, cover, and set aside for 1 to 4 hours. This dough can be refrigerated for 3 to 4 days.

Heat the oil in a wok or skillet over high heat until it reaches 350° to 375° F. (Drop a piece of the dough into the hot oil, and if it bubbles and rises to the top, then the oil is ready to be used. Cool the oil if it becomes too hot.)

Coat your hands lightly with oil (to prevent the dough from sticking to them) and divide the dough into 20 round balls. Cover and set aside. Working with each ball individually, press lightly to form a disc and then coat with flour. Roll into a 5- to 6-inch circle and carefully slide it into the wok. Press lightly on the poori with back of a large slotted spoon, guiding the air as it starts to puff up, until it puffs up into a complete round, 10 to 15 seconds. It should be golden and crisp, not too brown. Turn the poori over once to cook the other side. Remove to paper towels to drain and serve immediately.

Poori making is really quick if two people do it together, with one person rolling and the other frying.

MAKES 20 POORIS

CRISPY FRIED STUFFED PUFFY BREAD

BHARI HUI POORIAN

Most of the stuffings for paranthas (see pages 335–340) can also be used for pooris. These stuffings transform them into easy sandwiches that can be enjoyed by themselves or with various pickles and chutneys. They are superb as picnic fare and in packed lunches.

Stuffed pooris can be made up to 2 days ahead of time and stored in the refrigerator. To reheat, place them on an ungreased cookie sheet in a single layer and heat 5 to 6 inches under the broiler. Drain on paper towels and serve.

1 recipe Crispy Fried Bread with Carom Seeds (see page 340)
1 cup stuffing of your choice (see pages 335–340)

Coat your hands lightly with oil to prevent the dough from sticking to them and divide the dough into 20 round balls. Cover and set aside. Working with each ball individually, press lightly to form a disc and then coat with flour. Roll into a 3- to 4-inch circle. Place 1 tablespoon of the stuffing in the center and shape into a ball once again. Press the ball lightly to form a disk, coat with flour, and roll it out into a 6- to 7-inch circle. Deep-fry according to the instructions on page 341.

MAKES 20 POORIS

VARIATION: You could also use 1 teaspoon of urad bean batter (see page 63) as a stuffing. If the batter seems too thin, add some garbanzo bean flour to thicken it.

CRISPY FRIED GREEN SPLIT PEA PUFFY BREAD

SUKHÉ HARÉ MATTAR KI POORI

The combination of green split peas and whole-wheat flour makes this puffy poori variation green. The peas also transform this bread into a complete protein, so they can be served by themselves or as part of a larger menu.

Any type of leftover bean or lentil preparation can be used to make pooris in this manner. By varying the rolling and cooking techniques, this dough can be made into chapatis (see page 320) or paranthas (page 322).

1 tablespoon corn or peanut oil
1 teaspoon cumin seeds
2 teaspoons ground coriander
1 teaspoon ground cumin
½ teaspoon turmeric
¼ cup loosely packed finely chopped cilantro (fresh coriander), soft stems included
1 tablespoon peeled and minced fresh ginger
½ cup dried green split peas, picked over and washed
2 ¾ to 3 cups water
1 cup stone-ground durum whole-wheat flour
½ cup all-purpose flour
½ teaspoon carom seeds (see page 14)
2 cups whole-wheat flour for coating
2 to 3 cups peanut oil for deep-frying

Heat the oil in a small nonstick saucepan over moderately high heat and fry the cumin seeds until they sizzle, 10 seconds. Stir in the coriander, ground cumin, turmeric, cilantro, and ginger, then add the peas and 2 ½ cups of the water. Bring to a boil, then reduce the heat to medium, cover the pan, and simmer until the peas are soft and most of the water has been absorbed by the peas, 35 to 40 minutes. (Reduce the heat to low after 15 to 20 minutes.) Set aside to cool for 5 to 10 minutes.

Transfer the cooked peas to a food processor fitted with the metal S-blade and process until pureed. Add the whole-wheat and all-purpose flours and the carom seeds and process once again. (You will have to scrape the sides of the work bowl with a spatula.) Pour in the remaining water in a thin stream through the feed tube, stopping a few seconds after the dough gathers into a ball and the sides of the work bowl look clean.

Lightly oil your hands and remove the dough to a bowl and set aside for 1 to 4 hours.

Heat the oil in a wok or skillet over high heat until it reaches 350° to 375° F. (Drop a piece of the dough into the hot oil, and if it bubbles and rises to the top, then the oil is ready to be used. Cool the oil if it becomes too hot.)

Coat your hands lightly with oil (to prevent the dough from sticking to them) and divide the dough into 15 round balls. Cover and set aside. Working with each ball individually, press lightly to form a disk and then coat with flour. Roll into a 5- to 6-inch circle and carefully slide it into the wok. Press lightly on the poori with back of a large slotted spoon, guiding the air as it starts to puff up, until it puffs up into a complete round, 10 to 15 seconds. It should be golden and crisp, not too brown. Turn the poori over once to cook the other side. Remove to paper towels to drain and serve immediately.

MAKES 15 POORIS

LEAVENED DEEP-FRIED BREAD

BHATURA

Made with a leavened dough that is similar to that of naan (see page 346) and deep-fried like poori (page 340), bhaturas are another authentic and priceless addition to your bread recipes.

As kids, we used to eat these with garbanzo beans, much in the same way as kids in this country eat hamburgers.

FOR THE BREAD
3 cups unbleached all-purpose flour
1 cup fine semolina
1 teaspoon sugar
½ teaspoon salt, or to taste
1 tablespoon dry yeast
¾ cup nonfat plain yogurt, whisked until smooth
¾ cup scalded milk

FOR FRYING
3 to 4 cups peanut oil for deep-frying
3 cups unbleached all-purpose flour

Place the flour, semolina, sugar, salt, and yeast in a food processor fitted with the metal S-blade and process for a few seconds to mix.

Mix together the yogurt and milk. With the motor running, pour the yogurt-milk mixture through the feed tube in a thin stream and continue to process until the dough gathers into a ball and the sides of the work bowl look clean. Remove to a large bowl, cover, and place in a warm draft-free place until it doubles in volume, 3 to 4 hours.

Heat the oil in a wok or skillet over high heat until it reaches 350° to 375° F. (Drop a piece of the dough into the hot oil, and if it bubbles and rises to the top, the oil is ready to be used. Let it cool if it becomes too hot.)

Coat your hands lightly with oil and divide the dough into 16 to 18 round balls. Cover and set aside. Working with each ball individually, press lightly to form a disc and then coat with flour. Roll into a 6- to 7-inch circle and carefully slide it into the wok. Press lightly on the bhatura with the back of a large slotted spoon, guiding the air as it starts to puff up, until it puffs up into a complete round, 10 to 15 seconds. Turn it over once to cook the other side. They should be lightly golden on both sides, not too brown. Remove to paper towels to drain and serve immediately with Garbanzo Beans with Roasted Pomegranate Seeds (see page372) and Yogurt Mint Chutney (page 88).

Bhaturas can be made 2 to 3 days ahead of time and stacked until ready to use in the refrigerator. Spread on ungreased cookie sheets and reheat under the broiler. Drain on paper towels and serve.

MAKES 16 TO 18 BHATURAS

LAYERED AND OVEN-GRILLED BREAD

TANDOORI OVEN VALA PARANTHA

When cooking breads in the Indian *tandoor* (a cylindrical clay oven; see below), the word *parantha* takes on a new definition. The dough of these breads is always enriched with oil, layered with additional oil, and then baked by slapping it on the walls of the hot *tandoor*. These paranthas are generally brushed lightly with clarified butter (see page 30) after they are cooked.

When baked in a tandoor, these breads cook in a few seconds because of the intense heat, and they also take on an intoxicating smoky aroma from the live coals of the oven. This results in extraordinarily moist and flavorful breads that are almost impossible to reproduce without a tandoor and a *tandooriya* (someone who is adept at using the *tandoor*).

Since the tandoor is not accessible to most of us, making similar paranthas in a conventional oven is the next best thing. Paranthas grilled under the oven broiler are excellent substitutes for the real ones. To ensure that they remain moist, I brush them with water before grilling.

To make tandoori breads, use almost any type of enriched dough (plain, with spices, herbs, or vegetables) that has been mentioned in the parantha recipes (see pages 325–334) and roll them into triangles, squares, or rounds according to the directions on page 322.

Preheat the broiler. Place the rolled out breads in a single layer on ungreased cookie sheets and brush the tops with water. Place the cookie sheets one at a time 3 to 4 inches below the broiler heat and grill until the tops start to brown. (Reposition the paranthas to ensure that each one gets enough heat.) Turn the paranthas over once and cook lightly on the other side.

When they are done, remove each parantha to aluminum foil. Brush the top surface with butter and serve hot with any Indian meal.

GRILLED LEAVENED BREAD WITH NIGELLA SEEDS

KALONJI VALÉ TANDOORI NAAN

This familiar bread made with leavened all-purpose flour is an integral part of Indian restaurant–style cuisine. The lure of freshly baked naan catches people like spiders in its fragrant web.

When I was growing up, naan was never baked at home, even by people who had tandoors. Today, however, I am able to reproduce almost authentic naan at home, though they lack the smoky flavor of the coals of the tandoor.

Naan is incomparably marvelous with curries, lentils and beans, vegetable side dishes, barbecued foods, or just by itself. I have, on occasion, used it as a pizza crust.

1 tablespoon dry yeast
1 teaspoon sugar
½ cup warm water (about 130° F)
1 large egg (optional)
½ cup nonfat plain yogurt, whisked until smooth
½ cup warm milk (about 130° F)
4 cups unbleached all-purpose flour
3 tablespoons butter, at room temperature, plus 1 additional tablespoon, if making dough by hand
½ teaspoon salt, or to taste
1 cup unbleached all-purpose flour for coating
½ cup water for brushing
1 teaspoon nigella seeds (see page 19)
2 tablespoons melted regular or clarified (see page 30) or butter for brushing (optional)

To make the dough, dissolve the yeast and sugar in the warm water and set aside until frothy, 3 to 4 minutes. Mix the egg, yogurt, and milk together and set aside. (Do not worry if the milk curdles.) Add some extra yogurt if you are not using the egg.

Place the flour and butter in a food processor fitted with the metal S-blade and process until mixed. With the motor running, pour the yeast mixture through the feed tube, followed by the egg mixture, and process until the flour gathers into a ball and the sides of the work bowl look clean. (If the dough seems too sticky, add some more flour through the feed tube.) Remove to a large bowl, cover, and place in a warm draft-free spot until it doubles in volume, 2 to 3 hours. (If the dough is made by hand, oil your hands with butter to prevent the dough from sticking to them.)

Divide the dough into 16 round balls. Keep covered to prevent them from drying out. Working with each ball separately, press it into a flat disk, then coat completely in flour from the bowl. Roll each disk into a 5- to 6-inch circle, then pull from one side to make a triangle. Place on an ungreased cookie sheet and finish rolling all the other naan. (The naan can be made into rounds also.)

Preheat the broiler. Brush the top of each naan with water and sprinkle and press some nigella seeds into it. Place the cookie sheets, one at a time, 3 to 4 inches below the broiler heat until brown spots appear and the tops look done, about 1 minute. (You may have to reposition each naan, depending on the heat distribution of the broiler.) Turn each naan over and cook the bottoms slightly. Remove to a platter, brush lightly with the butter, and serve hot.

Naan can be made ahead of time, stacked one on top of another, and covered with aluminum foil, or be cooked lightly on one side, then cooled and stored in the refrigerator for 5 to 6 days (or frozen for 2 to 3 months). To reheat, place on cookie sheets in a single layer and place under the broiler until heated through. (They can be heated individually in a regular toaster also.) Reheating naan in a microwave oven makes them chewy.

MAKES 16 NAAN

GARLIC NAAN: Mince 3 to 5 cloves of garlic in the food processor, then proceed with the recipe. Substitute slivers of garlic (as many as you like) for the nigella seeds.

GINGER-SESAME NAAN: Mince a 1 ½-inch piece of peeled fresh ginger in the food processor, then proceed with the recipe. Substitute sesame seeds for the nigella seeds.

SCALLION AND MINT NAAN: Mince 3 to 4 whole scallions and ¼ cup lightly packed fresh mint leaves in the food processor, then proceed with the recipe. After the naan are baked, brush lightly with melted butter or clarified butter and sprinkle some ground dried mint leaves on top.

FENUGREEK NAAN: Mince 1 cup loosely packed fresh fenugreek leaves (see page 17) in the food processor, then proceed with the recipe. After the naan are baked, brush lightly with melted butter or clarified butter and sprinkle some ground dried fenugreek leaves on top.

SEMOLINA BREAD

SOOJI KA KULCHA

This leavened flatbread is partially baked in the oven, then finished on a griddle. The authentic recipe uses only all-purpose flour. The dough is made in exactly the same way as naan (see page 346), but the actual finished bread is very different.

Customarily served with Garbanzo Beans with Roasted Pomegranate Seeds (see page 272) or Black Garbanzo Beans (page 275), this bread is also appropriate as a base for individual pizzas or on the side with soup and salad (see variation at the end of the recipe).

1 tablespoon dry yeast
1 teaspoon sugar
⅓ cup warm water (130° F)
¾ cup nonfat plain yogurt
1 large egg (optional)
½ cup scalded milk
2 cups fine semolina
2 cups unbleached all-purpose flour
2 tablespoons unsalted butter, at room temperature
½ teaspoon salt
1 cup unbleached all-purpose flour for coating
¼ cup water for brushing

Dissolve the yeast and sugar in the warm water and set aside until frothy, 3 to 4 minutes. Mix together the yogurt, egg, and milk and set aside. (Do not worry if the milk curdles.) Add some extra yogurt if you are not using the egg.

Place the semolina, flour, butter, and salt in a food processor fitted with the metal S-blade and process until mixed.

With the motor running, pour the yeast mixture through the feed tube, then the egg mixture, and process until the flour gathers into a ball and the sides of the work bowl look clean. (If the dough seems too sticky, add 1 or 2 tablespoons additional flour through the feed tube.) Remove to a large bowl, cover, and place in a warm, draft-free spot until it doubles in volume, about 2 to 3 hours. (If the dough is made by hand, oil your hands with butter to prevent the dough from sticking to them.)

Divide the dough into 24 round balls. Keep covered to prevent them from drying out. Working with each ball separately, press it into a flat disc, and then coat completely in flour from the bowl. Roll each disc into a 5- to 6-inch circle, then place it on an ungreased cookie sheet. Repeat with the remaining balls.

Preheat the oven to 150° F and place all the cookie sheets in it until the kulchas rise, about 30 minutes or longer.

Remove from the oven and brush some water on each kulcha. Preheat the oven to 350° F, and bake (not more than two cookie sheets at a time), until the kulchas become slightly golden and firm, 3 to 5 minutes. Remove from the oven and finish baking the remainder.

(These partially baked kulchas can be cooled completely and refrigerated until required. They can also be frozen for 2 to 3 months.)

To finish cooking, heat a *tava*, pancake griddle, or skillet over moderately high heat, until a sprinkling of flour immediately turns brown (if it turns black, let the *tava* cool down). Wipe off the browned flour.

Brush both the sides of the partially baked kulchas with a touch of vegetable oil and place on the *tava*. Press lightly with a spatula until it gets flecked with golden dots, then turn over and cook the other side in the same way. Finish reheating the remaining kulchas. Individual reheating in this way ensures the silky softness that is associated with this unique bread.

MAKES 24 KULCHAS

VARIATIONS: To serve as a side bread with soup and salad, just finish baking it in the oven (reheating on the griddle is not necessary).

To make carom seed kulchas, add 1 teaspoon carom seeds (see page 14) along with the salt and proceed with the recipe.

STUFFED ONION BREAD

PYAZ KA KULCHA

These kulchas are very popular in most Indian restaurants. Traditionally they are baked in the tandoor, but at home the broiler gives wonderful results.

Serve them with barbecued foods, with curries or vegetables, or cut them into wedges and serve as appetizers with a glass of chilled chardonnay.

1 recipe Semolina Bread (see page 348)
1 cup unbleached all-purpose flour for coating
2 cups finely chopped onion
1 tablespoon melted regular or clarified butter (see page 30)

Lightly oil your hands to prevent the dough from sticking to them, and divide the dough into sixteen 1 ½-inch balls. Cover and set aside. Working with each ball separately, flatten into a disk with your fingertips, coat with flour, and roll it into a 4- to 5-inch circle. Place 2 tablespoons of the chopped onion in the center. Bring the edges together, pinch to seal, and then shape into a ball once again.

Flatten and coat this stuffed ball with flour and roll it into a 7- to 8-inch circle of even thickness. Keep turning and dusting the kulcha while rolling or it may stick to the rolling surface. If the stuffing has excess moisture, the kulchas may develop tiny holes as you roll them. If that happens, seal the holes by putting a pinch of dry flour on them. That should absorb all the excess moisture.

Place on an ungreased cookie sheet and finish rolling all the other kulchas.

Preheat the broiler. Brush the tops of the kulchas with water. Place the cookie sheets, one at a time, 3 to 4 inches below the broiler heat until brown spots appear and the tops look done, about 1 minute. (You may have to reposition each kulcha, depending on the heat distribution of the broiler.) Turn each kulcha over and cook slightly on the bottom. Remove to a platter, brush lightly with butter, and serve hot.

Kulchas can be made ahead of time, stacked one on top of another, and covered with aluminum foil, or be cooked lightly on one side, then cooled and stored in the refrigerator for 5 to 6 days (or frozen for 2 to 3 months). To reheat, place on cookie sheets in a single layer and place under the broiler until heated through. (They can be heated individually in a regular toaster also.) Reheating in a microwave oven makes them chewy.

MAKES 16 KULCHAS

VARIATION: Kulchas can also be stuffed with spinach, paneer cheese, or yellow mung beans.

CRISSCROSS POTATO BREAD

ALU VALI DOUBLE ROTI

The concept is Western, the filling is Indian, and this bread is a perfect example of how beautifully the two cuisines complement each other.

This bread, with a variety of different fillings, can easily become a staple in both Indian and American households. Instead of one large loaf, smaller individual loaves can be made. The stuffing in Puff Pastry Stuffed with Fresh Morel Mushrooms (see page 58) is also wonderful in this bread.

1 tablespoon peanut oil

1 tablespoon peeled and minced fresh ginger

¼ teaspoon minced garlic

1 teaspoon cumin seeds

1 teaspoon ground coriander

½ cup thinly sliced scallion greens

½ cup frozen peas, thawed

1 large potato, boiled until tender, peeled, and finely diced

½ cup loosely packed finely chopped cilantro (fresh coriander), soft stems included

½ teaspoon salt, or to taste

½ recipe Semolina Bread (see page 348)

1 teaspoon egg white for brushing

Heat the oil in a medium-size skillet over moderately high heat and stir-fry the ginger and garlic until barely golden, about 1 minute. Stir in the cumin seeds, then add the coriander and scallion greens. Cook, stirring, for 2 to 3 minutes, then add the peas, potato, cilantro, and salt. Reduce the heat to medium and cook the potatoes, stirring as necessary, until they start to turn golden, 10 to 15 minutes. Set aside to cool.

Roll out the dough to make a 10- by 12-inch rectangle. Place the filling along the center length. Cut the uncovered side flaps into diagonal 1 ¼-inch-wide strips still attached to the center dough. Starting from the top, place one strip from each side over the filling (somewhat like braiding). Do the same with the remaining strips, alternating between the sides, to form a lattice over the filling.

Brush the top with the egg white and place, covered, in a warm, draft-free spot for 2 to 3 hours.

Preheat the oven to 400° F. Place the bread on an ungreased cookie sheet on the center rack and bake until golden. Remove from the oven and serve hot or at room temperature. This bread can be served as an appetizer or with the main meal. Serve with Hot and Sour Chili Pepper Chutney (see page 91) or Mint and Tomato Chutney (page 87).

MAKES ONE 12- BY 4-INCH LOAF

Bread Loaves with Indian Flavors

DOUBLE ROTI MEIN HINDUSTANI ZAYAKA

To add a new romance to ordinary breads, bake your bread loaves with a touch of Indian spices. These flavorings add an uncommon character to familiar breads and can also be added to breads that are made in commercial bread machines. Start with your favorite bread recipe and add any one of the following herbs and spices along with the flour and other ingredients. You could also add some minced garlic, ginger, or onion along with the spices.

- 1 teaspoon coarsely crushed carom seeds (see page 14)
- ½ teaspoon nigella seeds (see page 19)
- 1 teaspoon coarsely crushed pan-toasted black peppercorns (see page 13), or to taste
- 1 teaspoon ground or whole pan-roasted cumin seeds (see page 16)
- 1 teaspoon dried fenugreek leaves (see page 17)
- 2 teaspoons dried mint leaves

(These measurements are enough for a 1-pound loaf of bread.)

For the Sweet Tooth

There are some tastes that take time to acquire, and many traditional Indian desserts fall into this category. Through the years, observing the various reactions to certain desserts, I quickly learned which Indian treats were "user-friendly" in America. In deference to my Western students and friends I have modified and selected those recipes that have a more accessible and universal appeal.

Of the desserts, ranging from halvah to puddings, custards to fudge, all but three have one common denominator—no baking. Remember, gas or electric ovens are still a rarity in India, so you won't find cakes or pies there. These homemade desserts are mostly stove-top prepared and then refrigerated. Thanks to condensed and evaporated milk, the most tedious part of preparing many of these thickened milk-based desserts has been virtually eliminated.

Wait till you taste the paneer or ricotta cheese desserts, so refreshing, light and relatively easy on the sugar intake. There is a light chocolate fudgelike dessert that will delight even the most ardent chocoholic and lots of sweets made from all varieties of nuts.

New Delhi Rice Pudding

CHAVAL KI KHEER

This traditional dessert, with a hint of rose water or saffron and a garnish of pure silver leaves, lightly lingers in the mind and on the palate long after the meal. Though Indians love this dessert just by itself, you could swirl in your favorite berry sauce and fresh berries and create an exotic yet familiar dessert of your own. This is an easy dessert to make for large gatherings.

Regulating the heat and constant stirring are very crucial when you make this pudding. The goal is to cook it as quickly as possible without burning the milk or allowing it to spill, more easily said than done without constant attention.

½ cup blanched almond slivers
¾ cup water
1 cup basmati rice, picked over
1 gallon regular milk
One 14-ounce can sweetened condensed milk
½ teaspoon ground green cardamom seeds
½ cup dessert masala (see page 29), plus 2 tablespoons for garnish
1 tablespoon pure rose water or 2 drops rose essence (see page 20) or ¼ teaspoon saffron threads soaked in 2 tablespoons milk for 30 minutes or longer
Six 4-inch silver leaves (see page 10) for garnish (optional)

Soak the almond slivers in the water to soften them for 1 hour or longer. Wash the rice in three to four changes of water, stirring lightly with your fingertips, until the water runs almost clear.

Place the rice and half of the regular milk in a large, heavy aluminum wok or saucepan (nonstick but not Teflon coated) and bring it to a boil over high heat. (Watch carefully, or the milk will boil over.) Reduce the heat to medium and simmer the pudding, stirring often, until thickened, 15 to 20 minutes. Then add another cup of milk and simmer until it is absorbed. Keep adding more milk until all of it is used up. At this stage the rice pudding should be thick and creamy. (The total time to cook this pudding is 50 to 60 minutes. Stirring the contents and scraping the sides often with a spatula are essential or the milk will burn on the bottom and sides of the pan.)

Drain and add the almond slivers. Stir in the condensed milk, then add the cardamom and dessert masala. Cook, stirring, for another 5 to 7 minutes, then remove the pan from the heat. Stir in the rose water and transfer the rice pudding to a serving bowl. Bring to room temperature, then chill for 8 to 10 hours or longer. Garnish with the silver leaves and dessert masala and serve.

Rice pudding stays fresh in the refrigerator for 5 to 6 days. I like to serve it in a silver bowl, but any type of serving bowl is acceptable.

MAKES 8 SERVINGS

GROUND RICE CUSTARD

FIRNI

Made with soaked and ground basmati rice, this custardlike dessert is very cool and refreshing. Its slightly granular texture makes it distinctive. *Firni* can also be made with rice flour or cornstarch. It is traditionally served in small individual dishes or large round and slightly concave unglazed clay containers.

1 cup basmati rice, picked over
2 cups water
½ gallon plus ¾ cup regular or low-fat milk
¾ cup sugar
2 tablespoons dessert masala (see page 29) or 1 tablespoon each ground raw pistachios
    and almonds
½ teaspoon ground green cardamom seeds
1 tablespoon rose water or 2 drops rose essence (see page 20)
4 or more 4-inch squares silver leaves (see page 10) for garnish
Ground or finely chopped pistachios and almonds for garnish

Wash the rice in three to four changes of water, stirring lightly with your fingertips, until the water runs almost clear. Soak it in the water overnight.

Boil the milk in a large heavy aluminum wok or saucepan (they are the best conductors of heat) over high heat. Reduce the heat to medium and simmer the milk for 5 to 7 minutes, stirring constantly with a large slotted spatula.

Meanwhile, drain and place the rice in a blender with ¾ cup milk and grind until it becomes fine. (It will still have a grain.) Then add the ground rice to the simmering milk in a slow stream, stirring constantly to prevent the formation of lumps. (If lumps develop, process in a blender until smooth. Then return everything to the pot.) Cook on medium heat for another 5 minutes, stirring constantly and scraping the bottom and sides. Add the sugar, dessert masala, and cardamom. Cook for 2 to 4 minutes over low heat, then remove from the heat. Stir in the rose water.

The *firni* should be of a medium custard consistency. (If it thickens too much while cooking, add some more milk.) It will thicken as it cools. While it is still hot, transfer to a serving bowl. Bring to room temperature, then chill for 8 to 10 hours or longer. Garnish with the silver leaves and nuts and serve. *Firni* stays fresh in the refrigerator for 5 to 6 days.

MAKES 8 TO 10 SERVINGS

CARAMEL CUSTARD

ANGREZI MISHTAAN

This dessert does not "officially" belong in an Indian cookbook, but over the years it has become one of the best-liked desserts served by Indian people. All the recipes for this dessert call for placing it in a water bath and then baking it in the oven, but my mother's Indian way is much faster. We "bake" it in a pressure cooker. You can actually assemble the custard according to your favorite recipe and cut your cooking time by three quarters by following the pressure cooker method.

(If you have an old flat-bottomed saucepan, remove its handle or buy a metal *patilla*— an Indian pan without handles—with a lid at an Indian market. Make sure it fits in your pressure cooker.)

4 cups milk
6 large eggs, lightly beaten with a fork
¾ cup sugar
1 teaspoon pure vanilla extract

Boil the milk over high heat in a heavy saucepan or in a microwave oven (8 to 10 minutes on high power). Transfer to a bowl and cool for 8 to 10 minutes. Stir in the eggs, ½ cup of the sugar, and the vanilla. Set aside.

Place the remaining sugar in a flat-bottomed pan that has a lid but no handles (choose a pan that will fit comfortably in your pressure cooker) and heat it over low heat, stirring constantly, until it becomes golden brown. With oven mitts on your hands, swirl the caramelized sugar by rotating the pan until the sugar hardens. (To speed the hardening of the sugar, swirl and immediately dip the bottom of the pan into a bowl of water; this may cause some crackling but the caramelized sugar will be fine.)

Pour the prepared custard over the sugar and cover the pan first with aluminum foil and then with the lid. Put 2 to 3 cups water in the pressure cooker and then place the custard pan in it. The water should cover about one third of the pan. Secure the lid of the pressure cooker, and cook over high heat for 40 to 50 seconds after the pressure regulator starts rocking. Remove from the heat and let the pressure drop by itself, 15 to 20 minutes.

Open the pressure cooker and remove the custard pan. (If it seems too hot to remove, let it remain inside until it is cool enough to handle.) Bring to room temperature, then refrigerate until chilled. Invert on to a platter and serve.

MAKES 8 SERVINGS

Indian Bread Pudding

SHAHI TUKRI

My friend Reita makes this dessert with French bread flutes (thin long rolls) but the smaller rolls also work fine. To make this recipe a real standout, cut the bread into triangles or rectangles, ensuring that each piece has part of the crust. Definitely not for dieters!

2 to 3 cups peanut oil for deep-frying
One 8-ounce French bread flute or rolls, cut into 2- by 1-inch pieces
Half 12-ounce can evaporated milk
Half 14-ounce can sweetened condensed milk
½ teaspoon ground green cardamom seeds
1 cup water
1 cup sugar
Four to six 4-inch silver leaves (see page 10)
1 tablespoon dessert masala (see page 29), or to taste

Heat the oil in a large wok or skillet over high heat until it reaches 325° to 350° F or until a piece of bread dropped into it bubbles and immediately rises to the top. Add the bread pieces and fry, stirring with a large slotted spoon, until they are golden (not brown), 4 to 5 minutes. (You may have to do this in two or three batches; don't crowd them in the pan.) Drain and remove to paper towels to drain further.

Place the evaporated milk in a large microwave-proof bowl and cook on high power for 4 minutes to reduce it by a third. Add the condensed milk and cook in the microwave for another 4 minutes on high power. (This can also be done over moderately high heat in a heavy saucepan, stirring, until reduced by a third.) Remove from the oven and stir in the ground cardamom. Set aside.

While the milk is cooking, combine the water and sugar in a small saucepan and boil over high heat for 2 to 3 minutes. With the help of kitchen tongs, dip each fried bread piece in this syrup and transfer to a platter. Arrange all the soaked bread pieces in an overlapping manner, making a "plateau."

Pour the thickened milk over the bread pieces in a thin stream, making sure all the pieces are covered. Garnish with the silver leaves and dessert masala and serve chilled or at room temperature.

Shahi tukri should not be made more than 4 to 6 hours ahead of time. If left for too long, the bread loses its crunch (though the leftovers taste good for 5 to 6 days).

MAKES 8 SERVINGS

DRIED VERMICELLI WITH ALMONDS AND PISTACHIOS

BADAAM AUR PISTÉ VALI SUKHI SEVIAN

The authentic version of this dessert calls for homemade vermicelli that is very thin (almost like angel hair pasta), slightly curly, and about ½ inch long. Making this type of vermicelli is a favorite pastime of the older women of the family. They sit with a container full of prepared flour dough, spread a sheet of newspaper or muslin in front of them, and keep "twisting" the dough between their forefinger and thumb into thin, long, little noodles. These noodles are air dried, roasted lightly, and then used to create a quick dessert.

If this kind is not available, you can use the longer commercial variety sold at Indian markets. Italian *zitoni tagliati* (broken semolina noodles) work well also.

2 tablespoons clarified butter (see page 30) or 3 tablespoons unsalted butter
2 cups vermicelli
4 cups boiling water
¾ cup sugar, or to taste
¾ teaspoon ground green cardamom seeds
2 tablespoons blanched almond slivers
2 tablespoons pistachio slivers or 3 tablespoons dessert masala (see page 29)

Heat the clarified butter over moderately high heat in a medium-size heavy wok or saucepan, add the vermicelli and cook, stirring constantly with a round slotted spoon, over high heat for 2 to 3 minutes, then over low until it turns medium brown, 8 to 10 minutes. Add the water (it will splatter upon contact with the hot pan), increase the heat to medium-high, cover the pan, and cook, stirring occasionally, until all the water evaporates and the noodles become soft, 5 to 7 minutes.

Reduce the heat to low, stir in the sugar, cover the pan, and cook until all the sugar is absorbed, 4 to 5 minutes. Turn off the heat and let the vermicelli rest for 5 to 7 minutes or more. Transfer to a serving dish, garnish with cardamom seeds and nut slivers, and serve.

MAKES 8 SERVINGS

SEMOLINA PUDDING

SOOJI KI KHEER

This quick and easy family-style dessert doubles as breakfast food. It is nutritious and light and is somewhat like Cream of Wheat cereal.

1 tablespoon unsalted butter
½ cup fine semolina
1 tablespoon golden raisins
1 tablespoon coarsely chopped blanched almonds
1 tablespoon coarsely chopped pistachios
5 cups low-fat or regular milk
⅓ cup sugar, or to taste
½ teaspoon ground green cardamom seeds
1 tablespoon dessert masala for garnish (see page 29)

Heat the butter in a medium-size heavy wok or saucepan over moderately high heat, add the semolina and raisins, and cook, stirring, until the semolina is golden and the raisins swell up, 5 to 7 minutes. (Reduce the heat if it seems too high.) Stir in the almonds and pistachios, then add the milk and bring to a boil, stirring constantly. Reduce the heat to medium and simmer for 5 to 7 minutes. Stir in the sugar and cook for another 2 to 3 minutes.

Transfer to a serving bowl, mix in the cardamom, garnish with the dessert masala, and serve hot or chilled. It is excellent both ways.

MAKES 8 SERVINGS

VARIATION: This recipe can be made with dried vermicelli also.

SEMOLINA HALVAH

SOOJI KA HALVA

This halvah bears no resemblance to the fudgelike halvah available in grocery stores. On the contrary, it is served hot, while it is soft and fluffy.

This dessert is associated with happy and auspicious occasions, and celebrations of all kinds. During special prayer ceremonies (*pujas*), it is presented to the gods for a blessing. This holy halvah (*prashad*) is then distributed among family and friends. Mothers and grandmothers make it on birthdays and anniversaries (it's the equivalent of birthday cake) and sometimes it is made just for the aroma it spreads throughout the house.

Authentic *halva* is made with equal amounts of semolina, butter (or ghee), and sugar, but I have cut back the butter and sugar as much as possible without disturbing its true character. This *halva* can also be made with whole-wheat flour.

⅓ cup or more unsalted butter
¾ cup fine semolina
½ cup garbanzo bean flour (see page 254)
3 tablespoons raisins
4 cups boiling water
1 cup sugar
½ teaspoon ground green cardamom seeds
¼ cup coarsely chopped blanched almonds
2 tablespoons coarsely chopped pistachios
Four 4-inch silver leaves (see page 10) for garnish (optional)

Melt the butter in a medium-size saucepan over medium to low heat and add the semolina, flour, and raisins. Cook, stirring, until the semolina turns a rich brown color, 20 to 25 minutes. Add the water, cover the pan, and simmer, stirring occasionally, until all the water is absorbed, 7 to 10 minutes. (Use caution when adding the water, because upon initial contact it starts to steam; this lasts for 5 to 10 seconds only.) Add the sugar and continue to cook until it is absorbed, 5 to 7 minutes.

Add the ground cardamom, almonds, and pistachios. Transfer to a serving bowl, garnish with the silver leaves, and serve hot. This dish can be made a few hours ahead of time and reheated with additional water in the pan in which it was cooked or in a microwave oven.

MAKES 8 SERVINGS

Carrot Halvah with Dark Brown Sugar

GAJJERELLA

This is a scrumptious dessert prized above most others, particularly in the cold winter months, when lovely red carrots flood the vegetable markets. Traditionally, this dessert is served hot after a hearty Indian meal, but it also tastes divine at room temperature. It is a healthful after-school snack, especially with a glass of milk or in the evening with samosas (see page 53) and a hot cup of tea.

The carrot halvah made in India is visually different from the one made by Indians in America, mainly because of the difference in the color of the carrots. The deep red color and sweetness of carrots in India produce a spectacular and rich-looking halvah that is almost impossible to reproduce. The use of dark brown sugar makes our "American" carrot halvah a close second. Buy organic, naturally sweet, young, and tender carrots, 6 to 8 inches long and ¾ inch wide at the top. Freshness can be judged by their feathery green leaves.

When using young and tender carrots, scrape them lightly with a knife to remove their rootlets and wash them thoroughly. Don't peel them or most of the "carrot" will be lost.

¼ cup unblanched almond slices
2 pounds young carrots (without leaves)
1 cup firmly packed dark brown sugar, or to taste
1 ¾ cups whipping or heavy cream
3 cups nonfat dry milk
1 cup ricotta cheese
2 tablespoons pistachios halves
Four to six 4-inch squares silver leaves (see page 10) for garnish
1 tablespoon dessert masala (see page 29) for garnish

Soak the almond slices in water to cover for 30 to 40 minutes or longer to soften them. Drain and set aside.

Scrape, wash, and dry the carrots. Then grate and place them in a large, heavy aluminum wok or a saucepan (not Teflon coated). Cover the pan and cook over moderately high heat for 4 to 5 minutes, stirring occasionally. Reduce the heat to low and cook another 5 minutes, stirring occasionally. Add the sugar and cook until the sugar melts, 2 to 3 minutes. Increase the heat to medium and continue to cook, stirring as necessary, until the sugar dries up and is absorbed into the carrots, 15 to 20 minutes.

While the carrots are cooking, combine the cream, dry milk, and ricotta cheese in a heavy nonstick saucepan and cook over medium heat until it becomes smooth like a thick batter, 3 to 5 minutes. Reduce the heat to low and cook, stirring often, until it starts to get very thick, 3 to 5 minutes. (At this point it may start to stick to the bottom of the pan.) Remove from the heat.

When all the sugar in the carrots dries up, stir them for 2 to 3 minutes. Add the thickened cream mixture, the almonds, and pistachios and cook over low heat until the mixture is completely dry, 3 to 4 minutes.

Transfer to a serving dish, garnish with the silver leaves and dessert masala, and serve hot. This dessert can be cooked 8 to 10 days ahead of time. (Do not reheat in a microwave oven if it has been garnished with the silver leaves, because they can damage the oven.)

MAKES 8 SERVINGS

VARIATION: CARROT FUDGE *(Gajjar Ki Burfee):* Spread any amount of Carrot Halvah on a cookie sheet while it is still warm. Top with silver leaves and set aside until it becomes cold.

Cut into 1-inch cubes or diamonds. Sprinkle some dessert masala on top and decorate on a platter lined with paper doilies. Serve with a cup of hot tea. They will stay fresh in the refrigerator for 8 to 10 days.

BASIC MILK FUDGE

SAADI BURFEE

A dessert that is surprisingly light, sweet, and should not be confused with the heavy American style of fudge. *Burfee* is to Indians what brownies are to the Western world. Authentic *burfee* is made with thickened milk, sugar, and butter. To this are added a whole array of nuts, flavorings, and selected vegetables to create an infinite variety of *burfee*s, which, though similar in name, are uniquely distinct in flavor (almost like muffins).

Start with this fast and easy basic recipe and then choose your own favorite flavorings from the recipes that follow.

Burfee stays fresh in the refrigerator for 15 to 20 days. Serve cold or at room temperature at the end of a meal, or as a part of an afternoon teatime menu. It also makes a lovely hostess gift in place of chocolates. Allow 2 to 4 pieces per person.

6 tablespoons (¾ stick) unsalted butter
One 2-pound container part-skim ricotta cheese
One 14-ounce can sweetened condensed milk
2 teaspoons pure vanilla extract

Melt the butter in a large heavy wok or saucepan over high heat. Add the ricotta cheese and cook, stirring often, with a large round or triangular slotted spatula until all the liquid evaporates, 20 to 25 minutes. (Reduce the heat as the cheese dries.) Add the milk and vanilla and continue to cook until all the liquid evaporates once again, 20 to 25 minutes.

Choose any of the following flavorings and finish making the *burfee.*

Layered Vanilla and Chocolate Fudge

CHAACLATE BURFEE

Tiny 1-inch squares of layered vanilla and chocolate fudge topped with edible pure silver are offered in individual candy cups, like chocolate bonbons.

> 1 recipe Basic Milk Fudge (above)
> ¾ cup semisweet chocolate chips
> Six to eight 4-inch squares silver leaves (see page 10) or 1 tablespoon Dessert Masala (page 29) for garnish

Place half of the fudge in an ungreased 11- by 8-inch cookie sheet with raised edges (or any dish of this size) and flatten into a smooth ¼-inch-thick layer.

Add the chocolate chips to the remaining mixture in the wok and cook, stirring, over medium heat until it becomes smooth, another 1 to 2 minutes.

Spread the chocolate mixture over the vanilla mixture in a smooth layer. Garnish and refrigerate for 1 to 2 hours or longer. Cut into 1-inch (or larger) squares. Place each square in a colorful paper candy cup and serve.

MAKES 60 TO 80 SQUARES

Pink and White Coconut Fudge Hearts

NARIYAL KI BURFEE

Perfect for Valentine's Day or any other day when you want to send a special message to your loved one, these dainty pink-and-white hearts are an edible love note.

> 1 recipe Basic Milk Fudge (see page 362)
> ½ cup sweetened shredded coconut, minced in a food processor until fine
> 2 to 3 drops artificial red food coloring

Make the basic *burfee* and mix in ¼ cup of the coconut. Divide the mixture into two parts. Place one in an ungreased 11- by 8-inch cookie sheet with raised edges (or any dish of this size) and flatten it into a smooth ¼-inch-thick layer.

Add the red food coloring to the second half, then spread it over the white layer. Garnish with the remaining coconut flakes and refrigerate for 1 to 2 hours or longer.

With a 1- to 1 ½-inch heart-shaped cookie cutter, cut the *burfee* into hearts. Place in paper candy cups, on a silver platter, or in decorative boxes and serve.

MAKES 50 TO 60 HEARTS

WHITE PISTACHIO DIAMONDS

SAFAID PISTA BURFEE

This is a basic white *burfee*, embellished with pistachios, crushed cardamom seeds, and a hint of rose essence.

½ cup shelled pistachios
1 cup boiling water
20 green cardamom pods
3 drops rose essence or 1 tablespoon rose water (see page 20)
1 recipe Basic Milk Fudge (see page 362)
Six to eight 4-inch square silver leaves (see page 10) or 1 tablespoon dessert masala
    (see page 29) for garnish

Soak the pistachios in the water for 30 minutes to 1 hour. Drain, then place on a kitchen towel and rub hard to remove the softened skins. Cut the nuts into quarters lengthwise.

Remove the seeds from the cardamom pods and grind them into a fine powder in a small spice or coffee grinder.

Add the pistachios, ground cardamom seeds, and rose essence to the *burfee* mixture while it is still hot. Place on an ungreased 11- by 8-inch cookie sheet with raised edges (or any dish of this size) and flatten into a smooth ½-inch-thick layer. Garnish and refrigerate for 1 to 2 hours or longer. Then cut into 1-inch diamonds. (To cut into diamonds, make eight parallel cuts 1 inch apart on the *burfee*. Then make 1-inch diagonal cuts, starting from one corner and ending on the other.) Arrange on a crystal or colorful platter and serve.

MAKES 60 TO 80 PIECES

No-Cook Pistachio Squares

PISTÉ KI LAUNGE

Also a part of the *burfee* family (see page 362), this green toffeelike dessert is made with ground raw pistachio nuts and sugar. It is served mostly by the affluent people in India (because of the high cost of pistachios), or included as a fancy dessert at more auspicious ceremonies like weddings and childbirth, when a little extra expenditure is customary.

The authentic version of this dessert is very tricky to make, as candy is, so when my friend Chanchal Runchal gave me a no-cook suggestion, I was excited. The results were phenomenal.

20 to 25 green cardamom pods
2 cups shelled pistachios
½ cup plus 2 tablespoons confectioners' sugar
2 to 3 tablespoons water
½ teaspoon butter
Four 4-inch squares silver leaves (see page 10) for garnish

Remove the seeds from the cardamom pods and grind them to a powder in a small spice or coffee grinder. Remove to a medium-size bowl. In the same grinder, grind the pistachios (in three to four batches) until powdered. Transfer to the bowl with the cardamom. Stir in the sugar, then add 2 tablespoons of the water. Mix with your fingertips until everything gathers into a stiff dough. Add more water if necessary. (At first the mixture seems too dry, but as you mix with your fingers, it will start to come together. If the dough seems too wet, add some more ground pistachios.)

Rub your hands with the butter and mold the mixture into a smooth ball. Flatten into a square with your hands. Place between two sheets of waxed paper and with a rolling pin roll it out to make a 7- to 8-inch square. Garnish with silver leaves and then cut into 1-inch or larger squares. Place in paper candy cups or on a platter lined with silver or gold paper doilies and serve. This stays fresh in the refrigerator for 10 to 15 days. Serve cold or at room temperature.

Makes 40 to 50 pieces

CASHEW AND SAFFRON ROLLS

KAJU KESAR BURFEE

Saffron, the most prized spice in the world, is at its fragrant best in this easy-to-make version of a classic Indian favorite. This variation of the No-Cook Pistachio Squares (above) provides a delicate and sweet ending to any meal. This is India's version of marzipan.

This exact recipe can be made with blanched almonds also.

½ heaping teaspoon saffron threads
3 tablespoons warm milk (any kind)
1 ½ cups coarsely chopped cashews
½ cup confectioners' sugar
¼ cup nonfat dry milk
½ teaspoon butter
Four 4-inch squares silver leaves (see page 10) for garnish

Dissolve the saffron in the warm milk for 10 to 15 minutes or longer.

In a coffee grinder, grind the cashews (in three to four batches) until powdered. (The food processor does not grind them fine enough.) Transfer to a medium-size bowl. Mix in the sugar and dry milk, then add the saffron milk. Mix with your fingertips until everything gathers into a stiff dough. Add more milk if necessary. (At first the mixture may seem too dry, but as you mix with your fingers, it will start to come together. If the dough seems too wet, add some more dry milk.)

Rub your hands with the butter and mold the mixture into a smooth ball. Divide into four parts. Working on a sheet of waxed paper, with a light coating of butter on your hands, roll each part into a 10- to 12-inch-long and ½-inch-thick roll. Then cut into eight to ten pieces each. Smooth the cut edges by applying gentle pressure with your finger and lay all the rolls on a platter. Garnish with the silver leaves and serve as a delicious dessert as you would chocolate truffles.

This *burfee* stays fresh in the refrigerator for 10 to 15 days. Serve cold or at room temperature.

MAKES 35 TO 40 PIECES

Dark Brown Milk Balls in Fragrant Syrup

GULAB JAMUN

"Poached plums in sugar syrup," remarked my daughter's friend Erica when she saw a bowl of *gulab jamuns* on the dessert table. Her first taste told her that her observation was not completely accurate. Definitely, the sugar syrup part was correct, but the "plums" turned out to be "cakelike, spongy, and unexpectedly delicious."

These caramel-colored milk balls are the Indian version of tea cakes and are served as part of the evening teatime ritual, along with samosas (see page 53) and pakoras (see page 42). They are very popular as a dessert also.

½ cup all-purpose flour
1 cup nonfat dry milk
¾ teaspoon baking powder
½ teaspoon crushed green cardamom seeds
1 ½ cups sugar plus 1 teaspoon
¼ cup (½ stick) unsalted butter, at room temperature
⅓ cup nonfat plain yogurt
2 to 3 cups vegetable shortening (not oil)
2 cups water
1 teaspoon slivered or coarsely chopped pistachios for garnish
¼ teaspoon ground green cardamom seeds for garnish

Place the flour, dry milk, baking powder, ¼ teaspoon of the cardamom seeds, and 1 teaspoon of the sugar in a food processor fitted with the metal S-blade and process until mixed. Add the butter and process until it is well mixed into the flour. With the motor running, add the yogurt in a thin stream through the feed tube and process until everything gathers into a ball. (The dough should be soft and somewhat sticky; if it seems too sticky, add some more dry milk.)

Transfer the dough to a bowl. With lightly buttered hands, shape the dough into 15 to 20 smooth and crack-free 1-inch balls. Cover and set aside.

Heat the shortening in a heavy wok to 325° F as measured on a meat thermometer. Add half the balls to the hot oil and fry, stirring gently with a large round or triangular slotted spoon, until they turn dark brown, 5 to 7 minutes. Let the thermometer remain in the wok, and carefully monitor the temperature; it should remain between 275° and 325° F. (Turn the heat off if the shortening becomes too hot.) It is essential for the balls to be fried at a low temperature for a long time to ensure that their centers get cooked and the balls don't collapse when they are added to the syrup. Remove the fried balls to a bowl lined with paper towels.

Prepare the syrup by placing the water and the remaining sugar and cardamom seeds in a wok or a wide saucepan. Stir to mix, then bring to a boil over high heat. Reduce to medium-low and simmer for about 5 minutes. Add the fried balls to the syrup and continue to simmer until the syrup becomes much thicker and the balls soak up the syrup and become soft, 15 to 20 minutes.

Transfer to a serving dish, garnish with the pistachios and ground cardamom seeds, and serve. *Gulab jamuns* are best when served hot, though they can be served at room temperature also. The unfinished fried balls can be refrigerated for up to 2 weeks, or frozen for 3 to 4 months. Simmer the refrigerated or frozen *gulab jamun*s in the syrup until they become soft.

MAKES 15 TO 20 GULAB JAMUN

CARAMELIZED MILK BALLS IN THICK SYRUP

KALA JAAM

This is a less syrupy, firmer variation of *Gulab Jamun*. *Kala jaam* are actually caramelized; prior to being fried, the balls are coated with sugar. As they fry, the sugar coating gradually melts, cooks slowly, and imparts a rich caramel color and flavor.

Kala jaam are customarily garnished with a small mound of thickened milk, on top of which rests a green pistachio nut.

½ recipe Basic Paneer Cheese (see page 230), at room temperature
1 recipe *Gulab Jamun* dough (see preceding recipe)
4 cups sugar, plus 1 to 2 extra tablespoons for coating
3 cups vegetable shortening
4 cups water
Seeds from 6 green cardamom pods
20 shelled green pistachios
½ teaspoon ground green cardamom seeds for garnish

Place the paneer cheese in a food processor fitted with a metal blade and process until it gathers into a ball. Remove 2 tablespoons and reserve for garnish. Break the *gulab jamun* dough into seven to eight pieces, and process it with the paneer cheese by dropping it through the feed tube with the motor running until everything gathers into a ball once again.

Transfer the dough to a bowl. With lightly buttered hands, shape the dough into 20 smooth, crack-free balls. Cover and set aside. (If a crack appears, press between the palms of your hands and then reshape.) Roll each ball in the coating sugar. Set aside.

Heat the shortening in a heavy wok to 325° F as measured on a meat thermometer. Add half the balls to the hot oil and fry, stirring gently with a large round or triangular slotted spoon, until they turn dark brown, 5 to 7 minutes. Let the thermometer remain in the wok and carefully monitor the temperature. It should remain between 275° and 300° F. (Turn the heat off if the shortening becomes too hot.) It is essential for the balls to be fried at a low temperature for a long time to ensure that their centers get cooked so they don't collapse when they are added to the syrup. Remove the fried balls to a bowl lined with paper towels.

Prepare the syrup by placing the water, the remaining sugar, and the cardamom seeds in a wok or a wide saucepan. Stir to mix, then bring to a boil over high heat. Reduce the heat to low and simmer for about 5 minutes. Add the fried balls to the syrup and continue to simmer, turning them as necessary until they soak up most of the syrup and become soft, 15 to 20 minutes.

Transfer to a serving dish, garnish with a dime-size dollop of the reserved paneer cheese, and top each with one pistachio nut. Sprinkle the ground cardamom on top and serve hot or at room temperature as a dessert or with evening tea. The unsoaked fried balls can be stored for up to 2 weeks in the refrigerator or in the freezer for 3 to 4 months. Simmer the refrigerated or frozen balls in the syrup until they are soft.

MAKES 20 KALA JAAMS

VARIATION: Instead of topping the balls with paneer cheese and pistachios, roll them in sweetened shredded coconut flakes or cut in half and top the round side with mashed paneer cheese and pistachios. (This gives you twice as many pieces.)

CHEESE BALLS IN CARDAMOM-FLAVORED SYRUP

RASGULLÉ

Rasgullas are a precious gift from the Bengali people. These white "Ping-Pong" balls floating in a cardamom-scented syrup are absolutely heavenly, especially when served thoroughly chilled. They are made with mashed paneer cheese and cooked in a syrup that penetrates and transforms them into soft and spongy delights.

1 recipe Basic Paneer Cheese made with regular or low-fat milk (see page 230), at
    room temperature
5 ½ cups water
1 ½ cups sugar plus 2 tablespoons
8 green cardamom pods, pounded lightly to break the skin, or broken open
1 teaspoon rose water (see page 20; optional)

Place the paneer cheese in a food processor fitted with the metal S-blade and process until it starts to gather into a soft and pliable dough (just before a ball is formed). Remove to a bowl and shape into thirty 1-inch crack-free balls. (This should be done between the palms of your hands, applying gentle pressure as you shape them.)

Place 5 cups of the water, 1 ½ cups of the sugar, and five of the cardamom pods in a pressure cooker and bring to a boil. Add fifteen of the balls, secure the lid of the pressure cooker, and cook over high heat for 30 to 40 seconds after the pressure regulator starts rocking. Remove from the heat and let the pressure drop by itself, 15 to 20 minutes. Open the pressure cooker and let the *rasgullé* cool down for at least 7 to 10 minutes. Then remove them to a medium-size bowl, with about ½ cup of the syrup. Set aside.

Add the remaining water, sugar, cardamom pods, and *rasgullé* to the pressure cooker and cook exactly as you did the first batch. Transfer everything to the bowl with the *rasgullé* and set aside to cool for about 1 hour or longer. Refrigerate until completely chilled, 8 to 10 hours or longer. *Rasgullé* stay fresh in the refrigerator for 10 to 12 days.

Sprinkle the rose water on the cold *rasgullé* if desired.

MAKES 30 RASGULLE

MULTICOLORED PETITE PANEER CHEESE BALLS

RANGEEN RASGULLIAN

These dainty pink, green, yellow, and white dime-size balls of cheese are a drier, sweeter, and firmer version of *rasgullé*. They provide pastel elegance when added to ordinary menus.

Making *rasgullian* is definitely more time-consuming than making *rasgullé*, but it all seems so rewarding when you see them positively shining on the dessert table.

1 recipe Basic Paneer Cheese made with regular or low-fat milk (see page 230), at
   room temperature
3 drops each red, yellow, and green food coloring
2 ½ cups sugar
6 cups water
8 green cardamom pods, pounded lightly to break the skin or broken open
1 teaspoon rose water (see page 20; optional)
Four 4-inch squares silver leaves (see page 10) for garnish

Place the paneer cheese in a food processor fitted with the metal S-blade and process until it starts to gather into a soft and pliable dough (just before a ball is formed). Remove to a bowl and divide into four batches. Mix the first batch with 2 drops of red color, the second with yellow, the third with green, and let the fourth remain white. Make twenty ⅓-inch crack-free balls from each batch.

Dissolve the sugar in the water and divide evenly into four portions. Place one portion, along with 2 of the cardamom pods and 1 drop of red coloring, in a pressure cooker and add the red balls to it. Secure the lid of the pressure cooker and cook over high heat for 30 to 40 seconds after the pressure regulator starts rocking. Remove from the heat and let the pressure drop by itself, 15 to 20 minutes. Open the pressure cooker and bring to a boil once again over high heat. Continue to boil until most of the water evaporates, 4 to 5 minutes. Remove the *rasgullian* to a medium-size bowl. Set aside to cool. Repeat this procedure with each color. Then refrigerate, covered, for 10 to 12 days. Store the different colors in separate bowls to prevent color overlaps.

Before serving, combine the *rasgullian* on an attractive platter, add the rose water if desired, garnish with the silver leaves, and serve chilled. This can be done 2 to 3 hours ahead of time. If it is done too much in advance, the colors start to overlap.

To maximize on your time and effort, double the recipe. *Rasgullian* can be frozen for 2 to 3 months.

MAKES 80 RASGULLIAN

VARIATION: Make larger multicolored *rasgullé* in the above manner. Before serving, roll them in sweetened shredded coconut.

Vanilla and Mango Ice Cream

AAM KI BURAF MALAI

Mangoes are by far the most popular fruit in India. Unfortunately, they are available only in the hot summer months. Besides eating them raw (I love to peel off the skin and bite into a whole mango), they are also used in a variety of drinks, pickles, chutneys, desserts, and main dishes.

This effortless dessert provides a charming last touch to any meal. Serve it with slices of fresh mangoes, sprigs of fresh mint, and the petals of red roses (make sure they haven't been sprayed).

Use fresh mangoes only if you can find the highly fragrant and ripe ones, otherwise stick to the canned mango pulp available in Indian markets.

½ gallon vanilla ice cream
2 cups pureed mangoes (from 2 to 3 peeled fresh mangoes)
Sprigs fresh mint for garnish

Transfer the ice cream to a medium-size bowl and keep at room temperature until melted, about 1 hour. Stir in the mango puree, then pour into individual cups and freeze.

Transfer the ice cream to individual plates, garnish with fresh mint, and serve.

MAKES ¾ GALLON

VARIATION: Instead of combining the ice cream with the mangoes, serve scoops of it with slices or small cubes of fresh ripe mango. A cup of perfectly brewed hot Darjeeling tea is ideal with this dessert.

Pistachio and Almond Ice Cream

PISTA AUR BADAAM KI KULFI

Authentic *kulfi* is an eggless ice cream made with whole milk that is simmered over low heat until it becomes thick and creamy. It is a little heavier than ice cream (in texture, not calories, because it is made with whole milk and not cream).

Ideally, *kulfi* should be smooth and creamy, with no ice particles. To achieve this, some families add thickeners such as cornstarch and slices of soaked bread, but the *kulfi* in my family in India was made with whole buffalo milk, which was painstakingly thickened by my grandmother until it was just perfect.

Since making *kulfi* in the traditional manner is quite cumbersome and time-consuming, I am offering you this no-cook recipe, which makes an outstanding *kulfi* that is even more delicious than the *kulfi* I remember.

Two 12-ounce cans evaporated milk (whole or low-fat)
Two 14-ounce cans sweetened condensed milk
2 cups fat-free Cool Whip or vanilla ice cream
1/4 cup dessert masala (see page 29) or 2 tablespoons each ground pistachios and almonds
1 teaspoon ground green cardamom seeds
2 teaspoons rose water or 4 drops rose essence (see page 20)
Slices of fresh strawberries (or other berries) for garnish

Place the milks and Cool Whip in a blender and process until smooth. Stir in the dessert masala, cardamom, and rose water.

Transfer to conical *kulfi* molds (these are similar to popsicle molds and are available in Indian markets) or 5 1/2-ounce plastic soufflé cups. Cover and place in the freezer for at least 4 to 5 hours or until needed. Frozen *kulfi* stays fresh for about 2 months.

To serve, dip the *kulfi* molds in hot water for 10 seconds, run a knife along the inside surface, and transfer immediately to a dessert plate. Cut into smaller pieces, garnish with sliced fresh strawberries (or any other berries), and serve. The plastic cups can be served as they are. They are a blessing especially at large gatherings. *Kulfi* can also be frozen in ice cube trays or cake pans.

MAKES 16 SOUFFLÉ CUPS

MANGO KULFI: Puree 2 cups canned mango slices with the milks and Cool Whip and proceed with the recipe.

SAFFRON KULFI: Soak 1/2 teaspoon or more saffron threads in 1/4 cup evaporated milk for about 15 minutes, then add to the above recipe with the milks and the Cool Whip.

KULFI FLAMBÉ: Our friends Ashok and Anju Khanna are always trying fun and crazy food experiments to impress their friends. During one of our visits to India, Ashok created a fascinating new dessert when he poured some cognac over frozen *kulfi* and set it ablaze. *Kulfi* never tasted so good. Ashok, thank you for this ingenious idea.

Ricotta Cheese Cake

RICOTTA PANEER KA RASGULLA-KAKE

When eggs are an issue and the occasion calls for a cake, present this perfect cardamom-flavored, eggless cake. Made with part-skim ricotta cheese, almonds, and pistachios, it has a hint of the popular Indian dessert Cheese Balls in Cardamom-Flavored Syrup (see page 369).

4 cups part-skim ricotta cheese
1 cup sugar, plus 1 tablespoon for sprinkling
½ cup dessert masala (see page 29), plus 2 tablespoons for garnish
2 or more 4-inch silver leaves (see page 10) for garnish

Preheat the oven to 375° F. Mix the ricotta cheese, sugar, and dessert masala in a bowl, then transfer it to an ungreased 11-inch pie dish or cake pan. Sprinkle the sugar on the top and bake until the edges are medium brown and the center feels firm, 1 to 1 ¼ hours. (The edges rise and start to turn brown quite rapidly, but don't panic if the center does not. It will eventually.) Remove from the oven when the top is a rich brown color (from the sugar that was sprinkled on top). Bring to room temperature.

Transfer to a platter lined with a paper doily. (To do this, first run a knife along the sides and invert the cake onto a large plate. Then reinvert it onto the platter to expose the top surface of the cake.) Garnish with the dessert masala and silver leaves and serve. This cake can be served chilled or at room temperature.

MAKES 12 TO 16 SERVINGS

Bharti's Eggless Cashew Nut Cookies

KAJU KE BISCUT

My friend Bharti Dhalwala, an excellent cook, is also very generous with her recipes. Her original recipe contained eggs, but at my suggestion, we substituted whipping cream and developed this authentic eggless recipe.

½ cup cashew nut halves
2 cups boiling water

1 ⅓ cups all-purpose flour
2 tablespoons nonfat dry milk
¼ teaspoon baking soda
¼ teaspoon salt
½ cup (1 stick) sweet unsalted butter, softened
½ cup sugar
½ cup whipping or heavy cream
1 teaspoon pure vanilla extract

Soak the cashew nuts in the boiling water for 15 to 20 minutes to soften. Drain and chop coarsely.

Sift the flour, dry milk, baking soda, and salt together in a medium-size bowl.

With a hand mixer, cream the butter and sugar together in a large bowl until it becomes light and fluffy. Mix in the cream, vanilla, and cashews. Fold in the sifted flour and mix gently until it gathers into a soft dough.

Divide the dough into two parts and shape each one into 5- to 6-inch-long 1 ½-inch-wide log. Wrap each one in plastic wrap and place in the freezer until it becomes firm, 20 to 30 minutes.

Cut each log into ¼-inch slices and place ½ inch apart on ungreased cookie sheets. Bake on the center rack in a preheated 375° F oven until golden, 20 to 25 minutes. Remove from the cookie sheet, cool, and store in airtight containers 10 to 15 days. This cookie dough can be frozen for up to 2 months. Thaw in the refrigerator overnight, or at room temperature for 2 to 3 hours. (The dough logs should be thawed completely, yet be firm enough to be sliced.)

MAKES 30 TO 35 COOKIES

ORANGE PEEL AND ALMOND COOKIES

SANTARA AUR BADAAM KE BISCUT

This is another masterpiece from Bharti. Made with whole-wheat flour and orange peel, these light and crispy cookies (almost like shortbread) have a terrific flavor. The dough for these is made in the food processor and can be frozen.

½ cup blanched almonds
2 cups boiling water
3 large oranges
½ cup sugar
½ cup (1 stick) sweet unsalted butter, softened
1 large egg white
1 cup stone-ground durum whole-wheat flour
½ cup all-purpose unbleached flour
2 tablespoons nonfat dry milk
¼ heaping teaspoon baking soda
¼ teaspoon salt
1 teaspoon pure orange extract

Soak the almonds in the boiling water for 15 to 20 minutes to soften. Drain and chop coarsely in a food processor fitted with the metal S-blade or by hand. Set aside.

With a peeler, remove the rind from the oranges, being careful not to include any of the bitter white pith. Place the orange rind and sugar in the unwashed food processor and process until finely minced. Add the butter and process until it becomes light and fluffy, about 1 minute. Add the egg white and continue to process for another 30 seconds.

Sift together the flours, dry milk, baking soda, and salt and add to the food processor along with the orange extract and reserved almonds. Pulse 8 to 10 times until the dough starts to gather. (Scrape the sides once or twice while pulsing.) Transfer to a bowl.

Divide the dough into two parts and shape each one into a 5- to 6-inch-long by 1 ½-inch-wide log. Wrap each log in plastic wrap and place in the freezer until it becomes firm, 20 to 30 minutes.

With a sharp knife, cut each log into ¼-inch slices and place ½ inch apart on ungreased cookie sheets. Bake on the center rack in a preheated 375° F oven until golden, 15 to 20 minutes.

Remove from the cookie sheet, cool, and store in airtight containers 10 to 15 days. The dough for these cookies can be frozen for up to 2 months. Thaw in the refrigerator, overnight, or at room temperature for 2 to 3 hours. (The dough logs should be thawed completely, yet be firm enough to be sliced.)

MAKES 30 TO 35 COOKIES

Mail Order Sources

CALIFORNIA

Bharat Bazar
11510 W. Washington Blvd.
Los Angeles, CA 90066
(310) 398-6766

Khalsa Fabric Plus
2021 W. Capitol Ave.
W. Sacramento, CA 95691
(916) 372-4643

Bazar of India
1810 University Ave.
Berkeley, CA 94702
(510) 548-4100

GEORGIA

Sona Imports
2D 1248 Clairmont Rd.
Decatur, GA 30030
(404) 292-7979

MASSACHUSETTS

India Grocery
199 Concord Street
Framingham, MA 01701
(508) 872-6120

NEW HAMPSHIRE

East West Foods
Lamplighter Square
South Nashua, NH 03062
(603) 888-7521

NEW YORK

Annapurna
127 East 28th Street
New York, NY 10016
(212) 889-7540

TEXAS

India Grocers
15 Richardson Heights North
Richardson, TX 75080
(972) 234-8051

House of Spices (India) Inc.
Keystone Park Shopping Center
13929 N. Central Expwy., Suite 419
Dallas, TX 75243
(972) 783-7544

INDEX